National Theatre ~~~~
2013

PLAYS FOR YOUNG PEOPLE

The Guffin

Mobile Phone Show

What Are They Like?

We Lost Elijah

I'm Spilling My Heart Out Here

Tomorrow I'll Be Happy

Soundclash

Don't Feed the Animals

Ailie and the Alien

Forty-Five Minutes

with an introduction by
ANTHONY BANKS

Methuen Drama

Bloomsbury Methuen Drama

An imprint of Bloomsbury Publishing Plc

50 Bedford Square	175 Fifth Avenue
London	New York
WC1B 3DP	NY 10010
UK	USA

www.bloomsbury.com

This collection first published in 2013

The Guffin © Howard Brenton 2013
Mobile Phone Show © Jim Cartwright 2013
What Are They Like? © Lucinda Coxon 2013
We Lost Elijah © Ryan Craig 2013
I'm Spilling My Heart Out Here © Stacey Gregg 2013
Tomorrow I'll Be Happy © Jonathan Harvey 2013
Soundclash © Lenny Henry 2013
Don't Feed the Animals © Jemma Kennedy 2013
Ailie and the Alien © Morna Pearson 2013
Forty-Five Minutes © Anya Reiss 2013
Introduction copyright © Anthony Banks 2013

Resource material copyright © National Theatre 2012

A catalogue record for this book is available from the British Library

ISBN
PB: 978-1-4081-8436-3
ePDF: 978-1-4081-8494-3
ePub: 978-1-4081-8458-5

Typeset by Country Setting, Kingsdown, Kent CT14 8ES
Printed and bound in Great Britain

Contents

Introduction by Anthony Banks, v

The Guffin by Howard Brenton, 1
Production Notes, 40

Mobile Phone Show by Jim Cartwright, 47
Production Notes, 89

What Are They Like? by Lucinda Coxon, 99
Production Notes, 124

We Lost Elijah by Ryan Craig, 137
Production Notes, 190

I'm Spilling My Heart Out Here by Stacey Gregg, 207
Production Notes, 262

Tomorrow I'll Be Happy by Jonathan Harvey, 275
Production Notes, 321

Soundclash by Lenny Henry, 333
Production Notes, 374

Don't Feed the Animals by Jemma Kennedy, 383
Production Notes, 428

Ailie and the Alien by Morna Pearson, 439
Production Notes, 480

Forty-Five Minutes by Anya Reiss, 489
Production Notes, 551

Participating Companies, 567

Partner Theatres, 570

Performing Rights, 571

National Theatre, 572

Introduction

In 2013 the National Theatre celebrates its fiftieth birthday. It's a year when we will be exploring what it means to be a national theatre, working to involve more young people across the nation in making theatre, and telling stories from across the country.

It also marks five decades in which young characters and young people have moved centre stage, taking their place in plays, TV series and films, in youth theatres and as audiences and participants in theatres across the country. Connections has been part of this movement since it was launched in 1995, with 142 new plays published for young performers aged thirteen to nineteen.

For the 2013 Connections programme, we invited ten writers to travel across the country, most to their home town, and to develop a play there with young people. From these encounters emerged stories of contemporary technology, of circuses and aliens, of parents, bullying and hate crime. The plays in this collection offer young theatre companies an infinite variety of inspiration: in their stories, themes, characters and styles.

Between February and May 2013, 230 youth theatre companies will give the premieres of these plays, from the North of Scotland to Truro and from Northern Ireland to Felixstowe, and at Connections festivals in twenty-two professional theatres. The programme culminates in a final festival at the National Theatre, with one production of each play presented on our stages.

HOWARD BRENTON began the idea for his play *The Guffin* with eight thirteen-year-olds from eight different towns in the UK. They spent a day in the National Theatre Studio exploring the theme of 'playing' and the time during childhood when it no longer seems appropriate to play. Howard's science-fiction adventure grew from there.

Four young people hanging out in a derelict house find a strange object; it's the Guffin. Touch it and your life is changed for ever.

JIM CARTWRIGHT began the research for *Mobile Phone Show* in his home county of Lancashire, where a talented group of young actors at the Dukes Theatre, Lancaster, improvised short scenes around mobile phones. Jim then interviewed several students at Southwark College, London, about their use of mobiles, and his research, investigation and invention continued from there.

A communication cacophony, a fully charged-up chorus line of chaos in a rhapsody of text, tweet and gabble.

LUCINDA COXON's *What Are They Like?* conjures a weird and wonderful universe in which twelve teenagers put on shoes and clothes that belong to their parents. Magically they become the older generation, revealing answers to the question in the play's title. Lucinda went back to her home town of Derby to workshop her play with Cast Ensemble Youth Theatre in Chellaston.

Adolescence is a rough ride. You've got existential angst, mood swings, fashion fiascos, terrifying physical changes, never enough money . . . And that's just the parents. How well do you know yours?

RYAN CRAIG's inspiration for *We Lost Elijah*, an extraordinary suburban adventure, began with research about the consequences which faced the young people involved in the nationwide summer riots of 2011.

Elijah's older brother and two friends were charged with getting him home safely while the riots were raging. Somehow, though, somewhere en route something happened and they didn't make it home together. Did Elijah get caught up in the events or was there another reason for his disappearance?

STACEY GREGG went back to her native Belfast to listen to young people chat about their everyday routines. She also visited amusement arcades on Brighton pier. She already knew that she wanted to write about the stresses and strains of adolescence and gradually shaped a story with a tomboy at its centre.

I'm Spilling My Heart Out Here was read and discussed by the young actors in Hertfordshire County Youth Theatre.

It's the daily scramble across no-man's-land: you flinch as you pass those even more clueless than you, strewn from the barbed wire of exams, first dates, evil former best mates . . . but hell's okay if you stick together.

JONATHAN HARVEY returned to his home town, Liverpool, to find the story for his Connections play *Tomorrow I'll Be Happy*, and developed it with a group of young people from the Theatre Royal Plymouth's Young Company.

When a stranger comes to a crumbling seaside town looking for his friend Darren, he discovers that he was killed in a homophobic hate crime. As the secrets of the past come spilling out, we learn that for Darren's group of friends all is not quite as it first seems.

LENNY HENRY wrote his hip-hop musical *Soundclash* because he was keen to create a big ensemble show that would appeal to young performers who enjoyed MCing. Reading reports of knife crime in the press led Lenny to his theme, and the play was workshopped with performing arts students at Walsall College Birmingham, with the help of ZooNation choreographer Kate Prince and lyric writer Akala.

A bunch of mates have been challenged to put together a reggae sound system to perform at a 'sound clash', a re-creation of a legendary music competition between DJs and MCs. None of them has the money or the equipment. But they do know a little kid whose dad used to be a DJ. Deep in the cellar of Lil Kid's house they find out more about music than they could possibly have imagined.

JEMMA KENNEDY was intrigued to find out what circuses were like these days. She travelled to a circus pitched for half-term week in an airfield in Essex, where local kids came into contact with kids who lived in caravans and travelled around the country with the circus. A lot of the themes, characters and stories in her play came from that visit, and she also enjoyed observing young people learning circus skills at Circus Space Workshops in London. Her play *Don't Feed the Animals* contains great silent comedy parts for the clowns, as well as opportunities for physical circus performance in the grand finale.

Sparks' Circus is on its way down. The owners have been forced to sell their star attraction, Tiny (the elephant) and a rival circus is poaching their artistes. With a busy bank holiday weekend ahead, it's down to acrobatic twins Zack and Missy to fill the house and stop their family business from going under. When a local gang of bored youths volunteers to help them, the twins are faced with the task of training an untrainable mob in circus skills.

MORNA PEARSON is from Elgin in the Highlands of Scotland, and travelled to Eden Court Theatre in Inverness to work with the youth theatre there to develop the ideas for her play *Ailie and the Alien*. Morna worked with a group of young people from eleven to fourteen years old, mostly from the Highlands, but including a few who had moved from overseas with parents working in the oil industry. Discussions about migration and living in remote places, as well the phenomenon of the Aurora Borealis, were influences in the creation of her play.

Ailie is a human and things have been going wrong for her for a while now. Finn is an alien who has crash-landed on earth. When Finn takes a shine to Ailie things suddenly start going right in her life. But when Finn is summoned to return home everything begins to unravel.

ANYA REISS started school in the year that NT Connections began, and as a teenager was a member of the NT Young Company, developing some of the early Connections plays. Shortly after this time, Anya was faced with the challenge of deciding whether or not to go to university. This period in her life and the discussions she had about the decision fuelled her to write her Connections play *Forty-Five Minutes*.

The deadline was wrong, so now there's just forty-five minutes till the bell goes and the UCAS forms must be sent and futures secured . . .

These plays are collected here and published for other young theatre companies and schools, beyond the 230 taking part in this year's National Theatre Connections and the end of this year's festival. We hope that you will enjoy reading and performing them.

And if you would like to be part of the next Connections programme, visit nationaltheatre.org.uk/connections.

ANTHONY BANKS
National Theatre, March 2013

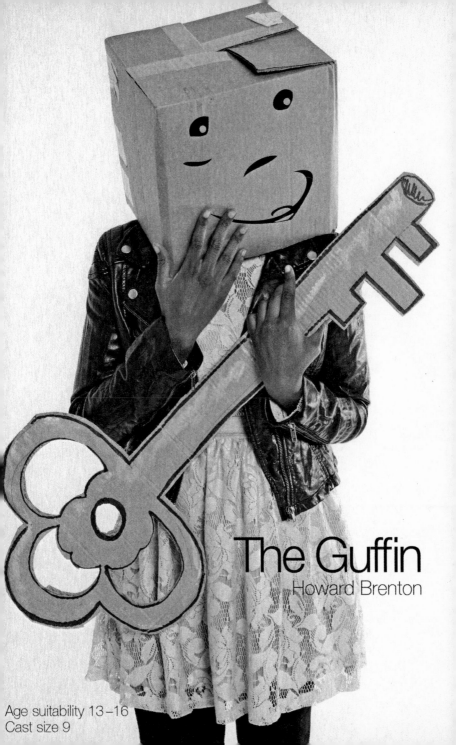

The Guffin
Howard Brenton

Age suitability 13–16
Cast size 9

Howard Brenton was born in Portsmouth in 1942. He and his wife Jane live in south London and they have two sons. His many plays include *Christie in Love* (Portable Theatre, 1969); *Revenge* (Theatre Upstairs, 1969); *Magnificence* (the Royal Court Theatre, 1973); *The Churchill Play* (Nottingham Playhouse, 1974, twice revived by the RSC, 1978 and 1988); *Bloody Poetry* (Foco Novo, 1984, and the Royal Court Theatre, 1987); *Weapons of Happiness* (National Theatre, winner of the *Evening Standard* award 1976); *Epsom Downs* (Joint Stock Theatre, 1977); *Sore Throats* (RSC, 1978); *The Romans in Britain* (National Theatre, 1980, revived Sheffield Crucible Theatre, 2006); *Thirteenth Night* (RSC, 1981); *The Genius* (1983), *Greenland* (1988) and *Berlin Bertie* (1992), all presented by the Royal Court; *Kit's Play* (RADA Jerwood Theatre, 2000); *Paul* (National Theatre 2005, nominated for the Olivier award, 2006); *In Extremis* (Shakespeare's Globe, 2006); *Never So Good* (National Theatre, 2008); *The Ragged Trousered Philanthropists* (Chichester Festival Theatre/Liverpool Everyman, 2010), *Anne Boleyn* (Shakespeare's Globe 2010/2011); and *55 Days* (Hampstead Theatre, 2012).

Characters

YOUNG WOMEN
Jay
Kavi
Mal
Gerj

YOUNG MEN
Lax
Gau
Dan
Sat

The Guffin, *played by a young man or young woman*

ADULTS
Dexter
Security Guard } *unseen and unheard*

Scene One

An open stage without scenery.

Jay *is alone. She is angry.*

Jay *(aside)* I hate those boys, I hate them! I want to boil them! I want to . . . I want to . . . boil them like tea bags! Yeah, I want them to be soggy nothings! And I'll tear them apart and I'll wash them down the . . . down the . . . down the . . . thing!

She stamps.

She throws herself on the ground.

She hits the ground repeatedly with her fists.

She stops and looks at her wrists: they are grazed and bleeding.

She bursts into tears.

Enter **Lax** *and* **Kavi**.

Jay *holds up her grazed wrists for them to see.*

Jay   Lax! Kavi! I'm bleeding!

Lax   Oh no, not again.

Kavi   I think she's hurt . . .

Lax   Kavi, no.

Jay   Bleeding, I'm bleeding!

Kavi   Jay, what is it?

Lax   We'll be late for Dexter.

Kavi   So will she!

Jay   I'm bleeding, and it's blood and I hate it!

Kavi *goes to* **Jay**. *She looks at* **Lax**, *hangs back.*

Lax *(aside)*   There's always one. Why is there always one?

Kavi   Jay, what happened?

Jay   It's those boys.

Kavi   What boys?

Jay   They're tea bags!

Kavi   Let me see.

Jay   Careful!

Kavi   You need some antiseptic on this.

Jay *drags her hand away.*

Jay   No!

Kavi   I've got some Savlon – here.

Kavi *takes out tissues.*

Jay   Ow ow ow!

Kavi   Don't be such a kid, Jay.

Jay   I'm not a kid.

Kavi   I'll just . . .

Jay   Calling me a kid! Just cos your mum lets you . . .

Kavi   Lets me what?

Jay   Sleep over. (*Nods at* **Lax**.) With him.

Lax   Working on our reputation?

Jay   You two better watch it, both of you being underaged, someone'll ring the Feds.

Lax   And who'd be that someone? What crapola little kid would that be?

Jay   No one'd know, it'd be anonymous, wouldn't it?

Lax   You are a waste of space, Jay.

Kavi   Just keep still, will you?

Kavi *dabs Savlon on* **Jay**'s *wrist.*

Jay   Ow!

Jay *withdraws.*

Lax (*aside*)   There's always one. With funny teeth, or some horrible body thing, or boils, or smell.

Jay   Ow ow!

Lax (*aside*)   I mean, I know there in't no rule that horrible people should look horrible. There's that Alicia in Mrs Baker's class, a great looker, oh the body, fit or what . . . and she's just about the most evil-minded cow on the planet. But with Jay . . . I mean I know I should be all like friendly and smiley and love your hair or whatever, but then she says something and I just want to kick her. And that's me . . . being horrible.

Jay   Ow!

Kavi   Keep still!

Jay   No, get off.

She pulls herself away.

Kavi   You're such a crashy bitch, Jay.

Jay   Yeah yeah yeah! That's what I am to you, in't I! I mean, you're the nipples, in't you, you two, all so tight and fly and sexy and lovey-dove, like the world belongs to you! I hate you!

Kavi   Well thank you very much.

Lax (*aside*)   Please, please, it's so boring to be a good person, but I am going to be a good person.

He turns to them.

Jay. These boys. Do you know their names?

A moment.

Jay   Skeggy and Dump.

Kavi   Who?

Jay   Skeggy and Dump! And they're tea bags! And I'm going to pull them all apart, all soggy, and theirs innards is going to go all over the sink!

Lax   Are they from down the dip?

Jay   Maybe.

Lax   This happen down the dip?

Kavi   A little kid got knifed down there.

Fear.

Jay *looks away.*

A beat.

Kavi   Jay, tell Dexter.

Jay   No way.

Kavi   Tell him.

Lax *pulls* **Kavi** *away from* **Jay**.

Lax   May not be a good idea, Kavi.

Kavi   Why not?

Lax   Dexter will tell the Feds.

Kavi   What are you like? He should tell the Feds.

Lax   But if, you know . . .

Kavi   No. What?

Lax   If it got back to us.

Kavi   But look what this Skeg and whatsit did to her.

Lax   Actually, she fell over and did that to herself, didn't she? I'm trying to be helpful here.

Kavi   Lax, sometimes you . . .

She turns to **Jay**.

Kavi   Jay, did those boys, you know, touch you?

A beat. All still.

*Then **Jay** shakes her head.*

Jay   Said things, didn't they.

Kavi   Said things, that all?

Lax   Big mouths, small dicks.

Jay   It's *what* they said, it matters, what's said, it sticks in you. Once it's in there, in your head, in you, you can't pull it out.

Lax   We are late for Dexter.

Kavi   Jay, what things?

Jay   Crapola 'bout us, 'bout Dexter. They were like, they were like, 'You're Dexter's hos.' They were like, 'The boys are Dexter's bumshots.' They were like, 'Dexter's a ponce.' They were like, 'We're going to . . . going to . . . going to . . . '

Kavi   Going to what?

Jay *cannot say it.*

A beat.

Kavi (*to* **Lax**)   We've got to tell Dexter.

Jay *backs away.*

Jay   Don't do that!

Kavi   Jay . . .

Jay   Swear you won't!

Kavi   It's heavy, Jay . . .

Jay   Tell Dexter and he'll steal.

Kavi   No he won't.

Jay   He'll steal my life. That's what his poxy workshop's for, he wants to steal our lives.

Lax   Don't do the workshop down, it's great . . .

Jay   Dexter's like, 'Ooh, tell me what you really feel,' 'Find the real you,' and he steals it, twists it and . . . and . . . Skeg and Dump, they got a point, Dexter is a ponce, and you fancy him and all, don't you? . . .

Kavi   Shut up, Jay . . .

Jay   How can you? I mean he's really old, I mean like . . . twenty-five!

Kavi   Dexter's great.

Jay   He's stealing from us, he wants to suck us dry, he wants to stuff things in us, put us up there so people can go 'Ooh! Ooh! How real!'

Kavi   It's a workshop, we're all doing it . . .

Jay   He's a bloodsucker, you all are . . .

Lax   That's just bollocks.

Jay (*to* **Kavi**)   You want to do him, you do, do, you want to do him . . .

Kavi *lashes out at* **Jay**.

Jay *lashes back.*

Lax *pulls* **Kavi** *away.*

Lax   No, no, no.

Jay *begins to run away.*

Kavi   Where you going?

Jay *stops and turns on her.*

Just cos you're a looker, you think you can do anything, don't you? And him, just cos you're lookers. It in't fair! It in't fair! I wish you . . . I wish you had cancer!

Kavi   You little cow!

Jay *runs off.*

Lax   Dear oh dear.

Kavi   Little cow! I was trying to help her.

Lax   She's a hater, hates everybody, everything.

Kavi   We going to tell Dexter? About her and those boys?

Lax   She's lying. There's no Skeggy and Dump. You know Jay, always into some kind of madness in her head.

Kavi   I don't know. I sort of believed her. But what a little . . .

Lax   Forget her. Come on.

He takes her arm.

Lax   So, fancy Dexter, do you?

Kavi *laughs.*

Kavi   You're joking.

Lax   Didn't know you're into old men.

Kavi   He's got a hair hanging out of his nose.

Lax   Dreaming of his nose hairs? Must be love.

Kavi   Get off.

She pushes him. They run off hand in hand, laughing, swinging each other around, having fun.

Scene Two

Empty stage.

Two Male Voices (*off*)   Slag! / Come here! / Slag! / Ho! / Come here, ho! / Slag!

Jay *runs on as if being chased.*

She looks around, crouched, hunted, breathing heavily.

Then she runs off.

Empty stage.

Two Male Voices (*off*)   Slag! Slag!

Jay *runs back on, panicky.*

Jay   No, no, no, no, no. Hide, hide.

She looks around, desperate.

Two Male Voices (*off*)   We're coming! / Slag! / Slag!

Jay *mimes breaking into an empty derelict house to escape from her pursuers.*

She pulls at the bottom of a rotten door. It breaks off and she throws it aside.

She goes down on her front and pulls herself through the gap beneath the imaginary door.

She goes up on to all fours and is still, listening.

Then she stands and scampers a distance.

She treads in some muck.

Jay   Urrgh.

She goes across the room.

She pushes open another door, with difficulty.

She goes into another room. She squints — the room is dim.

She crouches down, puts her hands to her face and cries.

A metal object, the Guffin — about the size and appearance of a metal boule — rolls across the stage and stops against her.

She starts and moves away.

Then she looks at the object.

She is still for a moment.

Then she picks it up and holds it up in front of her face.

The Guffin *enters. She/he has a skipping rope and is doing wonderful steps.*

The Guffin object becomes difficult to handle. **Jay** *juggles with it.*

Jay   Ow ow!

She cannot hear **The Guffin**, *who stops skipping.*

The Guffin   Stop it! Stop it! Don't be scared! If you're scared, it won't work!

Jay *controls herself.*

The Guffin   That's good, that's good, that's good, you can do it. Just cos I'm the thing that don't fit, don't be scared.

Jay *sits up straight, the Guffin cupped in her hands.*

The Guffin   You've nearly got it, Jay, you're nearly there. Ask it. Ask it. And you'll see me and we'll chill and we'll be great, we'll have a great time and I'll get you out of here, I will, I will, I will. The question, ask it.

Jay   What are you?

The Guffin *is furious and goes into contortions.*

The Guffin   No no no no no, wrong wrong wrong wrong!

Two Male Voices (*off*)   Slag, slag, little slag, know you're in there! / Little slag, know what we're going to, do ya, do ya?

The Guffin   Ask the question!

Jay   What . . . ?

The Guffin   What . . .

Jay   What . . . ?

The Guffin   Yes yes yes! What . . .

Jay   What am I?

The Guffin   You're me.

Startled, **Jay** *stands and turns. Now she can see* **The Guffin**.

They stare at each other.

Jay   Where did you come from?

The Guffin   You.

Jay *puts out a hand.*

The Guffin *puts out a hand.*

They touch fingers.

But **Jay**, *frightened, pulls her hand away.*

Jay   What, you sneaked in after me? You following me?

The Guffin   Oh, don't want things explained all the time, it's so boring explaining things. Plink!

The Guffin *clicks his/her fingers.*

Jay *cannot see him/her any more.*

Jay   Where are you?

She steps forward to where **The Guffin** *was and waves her hands in the thin air.*

The Guffin *walks around to behind her.*

The Guffin (*aside*)   Always fun, this bit.

She/he walks round **Jay** *until he/she is behind her, then clicks fingers.*

The Guffin   Plink! Over here!

Jay *whirls round.*

Jay   How do you do that?

The Guffin   I make a tiny wave in the probability mist so it refracts with the Higgs field.

Jay   What?

The Guffin   Said it was boring. Those boys outside, do you want me to kill them?

Jay   Yeah!

The Guffin   Right.

Horrible screams offstage. Then a silence.

Jay   What did you do?

The Guffin   I blinded them with needles of light that went right into their brains and boiled them. Their brains are very hot now, like soggy tea bags. Actually, *you* blinded them with needles of light that went right into their brains and boiled them. So that their brains are very hot now, like soggy tea bags. Happy?

Jay   I don't want to kill nobody.

The Guffin   You want Kavi to have cancer.

Jay   No. No . . .

The Guffin   Them's just words, I'm what you really want, cos I'm really you. Lovely stuff, reality. Bone cancer's tasty.

Clicks fingers.

Blink!

*Enter **Lax** and **Kavi**. **Kavi** hobbles on crutches.*

Lax *is helping her. Then he steps back.*

Kavi (*to **Jay***)   It hurts me. It hurts me. It hurts me. It's burning.

The Guffin   Want Lax to fancy you and all, don't you?

Lax *produces a magician's bunch of flowers 'out of thin air' and offers them shyly to **Jay**.*

Jay   No.

The Guffin   Yes.

Jay   No.

The Guffin   Yes.

Lax   I love your hair, Jay.

Jay   Get away!

Lax   You got great eyes and all.

Jay   No.

Lax   And I love the way when you wear dresses, they sort of . . . lilt when you walk.

He puts his hand out to her.

Jay   Get off!

Lax   Come up One Tree Park tonight. Wear that dress with blue spots.

Jay   Get off! You're not Lax, you're not!

The Guffin   He nearly is. Just try harder.

Jay *looks at* **The Guffin** *object in her hand.*

Jay   It's this, in't it? You're this.

The Guffin   Killer, lover, that's what you can be.

Jay   How do I turn it off?

The Guffin   You don't want to do that.

Jay   Go away!

The Guffin   All you need is the power. I'm the power.

Jay   No.

She throws the Guffin object down on the ground. To her surprise it bounces straight back into her hand.

The Guffin *skips around* **Jay**, *who follows her warily.*

The Guffin   Be the real you, be me, killer, lover . . .

Jay   No!

The Guffin *pulls* **Jay** *to him/her around the waist.*

The Guffin   There are other worlds. There's one with a Jay who doesn't have glaucoma, doesn't have fat knees, doesn't have a mum drunk-dialling you all the time. A Jay who does anything she wants.

Jay   No.

The Guffin   All right. Leave Skeggy and Dump dead, though, shall I? They're lying on the ground out there. It's really good the way their brains have, sort of, bubbled out of their eye sockets.

Jay   No. Get them back.

The Guffin   You know what they'll do to you.

Jay *pushes* **The Guffin** *away.*

Jay   I want to be me.

The Guffin   Oh, skankaroo. (*Clicks fingers.*) Plink!

Jay *turns on* **The Guffin**.

Jay   I'm not scared. I'm not.

She cannot see him/her.

Two Male Voices (*off*)   Slag, Slag, you're in there Slag! / Know you're in there, Slag!

Jay *stands. She looks around her. She runs off with the Guffin object.*

The Guffin (*alone, aside*)   Oh well.

She/he draws a pattern with his/her toe on the ground.

It's nicer in here. Not being anything. Rather than being out there with you bad jokes.

He/she skips off.

Scene Three

Workshop.

Mal, **Gerj**, **Sat**, **Gau**, **Dan**. *They are in rehearsal clothes.*

Dexter, *the adult leader of the workshop, is not seen or heard by the audience. When he speaks there is a loud, sharp crack from a percussive instrument (I believe classical orchestras use one called a whip). The young people in the workshop hear and react to* **Dexter** *as if he has spoken. They stare at where he is imagined to be standing. To help the actors, his name appears in italics, and his unheard lines are printed in brackets.*

Mal *and* **Gau**, **Gerj** *and* **Dan** *are in pairs, doing mirror exercises.*

Sat, *fed up, scowls around at the back.*

The percussive sound: Crack!

Dexter   (Sat, get into it.)

Sat   Can't get into it, Dexter. Can't do mirrors on my own, can I?

Mal   Do it with us.

Sat   Can't have a three-way mirror.

Mal   Why not?

Gau   Yeah, why not?

Dan   You're meant to be the genius round here.

Gau   Yeah, do it with yourself.

Dan   Wanker.

Crack!

Dexter   (Gau . . .)

Dan   Yeah, language. Sorry.

They continue the mirror exercises.

Let this run a while.

*Then **Lax** and **Kavi** rush in, pulling off outer clothes, dropping their bags.*

The others are continuing the exercise.

Crack!

Dexter   (Hey, hey, Kavi, Lax. Try not to be late, right?)

Kavi   Sorry, Dexter.

Lax   Yeah, sorry, Dexter.

Crack!

Dexter   (It's unfair on the others.)

Lax   Yeah, we said sorry!

Kavi *touches his arm to calm him down.*

Crack!

Dexter   (Is everything all right?)

Kavi   No, not all right really. Actually . . .

Lax   Everything's fine, Dexter, no worries.

Crack!

Dexter   (Sure?)

Lax   Yeah, sure. Shall we warm up?

Dexter   (Yeah, off you go. Do you know where Jay is?)

Kavi   No. Haven't seen her.

Lax   I mean if we had, we'd say.

Lax *and* **Kavi** *begin a warm-up, a distance from the others. Their mirror exercises become more contorted.*

Mal *stifles a giggle.*

Dan *stifles a giggle.*

Sat   Where is Jay then?

Lax   Why ask us?

Sat   She's my workshop partner, can't work without her. can I? Hey, Dexter, since Jay's not here, why don't I just do my presentation?

Crack!

Dexter   (You can't without Jay, you've been working on it with her.)

Sat   No, I'm cool. I don't need her, I'll do it with Mal.

Mal   No way.

Sat   Gerj then.

Gerj   No way.

Mal   It's you and Jay's stuff.

Gerj   Crapola, must be.

Mal   Major crapola.

Crack!

Dexter   (Mal, Gerj. The workshop rule.)

Sat   Yeah, workshop rule number one.

Mal   Sorry Dexter.

Gerj   Yeah, but it's Jay's stuff, with him.

Mal   I know it's workshop rule number one, support each other and that, but I just don't want to go there.

Gerj   No.

Mal   Not with this.

Gerj   Too . . .

Mal   Crap . . .

Gerj   Weird.

Sat   How do you know?

Mal   Cos it's you and Jay!

Sat   I'll do it with Gau.

Gau   Me? Stand in for Jay? No way.

Sat   Dan?

Dan   Yuckaroo, I'm not being like, you know, a girl.

Sat   I can act a girl. Girls can act me, can't they? Dexter, help us out here.

Crack!

Dexter *now goes into a complex explanation. They all look at him with increasing levels of puzzlement and confusion.*

A giggle from **Mal**, *then from* **Gerj** *as they lose* **Dexter**.

Even **Sat** *is lost by the end.*

Sat   Right. Cross-casting as a trans-sexual alienation technique. Yeah. Look, Dexter, I've been flat-roofing this for weeks. Can't I just . . . give it to you? I mean, tell you it?

Mal   Let him, Dexter.

Gau   Yeah, let him.

They look at **Dexter** *to see what he will say. A moment, then . . .*

Crack!

Dexter   (Okay all of you, listen up. And give Sat a chance.)

They all sit on the floor facing **Sat**. *Who stands.*

Gerj (*low*)   This'll be such kaka.

Dan (*low*)   All the way.

Sat   I. Yeah. I. It's. Yeah.

Fumbles with his notebook. Reads. Closes it.

Yeah.

He lets the notebook drop to the ground. He looks at it. Then he looks up.

He is tense at first but becomes increasingly confident.

There's this kid. Everyone hates her. And she's annoying, like *very* annoying, always butting in. And she says really stupid things, and you try to be nice to her because she's, you know, her hair's all over, and there's something about her that really gives you brain damage, and you try to be nice to her but she screams in your face. So she is not a very popular bunny. But something's driving her mad, you see, inside her. Because she sees things differently. She sees colours that aren't there, aren't there for us, but are there for her. And if you could see a new colour, that others can't, how could you describe it? You say 'green' and green is green, but she'd have to say 'blug' or 'doob' or 'selt'. And when people look at her, they

know that she's not seeing the world like we do. And it makes
her feel so bad inside she could die. And because of what she
is, she's a trouble magnet. And trouble she gets.

A beat.

They are mesmerised.

Sat   She's going home one day. And she's seeing the world
as all . . . 'blug' and 'doob' and 'selt'. She doesn't realise
where she's going. She ends up down the dip.

Lax *and* **Kavi** *look at each other.*

Sat   There are these two thugs. Skeggy and Dump.

Kavi   This is from Jay. Jay made this up.

Sat   Both of us did.

Kavi   Bet it was all her.

Sat   It's a collaboration.

Lax (*to* **Kavi**)   So, what she said to us, it was all out of her
head . . . ?

Sat   What do you mean, what she said to you?

Kavi   Don't matter.

Crack!

Dexter   (People, let Sat finish.)

Lax   Sorry.

Sat   There are those brick flats, boarded up. By the railway.
She runs down there. There's a door, the bottom rotted. She
ducks down and gets under and in. It's dim. Outside, she can
hear Skaggy and Dump shouting out for her: 'Slag! Come
here! Slag! Ho! Come here ho! Slag!' Door. She pushes it.
Dark room. Wet floor. She can just see a colour. One of hers.
She tries to be still. Not breathe. Not think. Then . . .
something moves. Across the floor? Rat? Rat? But it shines.
No, it sort of glints. For a moment. It rolls beside her. She . . .

reaches and touches it. It's hard. It's stone, it's not stone, it's metal, it's not metal. She lifts it up and looks at it. And it . . . it's alive and it . . .

A silence.

Again he has mesmerised them.

Gerj And it what?

Gau Yeah, what?

Sat That's as far as we got.

Gau What a let-down.

Dan What is the thing?

Gau Bomb. It's a bomb.

Crack!

Dexter (Come on guys!)

They ignore him.

Sat No.

Mal Maybe it's a big diamond. That's why it glints.

Sat No.

Gerj And it's a diamond. And the girl gets fabulously rich.

Mal And she buys the derelict flats. And makes them into a club.

Gau And the club goes mega, then one night . . .

Dan Got it. Got it! Skeggy and Dump turn up . . .

Gerj Turn up to wreck the place . . .

Mal But she's hired a real heavy.

Gerj This French girl. Assassin. And she takes them out. On the dance floor. Zap zap. And they dance on and no one notices and when the floor clears, there they are. Dead. As if . . .

Mal   As if dead by dancing.

Crack!

Dexter   (Guys!)

Crack!

Dan   That's great! Call it that! 'Dead by Dancing'!

Sat '   No, no. It's not a diamond. The thing, it's . . .

Enter **Jay**.

She has been mortally wounded, stabbed.

She staggers, clutching her side.

She drops her bag and staggers on.

A stage picture, like a tableau: for a moment they are all frozen at the sight of her.

Jay   I'm not afraid.

They break from the tableau and run to **Jay**.

Kavi *gets to her first. Only she hears* **Jay** *say:*

Jay (*to* **Kavi**)   In my bag.

Many 'Cracks!' But they ignore **Dexter** *and all speak at once.*

Mal   Oh my God, oh my God, oh my God /

Gerj   Oh my God, oh my God, oh my God /

Lax   Get somebody, get somebody /

Sat   Jay, what happened? Jay, what happened? /

Dan   There's blood, there's blood /

Gau   Don't go near her, don't go near her /

Crack!

Dexter   (All of you get back, give her space!)

They step back. **Jay** *lies dead. They freeze.*

Kavi *takes the Guffin out of* **Jay**'s *bag and looks at it.*

She remains still as the others scatter, taking out mobile phones. Again, they all speak at once, repeating lines. Greatly distressed.

Mal   Chandra, come and get me, please /

Gerj   Mum, Mum, Mum, are you there? Mum /

Lax   Dad, are you there? Dad, pick up. Dad, Dad, pick up /

Sat   Joanie, get down here now. Sis, please /

Dan   Mum, Mum, switch on. Switch on /

Gau   Dad, come down here. Dad, come down here /

Crack!

Dexter   (All right listen up! Everyone! Listen! The police are coming here and I want you all outside, but stick with me. Right?)

Their calls peter out.

They look at **Dexter**. *Wrecked faces.*

Kavi *is still looking at the object. Slowly, she puts it into her bag and takes out a phone.*

She presses a button. Listens for a moment.

Kavi   Mum . . . No, Mum . . . Mum, just come and get me home.

Lax, *phone to his ear, turns and looks at* **Kavi**.

All still in a tableau.

Then the scene ends and they all go off.

Scene Four

Empty stage for a moment.

Enter **Dan** *and* **Gau**. *They are carrying cardboard boxes.*

Dan *(aside)*   Back of Sainsbury's.

Gau (*aside*)   One of them scruffy bits you find. Where you can hang. Where you can . . .

And he kicks a cardboard box hard across the stage.

Then, both of them kick boxes about the stage in a fury.

Dan   That security guard – see him around?

Gau   Buster? He's all fluff and muff.

Dan   Massive guy, though.

They sag, their fury evaporated.

Sat *enters. He has the tabloid papers and is absorbed in reading them.*

Dan   Is it in there?

Sat   Yeah. We're all like famous.

Dan *pulls at the papers and reads.*

Gau   It was on the TV, local news. My dad recorded it.

Dan   (*reads*)   'Kiddie Crime Plague. Thirteen-year-old girl knifed to death.'

Gau   Dexter was on. He looked really wrecked.

Dan *has the* Daily Mail.

Dan   His picture's here. 'Twenty-five-year-old youth leader, Alistair Dexter said: "not all kids are thugs".'

Sat   Thanks, Dexter.

The three of them read the papers.

Enter **Mal** *and* **Gerj**.

Gerj   Hey, there's Sat, and Dan, and Gau . . .

Mal   Don't want to see 'em.

Gerj   Why not?

Mal   My big sister told my dad. He said I can't go to the workshop no more.

Gerj   Why not?

Mal   Because of the boys there.

Gerj   Yeah, my mum says I'm not to go either. But it's not their fault.

Mal   We don't know that.

Gerj   We were with them. When she got . . .

Mal   They could have done it before.

Gerj   What do you mean, 'before'? . . .

Mal   Before we got to the workshop.

Gerj   Mal, you're talking about Sat, Dan and Gau: three big Mr Softees.

Mal   They hated Jay.

Gerj   We all hated Jay.

Mal   They said horrible things about her.

Gerj   We all said horrible things about her.

Mal   Didn't.

Gerj   You did.

Mal   Didn't.

Gerj   You said she was a waste of space, skankaroo and a load of kaka on legs.

Mal   I never! Never! When did I say that?

Gerj   All the time.

Mal   No way, Jay was my best friend!

Gerj   No, she weren't.

Mal   She was! She was great! She . . . she . . .

Gerj   All right. All right.

They hug. **Mal** *is sobbing.*

Dan   Mal, Gerj.

But **Mal** *and* **Gerj** *don't want to talk to them. They back away and run off.*

Dan   What's the matter with them?

Gau   Hey, read this.

It is a local paper.

Dan *is a plodding reader:*

Dan   'Councillor Jeremy Salter, of the Health, Youth and Cultural Recreation Committee, said the theatre workshop which the murdered teenager attended is suspended indefinitely while police investigations continue. Mr Alistair Dexter, the workshop leader, protested that the council was hostile to the workshop and was using the investigation into the tragedy to close the workshop for good.'

Sat   It's like they're blaming us.

They stare at him.

What?

A beat.

Sat   What?

Gau   The story you told.

Dan   About the kid.

Gau   Her being chased.

Dan   That's what happened to Jay.

Sat   It was a story. We made it up.

Dan   Yeah.

Gau   How did you know it was going to happen, though?

Sat   It was a story.

Gau   But how did you know?

Sat   I didn't know! And Dexter said to me, do something about knife crime. It does happen round here. And Dexter said do something relevant, for the funders.

Dan   For who?

Sat   The funders! Dexter said they want a bit of knifing in theatre, cos it's relevant. So Jay and I, we made it up. Didn't want it to happen. It just did. It happened to her.

They will not look at him.

Gau   I got to go.

Dan   Me too.

Sat   Aren't we going up to One Tree?

Gau   My dad doesn't want me hanging in the parks.

Dan   I got to get in. My mum, you know she . . . yeah.

Dan *and* **Gau** *step back.*

Sat   Dan, Gau, we tight about this?

Dan   Sure.

Gau   Yeah.

Sat   See you then.

Dan   Yeah.

Gau   Sure.

They walk away.

Dan   You still playing Assassin's Creed III?

Gau   Nah, I'm into Resident Evil 6.

Dan   Any good?

Gau   It's a beast. Want to come round to mine?

Dan   Yeah.

Sat *calls after them, holding up the papers in his fists.*

Sat   Hey! We're famous!

Dan *and* **Gau** *run off.*

Sat   Heh, want to come round? Dan, Gau!

A beat.

Yeah, famous.

He throws the papers away.

He covers his face with his hands, very upset.

He recovers. He runs his hands through his hair, then talks to us.

Sat (*aside*)   Jay liked really skanky things. She had these
True Blood box sets, she played them over and over. Funny,
cos she hated blood. I think she had a thing about her knees.
She thought they were full of it – blood, she thought it was
running down in her, collecting in her knees. I mean, this was
a girl with problems. But I liked her. And . . .

He thinks about it for a moment.

It's like she was standing in front of you going off on one,
then . . . there's just air. Closed over where she should be.
And no one cares, not really. Once, when I went round to
hers, when her mum wasn't there, she wore this dress with
blue spots. It was very . . . Jay.

Sat *exits.*

Enter **Lax**, *mobile phone to his ear.*

A beat, then enter **Kavi**.

Lax   Yeah, Dexter, yeah . . . Yeah, I'm all right . . . Well,
the others are sort of scattered, you know? . . . Yeah, I'm
seeing Kavi now . . . Right.

He rings off.

You okay?

Kavi *nods.*

Kavi   You?

Lax   Yeah.

They find it difficult to talk to each other. Then a flood.

Kavi   My mum just hates seeing where we live on the telly.
And people saying, 'Did Kavi know that girl that got . . . '
You know.

Lax   I had this kind of flash. I saw Jay, in the middle of the
road, on the roundabout outside Sainsbury's. She reached out
her arms and there was blood all down her. And she stepped
into the traffic . . . then she wasn't there.

And again, they find it difficult.

Did you tell the police about seeing her before the . . . ?

Kavi *shakes her head.*

Kavi   You?

Lax *shakes his head.*

Kavi   Think we should?

Lax   Too late now. Anyway, she's . . .

Kavi   Yeah.

A beat.

Lax   I miss her.

Kavi   Yeah.

A beat.

Lax   I couldn't stand her.

Kavi   No.

Lax   And I can't handle it.

Kavi   My mum's, you know, at my aunt's. Do you want to
come round?

Lax   I don't know. What Jay said about us. I mean, maybe everyone says it.

Kavi   Not true, though.

Lax *can't handle this.*

He looks away, kicking at the ground.

Kavi   Wish it were.

Lax   Look, I'll see you.

He walks away.

Kavi   Lax, Jay gave me something.

He stops.

Lax   What?

Kavi   When she came in, you know . . . She said it was in her bag, so I went and got it.

She takes out **The Guffin** *object. They look at it.*

Lax   What is that?

Kavi   The thing in the play they were making up.

Lax   I s'pose she got it as a prop.

Kavi   S'pose so.

Lax *takes it.*

Lax   It looks smooth but feels rough.

Kavi   It doesn't feel sort of wet, to you?

Lax   No.

Enter **Sat**.

He goes to one of the tabloids he threw away and tears out an article.

Kavi   What is there, something about you?

Sat   Oh Lax, Kavi.

Kavi   You love it, don't you?

Sat   What do you mean?

Kavi   You love it cos it's just a story to you.

Sat   No.

Kavi   Here, this is yours.

She takes **The Guffin** *object from* **Lax** *and gives it to* **Sat**.

Sat   What is it?

Kavi   The prop. For your thing with Jay.

Sat   I've not seen it before.

Kavi   Jay must have got it.

Sat   It's hot.

Lax   Is it?

Sat   Maybe it's got a battery in it.

Lax   Maybe it's from some kind of joke shop. Maybe it's going to go 'bang'. And a thing'll come out of it, stupid little flag or something.

Sat *tries to open the Guffin object, twisting it.*

The Guffin *skips on to the stage.*

Lax   Yeah, there's got to be a battery.

The Guffin   Here we go, explain explain explain.

Sat   It's getting really . . . Ow!

He drops the Guffin object as if it were hot. **Lax** *flinches.*

It bounces back into his hands.

The Guffin *hops and skips back and forth across the stage during the following.*

Sat   Now it's cold.

Kavi   Oh, don't be pathetic.

Sat No, no, you see . . . the story we made up. The thing the kid found. We called it The Guffin. And it's the door to other worlds. It was all Jay's idea. She was brilliant. And we treated her crapola.

Kavi Door?

Sat To anything you want. A door to you, inside you, that was Jay's idea.

The Guffin C'mon, people. C'mon, c'mon.

She/he begins to hopscotch up and down.

Sat A door, and you opened it with a key. That was Jay's idea. And the key was going to be a question.

Kavi Great. So ask it.

Sat We hadn't decided what it was.

Lax Look, hang on. That thing's just a thing.

Kavi You said it was rough and dry, but it was wet.

Sat Yeah, it was hot, now it's cold. Oh, it's getting hot again.

The Guffin *skips in a circle.*

The Guffin Hot, cold. Dry, wet. Up, down. Near, far . . . C'mon folks, it's easy. Easy!

Lax All right, all right! You want a question?

*He leans into the Guffin object on the palm of **Sat**'s hand. He asks the question in a mocking way.*

Lax What is the meaning of life?

The Guffin Oh puke, puke, puke.

She/he holds his/her stomach and pretends to retch.

Lax There we go. Door open. Great. Let's walk right into some alien planet's garden, have sex with green women with super pink tits.

The Guffin *does a number of forward rolls, stands and goes into classical ballet steps.*

Kavi   I hate you, Lax.

Lax   Time to grow up, Kavi.

Kavi   Don't you see? You asked the wrong question.

Lax   What are you on?

Sat   Jay would have thought something like . . . like . . .

Lax   This is kids' stuff, Kavi. I mean, it's like playing – personally, I am no longer nine years old.

Sat   Like . . .

Kavi   I don't know, if it's a door . . .

Sat   Like what am I?

The Guffin *is suddenly dead still.*

Sat *is staring straight ahead.*

Lax   I'm out of here.

Kavi (*to* **Sat**)   What is it?

Lax   Kavi, come on.

Kavi *ignores him and is staring at* **Sat**.

Sat   Get lost, both of you.

Lax *exits.*

The Guffin *clicks his/her fingers.*

Sat *whirls round and sees him/her.* **Kavi** *cannot.*

The Guffin (*fingers to lips*)   Shh.

Kavi   Sat?

Sat   Can you . . . ?

The Guffin   Shh!

Kavi   Would have been a great presentation, you know? If . . .

Sat   If it hadn't got real?

Kavi   Well . . .

Sat   Don't want it real, do we? Cos real is pissy. In't it? Kack, piss – that's real.

Kavi *steps back.*

Kavi   I'm going to catch Lax. You know . . . he's coming round mine, cos my mum's . . . Sorry.

Turns away, turns back.

What did you call that thing?

Sat   The guffin.

Kavi   Yeah? Right.

She runs and exits.

Sat   You're not real, are you?

The Guffin   Course I am. Want to see her?

S/he raises an arm.

Enter **Jay**. *She is wearing her blue spotted dress.*

Jay   There's a waterfall up there.

Sat   Where?

Jay   Up through the trees. Let's go. We can swim.

Sat   All right.

They don't move.

Jay   Shall we get married?

Sat   Yeah.

Jay   We'll live in a house in a park. We won't have kids, cos they're horrible, but there'll be deer and we'd have a lake.

Sat   That'll cost.

Jay   Oh, you'll be loaded, cos of your crapola videos.

Sat   Will I?

Jay Yeah, and the first one will be about me, won't it?

Sat Yeah.

Jay Better get it on to YouTube then, before Dexter writes his poncy thing, cos poncy thing he will write.

Sat But I'm fourteen.

Jay Puts you light years ahead then, don't it?

Sat Yeah.

Jay Waterfall. C'mon. There's a pool, we can skinny dip.

Sat I want to.

Jay My knees look great, no worries. Bet your bum's got a bit of flab though.

Sat No way!

Jay Have a look, dumbo: get two mirrors, hold one sideways so you can see. Got to know who you are, haven't you?

Sat Why?

Jay Cos you asked the guffin the question!

The Guffin *gives a little wave.*

The Guffin Hello!

Jay Come on, I won't look at your bum if you don't want. Pity though.

She giggles.

Bet it flobbles.

Sat Jay . . .

A beat.

There're no trees, no waterfall, just bricks in the wall the back of Sainsbury's.

Jay Walk through it then.

She holds her hand out.

You want to.

The Guffin   You do.

Jay   C'mon.

The Guffin   C'mon.

Sat   You're not there.

Jay   You can do it.

Sat   It's just Sainsbury's toilets through that wall.

The Guffin   What wall are you looking at? That one? Or the wall of trees?

Sat   I can't see it any more.

The Guffin   You did though. I'll always be in, Sat. A door, you'll always know it's there. A tiny crack of light.

Crack! Very loud.

Sat   Kids' stuff! It's all kids' stuff!

Crack!

He throws the Guffin object to **The Guffin**, *who catches it.*

Jay   I loved you. Still do.

Crack!

Sat   Me too.

Crack!

Jay   Always, always. For never and ever, and never and ever.

Crack! Crack!

Sat   Ever for never.

Crack! Crack! Crack!

As with **Dexter**, *a* **Security Guard** *is unseen and unheard.*

Sat *turns.*

Security Guard   (You little runt, what you doing back here?)

Sat   I'm not doing nothing.

Security Guard   (Drugs is it?)

Sat   Not drugs, no. No way . . . no way.

Security Guard   (I'm pulling you in. Or give me a tenner.)

Sat   I haven't got a tenner.

Security Guard   (Come on.)

Sat *kicks out at him.*

Sat   Ever and ever!

He runs and exits.

Crack! Crack! A beat. Weaker. Crack! A beat. Weak. Crack.

The Guffin (*aside*)   Play done.

She throws **The Guffin** *into the audience.*

Jay (*aside*)   But can we have our ball back?

The Guffin

BY HOWARD BRENTON

*Notes on rehearsal and staging, drawn from a workshop
with the writer held at the National Theatre, November 2012*

How the writer came to write the play

Howard Brenton has recently written a string of plays with
history at the heart of the narratives. This sense of capturing
the past left him in a place where he was keen to get back to
the present moment. So, at the time he was writing, *directly*
capturing the 'present' was out of Howard's comfort zone.
When offered the opportunity to write for Connections, he
was keen to find a different approach to the canon of new
plays to be performed by young people.

He has always been fascinated with the idea of 'MacGuffin'.
This is a plot device invented by the filmmaker Alfred
Hitchcock. Simply put, the 'MacGuffin' is an object or event
in a film or book which serves as the impetus for the plot.
For Howard, the 'MacGuffin' is an object in a scenario
which has the power to explode a story. It is a trailblazing,
horizontal drive across the landscape of a play but also
provides the narrative space to 'sink down into the psychological
murk'.

'Without getting too abstract,' Howard explained, 'it is about
the object in the play becoming something uncontrollable, a
force within us which is difficult to quantify.' He wanted to
write a play which would encourage directors to reach right
into the ideas of the play and pull out what you see. *The Guffin*
is a piece of writing for the modern, filmic imagination.
Howard encourages those staging it to be brave and fearless.

Approaching the play

Nadia Fall (durector) spoke about the importance of 'unpicking the knots' of the play via *playing*. She presented a series of games so that the energies of the young people involved in the play are harnessed on their feet rather than around the table. This is the suggested approach towards development of ideas into rehearsals: creating a vast palette of approaches and then honing the responses of the young performers down into the forty minutes.

Themes

Self-awareness

After workshopping his ideas with young people at the National Theatre Studio, Howard was interested in excavating the moment when we 'stop playing'. He was fascinated by the array of answers given to this question and yet bewildered by the consciously/unconsciously wise responses. (On a wider level, outside the text, it is a theme worth exploring with the young performers by way of a personal route into the personalities of the characters they may well be playing in the production.)

Taking this question, he began to build characters out of it, suggesting that Lax and Kavi are almost grown up, on the edge of maturity, almost a couple; whereas the idea was that the other characters carry with them a sense of being a child.

With Jay and Sat we see a couple in opposition, struggling to understand one another until it is too late. So for Sat, by the end of the play there is a sense of emotional loss.

Identity

With Jay at the centre of things Howard has created a character who is 'quite simply awful to be around'. For Jay, it is just her nature; how she sees the world. But for the others, who openly explain how they find it difficult to be around her, Jay represents someone who doesn't quite fit into the norm.

Magic / reality
Nadia mentioned that an interesting production would excavate the '*measurements* between reality and imagination'. The Guffin is an intervention, starting its own narrative when it arrives in the play; an object that changes the rules.

Structure

Routines
Within the four-scene structure, Howard was keen to examine the architecture of the play as being a set of nine or ten 'routines'. These routines have a natural activity to them and there was a deliberate attempt to define more clearly 'things that the cast can be doing' rather than just the literary text. There was an encouragement to take the approach that there are lots of suggestions within these routines, but the creative team must invest time to make their own mark on the play. One routine could be interpreted as a short moment, or stretched out to the time and space of an operatic aria.

The simple advice is to identify the 'routines' and then divide them up into manageable, active explorations during rehearsals. Perhaps attack two routines per rehearsal and allow the students to have a think in advance about their reactions to the tasks. This combines a considered reaction with an instinctive exploration during the rehearsal.

Story within the story
With the Guffin as an object, there is the natural structure of an internal narrative within the piece. For Howard and Nadia, workshopping, analysing and finally making specific choices about the Guffin is important to make the most of the structure of the play.

Asides
One participant asked about the use of asides. Howard responded that he often uses them because they're a 'quick

fix' into what a character is thinking, be it contradictory to
the stage action or a declaration of partnership with another
character on stage.

Language

Invented words
The use of invented words within the pieces comes from an
urge to break the 'classroom' society from the use of a
standardised vernacular. The aim is to use the text as a
blueprint and twist it into the dialect of the young actors
involved all across the UK.

Physical
Nadia was keen to encourage directors to spend as much time
on the physical language of the play as on the textual work.
She talked about the young actors listening to each other
physically and ensuring that as much attention or logic was
applied to the physical language of the staging.

Characters and characterisation

THE GUFFIN – Howard explained that the Guffin is a major
energy and driving force through the play. The discussions
revolved around what that could mean for the characterisation.
Howard was keen to break from the obvious tropes of
characterisation for these sorts of magical devices. He asked,
'Where do the boundaries lie with the Guffin?' Nadia
suggested that the Guffin can mostly be shown through the
behaviour of others; the rest of the characters do the work for
the Guffin.

JAY – 'The visionary': the others react off her.

LAX/KAVI – 'A functioning couple . . . some heavy petting
when Mum is out.'

Casting

Simple decisions
With such a dense set of possibilities, there was a discussion
about not overcomplicating the casting process. Howard
actively felt that the actor playing Jay has to drive the play,
with the pace very much being defined by her choices. He
therefore felt that casting a young actor in this role will be
demanding and require a significant level of commitment and
engagement with the matrix of questions to bring a whole,
rounded and assured performance.

Production, staging and design

Spaces
Howard wrote the space the characters inhabit to be 'Brit
Universal' (places found all over Britain). He wants the actors
to find ways of painting what these places are like with the
words he has written. He used the example of 'the dip', which
he described as being like somewhere near where he lives:

> 'That deadly combination of railway arch, pub and
> Domino's pizza house. All wrapped around no street light.'

So painting the picture of what 'the dip' and the other places
in the play are like demands a great sense of inventiveness
from the actors, and for the directors to continue to ask
questions and gain clarity from the performances of the
young people.

Howard also mentioned that the simplest design will be the
best. Three cardboard vegetable crates can tell the story of
being outside Sainsbury's supermarket, for instance – there's
no need for elaborate design.

Staging
Howard explained that he conceived the production in-the-
round, but conceded that this might not be possible in some
of the productions.

Style and technique

There is no particular style in which Howard would like to see the play produced. Both he and Nadia pointed out that a sense of 'play' would feed into the rest of the play.

There was a discussion about creating the rules of the world in simple, dynamic ways.

Exercises for use in rehearsals

A significant amount of the workshop activity was spent on foot and revolved around the idea of exploring routines.

MIRRORING EXERCISE

Nadia took the participants through the process of building up a mirroring exercise.

Paired and named A and B, they started to explore what different types of mirroring could be used.

The next stage was to add some text plucked from the play and implemented in a call-and-response fashion.

From the play:
A: The question. Ask it.
B: What are you?

This layer of text on top of movement aimed to explore a rigour to the movement in the piece.

THE BALL EXERCISE

Nadia introduced different shapes and sizes of ball and asked the pairs to begin to play further with an object. Certain questions were asked:

'How does the Guffin appear/disappear?'

'What's the quality of its presence?'

FOREIGN LANGUAGE EXERCISE

Nadia introduced the idea of the meaning of language within the play being secondary for a moment. She asked the pairs to break off and improvise a short scene whereby one of the characters spoke in English and the other in a made-up language. This revealed the fact that sometimes we don't need two actors to 'sell' a scene to the audience. And so we arrived back at the simplicity of the young actors listening to each other. This is particularly the case in the scene with Dexter.

Suggested references

BOOKS
His Dark Materials by Philip Pulman (for alter egos).

Gormenghast by Mervyn Peake.

FILMS
Donnie Darko, written and directed by Richard Kelly (for the supernatural).

Alfred Hitchcock films (to look for where Hitchcock uses the MacGuffin).

MUSIC
Radiohead's 'Kid A'.

From a workshop led by Nadia Fall,
with notes by Jack Lowe

Mobile Phone Show

Jim Cartwright

Age suitability 13–19
Cast size 3–100

Jim Cartwright is a multi-award-winning play-wright whose work is consistently performed around the world and has been translated into over thirty-five languages. He has written successfully for film, television and radio and his stage work has been performed at the National Theatre, the Royal Court Theatre, in the West End and on Broadway. His plays for the theatre include: *Road, Bed, Two, The Rise and Fall of Little Voice, Prize Night* and *Hard Fruit*. Television and film work includes: *Road, Vroom, Wedded, June, Vacuuming Completely Nude in Paradise, Strumpet, Johnny Shakespeare* and *King of the Teds*. His plays are on both school and university curricula, and have been constantly in print since 1986.

Author's Notes

This play can be performed with no set whatsoever, no lighting, sound or props; or if desired it may be done with a set as elaborate as imagination or purse allow, back projections and effects, sound systems etc. – or anywhere in between the two.

It can be performed with three people or up to a hundred. All that is required of the actors is to turn up with a mobile phone.

It is genderless; the parts can be played by either sex or combination thereof.

No accent or region is stipulated, so it may be performed in any accent or combination of accents the group choose.

It is fluid enough in form – though the dialogue remains as written – that the group should be encouraged to add their own dances/songs/movement pieces: e.g. the group might become a massive human mobile phone – mobile phone juggling – mobile phone ballet/streetdance – mobile phone orchestra made up of ringtones, etc. etc.

This show is 'ours' – mine and the groups and the group leaders. All should share in its creation.

When it comes to the 'text haikus'. Perhaps the performers could write their own about their lives. Information on the haiku is on the internet and there are many good books, particularly *The Haiku Handbook: How to Write, Share and Teach Haiku* by William J. Higginson (Kodansha International, 2010).

When a line of dialogue is preceded by an em dash (—) it indicates an individual voice.

Characters

1
2
3
Voice
Phoner Loner
The Texter
Presenter
Brains
Georgie
Sammie
Billie
Dono
Natty
BB
TJ
Chorus
Others
Audience

An empty space. On the floor, spaced out, are a number of mobile phones.

From offstage an announcement is made.

'Ladies and gentlemen, the performance is about to begin, could I ask you all please to turn *on* your mobile phones, Thank you.'

The show begins . . .

Suddenly all the mobile phones start ringing, vibrating, jumping and buzzing.

The cast come on and pick up their own phones from the floor.

They each start talking into their phones as they move about the stage. A cacophony of voices.

— Oh my God, I don't believe it.

— No way.

— Liar.

— Yo, what's happening.

— What's next?

— Yes, way.

— I can't keep up.

— Never.

— I can't hear you.

— Oh my God.

— Him, he's the biggest keyboard warrior in the world!

— I'm not taking that, no, no.

— Are you under water!

— What? She said what? He said, what? What's what?

— How did you get this number!

— No.

— Yes.

— No.

— Yes.

— Don't keep me hanging on.

— There's more to life.

— Are you listening to me?

— Get out of it.

— What would you do? . . . You wouldn't!

— Twitter the tart.

— I'm going through a tunnel.

— Me three hundred minutes is nearly up and I've not spoke yet.

— You smell.

— Stop whispering.

— OMG, why have you forsaken me?

— Hello, are you 'withheld'? It sounds painful!

— Ten times over, mate, with bells on.

— My signal's bigger than yours.

— Just do it.

— I said speak when you're spoken to.

— Oh my God.

— Oh my God.

— Oh my God.

— You're breaking up.

— I'm hopeless.

— I can't get a word in.

— *Loud screaming down the phone with joy.*

— Tell them what I said.

— Oh my God.

— Knickers.

— Oh my God.

— Hold your nose and count to ten, that'll do it.

— The best text-kisser in town, I'm telling you.

— Fine then, fine, FINE!

— Whose call is this?!

— I shot the tariff.

— No not 'snow is coming' – Snowy's coming. Snowy the blond boy. Turn your volume up.

— Hurry up, my credit's low.

— Call me back.

— They're all coming.

— Who's going where?

— Who said what?

— She fancies you?

— Where did you go? Come back!

— Next time?

— I never.

— Oh my God.

The group begin to circle, tight and tighter in together as they speak, more and more – then, when tightly bound in scrum-like, the ringtones go off again . . .

Three performers break away and stand together. Against a wall or slouching in a line. Not looking at each other, talking as they text.

1   I need a new phone.

2   Yeah.

3   Nice.

1   Where do you get yours?

2   On line.

3   Bent Erika off the market.

1   Right.

2   I've just been down the shop.

3   Shop's good. Shops have 'em.

2   Yeah.

1   But this shop bloke, down there, he's asking me all these questions, questions, interrogation, third-degree type of thing.

2   Yeah.

3   Trying to fit the phone to the individual.

2   Yeah.

3   The individual to the phone.

2   Yeah.

3   Very important.

2 *starts to speak . . .*

1   Stop, you're gonna say 'Yeah', aren't you?

2   No.

1 *and* **3** *slow down their texting for a second, still without looking up.*

1 *and* **3**   Nothing like a change.

Back to full-speed texting.

2   I was gonna say . . .

3   Go on.

2   They are like a mobile matchmaker type of thing.

They all nod as they continue texting.

1   He's got his pen there ready to tick boxes.

2   Yeah.

3   They do like to tick.

2   Yeah, tick, tick, tickety.

1   First off, he says, he says, first off . . .

A loud voice from the crowd at the back.

Voice   Who do you talk to?

1 *jumps, almost stops texting but not quite.*

Voice   Do you have a wide circle of people you communicate with on a regular basis?

3   What, pray, did you say?

1   I said, I don't know what you're getting at, mush, but let's put it this way, I ain't no Billy no-mates.

2   Good call.

1   There's more than three in my contacts, pal.

3   Me, him, your mum, who's the other one?

1   Shut it!

The crowd advance holding their phones with tones ringing, the three merge into the crowd again, the crowd drive one of the performers off to the front corner of the stage, the performer has their hands over their ears.

The tones stop. The performer looks out at the audience . . . The others watch, onstage, in the background. From now on they act as a chorus to the performer's speech.

Phoner Loner   I was alone.

Chorus   Awwwwww.

Phoner Loner *gives them a dirty look.*

Phoner Loner   No one cared, noticed me, nothing. Not even bullied, nothing, no one.

One time I heard a word . . .

Chorus   Heard a word . . . What's the word you heard, nerd?

Phoner Loner   Non-descript . . .

Chorus (*whisper*)   Non-descript.

Phoner Loner   Non-descript, was the name I knew was mine.

The 'non' the small sharp 'hyphen' sign like a splinter in my soul, the 'descript', all mine.

Chorus (w*hisper into their phones*)   Non-descript. Non-descript.

Sounds like a . . . dry wind through dead leaves. A faint stink by the bin.

Phoner Loner   Non-descript, always in corners, almost invisible, on my own, at the back desk all alone.

Keeping my breathing quiet.

Keeping my eyes low.

If only I had a phone.

But Mother wouldn't let me have one.

Chorus   Mother wouldn't let me have one?

—   What?

All   What! Why? What! Why?

—   You can get one from Tesco for a tenner.

Phoner Loner   It's because of the radiation.

Chorus   The what?

They all laugh.

—   Turn you into an alien.

— Scorch your vitals.

— Crop circle your cranium.

— Twist your melon.

— Like a two-bar heater to the brain.

— Fry your head.

— Electric red.

The **Chorus** *rap a little.*

All
    Cook it, like Jamie, all a sizzle,
    with molten drizzle,
    micro-wizzled, ready in three –
    scrambled brains for tea.

More laughter.

Phoner Loner   Then one day – it was just there.

Chorus
    Answer to a prayer.

    'She found a phone' / 'Found it where!' / 'Found it on a
    bus seat' / 'Riding alone' / 'Right up there' / 'It was
    waiting on high'.

Phoner Loner   I know I should have . . .

Chorus
    'Gone to the driver' / 'Told someone older' / 'Found
    lost property' / 'Called the Coppers'.

Phoner Loner   But I slipped it away.

Chorus   Phoner Loner! You shouldna oughta!

Phoner Loner   I watched the back of the bus disappear and
I knew I was saved.

What now, I thought.

Chorus
Network Provider, dummy!
We all must have one.
A Provider who serves us,
who showers us with minutes of time, like thousands of
little ticking raindrops.
Who puts us everywhere, who flies us through the air.

Singing like Dominican monks.

Our Provider.

They bow.

Our Provider.

They bow.

Phoner Loner   Found my Provider.

Chorus   She found him in all his glory.

Again as the monks . . .

Five thousand free texts, three hundred minutes, unlimited
landlines and free web.

Phoner Loner   Felt more cared for than I ever did sitting
next to Mum in church. Cost less too, half of what we put on
the collection plate.

Now I have something with me at all times. To look at, to talk
in to, to listen from.

Chorus   A fount of freedom. A magic Mars Bar.

Phoner Loner   Suddenly awkwardness is impossible now,
my phone is always there. When it isn't on show it is swaddled
in my sleeve, against my pulse.

I have admiration now from all . . .

Chorus   Hark over there.

All nudging each other.

Phoner Loner   . . . as texts ping and calls come in, ringtones sing and twinkle and tweet around my head like Disney birds.

Attention is being paid, I'm 'Descript' now.

Chorus   Hark over there. (*Indicating* **Phoner.**) Friends by the phone full!! (*In admiration.*) How many texts can a person take!! The whole place shakes like earthquakes there's so many 'vibrates'.

Phoner Loner   But still they keep away.

They think me too popular for them, intimidated by me, in touch with a world none of them knows, exulted now. The Phoner Loner, who needs them not.

Pause.

But if they could only see.
The texts and calls are all from me to me.
The different ringtones I programme in separately.

I answer, then talk back to no one.
I press 'send', nothing's at the other end.

If they could only see.
The only real messages I get are from my NP.

'Your credit is low'.

'You have three free texts'.

'Thank you for your purchase'.

I'm more alone than when I started.

From one of the phones, suitable music is played.

The performer goes back into the crowd.

Silence.

The three are in their slouchy line again, talking and texting at the same time.

3   What else he ask ya?

2   Yeah.

1   He was on about allsorts, yeah . . . What was it now . . . Oh yeah . . .

Voice   How many texts on average do you send a day?

1   I ask ya?

2   What?

3 (*directed to* **2**)   No, not he asks 'you'.

3   Who?

1   I'm just saying. 'I ask you?'

2   What?

3   No.

2   Asked me what?

3   No, he's just saying 'I ask ya?' 'cause 'he' asked him.

2   Who?

1 *and* **3** *look at* **2**.

2   What?

3 (*to* **1**)   So that's what he said?

1   He did.

How many texts? I mean, who's counting, I ask ya?

3   Don't start that again!

Someone steps out of the **Chorus** *as a kind of* **Presenter**.

Presenter (*to audience*)   Excuse us, it's been five minutes, it's time for a T break.

(*aside*)   That's a 'text break', in mobile-phone-netics.

Suddenly the crowd are all in a straight line.

Presenter (*Sergeant Major*)   Texters, present mobiles.

They all get their phones in text position.

Half of them take a pace forward.

Presenter (*to audience*)   Texters are like eaters and lovers, quiet or noisy, fast or slow.

You get the silent senders . . .

He indicates those who have stepped forward.

They all suddenly start writing texts, thumbs going furiously, in silence.

They stop and send.

Presenter   Then you get the . . .

A Texter   Hang on, not finished yet.

Presenter (*Sergeant Major again*)   Hurry up, lad, or I'll snip your thumbs off and snap your sim.

The Texter *jumps to it and presses send.*

Presenter   Then you get the noisy ones.

The second half step forward and begin texting with their keyboard sounds on.

Presenter   A certain musicality to it, you must admit.

The **Presenter** *dances a little tap dance to the sounds.*

That twenty-first-century sound. Oh yeah. Little catchy keyboard there, man, if you're open to it.

Taps on.

They all press send.

At speed and through this speech, the **Presenter** *does the sound effects, like some demented Robin Williams/Lee Evans.*

Presenter   Gone now, like modern-day messenger pigeons, a million, zillion miles an hour, scorching the stratosphere, the clouds in bits, smoking, burnt mash . . . crispy on the ends maybe the way you like it . . . feathers in flames, winged messengers toasting the very wind, the very whooshing wind,

jet planes left for dead, zoooooooooooooooooo di doomdie –
(*Claps his hands.*) Splat on the phone screen of your mate in
London, Bradford, Paris or Mesopotamia.

Pause.

—   How do texts work really?

Presenter   I beg your pardon?

—   Really how do they work, like, texts?

Presenter   Really.

—   Really.

Presenter   Really and really . . . You want the *Blue Peter*
answer?

They all nod.

Brains   You don't know, do you?

Presenter   Sorry?

Brains (*sighs, then begins, at top speed*)   An SMS, message, as
specified by the Etsi organisation, seven-bit default alphabet,
used in OTA provisioning of WAP settings, Unicode UCS2
viewable on most phones as Flash SMS, is sent by protocol
description unit mod, which is just an encoding of the bit
stream represented by the PDU mode. All the octets are eight-
bit hexadecimal . . .

Presenter   Hang on, what?

Brains   Keep up, 'hexadecimal' . . .

—   Aren't they an eighties synth band?

—   Have you got their album?

—   No, but I'm sure me granddad has.

Presenter   Hang on, hang on. (*To* **Brains**.) And all that
what you said makes more sense than mine!!

Brains   It's facts.

Presenter   So what? I prefer mine.

Brains   Balderdash, you are nothing but a mobile-phoney.

Presenter   What! What! What! I'm not having that.

A Texter   Only one thing for it. A text-off.

Chorus   Yeah, yeah. Come on.

The two opponents separate off at either end of the stage, half the **Chorus** *around one, the other half around the other.*

—   Right then, exchange numbers . . .

They do, then back off again to their respective places.

—   Mobiles in pockets.

The two opponents obey.

—   You ready?

They both nod.

—   Okay, you know the rules of a text-out, I'm gonna call out a text term and you gotta send it and the first to arrive wins.

They nod.

Silence.

LOL . . . !

They both text it as fast as they can, send. The chorus sides watch. The exact same moment. Both sides raise their hands.

—   A draw. Alright . . .

—   Go again . . .

—   Mobiles in pockets . . .

—   Ready . . .

They nod.

Tense silence.

— 'K . . . !

They go for it, send. Same again, the 'pings' arrive at the same time. Cheers go up. Arguments . . .

— Settle down, settle down . . .

— Right. Return mobiles to pockets please . . .

They do . . . Really eyeballing, concentrating now.

Tense silence.

— OMG . . . !

*They go for it at top speed. Mobile pings. It hits **Brains**' phone first, he falls back into the crowd as if dead. **Presenter** whirls and jumps.*

Presenter   Stuff that up your hexadecimal!

He's lifted and bounced round the stage, as they all circle and whirl and merge.

The three are in their line again, still texting and talking at the same time.

1   Oh yeah . . . and then he's saying . . . 'Family and Friends'.

2   . . . What about 'em?

1   Do we talk a lot?

3   Blimey.

1   I know. I know . . . I said friends, yeah, family, not if I can flipping help it!

2   Good call.

2 high-fives 3 with one hand, while continuing to text with the other, 3, in same manner, manages the high-five slap.

2   I've blocked mine! Blocked 'em good and proper last Christmas. Bang! Stuff them.

1   That showed 'em, eh?

3   What did they say?

2   Don't know. They haven't noticed yet.

Three of the performers, **Sammie**, **Georgie**, **Billie** (*male, female or a mix*), *break off and move away to gather together, their phone screens illuminated and shining up under their faces.*

The others put their lights on their screens and follow them, gather around them. It's spooky like a mobile séance.

Georgie (*daft voice*)   Is there anybody there?

Sammie   Shut up.

Billie   Go on. Go on, text again.

Sammie *does.*

Georgie   Oh, this is mad.

Billie   Shhh.

Georgie   How many Network Providers have a signal on the 'Other Side'?

Sound of text going.

Sammie   It's gone. Quiet now.

Silence.

A sound from the **Chorus**.

Suddenly **Sammie** *jumps.*

Sammie   What was that?

Georgie   Nothing.

Silence.

They stare at the phone screen.

Nothing.

Georgie   See.

The **Chorus** *turn their screens off and back away.*

Sammie *still fixed on the screen.*

Georgie *takes* **Billie** *to one side.*

Georgie   Right, this has to stop.

Billie   What harm is it doing if it's helping?

Georgie   Plenty.

Billie   Why?

Georgie   Why? Why? Because we've got to face up to Mum's death and this is not the way!

Billie   I know other people who've carried on texting loved one's who've passed on.

Georgie   Oh yeah.

Billie   Yes, nothing wrong with it, it's like talking at the graveside.

Georgie   That's one thing, but this is something else, this is.

Looks over at **Sammie** *who is still staring at the screen.*

Georgie   Look.

Sammie.

No answer.

Sam!

Sammie   Shhh.

Georgie   Never mind all that. This has got to stop, you hear me?

Sammie (*carries on looking at screen*)   I can't.

Billie   We all feel it, we all love her, miss her . . .

Sammie   I just can't bear it.

Looks over at them, tears in eyes.

I can't go on without her.

Billie   Hey now. Hey.

Georgie   Snap out of it.

Billie   Have you no heart whatsoever?!

Georgie   Course I have, don't you think it's ripping me apart too, but I'm the only one seems to be moving this family along.

Billie   What are you on about?

Georgie   Well, look at Dad, no one's saying anything, but what's he doing to himself, to us? Working, working, non-stop. Then out every night. And Grandma . . .

Billie   She's in her own world.

Georgie   I know, but someone should be getting it through to her. All this hiding . . .

Billie   Is what you're doing not hiding?

Georgie   Sorry.

Billie   Running, hiding, all this 'Get on with it', 'Move on', not giving yourself or people a chance.

Georgie   Well, it's better than this craziness!

Sammie   It helps me.

Georgie   Helps! It's utter rubbish.

Billie   George!

Georgie   It is, and you know it is! You're making it worse!

Billie   How!

Georgie   Encouraging it!

Billie *jumps up and faces* **Georgie**.

Billie   Watch what you say!

Georgie   Or what?

Billie   You . . . (*Turns away.*) You are a piece of work, you are!

Georgie   Get real! Just get real!

Sammie   Stop it, stop it, both of you . . . I need quiet . . .
I'm going to try again . . .

Georgie   No.

Sammie *texts, not heeding, reads back while texting.*

Sammie   'Are you there, Mum?'

'Mum.'

'Are you there? We miss you so much, we can't live without
you.'

Silence.

Sammie*'s intensity has affected them all and they are stunned into
silence.*

They sit. And sit.

Georgie   Oh, I'm going.

Stands.

Suddenly a text comes. They all look at each other.

Sammie   I'm scared.

Billie   It will be from a mate.

Georgie   Don't read it!

Sammie *opens it.*

Billie   What does it say?

Fills up.

Sammie   It's her.

Reads.

'My little ones, I'm still here.'

It's her.

Billie   No.

Georgie   That's sick.

Snatches phone.

Who is this swine?

Looks who sent it.

Withheld. I thought as much.

This is some sick person.

Billie   It might not be.

Georgie   Course it is. She's dead. We went to her bloody funeral three weeks ago.

Billie   Hey!

Billie *turns to* **Sammie**.

Billie   What you going to do?

Sammie *starts texting back.*

Georgie   I don't believe this.

Billie   What did you put?

Sammie   'Mum, I love you. Please just give us a sign it's you.'

Georgie   Anything else?

Sammie   You can't text tears, can you?

Georgie   You shouldn't give them that, that's what these trolls want.

Suddenly a ping, the text has returned.

Slowly, apprehensively, **Sammie** *reads it.*

Billie   Well what does it say?

Sammie   'Night-night sleepy peepie.'

It's what she said to us. When we was kids, remember. Kiss us, then put her head back in the room and say . . .

Georgie   I know . . .

Billie   It's her.

Georgie   Others could know that.

Sammie   No.

Georgie *grabs phone, texts.*

Georgie   'Who are you! Sicko. Who is this?!'

Chorus *take up the cry as the three performers move away.*

Chorus (*speaking down their phones*)   Who is this?! Who is this?! WHO IS THIS?!

They come forward. They whisper.

— Days passed. More texts followed.
— Comforting.
— Loving.
— Could it be?

Georgie   NO.

Sammie   Can't you be glad?

Georgie   Someone's doing this! Playing with our heads. I can't stand it!

Sammie   But it's obvious she's with us now.

Georgie (*to* **Billie**)   Will you speak up!

Billie   Well it's . . . It's . . . I think it could be Mum.

Georgie   God help me!

Sammie   Perhaps he is helping.

At that **Georgie** *reaches for the phone.*

Georgie   Give me that!

Sammie   No!

Georgie (*snatches it, shouts out what is being typed*)   'Prove it's you. Conclusive. Prove it.'

Slams phone down.

Georgie   Will we hear again? I doubt it, unless they are more devious than I thought!

Sammie   Please get back. Please.

Billie   What's in it for anyone?

Georgie   These trolls, they love this kind of thing, screw people up or maybe it's money, that's what it's leading to.

Billie   What?

Georgie   No, no, listen, 'Send some money to such an account, they need it to help them with their important spiritual work' – all that, it happens.

Sammie   I'd hate to have your mind.

Georgie   I'd hate to be so weak and gullible.

Sammie   I pray you haven't frightened her away . . .

Georgie   It's not her! Don't be insane. It's not her!!

Suddenly the text sound.

They all look to phone.

Suddenly the **Chorus** *gather with their lights.*

Sammie *grabs up the phone.*

Holds it to heart.

Then slowly looks at it.

Sammie   Well . . .

Georgie   Read it, will you!

Billie   What does it say?

Sammie   'Five. Wings, tumbling, scaring sky.'

Georgie   What's that mean!

Billie   Preciously, none of us knows.

Georgie   We need to put this to someone. Get some clarity, some confirmation.

Sammie   Call Dad.

Billie   No, he'd hit the roof over the whole thing. Us trying to contact Mum, everything. No. No, he's coping with enough. Can't we just be content, have the messages as confirmation enough.

Georgie   No. Someone's got to confirm this or I'm going to the police.

Sammie   No.

Georgie   Watch me.

Sammie   What about asking Gran?

Billie   She wouldn't know, poor love, she just sits there knitting. Never mind séances, just mobiles and texts will have her befuddled even more.

Chorus   There were no more messages.

Georgie   See, scared them off.

Sammie   I know what it is, she's waiting for us to act on what she gave us.

Georgie   Rubbish.

Sammie   I'm going to ask Gran about what she said.

Billie   No.

Georgie   I'll go.

Billie   No, I'll do it. I don't want her frightened or shocked.

Chorus   So Gran was visited at the home. They drank tea, they talked of the old days, wool was held for her to unravel, as she unravelled the past . . . strand by woolly strand . . .

Billie *bursts back through the* **Chorus**.

Georgie   Well?

Sammie *looking up at* **Billie**.

Billie   Yes, when Mum was five she was an angel in a
Christmas play, they took her up on a wire, the sky gave way,
she fell, all panicked, but she fell in the manger by the baby
Jesus, all she got was a scar. A mini-miracle according to
Gran. She remembered the lot, she can't remember what
happened this morning but she knows the names of every kid
in it, what they wore, their . . .

Georgie   Okay, okay.

Sammie   Satisfied now?

Georgie *looks at her.*

The text sound goes again.

Sammie *reaches for it, picks it up.*

Opens it.

They are both staring at **Sammie**.

Sammie *turns slowly towards them and nods, it is her.*

Chorus   It's her. It is her.

The texts came more and more, and now they gave advice,
'Best to avoid that', 'Don't forget to . . . ', 'Wrap up warm . . . ',
'Remember . . . '. Just as Mother had done, and it was always
right . . .

The **Chorus** *change position. The three performers step through them
and stand facing the audience.*

And from then on they basked in the guidance and love of
their mother, texted back their thoughts, their problems, their
stories . . .

Time passed, life began again, grief took its place, the texts
grew less in number, bit by bit they petered out.

It was a secret they never told.

Dad too got better, began to live again.

All grew stronger, but Gran grew weaker . . .

One sad day she passed away . . .

After the funeral. The three of them had to go through her things.

Sammie *suddenly calls them* . . .

Sammie   In here. In here!

They gather.

Billie   What is it? What's the matter!

Sammie   Look at the bottom of her knitting bag.

Chorus   It was . . .

Billie   A brand-new mobile phone.

And look, Mum's sim in it.

She must have got it from her old one.

It dawns on them who was sending the texts.

Sammie   So that was it.

Georgie   But how did she know all that stuff about our lives, what we were doing, where we needed help, all that?

Sammie   Think I know.

Billie   What?

Sammie   I was talking to Dad recently, he was telling me about that time, how hard it was for him, how the only relief he got was going to see Gran every night . . .

Georgie   When we thought he was drinking . . .

Sammie   He was talking to her, and telling her about us, what we were doing, how we were coping . . .

Billie   When I think how destroyed we were.

Sammie   She knew we needed that comfort.

Billie   We needed that comfort so much.

Georgie   It was a con, but a good con.

Sammie   Thanks, Gran.

Sammie *picks up the mobile phone.*

Georgie   What you doing?

Sammie   Texting her. Texing our gran.

Georgie   Come on.

Sammie   Hey, I'm not daft, I know now, but it's symbolic, it makes me feel better.

Billie   Me too.

Sammie (*speaks as texts*)   'Thank you Gran, we love you.'

Sammie *gently puts the phone down.*

They walk away.

Phone suddenly pings, a text has arrived!

They all look at it.

Music plays from one of the phones.

The three again emerge, still at it, texting.

No talking.

Texting.

1   So Mr Tick-Tick's still at it.

2   Tickety.

3   Knocking off the boxes. A 'tick' boxer.

1   Yeah. Then he's like . . .

Voice   Would you say you use your phone for business mainly or personal matters?

2   What a liberty.

3   I'd have told them to stuff it.

1   I just said, personal, mush, personal, personal and more personal, and any business is none of your business, buster.

2   Good call. What's yours is yours.

2 *is looking over the shoulder of* **3**, *who covers the screen.*

3   Bug off.

AUDIENCE PARTICIPATION

An attempt to create some really real and possibly even personal moments on stage.

At this point the **Chorus** *begin filming the audience, walking towards them, then stop.*

They play it back, laughter maybe.

They stop.

Chorus   Call us, go on.

Holding up their phones.

If you have a number, for any of us, call. Be in our show.

Conversations can be had between the cast and audience members.

The cast can call people in the audience.

Someone from Chorus   I'm calling.

They ring someone in the audience.

Some other alternatives are below.

- *If inclined and someone has the nerve, a confession real or imagined could be made.*

- *'Mum I'm pregnant', 'It was me who broke the telly', 'Dad I don't want to go to University'.*

- *A truth might be told.*

- *Conversation with a parent in the audience, a friend, teacher, me if I am in the audience.*

- *Audience can hold their phones up with their ringtones.*

- *Suddenly one of them calls someone in the audience, someone in the audience calls someone on stage, then someone else calls someone in the audience, someone out there calls back and on the conversations go in a modern-day mobile round.*

- *The audience join in a chant, their voices coming through with the phones held by the cast.*

In whatever form it takes, the audience participation ends . . .

The three emerge again. Texting while talking, the same.

1   Then he's really warming up. Ticking away like a clock. Then he says to me . . .

Voice   Will you be doing anything creative with your phone?

3   What did you say?

1   I said I can think of a few creative things you could do with that pencil.

They all laugh.

*One of the performers (**Natty**) is off on their own; they are composing something on their phone, deep in thought. Another (**Dono**) comes to join them.*

Dono   What you doing?

Natty   Haiku.

Dono   Got a bit of a hack there, cough up.

Natty   No, it's a three-line poem, that sums up a moment in time.

Dono   Eh?

Natty   I text them to my friend in Japan and they text them back to me. Japan's where it was invented, like hundreds of years ago.

Dono   Oh yeah.

Natty   Here's some they sent me.

Reads from phone.

> On a barren branch
> a raven has perched –
> autumn dusk

> Old Pond –
> a frog leaps in,
> Plop!

> Evening breeze –
> water laps the
> legs of the blue heron

> Far fireworks –
> sounding, otherwise
> not a thing

Dono   Hey, nice.

Natty   Yes.

Dono
> My mate reads me Haiku
> from a mobile,
> others listen at a distance

Natty   You're getting it.

The others are gathering around bit by bit.

Natty   Here's some I sent over there, we do it every day.

> A note on the fridge,
> Mother's out,
> Cold fishfingers on a plate

> Once again your answer machine,
> I bite my thumbnail,
> to stop a tear

> The remote control
> on my homework book
> the weather man says more rain

Some of the others start typing and texting them.

Dad's slippers,
I want a lift,
He sighs, and the fire crackles

Midnight,
A skid on Morrison's car park,
through the car window, two fingers

Music through my earphones,
I look through the shop window
my best friend's in the Apple Store

Sun reflects off my phone screen,
I have two new apps –
A woman smiles, an old man doffs his cap

The three emerge again, talking while texting.

3   Anything else?

1   He pulls the protection racket, dun' he.

2   No.

1   Yeah.

Voice   Would you like protection in case of damage or loss?

1   Don't like the sound of that, I said.

3   Yeah, like making you an offer you can't refuse . . .

2   The mobile mafia.

1 *(waxing lyrical)*   I'll take me chances, mate, I said. I'm a gambler me.

2 *and* **3** *mumble agreement as they text away.*

1   I'll leave it, I says, leave it to that great lottery called life.

2   Let's hope you don't drop it down the lavvy like last time.

Suddenly the doors burst open. Someone comes into the auditorium.

BB   I've lost me mobile!

To members of the audience.

Anyone seen a phone?

You seen it! Phone? Phone? Arrrgh. You seen a phone? No idea where it is, looked everywhere! Me phone, seen it?

To someone in audience.

Can I borrow yours, mate, to call it?

They do. He dials.

It's ringing. (*Listens.*)

To audience.

Shhhh! (*To everyone.*) Listen, can you all listen. There's a life at stake here!

Silence.

No. No. No. Nothing.

Gives phone back. Moves on to stage.

It's gone.

My whole life has gone. I've been murdered, basically. My young life taken from me before my time!

Help me.

Think what's on there. Think. I don't want to!

It's my brain, everything I need to know comes from there. I've had a lobotomy basically, and my brain's been left on the sideboard or under a couch or a changing-room bench, on a wall, at a bus stop or in a bin . . . God forbid. It's my life. How can I go on!

How can anyone get to me! I've been off an hour, they'll think I died. I can't get hold of a soul. All me numbers, everything. GET A NEW ONE, YOU MIGHT SAY! But it's all the stuff. Reaming reams of my life. Scroll back the years and years of it. When you die they say your life flashes before you, well, mine's on there!

All the best texts I got or I sent, works of art they was, some of them.

Some of those tender, tender ones I was keeping too.

Christ, I've nothing now to show my kids!! When they come, if they come, I'll never meet anybody now, will I? Love life up the Swanee! Phoneless Romeo!

Without a phone, how do you date? Tell me that. Go on. Tell me!

I could have passed that sim down through the centuries.

A heirloom.

I don't have to use me brain if it's all on there, do I? I'll have to crank me human one up now.Where do you start?

It's the feel of it too, you get used to it, you know it and it knows you. Like a gunslinger and his Colt 45, Jimi Hendrix and his guitar, I could work it in the pitch dark, I know its every little phone foible, all its little ways.

Fills up. Suddenly in shock.

Oh God, all the pictures. Irreplaceable. Oh God, the parties, the holidays, the beaches – the one where I went like that . . .

Jumps in the air legs spread, arms up, the whole **Chorus** *do it behind.*

. . . Caught in mid-air I was. No one will ever see the like of that again, it's a moment in time. Oh God, my baby sister, our old dog that's gone, concerts, me with the famous, arms round ———— (*Here can be inserted a celebrity name if desired.*) Thumbs up. (*Puts his thumbs up like he's with them again.*) And even one of me and the phone I took in the mirror.

One-offs, originals, the only copies, the . . .

Suddenly in shock again.

OH GOD! And all the secrets, oh no, all the stuff, private. It can go public now. I remember this happened to someone

I heard of, they had to move away, start a new life. They needed
a complete new identity basically. Someone forwarded all the
photos and all the texts and all the messages to everyone.
Oh no! All the records of cheating and scamming and back-
stabbing and slagging, all the naughty pictures of others I
should never ever of took. That's me finished.

There's nothing for it, only one thing for it. I'm going to have
to go on Facebook and tell all, get it out before it gets out.

Can't even get on Facebook without it, have to use old Bessie
the school computer.

Where do I start? There was that text . . . (*Cringes.*)

That photo . . .

That . . .

Suddenly pauses, has heard something . . .

Wait a minute. Wait a cotton-picking minute . . .

What's that I hear?

What's that?

The sound of angels . . .

That's it . . .

*From a distance we hear a ringtone. It gets louder and louder, someone
approaching with a phone.*

BB *goes to take it, they lift it out of reach, then they run off laughing,* **BB**
gives chase.

BB   Come here.

Traps them.

Right!

Any frapeing?

They shake their head.

Any breaking in?

Shake head.

Okay.

BB *kisses them on the forehead.*

Thanks. Thank you. I owe you everything.

Takes the phone.

Holds it on high.

Then checks it.

It's only been off an hour and there's 101 messages.

OMG. OMG.

Makes a call.

I'm back. I'm back, it's like someone dying of thirst in the desert, suddenly drinking, drinking again . . .

Back . . . Back . . .

Turns away with the phone, still talking ten to the dozen . . .

The **Chorus** *are all on their phones as in the beginning.*

They swirl talking . . . ten to the dozen also. As they spin and move they leave the three in their line, all still texting and talking to each other at the same time.

2   I'm in love. Yes, it's the real thing.

1   How do you know?

3   They've been texting each other for three weeks.

1   What's your love look like?

2   Never met.

1   Eh?

3   Got a photo though.

1   Might not be them.

2   Don't say that.

1   Well, it happens.

2   I know.

1   Eh?

2   I sent them a picture of someone else!

1   You didn't!

2   Yes.

3   You shouldn't.

2   I know.

3   Who?

2   You.

3 chases 2 round the stage, as 3 calls after them.

1   Hey, hey, come back. I wanna tell you about his next question.

Voice   How about communication with the wider community?

TJ *steps forward talking into phone.*

TJ   I was there.

Someone at back is on their phone in conversation with **TJ**.

—   No

TJ   Oh yes

—   Was it like they said, they showed?

TJ   Not the full picture

—   Tell us, go on.

TJ   Atop the escalator, you know the place.

—   Second level?

TJ   That's it.

—   To the side River Island, and then Boots.

TJ   There I was.

Imagine it, I looking down from on high, from my chrome-railed, glassy, shopping mall, knoll.

Imagine it, looking down from there. See them swirl in, swirling in, the Saturday-morning shoppers.

Imagine it, sun beaming in through the glass dome roof, cathedral-like, seeing them swirl in, those pin-number pilgrims.

Are you seeing it? Seeing them swirl in to the music, the lulling, lilting music without meaning, music to shop to and nothing else.

The **Chorus** *begin to make the sounds of the pan-piped music.*

See them, there they go in a humdrum drift on a soulless rift, a pan-piped version of an ancient Abba.

The music gradually quieter, then fading away . . .

See them, like conjurers, whipping out the credit cards from pockets and purses, wallets and bags, at counters, continuous, whirling plastic squares, the only way to buy the wares beyond my reach and theirs. Magic, no one sees the money, till you're drowning in debt.

Then deep down below, I saw four teenagers, three lads and one girl, bright and happy, like jelly beans tossed in there, they was. They weren't doing no harm, know what I mean. Bit boisterous perhaps, different from the crowd, laughing too loud.

From nowhere, three security guards, pushing one of the boys about, no need for it, not right! Big and surly, hurly burly, forcing the kids into the wall, curly wurly, shove and crack, lad in a doorway arm up his back.

Chorus (*as the kids*)   'Get off!' 'Leave him alone!' 'Arrrrrrrr!' 'What have we done!' 'Get off'.

TJ   His mate started filming it, guard grabbed his phone. That did it! That was it! Lickety split, the other kid was on his mobile, all calm, looked like he was whispering into his palm.

Then from all sides they did come, young ones, streaming into the place, like those . . . what do they use in science experiments for molecules? – you know, bright coloured balls, injected in, rapid fire, changing one state of things to another.

The guards trapped by the sheer force of numbers, stacked carcasses up the back.

I saw it then, saw our power and our glory, the majesty of our mobility, never known to other generations, we don't care about politicians who don't care about us, we have what they don't, unity in a second, support in a trice, a community on call.

Pride filled me up, there we were showing our might, force but without violence, a Gandhi fight.

Then saw someone take some balloons from a card shop, just went in and out, a bear, a duck, a grinning cat, all floating on strings. Just a laugh.

But something started in me. 'No,' I said. 'No, don't!'

Something stirred in me, I said 'No.' 'No, don't.'

Next, shops were swamped, assistants trying to bolt the doors but no chance, saw one lad jam a descending shutter, then someone walking along with a flat screen, another there with trainers, another with boxes of brand-new phones.

I was calling from up there but nobody listened. Busting a gut, ripping my throat . . . 'No! No!'

A window went in, then another. Alarms going off, a crazy round mixed in with the ancient Abba sound.

Ahhhhhhhh!!

They'll take it from us. They'll take this freedom, can't you see? They'll take it . . .

The police came.

No. No.

The three balloons floated up in front of me, higher and higher and higher. Trailing their strings,

The **Chorus** *behind all look up as if watching them go.*

TJ Hit the glass roof, just beyond is the sky, where they could fly, but they bend against the block, crumpled faces now as if to cry . . . and then they popped and dropped.

I didn't look down where they fell. I heard though, shouts and scream a last mighty yell.

TJ *fades back into the crowd.*

The three are there again, talking and texting.

1 Then he started on about . . .

3 Tariffs.

2 Yeah.

1 How did you know?

3 They always do.

2 What did the man say?

1 The man said . . .

24 months – 400 minutes – unlimited texts – 250 MB – 22 quid.

One of the crowd takes the phone away from their ear and echoes this.

—   24 months – 400 minutes – unlimited texts – 250 MB – 22 quid.

They all voice it.

—   24 months – 400 minutes – unlimited texts – 250 MB – 22 quid.

Then they all begin chanting tariffs louder and louder, faster and faster. (Find as many variations as possible.)

—   200 minutes – 4,000 texts – 750 MB.

—   400 minutes – unlimited texts – 750 MB.

—   600 minutes – unlimited texts – 250 MB.

—   200 minutes – unlimited texts – 500 MB.

—   unlimited minutes – unlimited texts – 1 GB.

They carry on with tariffs until they reach a mad climax.

Then suddenly everything cuts out.

1   Last but not least he talks about . . .

All left speechless, phones at mouth.

Battery life.

The others all look at him.

Nothing.

They all look at each other.

All   NO CHARGE LEFT.

They meander about a bit.

They open their mouths but nothing comes out.

Slowly they start to leave the stage.

Gone.

Mobile Phone Show

BY JIM CARTWRIGHT

*Notes on rehearsal and staging, drawn from a workshop
with the writer held at the National Theatre, November 2012*

How the writer came to write the play

Jim Cartwright wanted to write something that young people
could apply their imagination and passion to. He looked to
his own children for inspiration – what did they spend their
time doing? The answer came in the form of mobile phones,
objects that have become so much a part of modern life. Nearly
everyone has one, and spends so much time on them, texting,
talking, playing games, checking emails, downloading ringtones . . . so why not make a piece of theatre about them? Jim
wrote *Mobile Phone Show* to be a vital, fluid and different piece
that young people could really make their own, requiring
nothing more than themselves and a mobile phone. He also
wanted to explore communication in the theatre and to look at
the relationship between actors and audience in a playful way.

Approaching the play

As Jim writes in his opening stage directions, you and your
company are encouraged and invited to take ownership of the
play. 'All should share in its creation.' Open it up; respond to
the skills, passions and imaginations of the young people you
are working with; they will often have the best ideas. Find your
own unique way of making the text work. Explore the theatrical
possibilities of the mobile phone (they are endless) and the ways
in which your chorus tell the story. Investigate each moment
fully and let your imaginations run free. Jim is excited by the
endless possibility of performance – every single show will be
different and this is to be embraced and celebrated.

Themes

- How dependent we have become on our phones/technology at our fingertips.
- How communication is evolving and changing with mobile phones.
- Instant communication.
- Intelligence. Information at our fingertips – if we don't know something we can very quickly find it out.
- Community and forming connections with others.
- Do we fight or embrace the presence of mobiles in daily life?
- Fitting in.
- Loneliness.
- Values of modern society.
- Text culture/phone etiquette.
- Our relationship to words and language.

Structure

Jim has deliberately kept the form fluid to allow more room for young people to make it their own. The ensemble is at its heart. There are fragments of stories and the three 'text talker' characters offer a basic throughline but, as the title indicates, it is a 'show' rather than a 'play'.

Casting

Jim has allowed for huge freedom in casting. It can be performed by as few as three people, or as many as a hundred. It is not region- or gender-specific, so use the accents and gender combinations of your group to make it work for you.

Production, staging and design

Your production can be as simple or as lavish as you see fit. It can be done with nothing more than a group of people and their mobile phones. It does not necessarily require set, lighting or sound, but if budget and resources will allow, see where your imagination can take you! Experiment with the theatrical possibilities of the mobile phones themselves – what can they offer in terms of lighting, sound effects, music, visual images?

Audience participation

Experiment with the possibilities of the audience participation moments and what can realistically be achieved with your company. If what is written in the text feels too complicated, don't be afraid to simplify the moment.

Suggestions for successful audience participation:

- Don't give phone numbers out, but make use of numbers you and your performers already know (for example, a performer's parent/friend/sibling might be in the audience).

- If you have the budget or the desire, you could buy 'plant' mobile phones, or SIM cards to use specifically for the show.

- If you want to try and contain audience participation to the specific moment in the text, bringing the house lights up/down at key moments might be a clear signal for an audience to know when they can/can't join in.

- Use your chorus to tell your audience what to do, or to rein them in if they get too rowdy. Or use projections/signs/announcements: 'Phones on' and 'Phones off'.

- Embrace all the non-show-related mobile phone sounds that might go off during the show as a result of having many mobile phones switched on. Enjoy the potential for spontaneous theatrical moments/conversations that might occur as a result!

- Have a few tricks up your sleeve should a moment become a bit unruly. For example, the chorus could break out into a song, or you could change the lighting state to create a moment that diverts attention back on to the stage.

- Audiences love the idea of improvised/unexpected moments during a performance. Play with that and create moments that give the impression of something that is on the spot and chaotic, but actually is rehearsed and ready to go.
- A live Twitter feed could be used during the show.
- Before the show begins, there could be instructions/activities in the foyer to help the audience into the world of the show.

Style and technique

Anything goes! Be madly creative and smash styles against each other. Embrace the theatricality and difference, don't try to squeeze it all into the same style, or force a narrative. Explore a wide range of performance styles according to what your group enjoy doing; dancing, singing, movement, projection, circus skills, mime, stand-up comedy, film, live music, etc.

Language

Respect the text. There are lots of moments where there is room for improvisation, but don't let it get out of hand. Welcome suggestions from your company to reflect regional voices, or 'text/phone speak' that Jim might not have known about at the time of writing.

Whenever there is a dash ahead of a sentence in the text, this is meant for an individual speaker.

Experiment with different ways of splitting up the chorus sections and uncover the rhythms of the text. You might want to put some sections to music or percussion. You might want some of it to be sung/rapped.

Encourage everyone in the company to write their own haikus about their lives. It might be useful to think of a haiku as a bit like a tweet – a brief moment to sum up an individual experience.

Exercises for use in rehearsal

MOBILE PHONE EXPLORATION: WHAT DOES IT DO?

Perhaps a useful exercise to do on the first day of rehearsals to get your company really thinking and observing beyond the everyday.

Brainstorm everything about mobile phones.

- Ask everyone about their phones (style/make/model etc.). What different types are in the room?
- How do you choose your mobile phone? What marketing do you respond to?
- What are the physical properties of your mobile phone? Ask people to describe their mobile phone as if they have never seen it before/as if describing it to someone else who has never seen one.
- What does it mean socially?
- When do you use it?
- What do you use it for?
- What would you do if you couldn't use it?
- What does it mean for your relationships?
- What information is on your mobile phone?
- What has been the evolution of the mobile phone?
- Does anyone use a landline?
- What *don't* we know about the mobile phone?

OBSERVATION/IMITATION EXERCISE

An exercise to focus on the quality of observation, seeing beyond the everyday and developing chorus possibilities.

- Form pairs. Label A and B.
- A follows B around the room, using all the space.
- A has to observe how B walks and follow exactly what is happening in front of them. Copy what they see. Encourage

them to place all of their attention on their partner and not themselves.

- Then find an individual element to how B is walking and exaggerate it. Push as far as possible until it is grotesque.
- B then has to turn around and try and catch out A – to catch them in the act. A has to act the innocent, as if nothing is going on.
- Swap, so B now follows A.

Then ask the group to stand at one end of the room, except for two volunteers.

- Ask everyone to watch the exercise and see how the pair are playing the game. Gradually send more people to join in, so more and more in the group are following and imitating a single person. Encourage the group to stick as closely to each other and the person they are following as possible, creating something similar to a shoal of fish.
- Give simple actions to the 'leader' to develop the game (stop/check watch/tie shoelace/see something in the sky, etc.) and encourage the 'followers' to push levels of exaggeration to the extreme.

Other developments to include could be:

- Playing with speed/tempo of movement.
- Changing the leadership at any point, so sensing as a group when to choose a different person to follow and imitate.

CHORUS EXERCISE

Ask the group to walk around the room, making lots of eye contact and taking new journeys in the space.

- On a single clap, ask everyone to jump at the same time. Keep walking and clapping until they are jumping at exactly the same time.
- Explore different ways of walking – e.g., walk using the outside/inside of your feet.

- Then shout out a number and tell everyone to get into groups of that size.
- Then on a clap, ask the group to turn ninety degrees and keep walking in that new direction.
- Then ask the group to slow down altogether until they are stationary. Then very slowly, as a group, start walking until they are at normal pace.
- Then call out a number and that number of people have to start walking at the same time. Keep trying until the correct number of people start walking together.

IMPROVISATION EXERCISES

Split into groups. Ask one person in a group to tell everyone about their journey that morning, or to describe the happiest day of their life, in the most minute detail possible. The rest of the group have to imitate them exactly. Repeat the exercise and, at any point, ask someone else to take over the telling of the story.

Surprise half of the group with an unexpected scenario and ask them to play the scene immediately. For example: 'You are an award-winning professional *a cappella* choir and are about to perform the premiere of your new piece. Welcome to the stage, take your bow and begin.' You can develop this with the other half of the group by asking them now to perform their new piece, which has lyrics in it.

EXERCISES WITH MOBILE PHONES

These are starting points to unlock the theatrical possibilities of the mobile phone and came about as a result of experimenting in the workshop. Seize the opportunity to play around with your group to unlock and experiment with all the different ways a mobile phone can be used in a theatrical and visual way.

- Ask everyone to turn on their mobile phones and to play around with the different noises they can make – keypad tones, ringtones, message alerts, etc.

- Repeat the observation/imitation exercise above, but with mobile phones. This time, the 'leader' uses their phone while walking and everyone else imitates what they do.

- Play the same imitation game, but this time follow the movements of the phone instead of the person holding it.

- Turn the lights out so that people are only lit by the light of their mobile phones.

- Play around with journeys, shapes, formations, synchronised movement of phones in the dark. Give the group different actions for their phones: look left/look right/check your phone/show phones out front/move them in a circle, etc.

- Split the group in half and ask them to stand at either end of the room, with one 'leader' in each group. Ask one 'leader' to ring the other and have an improvised conversation on loudspeaker. Ask the rest of the group to repeat everything their 'leader' does physically and vocally.

- Ask everyone to play their favourite song on their phone at the same time. See what happens if everyone starts singing along to their own song.

- Put all phones on loudspeaker. Choose the phone number of one person in the group and ask everyone to ring them at the same time. See who gets through. What happens with everyone else's phones?

- Ask everyone to take a photograph of themselves on their phones and to get the photo on the phone screen. Get into a tight group and use the phones like puppets to make a chorus of phones. Experiment with formations: for example, in a straight line horizontally/vertically, in a particular shape, getting the phones to 'dance', turn, talk to each other, etc.

- Ask everyone to make a sentence by taking a picture of a single letter on their phones and then arranging the letters in order. Play around with how the words are presented. Are they in a straight line? Or one word below another?

Play around with how each word is revealed. One by one or all together? In a particular rhythm? Experiment with making an anagram out of your original sentence.

- Set up an improvised phone conversation between two people, where what is said can be used to reveal the subtext of a verbal conversation. Split into smaller groups and ask each group to come up with a little vignette/story, using a phone conversation between two people and seeing how the images/letters/music on the rest of the group's phones can be used to theatrical effect.

- Ask two people to record themselves on their phones as they play a scene, or have a conversation. Then play back both phones at the same time and put the phones together, so the phones are now 'performing' the scene.

- Ask everyone to take a picture of a fragment of an object, a face, etc., then put all the phones together to make one picture.

Suggested references

BOOKS
The Haiku Handbook: How to Write, Share and Teach Haiku by William J. Higginson.

FILMS
Alex Horne Presents: The Horne Section (a live comedy and music show that revels in seemingly off-the-cuff improvised moments. This might be useful to watch in relation to the audience participation sections.)

Magical Mystery Tour (film starring the Beatles. A great example of embracing many different styles and theatricality.)

PAINTING
The Treachery of Images by René Magritte. (Useful to think of a mobile phone in a similar way. If it isn't a mobile phone, what is it?)

From a workshop led by Facilitating Director Phillip Breen, with notes by Kate Budgen

What Are They Like?

Lucinda Coxon

Age suitability 15–19
Cast size 12

Lucinda Coxon's plays include *Herding Cats* (Theatre Royal Bath, Hampstead Theatre, Theatre Award UK nominee 2011), *The Eternal Not*, *Happy Now?* (National Theatre, Writer's Guild of Great Britain Best Play Award 2008, Drama Desk and Lortel Award nominee, NY 2010), *Nostalgia and Vesuvius* (South Coast Repertory Theatre), *Improbabilities* (Soho Poly), *Wishbones*, *Waiting at the Water's Edge* (Bush Theatre), and *Three Graces* (Lakeside Theatre/ Colchester Mercury). Lucinda's adaptations include *The Shoemaker's Incredible Wife* from the play by Federico García Lorca and *The Ice Palace* from the novel by Tarjei Vesaas, both for National Theatre Connections. Her screenplays include *Wild Target*, *The Heart of Me* and *The Danish Girl*. Her four-part version of Michel Faber's *The Crimson Petal and the White* was screened to critical acclaim on BBC2 in 2011. She is currently adapting Sarah Waters's *The Little Stranger* for film.

Author's Notes

The stage directions given in this play are sometimes very specific, sometimes very loose. They should, by and large, be viewed as suggestions. They are a way of scoring the play.

The most useful approach in rehearsal may be to discover the intention behind the direction, rather than adhere to it. This is not the way I work ordinarily, but much of the pleasure of this play will lie in exploring its physical life.

What Are They Like? features twelve performers who play twelve characters. The transition from performer to character occurs on stage. There might be a value in staging a short warm-up in view of the audience before 'the play' commences. A sense of bonding in the performer company might usefully inform the various forms of isolation and community found in the characters' experiences.

The toy box can be approached at any time by any character, within the time bracket specified in the text. Characters might approach more than once, changing their minds about taking their toy. They do each have a special toy, but what that toy might be (cuddly toy, ball, skipping rope, musical instrument, remote-control helicopter, doll, puppet, etc.) is something to be discovered in rehearsal. Attachment to, or absorption in, a toy might halt or interrupt the action of the play. Toys might be deliberately or inadvertently shared. The toy might or might not be referred to when the character is speaking.

I spoke to many parents of teenagers as part of the process of developing this play. I am indebted to all of them for the stories they were generous enough to share with me.   L.C.

Characters

Alison
Frances
Gary
Grace
Indira
Johnny
Meera
Nick
Patrick
Robert
Sarah
Steph

One

Lights up. A circle of shoes on the floor, widely spaced, neatly arranged in pairs, pointing towards the centre – five pairs of men's, seven pairs of women's. They might be formal or utility wear, but they are the shoes of people aged over thirty.

In the centre of the shoe circle is a large cardboard box. We cannot see inside it.

Twelve performers enter, stalk in an insistent rhythm around the shoes, eventually stopping, each in front of a pair. When the moment is right, they step into the shoes. The shoes (and thus, characters) and the performers do not need to share a gender. Nor do the shoes have to fit.

Once all shoes are on, the circle becomes ominously energised.
Something is about to begin:

Robert   Tick.

Frances   Tock.

Steph   Tick.

Grace   Tock.

Nick   Tick.

Gary   Tock.

Johnny   Tick.

Indira   Tock.

Alison   Tick.

Patrick   Tock.

Sarah   Tick.

Meera   Tock.

Robert   Get up! Come on, you're going to miss it!

Frances   For the last time, can you just go to bed!

Steph   Go out, go on, and get some fresh air /

Grace   I want you back in the house by /

Nick   You're not still doing that . . . ?

Gary   Haven't you even started yet . . . ?

Johnny   You need to eat something /

Indira   Who's eaten all this?

Alison   You need to work harder /

Patrick   You'll wear yourself out.

Sarah   You've got to take it seriously /

Meera   Hey, it's not the end of the world . . .

Nick *confesses.*

Nick   Y' lie t'them – of course – don't you? Right from the start! You've got to – you don't mean to, but really . . . Come on! As soon as they're born, y' start lying.

It's like when they're little, you say . . . 'There's nothing to be frightened of.' But there is. Of course. There's plenty.

Meera *looks out at the audience.*

Meera   There's plenty.

Nick   I remember when Alex was – what was he? – three, maybe? He got obsessed – I don't know where that came from – obsessed – with the idea of death. The idea I was going to die. He'd wake up screaming . . . some terrible dream: 'Hey – hey!' I'd tell him: 'I'm not going to die! I'm not going t'die! I promise.'

Nick *looks at* **Meera**.

Nick   Not *ever*.

He moves away.

Indira   She borrows things. I don't mind. Well, I do. A bit. Not really, you know, but . . .

As **Indira** *speaks,* **Nick** *looks into the cardboard box. At intervals during the play, each of the characters will approach the box and remove a child's toy. The rate and rhythm of this process is something to be discovered.*

Indira   She's always wanted to wear my clothes. But then her brother was the same!

The high-heels – 'clip-clop shoes', they called them.

I think that's just normal. Kids like dressing up, don't they?

But now it's different. At least . . . it seems different. I mean, there's an element still, of dressing up, but . . .

She'll try things on of mine, and she'll look in the mirror . . . and . . .

The way she looks . . .

She shies away from something.

It's cold.

So . . . critical.

And part of me thinks: good for you – not kidding yourself. Not making *that* mistake.

And part of me thinks:

Please . . . Don't be so hard on yourself.

Don't be so hard on me.

Indira *leaves.* **Gary** *begins – shy, almost apologetic:*

Gary   There's a sense, I suppose, of . . . of a clock ticking fast once they're born. You're . . . you're so conscious all the time of these things that you won't get to do again. All these *first* things. First steps, first words . . . you know! They feel so . . . precious.

Robert *chimes in . . .*

Robert   And you've got to hurry to keep up with them.

Gary   I think that's why you take all those pictures – it all feels so sort of . . . fleeting.

Then, I don't know, it flattens out a bit in the middle . . .

Robert   It's true . . . you relax a bit. Life settles down.

Gary   And then all of a sudden . . .

Robert   Tell me about it!

Gary *struggles a moment, then:*

Gary   He talks now, sometimes, about the years until he leaves. And I feel . . .

I feel at sea, if I'm honest.

I feel . . .

But **Gary**'s *interrupted as* **Sarah** *rushes in, furious.*

Sarah   This is the worst it's ever been. Actually, the other day, I just went in and said: Okay, I've done everything I could do. From now on, it's on you. That's it. It's on you. When the results come out on August 23rd and you've not got enough to stay on in the sixth form, it's

All

On

You.

She seems exhausted now. **Robert** *goes to speak but before he can:*

Sarah   It's impossible. Of course his dad basically left school with nothing but a cycling proficiency badge so he says 'he'll be alright' – and it makes me so angry! Because you don't know that.

You don't *know* that!

And then I think, why do I have to be the bloody bad guy all the time. Why is it always me?

Sarah *storms off.*

Robert *takes his chance.*

Robert   The most important thing is to let them know you get things wrong. Admit to your mistakes, don't try to keep your end up. Cos they see it anyway.

Our parents didn't do that. They belonged to a generation that thought you had to be . . . totally infallible. Or look that way at any rate. No way my kids think that about me. They've seen me mess things up too often.

He ambles off. **Johnny** *remembers with enormous pleasure.*

Johnny   I used t'go on trains all the time. I'd say to my parents:

'I don't know what time I'll be back, I'm going on the train!'

People think they're unreliable now – they were a lot worse then. I'd go all over – as far as I could afford. My parents didn't even know what county I was in!

If mobile phones had existed, I suppose they'd've been calling and asking. That would've ruined it – completely!

Patrick   Okay: I find the height thing difficult. If you'd told me before, that one day I'd . . .

Well I'd've laughed in your face.

But it matters. It just does.

I've always been tall. I'm not used to looking up at anyone.

Never mind my own son.

Johnny   Kira tends to be quite slow returning texts. Within an hour, I consider acceptable.

I tend not to bug her so I get more of a response, whereas her mother . . . well . . .

Frantic's not the right word, but . . .

For me, if she picks up, that's fine. I don't need to know where she is and who she's with. I just need to know she's alright.

Johnny *shrugs, sneaks off.*

Robert   Get up! Come on, you're going to miss it!

Frances   For the last time, can you just go to bed!

Steph   Go out, go on, and get some fresh air /

Grace   I want you back in the house by /

Nick   You're not still doing that . . . ?

Gary   Haven't you even started yet . . . ?

Johnny   You need to eat something /

Indira   Who's eaten all this?

Alison   You need to work harder /

Patrick   You'll wear yourself out.

Sarah   You've got to take it seriously /

Meera   Hey, it's not the end of the world . . .

Frances   Blah blah blah blah.

Grace *is on the phone. It might be a toy phone. Or a random toy being used as a phone. Or there might not be any kind of prop-phone.*

Grace   Hi, Arun, it's me. Can you give me a call?

Frances   I just feel like a broken record sometimes.

Grace   Hi, Arun, it's me again. Can you call home please?

Frances   I laugh in the middle of saying things sometimes, cos I've said them so often!

Grace *is testy now:*

Grace   Yep, me again. Phone. Please, Arun.

Frances   Or cos I sound like my own mum.

Grace *gives up.*

Steph   I *hate* that.

Grace *tries again. No joy – gives up.*

Frances   Except no way would she have put up with what I get!

Steph   I hear myself, you know? And I just think: shut up! That wasn't true when she said it to you, and it isn't any truer now!

Frances   I say to my girls: you see that word that just came out of your mouth, I wouldn't have even let it come into my head with my mother!

It's because they've never been battered – they've never feared that immediate reprisal. I've had to really *look* for ways to punish them!

Honestly, because we don't hit them – I know some people do, and that's their business – but because we don't, the question is, *what can you do?*

I said to Jasmine (it's always Jasmine) after this last incident:

Okay – here's the deal . . . you know I'm on flexitime, so that means I can choose my work hours . . . ? Let me promise you this: if you continue with this behaviour, even though you are fifteen years old, I will walk you to school every morning, and collect you every afternoon. I really mean it.

That worked.

Grace   He's got a girlfriend. He goes to her house all the time. Every day, straight from school.

She seems very nice, and in some ways we're thrilled – I mean that he's managed to make a relationship – but . . .

Well, we never know what time he's coming back!

I tell him: we only need a bit of communication. Just return our texts. But he doesn't even have his phone turned on when he's round there.

Steph   You can remember things about yourself at that age, that's what makes it hard, I think.

Grace   In the end, I rang her dad and said: 'Look, we really appreciate you having Arun so often. But would you please ask him to keep his phone on, and it would be great if we knew that when it got to half past nine you'd send him home.'

Steph   You don't remember your own first tooth, or learning to read – of course not. But your teenage years – you can remember that – O-levels . . . parties . . . *kissing*!

The recollection excites **Steph** . . .

Grace   When Arun found out, he went mad: 'I'm so embarrassed, you've embarrassed me so badly! I can't believe you did this!' On and on.

Completely out of control.

Steph   I remember the taste of boys who smoked! And I never want my kids to smoke – of course I don't – or their friends, but . . .

To be fifteen and kiss a boy who tastes of smoke . . .

It knocks your socks off!

Grace   'You've made me look like a complete idiot! It's so embarrassing!'

I said –

No!

What's embarrassing is

this

you

right now.

You're embarrassing yourself!

He said, it's different – there's no one here to see. I said I'm here, aren't I?

He looked astonished. As though that hadn't occurred to him.

He said, well if I can't embarrass myself in front of my own mother, what's the use of anything?

She falters.

'My own mother'. He said that.

Her tone changes.

And I was so relieved. Because . . . Because I'm always waiting for that whole thing to kick in.

'You're not my real mother.'

I'm always waiting for that.

Alison   For my eighteenth birthday, my parents bought me a set of suitcases.

They said it was traditional.

And when I left home, they did this thing where – I mean straight away – they redecorated. Completely. Everywhere.

And they started going on all these really . . . *different* holidays.

I was so . . . wounded. Honestly. I just . . . I just couldn't believe it.

Gary   He got mugged.

Meera   Zack did – they all do. The boys, that is.

Gary   It's as if there's a little window of opportunity where the bigger boys can pounce. Like when crabs shed their shells and all the birds are just waiting.

Meera   'A man stood in front of me, told me to give him my bike.' So he did. Just like that.

Gary   Some bigger boys just walked up to him and his friends, broad daylight, y'know . . . ?

Meera   'This boy asked me the time, so I took out my phone . . . '

She gestures the inevitable consequence.

Gary   Took what was in their pockets. They just let them, rather than lose face, make a fuss . . .

Meera   I said, good boy. Some things aren't worth fighting over.

Indira   She's not fat – I'll say that straight off. But she's not thin, either. Not like some of the skinny-skinny ones. I tell her it doesn't matter. At their age, your body's changing all the time! And what a person looks like is a very small part of who they are!

I can see she doesn't believe me. I don't believe myself sometimes. But it's what you're meant to say.

My husband used t' tell me I was beautiful, and I'd think – what are you –

A liar, or just stupid?

In the end, it made me hate him.

Meera   We're a tight little unit. We've not had much choice with their dad out of the picture.

So when I was diagnosed, I just told them: I'd had a test that said I needed an operation, and the operation would be in ten days' time.

I told them I wasn't going to die.

I felt pretty confident about that – we'd caught it very early, and my doctor seemed really positive. So I told them that. It seemed important to just say it.

I asked them to think if they had any questions they wanted me to ask the doctor – because I had lots of questions too – and if we pooled our questions, we might understand the illness better.

Zack didn't ask anything.

Nadia asked two things: 'What colour is the tumour?' and 'After they take it out, can I have it?'

Sarah   He hates me at the moment – really hates me.

I look on his computer.

There was a problem for a while, with what he was watching. I had to talk to him about it. I had to tell him:

This is nothing like the real world. This isn't what real women look like. Those women aren't enjoying it. They're just doing it to pay for a drug habit or feed their children.

I check his search history.

I tell him, if you've cleared it, I'll just assume that's what you were doing, and we'll be having this conversation again.

Frances   So last summer one day she came home in a rare old state – this is Jasmine again, I hardly need say. She could really hardly breathe to get her words out –

'They've been caught shoplifting – Darcy and Jenny-Rose! I knew they were going to do it, so I went next door to Boots.'

It was a proper saga . . . the parents were down at the police station and the girls were banned from H & M.

She shrugs.

That was all that happened in the end.

A shift.

But I had to have the talk with Jasmine.

I had to say:

Alright let me tell you, if *you* had been caught, it wouldn't have been the same.

It would have been a completely different outcome, and this is why:

Because you're black. And you need to learn this lesson:

You would have been treated completely differently.

You always will be.

Sarah   I know I'm hard on him, but . . . At least that's what he thinks. But you've got to draw the line. I'm just not always sure the line's in the right place.

Frances   I called a meeting in Costa with the other mums. I said I'm sorry, I really like your girls. But when my daughter's with them, when they're all together, there's something goes wrong. So my daughter won't be coming to your house again, and your children are no longer welcome in my home.

I've never regretted that.

You want them to learn the lessons, that actions have consequences. But they can be very hard lessons.

Robert   Our lives, before we had the boys . . . if they knew, it would kill them.

Drugs, for example. We've taken just about everything, both of us. I've never told them that. I don't want to endorse that behaviour – I mean, we don't take drugs now, and I don't think it did us any harm, but that's not the case for everyone.

So they need to understand it's not behaviour I approve of.

I think it's dangerous behaviour.

Johnny   I deliberately don't ask, to be honest. I'd rather not know. Who's this, who's that? How long have you known them?

The truth is there's a distance between us, and I quite like that. We respect each other's boundaries.

Once, in the kitchen, I found a lighter. I wondered about it.

But I just left it alone and it disappeared.

I think that's my policy really. Do nothing if you can. And things just tend to resolve themselves.

He looks down for a moment, then:

I still don't know whose lighter it was.

Patrick   If I'm honest, I've noticed myself competing with him more.

We'd always done running races in the park, but . . .

I started to make the distances shorter so I could still beat him.

Gary   I like to think he still needs me. I don't know if it's true. He'll ring for a lift sometimes, and actually, he's just being lazy – he doesn't want to walk, but I go.

And I'm glad to go. Cos how many more chances will there be? 'Thanks, Dad,' he says. But I'm doing it for me, not him.

I think more about my dad now. You think more about your parents when you're older. When they're not around any more.

Robert   Get up! Come on, you're going to miss it!

Frances   For the last time, can you just go to bed!

Steph   Go out, go on, and get some fresh air /

Grace   I want you back in the house by /

Nick   You're not still doing that . . . ?

Gary   Haven't you even started yet . . . ?

Johnny   You need to eat something /

Indira   Who's eaten all this?

Alison   You need to work harder /

Patrick   You'll wear yourself out.

Sarah   You've got to take it seriously /

Meera   Hey, it's not the end of the world . . .

Alison   For years, I was so jealous of people whose parents had kept their room the same for them. Their old posters on the walls even, some of them. Because honestly, mine . . . well, they couldn't disguise how excited they were . . . to be losing a daughter but gaining an en-suite.

So now, I just feel totally guilty. Because, if I'm honest . . .

I really badly want them out.

All of them.

I can't wait.

Grace   He doesn't ever want to talk about his birth family. He can remember it, that life – of course. He'll never forget it . . . But he keeps it to himself.

It's left him bad with change. Uncertainty. He worries.

He still hasn't called.

Sometimes, I think, if I did to him what he does to us . . . kept him hanging, in the dark, his world would just collapse.

Nick   Once or twice, I've admitted to something, from when I got it wrong, round about their age.

They're shocked – they can't handle it. They think they know everything about you. You're the one thing in the world they know everything about, that doesn't change.

It's 'cannot compute' when you introduce stuff that doesn't go with that picture.

I think they want you to lie. They lie too, of course. It's how we all protect each other.

Robert   I once, when I was young . . . seventeen, it was . . . I made a big mistake with something I took, something I got given at a club.

I had the classic bad trip – I was terrified, utterly. Completely out of my depth – it could have ended really badly . . but no way was I going to call my parents.

He shakes his head at the thought.

So what I say to mine is this:

If you're ever anywhere with people you feel unsure about, or where you start to feel uncomfortable, or if you just don't like what's going on – I don't care what it is – girls, drugs, police – doesn't matter.

You call me. I won't judge you.

Any time, day or night. You call me, and I sort it out.

Patrick   I asked him to show me how to get the iPod to play through the speakers.

He laughed at me. Then he did it really fast, so I couldn't see how.

Now I've got to ask him again.

Meera   When I was growing up, all I wanted was to get away.

It wasn't that I didn't love my parents . . . but . . . I hated that whole extended family thing you get in immigrant communities. I needed to get out – get on . . .

I know they've got to separate from you, but . . .

I can't bear the idea of a slow drifting away.

Johnny   She's not getting on with her mum. Occasionally, there's like a glimmer of some kind of bonding, but mostly they're at each other's throats. I'm the mediator.

I try not to lose my temper. I didn't know I had a temper until we had Kira!

She's quite a forceful character. When she was two, I'd use hostage negotiation techniques on her . . . But she still made mincemeat of me.

She can still turn the tables. Her mum can't do anything right . . .

But if she was here now, with you, she'd be absolutely charming.

Meera   When I told them I was having chemo, Zack asked if my hair would fall out. I said, yes. And it'll look weird at first, but you mustn't be frightened. It won't be for ever. He said:

I never ever want to be seen with you in public with no hair.

I said: I don't blame you. I'll always wear a hat or scarf.

And I did.

Nick   Apart from personal history, then, money and food would be the other main things.

I mean, like, they'll say, 'What's for pudding?' and we say a piece of fruit. Then, once they're gone, it's out with the Dairy Milk. Yeah, we lie about that.

And about how much Margaret earns. We tell them it's less. They can't understand what money's worth anyway. And I don't want them feeling too cosy.

We're not rich. It just sounds like a lot to a kid.

They're going to need to try in life. You look at the world now . . . they're going t' have to *really* try.

Gary   I remember the feel of his hand, small, in mine. The smell of the top of his head. Being able to pick him up!

When he was a tiny baby, I went to Mothercare in the High Road. They had these sleepsuits with the sun, moon and the stars on. I just thought they were fantastic.

I bought them in all the sizes: 0–3 months, 3–6 . . . all the way up to 36 months.

I went a bit mad, I suppose.

Alison   My greatest fear for the future is that if I don't watch it, by the time the last one moves out, first one'll be wanting t' move back in. The idea of that . . . well, it keeps me awake at night.

Gary   He wore them for years. You can imagine. I can see him in them, still . . .

Indira   I don't know how to help her. To make her understand that she is beautiful. Because she really is.

That's the hardest thing, I suppose.

I look at her and realise I was beautiful at her age. But I couldn't believe it then. And it's too late to start now.

Gary   It's like sand running through an hourglass . . . Near the end, it looks like it's going much faster. It isn't – I know that – but still . . .

Steph   It makes you feel totally out of control.

Gary   I'm making it all sound sad. It's not. I don't know why it sounds like it is.

Steph   I think that's all you can say about sex and so on: warn them that the body . . . the senses, if you like . . . have a mind of their own.

And they don't always want what's best for your long-term future.

You will not always feel in control of yourself. And nor will other people.

I said: 'I'm going to buy some condoms. Leave them in the bathroom, with the Tampax and the rest.' They were up in arms about it!

David went bonkers at me. He thinks of them as little girls still. I said, I'm not trying to encourage them to do it! But I don't want them too embarrassed to go and buy Durex and then . . .

You know.

They say –

We don't want to 'discuss' sex and drugs and stuff! We just want a rule. Why can't you be more like Grandma . . . ? Just tell us:

'No – You can't do *anything*! At all! Ever!'

I say: well you two are evidence of how well that approach worked.

Sarah   This year, when his birthday was coming up, I was hating him so much. I couldn't even stand the idea of making him a cake. Not that he'd ever admit to wanting one. Honestly. Really hating.

I thought, I've got to get out of this – for my sake as much as his. I've got to find a way to remember what it was like – before. What *we* were like.

So I thought I'd make him a photo album. Of his life, to date.

Then I worried – I thought, am I being mean, you know? Am I going: Oh, look you hate me, but see how much I love you with all my cutting and sticking, and . . . ?

And then I thought, Oh, just get on with it. He won't think that. He won't even be interested. So I did it.

I made him open his presents sitting on our bed, with Kelly there as well. I saved the album till last.

Beat.

Well, he couldn't stop looking at it. That was what he did, for about an hour. Just look through the pictures.

I said: there are plenty of pages in the back . . . for the future.

Patrick   I bought some clothes like his. I can't believe I did it.

Frances *starts to laugh, just thinking of what she's about to say.*

Frances   If Rick and me have a row –

Patrick   God knows what I look like in them.

Frances   – like one of the really vicious ones –

Patrick   He's been very nice about it.

Frances   – she says, 'I know I'm only sixteen, but I don't understand why you don't divorce him. Do it before you're too old to get someone else. Honestly, what do you see in him?'

That's when they're in a phase of hating their dad! Of course, sometimes, it's the other way, and I'm the villain.

Robert   The thing is, they've got to experiment with life. I know that. And they've got to feel as though they're doing something you disapprove of – because half the time that's the whole fun of it. So you've got to sort of take positions. On things you're not that bothered about.

They've got to think you're a bit of an old fart. That's sort of the job.

He shrugs, walks off.

Grace   He announced he was going on holiday with his girlfriend. Her grandma's in Croatia, near the sea. I said – hang on, we need to talk about this first! And there's the cost . . .

In the end, we agreed – if he paid half.

We set up jobs for him – cat-feeding, lawn-mowing, car-washing – all that.

Well, he didn't seem that interested. I felt riled. I really did. That he wouldn't make more of an effort. Time was getting on. I started nagging him. Then it dawned on me . . .

I talked to him about it, in the car. It's the best place. I said:

If you don't really want to go, it's alright. I'll say I've changed my mind, you're not allowed. I'll be the bad guy.

She notices that the others are now listening to her . . .

Silence. For miles. So I said:

Okay. I'll tell them. You're not going. It's alright, it's over.

The slightest nod he gave me.

What do you want for tea?

By this stage in the play, all of the characters have collected their toys.

Steph   I bought a new dress the other day. The youngest said: You can't wear that! Not at your age! I said: Don't think of me as thirty-six. Think of me as the same age as you but with twenty-two years' more experience!

Johnny   She changes so fast. She's really like a different person . . . You get used to one Kira, and six weeks later there's a new Kira. She's really like a different person . . . New . . . friends, new music, all changed. And you worry, but . . .

Well, you'll worry for the rest of their life, won't you?

Alison   I suppose the only thing worse is if they all move out and I'm too knackered by then to enjoy it.

Bloody hell.

Frances   The main thing is, they make me laugh. They really, really make me laugh. I can't tell you.

If I'm honest, I just think they're brilliant. That's the thing, in the end.

I just think they're great.

I really do.

Johnny   She looks older than she is. We went to the pub the other day. She asked for a pint of lager and I bought it for her.

It's the first drink we've ever had together.

He fails to stifle a smile.

She didn't finish it.

He looks at the others. A sense of something inescapable . . . a mood growing within the group, fear and excitement in the face of the unknown, as:

Robert   Tick.

Frances   Tock.

Steph   Tick.

Grace   Tock.

Nick   Tick.

Gary   Tock.

Johnny   Tick.

Indira   Tock.

Alison   Tick.

Patrick   Tock.

Sarah   Tick.

Meera   Tock.

The characters brace, clutching their toys as a sonic boom flowers in the air . . . announcing, simultaneously, an end and a beginning.

Shoes should be removed and hurled away for any curtain call.

What Are They Like?

BY LUCINDA COXON

*Notes on rehearsal and staging, drawn from a workshop
with the writer held at the National Theatre, November 2012*

How the writer came to write the play

The process of researching and writing *What Are They Like?*
began with Lucinda's reflections on the relationships between
parents and teenagers. Her experiences as a mother of a
teenager and those of other parents seemed to highlight a
commonly felt anxiety that young people's lives become more
mysterious to their parents as they enter their teens. From
their whereabouts and activities to their relationships and
sex lives, parents have to get used to knowing less about what
their offspring are up to. Lucinda also felt that for many
parents there is a gap between their understanding of what
other adolescents might get up to and their acknowledgement
of whether this behaviour applies to their own child.

In her research for the play, and conversations with GCSE
and A-level students in schools, Lucinda also began to see
that teenagers' knowledge of their parents' lives was even
more scanty. Adults at least had the advantage of having been
teenagers at one point in their lives. Some of the young
people with whom Lucinda spoke felt that their parents lied
to them rarely and only to protect their well-being. However,
for parents, lying to or concealing things from their children
was a more complicated issue. They often felt the need to
edit their personal history, make decisions about what their
teenagers could cope with or what information would be
useful to them. Lucinda noted that real honesty often kicks in
much later in relationships between parents and children.

Having observed that imagining their parents' lives was often
hard for teenagers, she came up with the idea of asking
teenagers to 'walk literally in their parents' shoes'. The play

asks its young performers to express the thoughts of adults as their own and to understand the joys and anxieties of being a parent. Lucinda's research involved conversations with a number of parents about their relationships with teenage children. As well as identifying common anxieties and issues surrounding parenting, this research also touched on specific issues raised by the play, including illness and adoption. The different themes and ideas that Lucinda had explored began to shape themselves into the twelve distinct voices and characters that form the basis of the play.

Approaching the play

Understanding and exploring the play's adult characters will be at the heart of working on a production of *What Are They Like?* Not only does each actor need to develop a detailed sense of who their character is, but the play also asks them to grasp the rhythms of adult speech. Different ways to begin work on the play might include:

- Reading it through with the company, allowing them to hear it and discuss what feels distinct about the way the adults express themselves.

- Reading the play for one character, with the group working through the play and speaking only their lines. This could be a way of encouraging initial ideas about what distinguishes the character.

- Ask the company to do some research into adults and the adult world, perhaps looking at films or images from the adolescence of their parents' generation.

- Get each actor to talk to a parent or another adult about their childhood, their teenage years or their experience of their own parents.

- Discussion in rehearsals could be prompted by asking actors to bring in photographs of their parents when they were teenagers.

Work involving actors' families and parents needs to be
conducted carefully and with warning, but it can also generate
a strong understanding of the subject matter within the
company.

Structure

The play has its own very distinctive structure and doesn't tell
a traditional, linear story. Its characters have only two things
in common: they all have children and were once children
themselves. The play's setting is explicitly theatrical rather than
naturalistic and acknowledges that we are in a performance
space. As a result, it raises a number of structural questions:

Where are the characters?
Lucinda imagined the characters coming from different
places around the country rather than living in the same town
or city. The theatrical space they inhabit is abstract rather
than a literal location they have all gathered in. Its only rules
are that we should see the characters in one space together
and that they should not leave that space during the
performance or disappear when not speaking. In working on
the play you might choose to give each individual character
their own specific real-world location or context. This might
be physically represented onstage or just imagined by the
actors.

Who are they speaking to?
The text leaves this question open to the interpretation of
each company rather than setting a rule. The more specific
you can be about this, the more each actor will be able to
animate his or her character. There's a danger that if they
choose to speak to the audience or other actors as a group in
general, the character's thoughts will feel less concrete and
their tone less varied. You might set up or experiment with
different scenarios for each character, whether that's speaking
to a friend in private, being interviewed more formally or
speaking with an imagined therapist.

Are they aware of each other?
At moments in the text, what two characters are talking about appears to connect. Ideas about the passage of time or being mugged are shared for a moment. Lucinda suggests that in general the characters are 'not aware of one another as people' but part of an onstage 'weather system' and so have a subliminal effect on each other. This means that occasionally there is a resonance of subject matter or that a particular topic is in the air for a moment.

What do the shoes represent?
The structure of the play acknowledges very clearly the distinction between 'performers' and 'characters'. The shoes that are part of the opening ritual of the play in some way represent each character. When the performers step into them, they become that character. Lucinda describes the shoes as part of the fairy-tale or magical aspect of the play, arguing that they create a very theatrical moment of transformation. You might also discuss who the actors are when they are out of the shoes, whether they are themselves, playing other teenage performers or representing the characters away from their roles as parents.

Themes

Time
How parents experience the passage of time was one of the questions Lucinda came across repeatedly in her research interviews. Many parents felt that the years were short but the days were long. Their children seemed to grow up quickly, but daily life was full of chores and constant negotiations. The play emphasises the significance of time in its opening and closing 'tick-tock' refrain, its twelve characters and the sequences of shorter lines that break up the monologues. These are full of everyday commands from parents – 'Get up,' 'You need to eat something.' They remind us that the characters experience their time with their children like sand slipping through an hourglass.

Performance/audience
Lucinda places the action of the play in a very theatrical context, making it clear that the audience are watching a performance. This was partly a response to her sense that being a parent involves performing or presenting a particular version of yourself. Several of the characters in the play catch themselves saying something their own parents said, and react in disbelief. Steph hears something her mother would have said and tells us, 'I just think: shut up!' Given that parents will form a large part of most audiences, in some respects the performance acts rather like a mirror.

Lying
The things that teenagers and parents lie to one another about were key inspirations behind the play. The characters' experiences give us examples of different kinds of lying. They lie to safeguard their children from harm or upset, to protect their own privacy or to obscure their past or sexual history. Lying is also part of the everyday negotiations with teenagers over boundaries: Nick lies about food and what's available for dinner, and several of the parents worry that their children are lying about where they are or when they will be home.

Language

The language in the play is shaped precisely to reflect the way characters reach for their thoughts, reveal their anxieties and allow private frustrations to burst out. Encouraging your company to be precise with the text and learning it will allow them to capture these details. You might use an exercise called 'walking the text' to develop this precision. Actors walk around the space while speaking their lines and change direction for commas, and stop at full stops or when the line trails off. This work allows them to develop a clear sense of the shape of each thought and see where characters change their minds or go back on themselves.

Characters

There is a decision for each company to make about how well
the performers inhabit the adult characters and how much to
emphasise the gap between. Even though these adults are
being played by a teenage company, there can be something
brilliantly uncanny about younger performers inhabiting
older characters' thoughts and their physicality. Equally,
Lucinda points out that any successful transformation will
always be balanced by an inability to deny the gap between
young performer and adult character. For her this is a
'double image' that allows us to see the child inside each
adult, the teenager they once were. Whatever approach is
taken, it is consistency of style that is important.

The process for developing character can be split into three
steps. To begin with it will be useful to establish the hard facts
about each character from the text. There may then be a list
of questions to be answered or inferences to be made that the
text doesn't answer directly. Finally, research may be needed
into the issues each character raises.

Taking ROBERT as an example, facts from the text would
include:

- He has more than one son.

- He and his partner have taken drugs in the past.

- He doesn't take drugs now.

- He has never told his children about taking drugs.

- He doesn't pretend to be infallible to his children, like his
  parents did to him.

Our questions about Robert might include why he advocates
being more honest and open with his children than his
parents were with him, but not on the subject of his drug
taking. These facts and the questions they raise could lead us
towards a sense of Robert as a man who struggles with the
distinction between his identity as a person and as a parent.

Here is a brief set of ideas about the characters from discussion with Lucinda:

FRANCES   While the text states that Frances's daughter Jasmine is black, her role might be read by a performer of any ethnicity. You might also decide that Frances is white, making Jasmine mixed race. She has a sense of humour and isn't averse to messing with her daughters' heads a little. The physical punishment she received from her parents isn't evidence of systematic abuse, but shows Frances confronted with the need to make a different choice with her children.

STEPH   Steph represents an antidote to the way adults talk to teenagers about sex as though it is something rational that can be controlled. Her decision to buy condoms and leave them in the bathroom is an acknowledgement that sex can be an irrational appetite that it is better to be prepared for than to be denied. She is willing to recall her excitement about boys as a teenager.

GRACE   Her son is adopted and as a result their relationship is subtly different. She is able to observe him with a level of objectivity that other parents cannot achieve. We see this in her description of his attitude towards his birth family and of the arguments they have about his girlfriend.

NICK   Nick struggles to have the relationship with his children that he might want and feels a little isolated from them. He thinks his children want protecting by his lies, whether they are about the reality of death or his past mistakes. His wife Margaret is the major wage-earner in the family.

GARY   He wrestles with how long you can offer your children protection and asks what can replace the closeness a parent feels with a child. Gary moves between describing the powerful impulse to protect his son when he was born and how, now his son is a teenager, he cannot defend him from mugging.

JOHNNY   There is something subversive about Johnny, demonstrated both in his childhood adventures on trains and in his resentment at needing to check up on his own children.

In taking his daughter for a drink he seems to advocate the benefits of letting things go as a parent, a sort of benign neglect.

INDIRA   Someone who is very conscious of image, Indira struggles to separate herself from her daughter. The issues her daughter experiences with body image and beauty are things that are too close to her, so she can't be objective about them.

ALISON   Alison is reaching a point where she is ready to get on with her future, beyond being a mother. We see her accepting that she has understood something about her own parents and their decision to redecorate her childhood room. She's processed her feelings about this and can be playful with the story.

PATRICK   During her research, Lucinda came across fathers who had experienced their sons growing taller than them. Patrick shows his humiliation and his crippling response. He is also willing to put his hands up and admit how ridiculous are his attempts to dress like and keep up with his son.

SARAH   Sarah's relationship with her son is becoming embattled as she tries to convince him to work harder and control what he looks at on the internet. She might have a partner who is more relaxed or less tuned in, and her journey is about finding a way to celebrate her son's birthday within this strained context.

MEERA   There is a frankness in Meera's relationship with her children. She is front-footed, strong and may have been quite rebellious when younger. These qualities seem to help her in managing her children's relationship with her cancer. Her son Zack is able to be open and honest with her about his feelings.

Casting

The opening ritual in the play and the device of the shoes make a clear distinction between the 'performers' and named characters. This means that actors of either gender and of any ethnicity could be cast in any of the roles. A production with an all-male or all-female company is absolutely possible.

Performing the play with a cast that is smaller or larger than the twelve named parts presents a different challenge. The contrasts and distinctions between characters are crucial to the play so, however you approach it, preserving their distinct identities is important:

- *Fewer than twelve*   With a smaller company, it may be useful to allow the shoes to dictate and define character very clearly, with actors voicing multiple characters rather than trying to cut anyone from the text.

- *More than twelve*   The challenge with a larger ensemble will be not to lose the personal and confessional quality in the audience's relationship with characters. One option is to allow actors to share a character, using the shoes to define the role. There may also be ways of using an ensemble to represent physical aspects of a character, or even the silent individuals to whom they are speaking. You might also consider having more than one cast, with different actors playing different roles on different nights.

Toys

The 'toy box' and twelve toys specified in the text give a physical life to the play that runs alongside the text. They should give characters access to a more private world of reflection, vulnerability and childlike playfulness. They also represent childhood as opposed to the worlds of teenagers and parents that dominate the play. Each toy could have a very different relationship with its character, and they don't all need to mean exactly the same thing. You might begin by asking the following questions:

- Do the toys belong to the characters, to their children or even to grandparents?
- What era is each toy from?
- What memories are attached to them?
- In what situation would an adult pick up a toy?
- How can each toy be played with in the space?

While playing with the toys is quite a private and personal act, there may be quicksilver moments of interaction as there are in the text. A toy car might invade another character's play or distract a character from speaking. Each production must find a balance so that the toys have a relationship with the action while never upstaging the words.

Rhythm

The opening ritual of the play and the sequences of shorter lines have a more rhythmic quality to them. The text should be followed precisely rather than allowing lines to overlap. It might be useful to think of these sequences building like a time bomb towards the next monologue or towards the sonic boom at the end. The rhythms could be regular or unpredictable but should give the audience the feeling that something is coming whether the characters are ready or not.

The rhythm in the way the play moves between different monologues includes moments of interruption and of characters fading away. These transitions are governed by a character's need or impulse to express something to the audience rather than taking turns. It might be useful to map out these journeys with actors, charting a graph to represent their contributions. There may be moments where someone wants to speak but decides not to, or where several characters are about to speak and one wins through. The text doesn't always need to run at speed and sometimes could benefit from some air around it, or a momentary lull before the next character speaks.

Production, staging and design

Staging
Other than elements like the opening ritual, the action with the shoes and the toy box, Lucinda's script leaves many choices to each company and their particular vision about design and how the space works. As long as the text is interpreted in the

spirit of the play and with clarity, there is scope for many
possible productions. Useful questions might include:

- Is there a distinction in the space between where characters
  are during private and public moments? Being specific
  about these spaces will allow moments of transition to feel
  like part of each character's journey rather than just
  blocking.

- Are there ways in which rituals or sequences of movement
  change and develop as the play moves forward?

- Are there ways of using levels in the blocking, contrasts
  between stillness and movement or different volumes to
  make the production feel dynamic rather than static?

Where stage directions are very specific, that usually indicates
that the order in which things happen is linked or connected.
For example, as the shoes are put on the text states that the
'circle becomes ominously energised' as though something is
about to begin. There is a clear suggestion here that the shoes
should in some way trigger the 'tick-tock' sequence that
begins the spoken text.

Costume

While the play gives characters' shoes a particular significance,
other elements of costume are open to interpretation. You
might decide that these should be the clothes of the teenage
performers, or that they are part of the adult identities they
assume. Selecting clothes could also form a useful rehearsal
exercise. You might ask actors to find their character's
costume and then examine how adult clothing shapes their
movement and physicality.

Sound

Music might be used to support different elements of the action
such as the opening warm-up. The only specified sound effect
is the 'sonic boom' at the end of the play. This is the sound of
shockwaves travelling at great speed rather than a bomb
explosion. It is a moment that should be marked, but one which

each production will find a significance for or interpretation of during rehearsals.

Exercises for use in rehearsals

OBSERVATION

To engage actors with the parents' world and the physicality of adults, you might ask them to make observations in the outside world comparing how adults move differently from teenagers. They could note different stances, what parts of the body they lead with, the pace of their walk. This information can feed into work that asks them to create each character's physicality and the way they move round the space onstage. These sessions might be developed by creating a private space for each character, a literal or imagined room where each actor can spend time discovering what they are like when they are alone.

SILENT SPEAKER

One way of working on each monologue might be to specify the individual to whom each character is speaking and decide what questions they have asked to prompt these replies. Rehearsing each character's text with a specific situation or location and another actor will help the actors make their lines feel concrete and personal rather than general and reflective.

CHARACTER QUESTIONS

Once you have established the hard facts about each character, hot-seating each actor might be an active way of developing a fuller sense of their character. Questions about what they fear most, when they were happy and what they want in the future will help pin down an objective that guides the character through the play. These questions might also help to reveal a clearer picture of each character's children, who are key roles in the play.

TIMELINES

The relationship between each character's own childhood and who they are as a parent is important in the play. There are various ways you might develop a sense of this in rehearsal. Actors could put together a shoe history for their character, charting pairs of shoes they wore at different ages. You might also select a set of landmark birthdays and ask actors to research what was happening in the world when their parents reached these ages, or what their character was doing.

IMPROVISATION

Improvisation could be a useful way to create a sense of who each parent is when they are away from their children. You might ask the company to improvise scenes in a social setting, allowing them to experience each character with friends or perhaps with their own parents. There are also specific events and even objects that are recalled in the text to which the actors could usefully ascribe a memory. For instance, the actor playing Grace may want to improvise the argument she has with Arun in the car; and the actor playing Sarah might want to create the birthday book she makes for her son.

From a workshop led by James Macdonald
with notes by Sam Pritchard

We Lost Elijah

Ryan Craig

Age suitability 13–19
Cast size 9

Ryan Craig was the Writer-in-Residence at the National Theatre Studio, 2012. He has written for television, film, radio and theatre. In 2005 he received a Most Promising Playwright Nomination at the *Evening Standard* awards for his play *What We Did to Weinstein* (Menier Chocolate Factory). Other plays include *The Holy Rosenbergs* and the English version of Tadeusz Slobodzianek's *Our Class* (National Theatre); *The Glass Room* (Hampstead Theatre); *Broken Road* (Edinburgh/Fringe First Award); *Happy Savages* (Lyric Studio/Underbelly); and a translation of *Portugal* (National Theatre). Television work includes the Channel 4 drama documentary *Saddam's Tribe*, and episodes of *Robin Hood*, *Hustle* and *Waterloo Road* (BBC). In 2005 he was Writer-in-Residence at BBC Radio Drama and his radio plays include *English in Afghanistan*, *The Lysistrata Project*, *Hold My Breath*, *Portugal*, *The Great Pursuit* and *Looking for Danny*.

Characters

Grace
Kara
Malachi
Maxwell
Titus
Holly
Shana
Becky
Elijah

The set should be as bare as possible and the action as fluid as possible. The characters should be onstage all the time.

A forward slash (/) denotes the point in a speaker's line at which the next speaker interrupts.

Garden

Kara   Elijah had been missing for ten days when my sister Grace made us all a meal in our garden.

Grace   Listen up, everyone. Tonight we're making a vigil. I've invited all of you here, all of you who were closest to him, if you like, the *core* group . . . to come together . . . to commemorate the passing of ten days without him.

Kara   Then she lit a candle for him and laid a place and poured him a drink. As if he were there . . .

Grace   Because he is here with us . . . in spirit.

All prepare a table. Except **Kara**, *who continues to address the audience.*

Kara   Titus and Maxwell, Holly and Shana, Becky, Malachi . . . It was a massively odd night to be honest. Everyone was quiet and tense, me most of all. The reality was just starting to dawn on people that maybe he'd really gone. Maybe something terrible really had happened to him . . . *is* happening to him. Maybe he's never coming back.

Once the table is laid, they all sit down to eat.

All night we traded stories and memories of our lost friend.

Maxwell   I knew him well. Really well. Well, not really well maybe . . . but quite well. Sat next to each other in History. Well, not next to . . . you know . . . / but really near . . .

Titus   I remember this one time, right. This one time . . . and we were like laughing so hard. About . . . what was it about . . . it was really funny . . . so funny . . . I was like hurting in my ears . . . You know when you get that? Hot ears from laughing. And Elijah was . . . what was it? It was so . . . I can't . . . But anyway, I turned to look at Elijah and I was like . . . / When was it . . . ?

Shana   He used to come over my house all the time. My mum would make a victoria sponge and everyone would come over.

Titus   But like I say, it really was that funny.

Shana   And Elijah had such a big chunk of cake, he got massively queasy. Vommed profusely. Me and him would often smile about that. When we saw each other at school. You know, one of those knowing smiles. We wouldn't speak much. I don't think he ever spoke that much. Actually, I can't remember his voice. It wasn't a distinctive voice, was it? But we definitely shared a look . . . you know . . . like we both knew what each other was thinking about. And that we were both thinking about that time he sicked victoria sponge all over my mum's Axminster.

Maxwell   I reckon we had a lot in common. Well, not a lot but we were in History together . . . or was it Geography? And we also had other things / that were the same . . .

Shana   My mum reckoned he probably had some sort of gluten intolerance.

Kara   Nobody really ate much. Not with the spectre of Elijah looming over us like that and the . . . that uneaten meal sitting there. Except Grace . . . she polished hers off like it was her last meal, like a condemned man, but the rest of us picked and pushed our food about the plate. It was Malachi I was most worried about.

Grace   Malachi, you haven't eaten any of your meal.

Kara   He wasn't himself. Hadn't been since it happened.

Grace   Babe, come on, eat some.

Malachi   I'm all right.

Kara   He blamed himself for what happened.

Grace   But I made it specially.

Kara   He was supposed to get his little brother home safe that night.

Grace   Chicken drumsticks with rice and sweetcorn. 'Lijah's favourite.

Malachi   I know.

Grace   And Diet Dr Pepper. His favourite drink.

Malachi   I know. I know it's his favourite.

Grace   D'you remember, Elijah used to add sugar to the Dr Pepper from a sachet and then shuckle it with a straw. He liked how the liquid would cloud up and fizz and change consistency. Then he'd admire it for a bit before downing it in one go.

Malachi   I remember.

Grace   That's why I've provided sachets for everyone. Canderel for those who're watching their figures.

She stands up and clinks a glass.

Everyone! Everyone listen. I want to say something. I'm so happy you're all here tonight for this sad but very special occasion. Elijah had such an impact on all of us who knew him. There have been so many messages of support. So many flowers and the candles and stuff on Eagle Road, where he was last seen . . . really gives you a brick in your throat. So I make this toast in the hope that somewhere . . . somehow . . . he hears this. This is for you, Elijah . . . wherever you are. We miss you.

All   Elijah!

Grace   Now I want everyone to add the sachets to the drink and stir.

They do so and the noise of the drinks fizzing builds and builds.

Kara   And that's when it happened. Hard and fast and utterly devastating.

The fizzing builds to an explosion. Everyone screams, then freezes.

But first we have to go back. Before it all changed.

The table is cleared as she continues to talk to the audience.

Kara   First I want to talk about Malachi. Before Elijah went missing and he was . . . God, he was . . . I mean, everyone loved Malachi . . . admired him . . . I mean, everyone. Kids, parents, teachers, and I need to say this before everything gets twisted and changed and people forget how he was . . . Oh God, he was so beautiful. Not how he looked . . . necessarily . . . but what came out of his eyes. And his smile, it was . . . so . . . Anyway I saw a lot of him cos he was dating my sister. He'd come to the house to see her, and my mum would get all giddy and fuss over him, and keep saying his name a lot. So obvious. Disgusting for a woman of her years. Forty-two.

Everyone gathers for a church service.

One day, we got news that Malachi was chosen to be on this big TV show. A proper show. About young entrepreneurs. He'd started this business investing in new energy-saving gadgets and stuff. So he had even more sparkle and swagger than usual. He had an energy force around him like he was a celebrity – a . . . a . . . a Beckham, or, or even an Andre, and there was this one time when Shana's baby was being baptised . . . yeah . . . and little baby Juniper is naked and being held over the font, and the priest is . . . / you know, he's doing his routine and everyone's listening . . .

Priest (*played by one of the cast; starting loud and getting softer*)
You are now stripped and naked, in this also imitating Christ, despoiled of His garments on His Cross, He who by His nakedness, / despoiled the principalities and powers, and fearlessly triumphed over them on the Cross . . .

Kara   And then, he walks in. Malachi. And everyone . . . that whole congregation turns their attention on to him. I remember thinking . . . just for that moment . . . and just to us who knew him . . . he's more famous than God.

Malachi's Bedroom

Grace   Gosh, you look so fine in that suit.

Malachi   Sorry I was late for the baptism. Had to do my last interview for the producers. Couldn't get out of it.

Grace   Course not. That show's important. I'm so proud of you.

Malachi   I hope I didn't disturb the service.

Grace   We were all just pleased you could make it.

Malachi   Priest looked pretty cheesed off when we came in like that.

Grace   Yeah, he was . . . Hold on. We?

Malachi   Me and Elijah. We came in together.

Grace   Oh. I didn't notice he was with you.

Malachi   Yeah. He waited for me outside. You know what Elijah's like.

Grace   Not really.

Malachi   Just he was too nervous to go in alone.

Grace   Loser.

Malachi   Hey. None of that. I won't have that.

Grace   Sorry, babe / I didn't mean . . .

Malachi   He's my little bro, right? He's my responsibility and I take nothing more serious. Yeah? It's my job to look out for him.

Grace   Oh. Okay. Sorry. Anyway, what about we celebrate you being on that TV show, just the two of us . . . ?

Malachi   Yeah . . . / well . . . Thing is . . .

Grace   Do something really despicable, really nasty . . .

Malachi   I'd really like to and everything . . .

Grace   Right. *But?*

Malachi   No . . . well . . . see, Becky and some of the guys . . .

Grace   Becky?

Malachi   Yeah. And some of the . . . Just . . . I'm only saying . . .

Grace   Becky? Becky / *Myers?*

Malachi   Yeah . . . and some of the . . . they was thinking of going bowling.

Grace   Bowling? You're going bowling? You're going bowling with *Becky Myers?*

Malachi   Yes. And some of the . . . Look, you . . . uh . . . you should come. Yeah, you should definitely come. You wanna come?

Grace   You know I hate bowling. You know it screws my nails up.

Malachi   Yeah, but like I'm like captain of the school bowling team, babe . . . I mean, *I* really should . . . and they organised it special.

Grace   Well, I've organised stuff too . . .

Malachi   But we can do that after.

Grace   She's got quite a rep you know? Becky Myers?

Malachi   Come on, Grace . . .

Grace   She's a massive skank. Made her way through half the school's male population. And she's pretentious. Which is worse.

Malachi   She's arty. Her writing's really interesting, actually.

Grace   What you mean that porny stuff she reads out in class –

Malachi   It's quirky.

Grace   – 'bout her pervy fantasies and her sordid little encounters? It isn't decent.

Malachi   Well, if you're not happy, babe, I won't go. If that's what you really want? I'll call them now and let them down . . . disappoint everyone . . .

Grace   No way, no, I don't want you to do that. You should go, I'm fine. It's just . . . you know, I thought me and you were gonna spend the night together.

Malachi   We are. After bowling. I'll make it worth your while, I promise.

Grace   Yeah?

Malachi   Have I ever let you down before? Now, come on. Look, it's late, yeah, I should get changed then and head off.

Grace   Malachi? Are we okay?

Malachi   What? Course we are.

Grace   No, because . . .

Malachi   Look at me. We're okay. You believe me?

Grace *smiles.*

Grace   Go. Enjoy. Smash them ten pins and come to my bed all sweaty and triumphant.

Malachi *smiles, kisses her chastely on the head and then goes. When he is gone,* **Grace***'s smile turns sour. Then she rummages through all his stuff in his room.*

Railroad Tracks

Trains can be heard chunting past. A boy in his Sunday-best throws stones at the trains. This is **Elijah***. He carries on for a while.* **Grace** *enters. He notices her, but carries on throwing the stones.*

Grace   All right?

Elijah *carries on throwing stones.*

Grace   Stop that now and come home.

Elijah *throws a stone. It hits at train.*

Elijah   Strike! Boom!

Grace   Elijah!

Elijah   Why aren't you bowling?

Grace   My nails.

Elijah   Least you're invited.

Grace   Course I'm invited. I'm Malachi's . . . and they're my friends, of course I was invited.

Elijah   I wasn't.

Grace   They probably just forgot to. I'm sure it wasn't personal.

Elijah   Right.

He throws a stone.

How d'you know I was here?

Grace   I think you should come home now, yeah? This place gets really dodgy at night.

Elijah   You read my diary, didn't you?

Grace   Elijah, please don't do suicide today.

Elijah   You shouldn't read people's private diaries.

Grace   It's not true what you wrote, you know? That no one cares if you live or die. And even if it is a bit true, it doesn't mean you should go doing . . . that. It's messy and inconveniences everyone.

Elijah   Oh well. I wouldn't want to put anyone out.

Grace   I'm actually worried about you . . .

Elijah   And I wanna know, no, seriously, I wanna know what gives you the right to go fingering through my personal stuff?

Grace   Don't be disgusting I don't wanna go fingering anything of yours. Personal or otherwise. You think I care about *your* stuff?

Elijah   Why d'you read my diary then?

Grace   Because.

Beat. **Grace** *sighs and gives in.*

Grace   Because I thought it was Malachi's. All right?

Elijah   Malachi's?

Grace   I go through his stuff now and again. Call the Feds.

Elijah   Now and again? You mean you regularly go through his stuff?

Grace   Sock drawers, pockets, text messages, emails . . .

Elijah   That's weird. Why?

Grace   See if he's cheating. So what? Go to the tabloids.

Elijah   Malachi cheat? I don't think so.

Grace   What do you know?

Elijah   I know him pretty well, he is my brother.

Grace   Boys aren't in control of who cheats. Girls are. Every skank at Stanley Street wants a bit of Malachi. You expect me to just sit on my arse and let that happen?

Elijah   So you go through his stuff?

Grace   I drop my guard for one second . . . I take my eye off the ball for one second . . .

Elijah   But he loves you.

Grace   So? You got to be vigilant with a boyfriend like that. Every minute.

Elijah   Sounds like a lot of work.

Grace   It is . . . and you can never ease up. You got to attend to it diligently. Feed it and water it.

Elijah   Like tropical fish?

Grace   Yes! Exactly. Exactly like tropical fish. Yes. You gotta . . . exactly like that . . . You got to constantly check the balance of power. The calibration. If he feels too powerful, he'll resent me for holding him back. But if he feels too weak, that's worse. Why? Cos then he'll look for validation elsewhere.

Elijah   You spend a lot of time on this, don't you?

Grace   Right now he's feeling vulnerable. I think I made myself too desirable. I've been too remote. I've developed a kind of glacial beauty. I worked so hard at not seeming desperate or needy, I may have pushed him too far the other way. I need to find something . . . some clues . . . I need figure out how to behave next.

Elijah   So basically, you keep looking through his stuff till you find something? You even go in my room?

Grace   Once I start, it's like a mission, like an addiction . . .

Elijah   That's pretty sick, do you know that?

Grace   Well, that's what love is. Sickness. Constant anxiety, constant fear . . . and if you'd ever had a relationship you'd know that. But you haven't have you, no, because you're a human bogey.

Elijah   That's not very friendly.

Grace   I can't lose him. Do you understand me? I will not lose him. Any of those bitches so much as sniff his hair, I will inject my finger through their lungs. 'Specially Becky Myers. She's got her beady little eye on him, I know it. I know her type, she'll pull out every stop to do him and he'll be helpless to resist.

Elijah *looks away, choked up.*

Grace   Oh. God Jesus. Sorry. I didn't think.

Elijah   You read that bit too, then? In my diary? About me and Becky?

Grace   Well . . . I mean, yes, I mean, it was there . . . it sort of . . . got in the way of my eyes.

Elijah   Fine.

Grace   Sorry.

Elijah   It's fine.

Grace   You don't wanna get worked up over Becky Myers.

Elijah   I don't want to talk about it.

Grace   I understand. I won't talk about it. Fine. But really Elijah, Becky Myers.

Elijah   Uhm . . . don't wanna talk about it.

Grace   But I can help. Tell you where you went wrong.

Elijah   Don't want your help, thanks.

Grace   But how will you learn for next time?

Elijah   There's not gonna be a next time.

Grace   Oh what, because you're gonna jump in front of the four fifty-two like you wrote in your stupid diary? I don't think so.

Elijah   You don't know anything about it.

Grace   Nobody throws themselves in front of a train for Becky Myers, Elijah. Not even a hopeless bozo like you.

Elijah   But she's so amazing, she's got like a hummingbird mind, you never know what she's gonna land on, or how she's gonna see something or respond to something. And she wears all these quirky hats and stuff.

Grace   Hats? Anyone can wear a hat. I can wear a hat.

Elijah   Not like Becky you can't. No one can wear a hat like Becky. No one can pull off a jaunty hat like Becky Myers.

Grace   She needs a hat to cover her lumpy skull.

Elijah   She's totally her own invention. I just . . . She floors me. And when we kissed after Citizenship, it was . . . I felt I, for the first time, I *was* someone.

Grace   You really are a lost little puppy aren't you, babe?

Elijah   So I followed her for a bit . . . Took me weeks to summon up all my guts and talk to her. Tell her how I felt.

Becky (*appearing*)   What did you say to me?

Elijah   I . . . Yeah, so . . . what was it again . . . ?

Becky   You just said you loved me?

Elijah   Right.

Becky   Oh, Elijah . . . oh, my dear, dear boy . . .

Elijah   So I want us to hang out. Like a proper couple. I mean, if you . . . you like me back and that.

Becky   Well. Well well well I think I need to take this piece of news in for a moment. Gosh. And you want us to . . . Golly, I really don't know how to respond.

Elijah   Oh. Right. Becky / I . . .

Becky *kisses him.* **Elijah** *melts.*

Elijah   Oh. Does that mean / that you . . .

Becky   Tell me, Elijah . . . answer me this . . .

Elijah   Yes?

Becky   Are you familiar with the word 'risible'?

Elijah   Uh . . . sure . . .

Becky   You're not, are you? Don't pretend.

Elijah   . . . Yeah it means like when you *ris* . . . no. No, I'm not.

Becky   Okay, look it up. I'll wait.

Elijah   Now?

Becky   Don't you have an iPhone?

Elijah   Nokia.

Becky   Oh my God. Use mine. I've got a dictionary app. Here.

Elijah *takes the phone.*

Elijah   Rigible?

Becky *(losing patience and spelling it out)*   R-I-S-I-B-L-E.

He types. Waits. Reads.

Elijah   'Not effective or useful; stupid. Such as provokes laughter.'

Becky   Not the exact definition I would use, but okay. Does it give you an example?

Elijah   Uh . . . yeah. 'She's been making risible attempts to learn the trumpet.'

Becky   Hmm. Okay. So how would we use risible in this context? In the context we're in right now.

Elijah   I dunno . . . Uhm . . . uh . . . 'Elijah's been using risible attempts to hook up with Becky.'

Becky   There you go.

Elijah   Huh. I guess you learn something every day.

Becky   Glad to help.

Elijah   Wait.

Becky   Yes?

Elijah   But you kissed me.

Becky   I kiss lots of boys. Life is to be experienced, Elijah.

Elijah   But it was really nice.

Becky (*contemptuous*)   Nice?

Elijah   No, really, it was great.

Becky   Of course it was, I know what I'm doing.

Elijah   There was . . . tingling. Bristling on my skin. It was new.

Becky   Okay. Let's sit down.

*She takes **Elijah**'s hand and sits him down.*

Becky   See . . . I do think you're sort of cute.

Elijah   Yeah?

Becky   And I tingled a bit too . . . when we kissed. I've long been intrigued to see what it would be like with you.

Elijah   Right. Then / why . . .

Becky   And I've noticed you following me. At school. Looking away whenever I try to catch your eye.

Elijah   No, I wasn't following you or / anything I . . .

Becky   It's okay. I like it.

Elijah   Oh?

Becky   I think it's endearing.

Elijah   Is it?

Becky   And when you're lurking outside my house. That makes me smile too.

Elijah   Oh . . . good then . . . but I was, you know, in the / area.

Becky   It's touching, I think, knowing you're there. Knowing you're so completely obsessed with me, it's sort of . . . comfortable.

Elijah   Right, so does that mean . . . me and you . . . I mean, are we going out then?

Becky   Okay, let me clarify things for you so there's no more confusion. I am Becky. I am popular and successful. I know how to dress, I know how to socialise. I have friends and career prospects and talents. When I walk into a room, people smile and notice me, they feel imperceptibly elevated by my very presence. You. Are a total irrelevance. I'm not blaming you, you can't *help* it, it's just how you came out of your mother. We inhabit separate universes.

Elijah   Right, so that's a no, then, is it?

Becky   I need a man of substance, Elijah. A man that will challenge me and teach me the ways of love and the world and perhaps even break my heart. Can you imagine what that's like? For someone you love to crush your heart so completely. Smash it into bits. I want to feel all the extremes of living.

Elijah   Well . . . thanks for clearing that up. I'll be off then. Take care.

Becky   But I do like you being there. You can carry on stalking me if you like. I'll pretend I don't see you. But we'll both know I'm smiling inside.

Elijah   Right. Thanks. I'll bear that in mind.

Becky   Oh, you really are very sweet.

Becky kisses **Elijah**. *More passionately this time. Then she goes.*

Grace   And this is why you're gonna catapult yourself in front of a train? For that trollop?

Elijah   It's not just her, it's everything. Everyone.

Grace   What d'you mean 'everyone'? Most people don't give you a second's thought.

Elijah   Exactly. Exactly my point. I'm like . . . I might as well be invisible. 'Specially when I'm with Malachi. The only

people who take any notice of me are Holly and Shana, and
that's so they can punch me in the ear and stick my head
down the bog. And the ladies' bog as well. Not even the
gents'. I almost wouldn't mind if it was the gents'. That's kind
of a rite of passage for a pathetic victim like me.

Grace   So tell Malachi. He'll get them to stop.

Elijah   I can't go to him.

Grace   Why not?

Elijah   I just can't.

Grace   They wouldn't dare upset Malachi.

Elijah   It's too humiliating. Don't you understand? I'm
ashamed. So please just . . . just go now . . . It's nearly time.

Grace   You're not gonna kill yourself, sweetie.

Elijah   I am.

Grace   No, because you gotta be heroic and mysterious for
that kind of caper and really, I think we'd all agree, wouldn't
we . . . you're none of those things.

*Beat. Sound of a train approaching from a distance. A small sound that
gradually builds.*

Elijah   I'm going to do it. I'm going to do it. I'm doing it,
I'm doing it. I'm jumping. So stay, don't stay, it's up to you.

Grace   Wait. Look. What if you could change things and
stay alive?

Elijah   Grace . . .

Grace   Make people care and not have to kill yourself?
Yeah?

Elijah   You can't help me. No one can help me.

Grace   Just hear me out, yeah? There'll be another train
any minute. Just let me tell you my idea. Yeah? Please, Elijah!

Train builds and builds until it becomes deafening. **Elijah** *doesn't move. Finally the train shoots past and the sound starts to lessen.*

Elijah   This had better be good . . .

Grace   Okay . . . so we had this gerbil when I was around five. George.

Elijah   George the gerbil? Jesus . . .

Grace   Just listen. Little ginger thing he was, and cute as a plum, and when we first got him, Kara and me, we made such a big fuss about him – grooming him and replenishing the straw in his hut so he was all cosy and happy. Mum was all like, 'That bloody rodent's not coming anywhere near this house,' so we put him in this shed . . . we had . . . way, way down at the end of the garden. One time, George got out of his cage, escaped. We had the whole street out looking for him – shouting his name, crawling under cars . . . Kara and me were distraught, on and on we went saying how special he was to us and how we felt so guilty . . . furious with ourselves for not securing his cage properly. It killed us, the thought we'd never see him again. So when our Uncle Eddie found him in a hedge, nibbling at some sick outside number twelve, we hugged him close and vowed to take extra special care of him from this day forth. After a bit, though, we started resenting him. Trudging all the way down the end of that garden, every morning, rain or shine . . . Then one morning, after it was bitter cold in the night . . . I went down to the shed to give George his feed and he was rock solid. Dead-eyed. Frozen to the bone.

Elijah   That's an awful story. I really can't see why you told me that.

Grace   Cos you need to do one. Like George did.

Elijah   Wait a minute, I'm the gerbil?

Grace   You need to get gone and allow people to notice. Let them miss you.

Elijah   I really believe that might be the stupidest idea I ever heard of.

Grace   Come on, it'll only be for a bit. Enough time for people to be . . . I don't know . . . seriously concerned about your well-being. Which, and tell me if I'm off the mark here, but right now . . . they are not.

Elijah   Forget it.

Grace   We'd have to think it through properly, though . . . long enough so it makes the biggest impact.

Elijah   It won't have any impact cos I'm not gonna do it.

Grace   But this could really work.

Elijah   It won't work cos nobody cares about me enough to miss me.

Grace   Okay, well why do you think that is? Eh? I'll tell you, shall I? Because you don't make the effort.

Elijah   Excuse me?

Grace   You don't contribute.

Elijah   I contribute.

Grace   What do you contribute to school life?

Elijah   I contribute.

Grace   What?

Elijah   I . . . I . . . look, I contribute, okay? / I contribute. All right? In my own way.

Grace   Name one thing. You in any teams? No. You in any groups? Drama? Debating, band, choir, any arts and crafts? No.

Elijah   So what, so I'm not in any groups. So I'm not good at stuff, does that make me a bad person? I don't really get music or art or sport, does that mean I don't deserve to live? I tried to join those clubs. I try out for the teams and I'm too slow, or I'm too weak. I audition for those shows, but I can't act or sing or dance. They don't even let me go in the chorus, cos I've got no co-ordination.

Grace   Exactly. Plus, a poor-to-average academic record, so you're not really punching your weight in that department.

Elijah   I did good in English. / And Chemistry.

Grace   How many friends do you have on Facebook? Hm? Facebook. How many friends?

Elijah   Enough.

Grace   How many exactly?

Elijah   Look . . . I'm a little bit busy committing suicide here . . .

Grace   Fourteen. It's tragic. And I bet a third of those are your immediate family. You know you can't count immediate family as friends, tosspot. They don't have a choice. I bet even your mum had to think about it before accepting you as a friend.

Elijah   Please leave me alone, Grace. / Please. Leave me alone . . .

Grace   How many people have ignored your friend requests? How many people have accepted your friend requests in order to bulk up their numbers, uh? Only to unfriend you later on when they've got a tolerable amount of friends? And by the way, fourteen is not a tolerable amount. You barely exist, Elijah. Why didn't you have a birthday party this year?

Elijah   What?

Grace   Why didn't you have a party for your birthday? Come on.

Elijah   My mum made shepherd's pie.

Grace   And who came?

Elijah   Wasn't that sort of party.

Grace   Who came to your party, Elijah?

Elijah   Well it was just me and Mum and Malachi.

Grace   And then Malachi had to go mountaineering or something, didn't he?

Elijah   Okay, look . . .

Grace   You might as well be dead or decaying, cos you don't make a mark. You heard what Becky said, you're always there. A sort of . . . everyday irritant . . . like a stench in the fridge . . . and you clean it out and you chuck away all the food that's gone bad and it's still there, the stench, you can't get rid of it, and that's you.

Elijah   A stench?

Grace   Is that what you want?

Elijah   And going missing will change all that?

Grace   You'll be the talk of the school. You'll be the mystery man, the subject of all the gossip. Every kid'll want to be connected to you in some way. They'll, all of them, be bigging up their friendships with you. Oh, me and 'Lijah, yeah, we were like that. Everyone loves to be close to tragedy, it makes them special. Plus, all the shitty horrible things people did to you . . . they'll all regret them. All the abuse they dished out, all the misery they made for you . . . inside, they'll feel terrible.

Elijah   You think so?

Grace   I guarantee it.

Elijah *seriously thinks about this for the first time.*

Elijah   . . . Where would I go?

Grace   I'll find somewhere. Somewhere close. But you'd have to go deep. No contact with anyone. No Facebook, no mobile, no Twitter, no emails, no texts, no internet; total blank out. Then . . . when you come back, when they see you're safe and well . . . the elation . . . Think of your mum's face – the joy, the tears of sweet relief. The new-found love in their hearts. And Malachi.

Pause. She can see she's getting through. She goes for the jugular.

And Becky.

Elijah Becky? Really.

Grace God, yes. The drama of it . . . Oh, she'll be beside herself.

Elijah I dunno, Grace . . .

Grace Don't you want things to change? Don't you want people to treat you different?

Elijah I suppose . . .

Grace Then give them the gift of missing you.

Pause.

Elijah No . . . No it's stupid. It's not happening. I'm peckish. I'm going home.

Elijah *shakes his head and goes.* **Grace** *sighs.*

Noise of smashing and sirens and general pandemonium across the stage.

Kara A few days after that the riots happened. First in London, then all over. There were rumours that some of our school were involved in the looting and the fighting with police.

Holly I remember being there. We got the feeling of power like we could stand up to the Man. I felt like I *was* someone.

Shana People were gonna hear us. They couldn't ignore this.

Holly I was gonna take stuff. I was gonna smash stuff up and no one could stop me. I was expressing myself. We watched buildings burn and cheered and the Feds just stood by and watched and they couldn't do nothing about it.

Shana   It was like the best party ever. We ruled our own streets for the first time. It was brilliant.

Holly   I felt so powerful. Like a celebrity. I could take what I wanted.

Shana   Then the Feds finally woke up and started charging us and battering us.

Holly   One of them got me by the throat and called me a fat bitch. I called him a dickhead and pushed him off me. He battered me with his truncheon but I didn't cry or give in and then I got swept up in the crowds. I stood up for myself.

Shana   No one can say we weren't alive that day. We didn't make a mark.

Holly   I reckon we'll go down in history.

Shana   And we were back in time for 'Enders.

Holly   Yeah . . . the repeat on BBC Three, though.

Shana   Yeah. But still . . . we got our stuff. That's the main thing. Though I only got a pair of Skechers two sizes too big and both for the left foot, and an Ericsson phone charger I can't use.

Holly   I got a pair of velour trackie bottoms, but they weren't in my colour so I gave them to my nan.

Grace and Kara's House

Kara   Grace and I were watching the rioting on the news . . . Mum was away and it was just us in the house. Someone started knocking at the back window.

Knocking.

Oh God!

Grace   Hello?!

Kara   I nearly jumped out of my skin.

Grace   Stay there, Kara.

Kara   Grace, don't go out there. Be careful. I'm scared.

Grace   I said just wait there!

Grace and Kara's Garden

Grace   What are you doing?

Elijah   Let's do it. Your plan. I want to do it.

Grace   What?

Elijah   I ran away from Malachi.

Grace   What?

Elijah   We got caught up in all this crazy shit. There's kids, masses of them, going bonkers on Eagle Road.

Grace   It's on the news.

Elijah   Everyone's wired. There's this feeling in the air . . . I can't describe it, but it makes you . . . I dunno . . . see a mad opportunity and want to take a leap at it . . .

Grace   What are you talking about, what did you do?

Elijah   I lost Malachi. In all the havoc. Gave him the slip. He was watching these kids smashing up the Millets . . . when his back was turned, I ran. Ran like fire. And I was running and I was thinking about what you said. If I hid for a bit and what people would think. No contact, if I just vanished. So I wanna do it. Invisible man.

Grace   God, I'm buzzing. Really? Okay. Let's do it. This is exciting and totally beyond insane. I love you. This is the best thing that's happened. Okay, I gotta think. I gotta think. Wait. What about your mobile? The Feds can trace it.

Elijah   Dumped it in a bin.

Grace   Good boy. What about cameras?

Elijah   There was a load of stuff on the street from this party shop. I took a mask and wore it and snuck off. If anything, the cameras'll pick up Barack Obama legging it.

Grace   Great. Right. You'll have to go in the shed. He'll be looking for you.

Elijah   What? The shed?

Grace   We can't risk you moving another millimetre.

Elijah   The gerbil shed?

Grace   It's right down the end of the garden, no one ever goes in there.

Elijah   I dunno, Grace . . .

Grace   My dad used to paint in there before he left.

Elijah   Is there a computer and games and stuff?

Grace   Took it all with him.

Elijah   Well, what would I do all day?

Grace   There's books and shit.

Elijah   Books? I'll go demented after half a day.

Grace   Do you wanna do this or not? Don't back out on me now. Are you gonna disappoint me? You do not wanna disappoint me, boy.

Elijah   I'm not your bloody gerbil, you know? Gordon.

Grace   George. Look, it won't be for ever.

Kara (*calling from the house*)   Grace!

Grace   Quick. Get in the shed.

Elijah (*whispering*)   Just make sure you bring me regular meals and stuff.

Kara   Grace, are you out there?

Grace   What is it?!

Kara   Malachi's here.

Grace   Just coming!

Elijah   Promise me, Grace.

Grace   Get in that shed and keep your mouth shut.

She locks the shed.

Elijah   Don't lock it. Oy.

Grace   For safety.

Elijah   What if you're in an accident? I'll rot in here and die.

Grace   There's only a very slim chance of that. Now keep quiet. This is brilliant.

Grace and Kara's House

Grace   Gone?

Malachi   Yes.

Grace   You sure?

Malachi   Course I'm sure. He's gone.

Grace   He's not sitting at home and no one's noticed?

Malachi   He's gone, he's gone.

Grace   I mean, he's not the most impressive-looking dude, is he?

Malachi   He's gone, Grace. Jesus. I searched, all right? I searched everywhere. I left a thousand messages.

Grace   Have you rung his mates? / That won't take long.

Malachi   We were walking . . . We'd been to our nan for dinner and Mum had called us and said to come straight home. She was freaked out about the looters . . .

Grace   It's all over the news what's happening . . .

Malachi   We have to walk through Eagle Road to get home. Right where it was all kicking off.

Grace   We've had it on Sky all night, ask Kara if you don't believe me, it's mental.

Malachi   This massive . . . it was mayhem, this huge crowd and glass everywhere and shouting and burning and police . . . Mum said, whatever you do Malachi, please, please get Elijah home safely. He's so helpless and he looks up to you. He'll feel safe with you. Jesus. What am I gonna do?

Beat. **Grace** *steels herself, then goes for the kill.*

Grace   Maybe you should call the police?

Malachi   What?

Grace   Inform the Feds, why not?

Malachi   . . . It hasn't been twenty-four hours yet.

Grace   Yeah, but if you're worried something's happened –

Malachi   Won't they have enough to deal with tonight?

Grace   This is pretty serious, though, don't you think?

Malachi   You really think something's happened?

Grace   You were there, babe. You're obviously concerned for his welfare.

Malachi   But I mean . . . what would anyone want with Elijah?

Grace   There are some sick people in this world, Malachi. Some very, very sick and strange people.

Malachi   You don't think something bad's happened? You don't think he's hurt, do you?

Grace   I really don't know. When was the last time you saw him alive?

Malachi   What? Alive? Jesus / Christ, Grace . . .

Grace   Well, you know what I mean? Saw him with your own eyes.

Malachi   Christ, I can't think. Okay. We were walking past the Millets on Eagle Road. These kids . . . they were gutting the place. I stopped to watch, I had to. They had all this kit out on the street, trainers, trackies, rackets, they *attacked* it all like pigeons swarming over a discarded KFC, big ones getting the prime pickings, smaller ones scrapping over the rest. It was all over in seconds, I swear. Then I turned to 'Lijah and said something, but he was nowhere. I shouted for him . . . Nothing. I scanned down the street, this way and that . . . He's nowhere. I phoned him, straight to voicemail. Phoned again. Third time. I was shouting for him . . . I was getting a bit para, you know, cos the air was, like, thick with threat and I didn't want to draw attention to myself. I picked a direction and jogged off to look for him. I swear to God, I looked everywhere for that kid.

Grace   Right. We need to act fast.

Malachi   What?

Grace   Get photos of him up online. Start a website.

Malachi   Grace . . .

Grace   Get some posters printed. Stick 'em up where people go. Eagle Arcade, Stanley Street lido, Captain Chicken's, the station . . .

Malachi   Just stop a minute . . .

Grace   Don't you see? We want as many people to know he's missing as possible. Widen the search.

Malachi   Grace . . . / Babe.

Grace   No, there's no time to lose, babe. Yeah? Okay. Now there'll be a police report. What was he wearing when you last saw him alive?

Malachi   A, like, a blue . . . Will you stop saying that? He's still alive, alright?

Grace   Come on, come on, what was he wearing?

Malachi   Jesus, what if he's not? What if he's . . . how the hell do I tell Mum? She's already got a nervous condition. This'll finish her off.

Grace   Keep focused. What was he dressed in?.

Malachi   I dunno, he was in, like, a vest thing . . . trackie bottoms . . .

Grace   You need to be specific, Malachi. Come on. For when they trawl through all the CCTV footage.

Malachi   I can't.

Grace   Maybe there are some clues in his room? On his computer?

Malachi   I can't do this.

Grace   Did he keep a diary? There may be clues in there. Things that upset him. People.

Malachi   I dunno. A diary? I don't think so.

Grace   I can help you Malachi. Baby. I can't make this okay. You have to trust me.

Malachi   I just had a thought. This'll be on the news.

Grace (*excited*)   You really think so?

Malachi   No, no. I can't have this hanging over me.

Grace   Maybe regional news, I don't think it'll make the nationals. Do you think it'll make the nationals?

Malachi   I'm supposed to be . . . How is this gonna affect the TV show?

Grace (*stoking him*)   It'll all be fine. Don't worry. Grace is here.

Malachi   You don't understand. The show's about responsible young people. Business leaders of the future. And

this'll be everywhere. I'll be blamed and everyone'll hate me
for it.

Grace   I won't hate you.

Malachi   I should have watched him. I should have
protected him. How could I let this happen?

Grace   You couldn't help it.

Malachi   This is my fault, Grace! I took my eye off him.
I was too busy watching those . . . I keep checking my phone.
Nothing. Jesus, I so screwed this up. I feel so stupid. Useless.

Grace   You shouldn't beat yourself up, baby. You have
every right to have these feelings. Everyone makes mistakes,
yeah?

Malachi   Not me.

Grace   Yes, you're not superhuman. You need to let
yourself off the hook, or you'll be no use to your mum or
anyone. You need to give yourself permission to feel idiotic
and worthless. They're perfectly normal feelings. Okay, babe?

Malachi   All I know's . . . if that kid doesn't pitch up, I'm
massively bolloxed. Jesus, I can't be responsible for this.

Grace   I'll stand by you whatever. You'll still have me,
Malachi. You'll always have your little Gracie. Look at me.

Malachi *looks at her as if for the first time in ages. Then he throws
himself into her arms.*

Malachi   Oh God.

Grace   That's it. That's better. Gracie's here. Gracie'll
make it all okay.

Park

Titus   D'you 'member . . . d'you 'member, right . . . like . . .
right . . . when 'Lijah . . . it was a really hot scorching day,

like, right, and we were out on Biology field trip and we was so bored, bored as hell, man, and 'Lijah looked up to the sky and he was like, 'I command you, sky, to rain.'

Maxwell   Yeah.

Titus   He reckoned he could make it rain. Just by . . .

Maxwell   I remember.

Titus   Just by willing it. Just by wanting it. And, oh my God, it only rained.

Maxwell   It did.

Titus   It was mental.

Maxwell   There was always something about him. Something . . . I don't know . . .

Titus   Special.

Maxwell   Not special.

Titus   Weird.

Maxwell   Not weird, yes, but not that.

Titus   Magical.

Maxwell   Yes. Sort of . . . *magical*. Yes. Does that sound dumb?

Titus   Doesn't sound dumb to me, bro . . .

Becky   Don't you think there's been a sort of eerie feeling around Stanley Street since poor Elijah was taken from us? A kind of ominous malaise.

Kara   Hang on, we don't know that.

Becky   Don't we . . . ?

Kara   We don't know he was taken.

Becky   Okay, but something happened.

Kara   We don't know he was taken. We don't have that information.

Becky   We know *something* happened, though.

Kara   We don't know anything. No one knows anything. At all. I don't. Do you?

Becky   No. But someone knows something.

Maxwell   I remember, once we were picking teams . . . five a side . . . and he was the last to be picked . . .

Titus   Always.

Maxwell   . . . always the last to be picked. But he didn't mind. He just kind of shrugged.

Titus   He was in goal.

Maxwell   Always. And he actually saved a goal . . . or someone kicked it wide . . . and we went on to win the match.

Titus   Yeah, we won, didn't we, that one time.

Maxwell   And I think now it was cos of him. Cos he was vibing us to win.

Shana   There was always something tragic about that kid. You know what I mean?

Holly   Sort of spooky?

Shana   A cloud round him. Walked about with a . . . yeah, now I think of it.

Shed

Elijah   Where've you been? I'm starving.

Grace   Eat this.

Elijah (*grabs at the food and eats hungrily*)   And there's this weird smell in here. I think it's all these old paint pots and crap of your dad's.

Grace   I got you some pants and a toothbrush.

Elijah (*chewing*)   . . . and there's all this old tat. Pliers and mugs and gas canister and brushes and shit, is it all safe? I mean . . .

Grace   You'll be pleased to know everyone's gone completely doolally cos of you. Talking about nothing else.

Elijah   Are people really missing me, then?

Grace   They've totally changed history. Turned you into some kind of wizard.

Elijah   Wizard?

Grace   Here, I got you a box of juice as well.

Elijah *drinks the juice.*

Grace   Police are all stopping people in the street. Searching houses. Even created an emergency hot line for anyone with information. Already got some cranks coming forward wanting money.

Elijah   What about Becky?

Grace   Oh, she's convinced you've been tortured, raped and cut into squares. She keeps telling everyone they're gonna find body parts floating in the canal.

Elijah   Is she upset, though?

Grace   She's enjoying it. Putting the heebie-jeebies up everyone. Wondering who's next.

Elijah   But she misses me?

Grace   Finish your juice, I wanna chuck the box away.

Elijah *finishes the drink.*

Grace   She thinks you're special for being taken.

Elijah   I can't wait to see her face when I show up.

Grace   Told you I was right about this, didn't I?

Elijah   What about Malachi? Is he all right?

Grace   You let me worry about Malachi.

Elijah   Is he blaming himself?

Grace   Give me the box.

Elijah   I don't want him to feel bad.

Grace   They dropped him from that TV show.

Elijah   What? Cos of me?

Grace   He's got so boring. All he goes on about is how he doesn't deserve to live.

Elijah   What? Hang on, Grace . . .

Grace   He's no fun any more.

Elijah   Doesn't deserve to live?

Grace   He's obsessed with what happened that night. Keeps going over and over it in his head, it's driving me potty. All he wants to talk about.

Elijah   Okay. I think . . . great . . . You know . . . Wow . . . This has been a . . . a really interesting experiment.

Grace   Where do you think you're going, sunshine?

Elijah   I'm gonna say I just had to get away, to, to think . . . get my head together . . . but I'm back now and I'm alright and everyone can go back to being normal.

Grace   No no no no no.

Elijah   Look, it's over, okay . . .

Grace   It's way too soon.

Elijah   Let me go, Grace.

Grace   You're staying where you are, this is just getting started.

Elijah   Malachi getting dropped . . . this is not what I wanted.

Grace   You'll ruin everything if you go now.

Elijah   Get out the way and let me out.

Grace   If you show up now, it won't mean anything.
Everyone'll just go back to how it was before.

Elijah   Good, this is stupid.

Grace   But it won't change anything. Remember George?

Elijah   Screw him. I gotta get out of this shed.

Grace   We found him too quick and we stopped caring and
he froze to death.

Elijah   I'm not a gerbil, Grace. I'm a human being!

Grace   Shhh, quiet! There's people in the next houses.

Elijah   Hello! / It's me!

Grace   Idiot.

Elijah   It's Elijah!

Grace   Stop it.

Elijah   I'm in the shed!

Grace   Fine then. Tell everyone. Tell everyone how you've
lied. How you've betrayed them. How you've duped them
and fooled them. How your mum's on pills cos of you, and
your brother wants to top himself. All cos of your stupid little
game.

Elijah   Now hang on a minute . . .

Grace   You come out now and it looks like you were never
serious. Like all you wanted to do was screw with people's
feelings. Laugh at them.

Elijah   That's not what this is about at all, I just . . .

Grace   Isn't it? Cos I'd have to tell people . . . you know . . .
He came to me. Elijah came to me. Told me he ran away

from his brother, how he wanted to take revenge on everyone for ignoring him . . .

Elijah   Revenge? / No . . .

Grace   How he *begged* me to let him shack in my dad's shed.

Elijah   Didn't beg you . . .

Grace   Just so he could take the piss. Out of the people who care about him. Huh? How would that go down?

Elijah   I just . . .

Grace   How would it go down, Elijah?

Elijah   Not well.

Grace   Right answer.

Elijah   But this was your idea!

Grace   Oh, you think people are gonna believe that, do you? If you pop up now? I'll tell you what they'll do, shall I? They'll *despise* you. They'll despise you for what you've done to them. Even more than they did before.

Elijah *ponders this gravely for a time.*

Elijah   . . . Right . . . well . . . Seeing as you put it like that. Maybe I could hang on a bit longer.

Grace   Thank you. Finally come to your senses. Now stay there like a good boy and I will let you know the optimum time for your revelation. Okay?

Elijah *nods.* **Grace** *goes.*

Kara   That whole time was like an out-of-body experience. The whole world talking about the riots and everyone we knew obsessing about Elijah. Things were getting so weird. Someone even came forward saying they knew where Elijah was and wanted twenty grand to give over information. Then one night I saw Grace, it was strange, she was coming up from the back of the garden with a torch and some dirty plates and cups. Grace?

Garden

Grace   Christ. Go back to bed.

Kara   Where've you been with that?

Grace   I told you to butt out.

Kara   Have you been by the shed?

Grace   No.

Kara   Is there someone down there? God. Wait. No.

Grace   Kara . . .

Kara   Is Dad back? Grace, tell me, please, is Dad here?

Grace   Don't be stupid.

Kara   You've got to tell me. I've got a right to know if he is. Grace?

Grace   It's not Dad, alright? Jesus.

Kara   So who were you taking food to . . . who's in the . . . Oh . . . oh God, it's him.

Grace   Kara . . .

Kara   Isn't it? Oh God, it's bloody him, isn't it?

Grace   Keep your voice down.

Kara   I don't believe it, you've got Elijah in our bloody shed.

Grace   I swear to God, you keep your gob shut about this or I'll shut it for you.

Kara (*whispering*)   But how . . . I don't . . . how . . . I don't . . . how . . . did this . . .

Grace   He ran away. Okay. Look, it's what he wants. It's . . . I'm helping him.

Kara   'What he wants'?

Grace   He's having some kind of nervous breakdown or something, yeah, so just . . . just have a bit of compassion, okay? And respect his wishes. Okay?

Malachi *steps forward and addresses the audience.*

Malachi   The police came round to ours again. Had to make what they called a 'risk assessment'. Wanted photos and stuff . . . asked loads of questions about the moments before he went. Places he's known to have gone, addresses and phone numbers of his mates. One of them searched his room. Took away his hard drive and his toothbrush. For DNA. I was getting really cheesed off at this point. They looked at me as if I was scum. Kept asking the same things over and over. Did I know any of the people causing the disturbances that night? Did I argue with Elijah before he went? Were we meeting anyone? If we spoke to anyone on route. Did he phone anyone? Did anyone phone him? Did he message anyone? Did anyone message him? Said they needed to know if it was serious enough for them to justify using a specialist search team. They gotta divert funds from other areas . . . Sniffer dogs and choppers don't come cheap, you know, they gotta be sure he's in proper peril. So I got really shirty, you know, really hacked off. I said, 'Look! He vanished during the biggest public disorder in a generation, how will that do? Is that peril enough for you?' Then I bolted out of there and went round to see Grace.

Kara   I was there when Malachi arrived.

Grace and Kara's House

Malachi   People are talking about him like he's not coming back. Do you think he's dead? Kara? Because if he's dead, then it's my fault. Isn't it? So what does that make me, his murderer?

Kara   Grace should be back any minute. Shall I make a cup of tea?

Malachi   I can't, you see I can't breathe until I find him.
I can't do anything. I can't eat or sleep or work until I find
him. I don't even know what I'm wearing today, what I put
on this morning. I don't remember dressing. See, I feel naked.

Kara   You look fine. More than fine.

Grace (*coming in suspiciously*)   What's going on here?

Kara   What? Nothing.

Grace   Got a lot to chat about, have we?

Kara   No, we just . . . Malachi was / just . . .

Malachi   I was about to tell Kara. The local news want me
to go on the telly.

Grace   The news?

Malachi   Mum's too doped up to do it. They want pictures
of Elijah. Home movies and stuff to show. Then I gotta make
a statement. Don't know how I'll cope.

Kara   You poor thing.

Grace   I can do it.

Kara   Grace.

Grace   You're very emotionally fragile right now, Malachi,
you're liable to choke up. I can speak on your behalf.

Malachi   Thanks, but I can't let you do that . . .

Grace   You know the way the news works, you got a few
precious seconds to make your mark. You gotta make it count.
Can't have you babbling like a teary wreck. Best if I do it.

Malachi   Oh . . . okay . . . thanks. What would I do
without you?

TV Studio

Grace (*reads a statement*)   Elijah is a cherished member of our community. Always mucking in with everything, helping his fellow students and old people and, also, academically . . . sound. He was last seen in Eagle Road at about half past seven on the ninth of August. He was wearing a red hoodie and jeans. If anyone knows anything at all about his disappearance, please contact the police hot line. (*Looks into the camera.*) Elijah. If you're listening. We all love you very much. Please let us know that you're safe and well. Everyone is desperate for news.

Street

Maxwell   There she is . . . come on . . . Grace. Wait up.

Titus   You're in with those TV guys, right?

Grace   Yeah. So?

Titus   We wrote a song.

Maxwell   For Elijah.

Titus
  Sing it. Sing it. One two (three four) two, two, three, four . . . (three), two, three, four . . .

Both
  Elijah, Elijah,
  We're comin' to find ya.
  Wherever you're hidin'
  Wherever you mindin'

Titus
  Like when they looked for Gadaffi in the desert hell –

Maxwell
  They found him!

Titus
Like when they looked for Saddam down the sewer well –

Maxwell
They found that one too!

Both
So we're definitely comin'
We're like the forty-nine bus
And like

Maxwell
Global warmin'

Both
There ain't no stoppin' us
We're gonna find ya
Eli-i-i-jah

Maxwell   And I do like a ya-ya-ya! On the end of it.

Titus   Well? What d'you think? Reckon you could speak to the TV dudes? Put in a word.

Maxwell   We need to get some broadcast time, isn't it.

Grace   You wanna know what I think? I think it's despicable.

Maxwell   What? Hold on.

Grace   Using his disappearance to further your music careers. I think it's a total disgrace.

Titus   No, but we wouldn't take any royalties. It would all go straight into this fund. Swear to God.

Grace   What? What fund?

Maxwell   They started this fund. 'Help Find Elijah'. You didn't hear?

Grace   A fund? Who started it?

Titus   Kara did.

Grace   Kara?

Titus   So, will you talk to them?

Grace   Kara started a fund? Kara started a fund? Kara? Started a fund?

Titus   So, will you talk to them?

Grace   Shit.

Maxwell   We think it'll move people.

Grace   Move people? Listen to me. Your song blows. It's dog-rotten.

She goes.

Titus (*calling after her*)   So you'll think about it, yeah?

Maxwell   We got a right to express our grief, you know?

Grace and Kara's House

Kara   I was at home with Malachi. He was in a frightening state.

Malachi   All the wonderful things people have been saying about my brother. I had no idea people felt that way about him. He had so many friends and admirers.

Kara   Yeah. I know.

Malachi   I had no idea he touched people so profoundly.

Kara   Well he . . . I mean . . . he did . . . uh . . . touch people.

Malachi   Yeah. He did, didn't he? Which is why I've decided . . . I think I'm gonna to pay the twenty grand.

Kara   What? No . . .

Malachi   These people say they got information.

Kara   Malachi . . . wait a minute . . .

Malachi   I got some money when my dad died. Plus, I can borrow some from this loan firm . . .

Kara   But you don't know if these people are scammers?

Malachi   We've got to pursue every avenue. Follow any lead.

Kara   Please think about this . . .

Malachi   If it costs me to do it . . . if it totally breaks me / I don't care.

Kara   You're upset. You're not thinking properly.

Grace (*storming in*)   Kara, I wanna word with you.

Kara   What?

Malachi   Grace, can we . . . I really need to talk.

Grace   Yeah, yeah. Later. I gotta speak to Kara now.

Malachi   It's really important. I need to make a really big decision.

Grace   Not now, Malachi. I can't be there for you every second, okay? Now go home will you, I have to talk to Kara.

Malachi   Okay. Sorry. Can I call you later then, yeah? Chat then?

Grace   Whatever.

Malachi *goes.*

Grace   He's so needy.

Kara   I can't believe you treat him like that.

Grace   You started a fund? Huh?

Kara   What? Now wait a minute.

Grace   You started a fund, Kara?

Kara   I didn't want to.

Grace   But you did? You started a fund?

Kara   Can you stop saying that?

Grace   I want to know what your game is here?

Kara   I haven't got a game.

Grace   You wait till my back is turned and you start cashing in on this thing. Is that it?

Kara   I'm not cashing in.

Grace   This was my idea, Kara. You always have to have what's mine.

Kara   It's because I've been spending more time with Malachi.

Grace   What? So that's what you're up to?

Kara   No.

Grace   You skank! You want my man.

Kara   I don't.

Grace   I'll tear your face off.

Kara   You've been totally ignoring him! You've been strutting about like the cat that ate the peacock. Going on telly, and signing autographs, and acting as spokesperson for the family, and you don't have time for anyone else, and he's there suffering. He's really struggling, Grace. He needs you.

Grace   I know, and it's making me sick. And who asked you to get involved, anyway?

Kara   People were coming to me. As Malachi's friend . . .

Grace   His *friend*?

Kara   What was I supposed to say . . . ? Huh? 'Oh yeah, screw Elijah. I'm not raising a penny for that tosser, I don't want your five hundred pounds. Take it back.'

Grace   What?

Kara   'Your money's no good here.'

Grace   Five hundred pounds?

Kara   That's what's been collected so far?

Grace   Five hundred pounds?

Kara   This isn't my fault, Grace. I didn't start all this. I'm not the kind of person who enjoys all this deceit. It's very unpleasant for me.

Grace   Shut up. I'm thinking.

Kara   It's horrible knowing. I wish I didn't.

Grace   We could triple that money if we get this right.

Kara   Get what right?

Grace   This fund-raiser. It could be a real event. Like a concert.

Kara   Grace . . .

Grace   People could . . . could, I dunno, read poems and stuff, and make speeches, sing songs. Invite the parents. They'll pay through the nose for all that rubbish.

Kara   What are you talking about?

Grace   It's an offering to the gods of luck, isn't it, Kara? 'Thank you for not taking my kid.'

Kara   No . . . no . . . you have to stop this right now, Grace.

Grace   What? When I'm just getting warmed up?

Kara   Yes. You have to tell people what happened. This isn't right. Even by your standards / this is going too far . . .

Grace   Now you listen to me, Kara. You say a word about this and I will hurt you. Okay? I'll tell everyone it was your idea.

Kara   My idea? But . . .

Grace   You could get a criminal record, you know? You won't go to college, you won't get a job. Might even get banged up.

Kara   Prison? Me?

Grace   Certainly. Perverting the course of justice, false imprisonment . . .

Kara   False imprisonment? I thought he wanted to be in there?

Grace   Christ. Why can't you ever support me? Huh? Why are you always sniping and holding me back and being negative? You stifle me.

Kara   Grace, can't you see this is crazy? There's police out looking for him, for heaven's sake . . . with helicopters and cocker spaniels.

Grace   Oh, you're such a . . . Why can't you be more enterprising? You've got no ambition. No hunger for experience. You're so wet.

Kara   Jesus, this isn't opportunity for growth, Grace. There's people worried to death about that kid.

Grace   Those people didn't give a shit about him when he was around. They didn't even notice he was alive. Let them sweat.

Kara (*getting much more upset now*)   And what about Malachi?

Grace   Stay off of him. I swear to God, Kara, stay off of him.

Kara   I won't. I won't. He's gonna destroy himself over this.

Grace   I told you to shut up! Shut your mouth! Cos you don't know anything about it. Elijah was gonna throw himself in front of a train and none of those bastards would've blinked. And I saved him. *Me*. I was the only one who cared!

Beat. Both calm down a little in the silence.

Grace   Look . . . People want to remember him, is that so bad? People want to put their hands in their pockets because it helps them to feel better. You want to take that away from them? What kind of a human being are you?

She storms off.

Kara   Posters started going up about the fund-raiser, sometimes covering the posters of Elijah's face saying he was missing. Grace threw herself into the organising. She became the centre of everything.

Holly   You get Grace's text about dinner at hers after the concert?

Shana   Yeah. Ten quid? For a chicken drumstick and bit of pasta salad. Is she having a joke?

Holly   Yeah. You going?

Shana   Course. It's for Elijah, isn't it?

Holly   Exactly.

Kara   One day, I noticed Grace was wearing this really expensive leather jacket. She told me it was from Primark, but even I could tell it was designer. She was so busy with arrangements I worried she might have forgotten to feed and water Elijah. So I went to the shed with some leftovers. It was really dark in there.

Shed

Elijah   Grace took the bulb away. She didn't want the light to raise any suspicions. Thanks for the food.

Kara   No problem. Grace would've come herself, she's just a bit busy right now.

Elijah   Yeah. Listen – all this stuff in here . . . it's all safe, yeah.

Kara   What? Oh. I never come down here really.

Elijah   No, but I mean it's not gonna poison me or . . . or anything? Do me harm in some way?

Kara   I've really got to head back in . . .

Elijah   I mean, what's her plan here, Kara? Yeah?

Kara   Oh . . . uh . . .

Elijah   I mean, how long does she expect me to survive in this shed? I've been in here a week now. Can you talk to her for me?

Kara   Me?

Elijah   Get some kind of estimate. I mean, Jesus, it's so stuffy and the smell . . . I'm choking. And Grace won't let me even crack a window.

Kara   I'm sure she knows what she's doing.

Elijah   Are you? Because . . . I've been thinking it through and . . . I understand that we've put people out and everything . . . but surely the longer we drag this out, the worse it's gonna be.

Kara   I really don't know / about that . . .

Elijah   I mean, think about it . . .

Kara   . . . You really need to /speak to Grace . . .

Elijah   It doesn't make sense to stay. Does it? So you need to tell her.

Kara   Me? No. I can't. Please don't ask me again. I want to, but I'm getting a bit scared of her to be honest.

Elijah   Right.

Kara   Thing is, she's really got her heart set on you being gone still. Can you last a bit longer, do you think?

Elijah   But I'm so bored . . . I was reading one of your dad's books before Grace took my light. *Tom Sawyer*. I'm really into it. Could you get me a torch?

Kara   Grace is using the torch. / She's always got it.

Elijah   Or some matches then. Please, Kara. I'm going crazy in here.

Singing is heard. It is **Maxwell** *and* **Titus** *doing their song. When it finishes, there is applause.*

Grace   Great stuff. That was Titus and Maxwell with their tribute single 'Everyone Mash up for Elijah'. And now, Shana and Holly have written a poem they'd like to share with us. Apparently, Shana will read the poem, while Holly acts out her loss through the medium of movement. Ladies.

Shana
      He wasn't a cool guy, a high flier
      He wasn't the cool cat.
      Or the top dog or the best dressed
      No he sure wasn't that.
      He wasn't the prettiest or the wittiest
      Or the fittest or hippest
      Or our bosom buddy
      Or our blood brother
      But he was our school mate
      And a friend.
      And now this poem has come to an end.

Applause.

Grace   Thank you, Shana and Holly. And now Becky Myers has kindly written a . . . an . . . (*She has to read it.*) An elegiac essay.

Becky   As some of you may know, Elijah and I were lovers. We had a deep and majestic bond that distance and separation and even – yes! – even death can never break. Since Elijah was so brutally taken from us, my soul has been black as night. A dark, dark night. I don't know how many of you have read Homer? A very important writer. He describes Night as a woman. Dressed in dark clothes, accompanied in her chariot by stars, and with such power and might she can subdue the great god Zeus. That is me. And like Night, *I* must be powerful. Brave. I must keep the faith. For I know my love is out there. And, one day, our spirits will dance again. Ride together again on my chariot. Oh Elijah, where you have gone, we know not of. Perhaps you were too delicate and mystical a creature for this world. Perhaps this life was too cruel . . . too cynical for someone as wondrous as you. Perhaps the truth is . . . we lost you even ere you were parted from us. I love you Elijah. Wherever you are!

Kara   It was gruesome. I nearly brought up my pasty. That night at the dinner in our garden, we were all shuckling the sugar round in our Diet Dr Peppers when Malachi stopped everything to say a prayer.

Garden

Malachi   Dear God or gods or Goddess or goddesses or evil genius scientist, or Darwin or Kurt Cobain or Buddha or Lady Di or Rupert Murdoch or Michael Jackson or whoever's up there and whoever decides these things . . . please . . . I'll give anything . . . I'll give my life . . . just please . . . please . . .

Kara   And that's when it happened. In the middle of the prayer. Bam.

Massive explosion.

I blame myself. But I blame Grace too. And Malachi. And Shana and Holly and Titus and Maxwell. And Elijah. We're all responsible in some way for what happened to us in that garden. We all could have stopped it. Each of us had the opportunity to change things, to resist things, to be kinder, or more truthful, or less greedy, or less cowardly. No, when I think about it . . . we're all guilty. So we all deserved what we got.

Blackout.

We Lost Elijah

BY RYAN CRAIG

*Notes on rehearsal and staging, drawn from a workshop
with the writer held at the National Theatre, November 2012*

What is the background to the play?

Ryan Craig knew from the outset that the play was about
someone going missing and the guilt when you are meant to
be in charge of that person. The initial idea came from the
Shannon Matthews case, an extraordinary missing person's
case where the mother and uncle had colluded to pretend the
girl had gone missing, in order to earn themselves money and
attention. It was from this that the character of Grace was
born.

The play came unconsciously, quickly and feverishly – and
the frenetic energy with which it was written mirrors the
energy with which it plays out. There was an almost dream-
like quality to the writing process, and indeed the piece itself.

The title was decided very early on, before the play was
written.

Themes and questions

Laurie Sansom (director) emphasised that rather than thinking
of a theme as a subject (for instance, schooldays, friendships),
it was useful to think of it as a question that the play explores.
This question can become the starting point for your directorial
and design process, and the question that you and your acting
company return to and work to answer together. Questions
help to focus the point of interest in the play. They are not
easy to articulate and are likely to change through the course
of the play but will absolutely influence the direction, playing
style and design. You want the direction and choices to come
from these questions. They don't need to be answered by the

play: it is through the character and the actions of the characters that we get to the heart of it. With characters it is crucial not simply to think about their qualities, but also what they are trying to do to one another.

There are a number of key themes/questions in the play:

- Friendships (what are the motivations of friendship?); manipulation (how do the characters manipulate one another?); identity (how do young people build their identity?)

- Absent adults (what happens when young people take on adult roles?); fear of consequences (why does no one in the play stop?); the role of the gods (what is the significance of names and the baptism?); celebrity, media and fame (what is the overarching framework and motivation for the characters? How are they seeking excitement?)

- How do teens get validation in society? How is identity expressed through the media? What methods do characters use to control others? Who is in control? What does each character have to lose? What happens at the end? Is it suicide? Is it planned?

- Does the play reflect society today? Do we really know anyone? Is society responsible for the identity crisis today/in the play? What does the play say about class?

There are also a number of themes that Ryan felt were missing from the play, including opportunity. This piece is about standing on the cusp between childhood and adulthood. The two major events in the play – Grace coming up with the idea and Elijah disappearing – both hinge on characters seeing an opportunity for changing their course.

Location

This play does not have to be set in London. Ryan has been careful to leave it open to you to make a choice. Although it does feel like an urban play, Laurie's suggestion would be to

start with finding the location nearest to you that experienced
the riots of the summer of 2011.

Approaching the play

Laurie suggested trying to get the company to learn lines
early (he asks actors to learn their lines before coming into a
rehearsal room). Once the lines are learnt you can start doing
the actual text work. The bulk of this work is about what one
character is actually going to do to the other. In order to get
the actors to speak the words naturally and effortlessly it is
important that they are thinking about what they are doing
rather than how they are saying the line.

Thinking that there's a right way of saying something is a
death knell for an actor and a line. All you will achieve is an
actor worrying they have got it wrong and feeling self-conscious
about the line. Never give a line reading. That is banned!

You want to feel that the line is happening for the first time
and is alive. Every group will have a unique set of obstacles to
achieving this, but the greater the ease of the delivery, the
more it will open up the comic potential. If inflections mean
that the text is not making sense, ask a simple question: what
is the most important word in the line? (Often the problem lies
in stressing too many words, which leads to over-deliberate
acting – permissible only in newsreaders and public speakers.)

There are no 'gags' in the piece. It is not looking for laughs,
so it is best simply to play the truth of the line, and focus on
what the character is trying to do on it. Fight the instinct to be
funny. Crucially, none of the characters thinks of themself as
funny and in fact they take themselves very seriously.

Language

The text is not entirely naturalistic. It is heightened.

But young people have fast, natural speech rhythms, and
often when delivering lines become very self-conscious.
Ideally you would try to key the text into their speech

patterns, and enjoy the heightened nature of the language without labouring it.

Some of the characters (Becky and Shana in particular) have very advanced language – and there is a question about where their phrases and syntax come from, and about playing with the idea of mimicry.

Characters

As much as possible, ask the characters questions that may lead them in a certain direction, but will also invest the actor with purpose and responsibility for the key decisions. It requires bravery to hand power to the group but will pay off in terms of ownership.

Character questions include:

- How do the characters perceive one another? How does this differ with how they perceive themselves? The biggest change during the play is in Malachi (between before and after Elijah disappearing) and how he perceives himself, and is perceived by Grace. But even Elijah changes: he has guts with Becky and there's a difference between how he perceives himself and how she perceives him.

- Where are the character contradictions? These and how they are played help to build rounded characters.

- How old are Grace, Malachi and Elijah? The general consensus in the workshop was that Grace and Malachi were around seventeen years old and Elijah between thirteen and fifteen. Ryan emphasised that he did not feel that Elijah was very much younger than Malachi, as that could take away from certain character decisions, motivations and imbalances in their relationships. One workshop participant suggested that they might even be twins, which Laurie agreed could be a possibility.

Doing the same amount of character work across the whole company can often provide a process to performers with smaller parts who have a 'blank cheque', and their journey can be hugely enriched.

Think about: what do they think they want? What is driving
their wants? Laurie calls the Stanislavskian 'super-objective'
the 'engine'. In deciding what the engine is, you create a
back-story of relationships and family history that will give
a sense of the world.

It will be informative to compare and contrast characters, for
instance Malachi and Elijah:

MALACHI (17?)	ELIJAH (13–15?)
High status	Inferiority complex
Focused/aspirations	Lost
Charismatic	Sensitive
Responsible	Low status
Sexual/sexually experienced	Average
Beautiful	Isolated
Popular	Perceptive
Alpha	Introverted
Girlfriend	Honest
Ambitions	Trapped
Successful	Sexual awakening
Presence	Naive
Father figure	Unhappy
Entrepreneur	No friends

How much of Elijah's list is a consequence of Malachi's?

Or list out characteristics, for instance Grace:

* Clever
* Manipulative
* Possessive
* Insecure
* Needy
* Control freak
* Sexual
* Aware
* Aspirational
* Sneaky
* Popular – is she? Why doesn't she go bowling?

Character journeys

MALACHI   At the beginning he seems to know who he is. Everyone aspires to be like him, but end up breaking him. Do you think of it as how far he falls? Or he gets to know himself better? Is Malachi genuinely beginning to understand his relationship to his brother? Is Malachi the innocent with an imposed downfall?

GRACE   Laurie pointed out the complexity of Grace and of charting through what she wants. What is going on with Grace to make her want what she wants? The journey that Grace goes on is extreme in its escalation. Is it all for social acceptance?

How much does Grace identify with Elijah? How much is she driven by a fear of losing Malachi? This plan is for both of them.

Grace ought to be subtle rather than 'bitchy'. On the surface she may enjoy the bitching but it is important to evoke sympathy and have a growing understanding of why she is doing what she is doing. She has to be a complex character and will be hugely challenging for the actor to play. She has many contradictions: her instinct is to go and help Elijah (she later says, 'And I saved him. Me. I was the only one who cared!'). It is more useful to think of that as a genuine instinct, rather than premeditated for her own gain. If Elijah is insignificant, why does she intervene?

Always with Grace, it is useful to ask what is she trying to do? And how does that differ with her tactics (the way she is trying to do it)? For instance, when she is mean is it a tactic, rather than necessarily an expression of wanting to hurt another character?

Generally give Grace a big break! Allow her to change her tactics. She needs to have femininity and softness, otherwise why would she be in a relationship with Malachi? What does Malachi see in Grace? What has happened to Dad? How has she been affected by the lack of a father figure? What are her limits/patterns of affection (for instance, she loved her gerbil but she didn't know how to look after it)?

For all the characters it will be useful to think about how they felt about Elijah before in comparison to how they feel about Elijah now. Was it useful for them to ostracise Elijah before?

Casting

You don't physically have to cast to type (e.g., Malachi doesn't have to be Adonis, nor Elijah Gollum). What is more important is that your cast channel the characters' qualities (hence the usefulness of the character lists).

There was a conversation with Ryan about the possibility of cross-casting/name-swapping (especially with Shana etc.). Ryan had liked that it was the girls who were involved in the riots, but felt that as long as the characters stayed true to the relationships and qualities inherent in the text and made sense of them, it was okay.

Laurie's rehearsal room tips

Exercises for use in rehearsals
You will lose the plot (literally) if the characters' tactics get merged with wants.

It is useful having one-on-one conversations with the actor. You don't necessarily want the full company knowing all the decisions. Some may well be secrets that only one actor knows. Doing one-on-one sessions can often engage with the actors' inner lives. The suggestion would be to do a session really early on, to inspire the decisions, and also at the end of the process, to see what has been discovered.

It is a really good exercise to get actors to write a monologue from the perspective of the character, either before or after the play, or at a particular moment in the play. It forces actors to engage with their voice. In setting up the writing exercise, make sure you determine who they are speaking to, as this will drastically alter the content of the monologue (e.g.

confession to a friend versus telling a policeman). It doesn't
matter as long as it is specific.

LAURIE'S 'ADD-WATER-AND-MIX' CHARACTER PROFILE

Use this exercise with your company to explore characters:

Write the first thing you can think of. This exercise will tell
you where your gaps are – what you don't know is as
important as what you do!

Decide on a character.

- Full name.
- Age.
- Family – brothers/sisters? Ages? Mum and Dad?
- Living situation? What kind of house do you live in?
  Where is it? Location?
- Physical appearance. What do you look like?
- What do you wear?
- What music do you listen to?
- Who is your best friend? Why?
- Academic record? What is your favourite subject?
- What is your most treasured possession?
- What's your secret (that no one else in the world knows)?
- What do you think you want to do when you leave school?
  Is this aspirational or practical?
- What do you do in your spare time?
- What is your favourite phrase or saying (habitual)?
- What is your super-objective (engine/driving force)? You
  may not even be aware of it.
- Any additional information that you instinctively think is
  essential to the character?

Read back over what you have written. If there is anything
wrong – change it. If there is anything extra – add it. Once
you have reviewed and edited – absorb it, and invest it into

the production. You should have a clearer sense of who the person is.

How to make a character physical

Choose a character. Start this exercise as yourself.

- Stand somewhere in the space: shake it out!
- Centre yourself – chin parallel to the floor, knees slightly bent, let out any tensions or stiffness.
- Close your eyes.
- You are walking down a street in the town where the character lives.
- Look around you. What kind of street is it? What are the houses like?
- Are there cars? What is the sky like? What is the weather like? Is it comfortable? Is it dangerous? How relaxed are you?
- Take a step forward.
- Two hundred yards in front of you is a house/building where the character lives. Turn to face it.
- Approach the building. What is the house like? It is a semi? Or a flat? Is there a garden?
- The front door is ajar. Push it open.
- How do you feel? What do you see? What are the walls like? How many doors are there? Are there stairs? Is there carpet or lino?
- Find your way to the character's bedroom.
- What is their door like? Open the door.
- The character is standing in front of you.
- Before you approach them, what is in the room? Is there a desk? Is there a chair? What colour are the walls?
- Look at the character – how do you feel? What are they wearing?
- Take two steps forward so you are nose-to-nose with the character.

- Imagine that you are stepping into the body of the character. After three: one – two – three.

- Let your body readjust – scan your body. How does it affect you? Your shoulders, your chin, knees, hips, face, ankles, feet.

- How does the character hold themself?

- When you are ready open your eyes and explore how they move. Find their rhythm – is it smooth or staccato? Fast or slow?

- Try sitting down – how do they sit?

- Explore the space.

- Find their voice – what is their 'watch-cry' (a phrase or line that they use a lot, like a motto)?

- Find an object that is interesting to them – how do they relate to this object? (Make this something real in the room rather than imagined.)

- Play with their voice. Play with register – highs and lows, fast and slow rhythms.

- Find three physical habits (they can be unconscious habits). Keep playing the habits; if they don't feel right, change them.

- Swap between these elements: fast, slow, sit, objects, habits, watch-cry.

- Now get the character to do an activity that they do regularly.

- Keep this activity going.

- Add a monologue to this – who are they talking to as they do their activity?

- Keep talking until it feels completely natural.

- Find an activity that they do that makes them happy. Keep the monologue going – commit to how they speak. Throw in their watch-cry.

- Include their habits.

- Let them surprise you. What do they do that seems contradictory to their character?
- Chop and change between all the exercises – don't stop talking through the exercise.
- Everyone is going to make their way to Grace's garden when you are ready.
- Make a circle once you are in the garden. Once you are there, you can see and interact with one another.

This exercise is useful because you have to make quick, active, physical decisions. We have a physical life that we aren't in control of. There are ways of setting up improvisations that can be very rewarding. The best results come from leading a company gently into being comfortable enough to get under the skin of the character. It is also hugely revealing what they can't answer in these exercises. It is always specificity that allows us to access who the character is.

'Watch-cry' phrases identified in the workshop included:

GRACE: Whatever! / Can I help with that? / You are such a loser!

MALACHI: That's so sorted. / Yes. / I can do that!

ELIJAH: I dunno. / When I'm older.

BECKY: I mean, seriously?! / That's luscious!

Staging

The directions in the script ask that the set be as bare as possible and the action as fluid as possible. Why is this?

Ryan's instinct for the piece is that it is fluid and physically frenetic, and not easily divided into this scene and then the next. The scenes should be allowed to crash into one another. Elijah notably traverses between time frames easily. Becky appears rather than enters. Blackouts are banned! But other than that, there aren't any hard-and-fast rules about staging.

The staging should point towards a decision about the world of the play. What are we watching? Why? Returning to Kara at the end implicating everyone and reviewing what happened – is she talking to the group? The choice is yours.

Choosing permutations and staging will likely be dictated by the spaces you are dealing with, but will also impact the definition of who an audience are, and how they receive a story. Laurie is partial to theatre-in-the-round (where there are the same number of people on all sides), but there are also possibilities of theatre in the oblong (a kind of traverse theatre, with smaller sections of audience on two sides).

You could experiment around the idea of set without using a set. What role do objects play?

Always ask of staging: what dramatic function is that moment serving? Is it making the story clearer?

Ryan emphasised that the stage action shouldn't mime what has already been said in the text. Imagination is better than crudely repeating physically what is simultaneously being spoken. We want the staging to offer new pieces of the puzzle and jolts in the energy.

Staging work

The scene between Grace and Elijah

Laurie set up a space in the round. He placed the railway track across the space and an oil drum (chair) on one side of it, near Elijah. The aim of staging is to focus on the detail in a scene. There is a balance to be sought between what you offer to the actors and what you are asking of them. With professional actors, the less you tell someone the better: give them space to make choices, and invest in those choices.

What might you want to establish before you start the scene?

Talk to the actors about the given circumstances of the scene. For instance, where are you? Where have you come from?

What time is it? (This question threw up that it was the 4:52 train and therefore it wasn't actually going to be dark soon.) Get the actors to describe the environment. How long has Elijah been there? Ask questions about their relationship. Why is Elijah in his Sunday best? Is there anything you need to know about the christening? What has just happened to Grace? When did she read the diary? How has she arrived at the railway track? How do the characters expect the scene to go (e.g. does Elijah expect company? And how does this affect his reaction when Grace arrives?) Where was the diary? Did he leave it in the room for Malachi to find?

Deal with the questions thrown up by the text. For instance, it was suggested that the line 'Don't do suicide today' might not be the first time that Elijah has tried this or threatened this. But the stakes are higher if it is the first time and he wants someone to know.

Note discoveries that have been made – e.g. Grace wants to know if Elijah has written anything about her; the fact that Elijah has written a diary at all and what it says about him; Grace's defence mechanism and how that reveals her insecurity about whether Malachi loves her, and establishes the fear and anxiety that is perhaps the engine for future actions.

If the company have lots of versions for why someone is doing something or what they are doing, it is up to you to pick one and try it.

Discover the basic relationships through the playing of the scene – e.g. Elijah clearly wouldn't have picked Grace to interrupt his suicide!

What are the unspoken questions in a scene? How quickly does Elijah figure out that she has read the diary? Why does he ask her about it? When does Grace have the idea?

A tool that can be useful is finding units in a scene:

- The simplest version of delineating a unit is when the subject of a conversation changes. This gives you a way

of finding the shape of a scene and the place where the
intention/actions might change.

- Units do not mean a pause in the rhythm; they often in
  fact mean the opposite – a change of gear.

- Units can bog you down at times but they are excellent for
  breaking down the trickier parts (might be very useful for
  this central scene, for example).

- The best thing is to get the actors to decide where the units
  are as this starts conversations about where the characters
  want change.

- Units also provide useful staging posts and so are often
  useful to do for yourself as a shorthand for the sections of a
  piece.

There is an infinite number of ways to move a scene physically
in a space. Ideally, the actor will be so immersed in the
character that they will respond instinctively, physically, in
character. This is obviously not so possible if there is a large
group of actors, when the staging may have to be more
choreographed. More freedom can be given to the actor to
decide what is physically demanded by the relationship that is
being played on stage. Get them to try options so that you
can see what works, and they can feel what is good. You may
have to make some decisions to help some actors unlock
physical choices, but staging should be something that can be
easily changed if the actors know what the scene is about.

The nature of subtext

Ryan said that when writing dialogue he is always trying to
find the pressure on top of a line (what is commonly referred
to as subtext). It is useful to think of it as a pressure that is the
real meaning, pushing on the line and forcing it out. People
rarely say what they mean, and yet words are deliberate. They
are not used to explain meaning but rather to obfuscate it.

Do we actually know who anyone is? On the surface, Grace
appears to know what to do, but she is riddled with anxiety

and self-doubt. Theatre is only interesting when we are party to someone's vulnerability. It is much harder to engage with an actor if they don't open up. It is something we try not to show to others. It is a challenge to lead young actors to reveal that vulnerability safely.

Laurie said: 'Always be suspicious of what characters say to one another in a Ryan Craig play! They are sometimes lying. And sometimes they don't even realise it isn't true!'

Questions for Ryan Craig

What is the relevance of the characters' names?

Ryan grew up in a Jewish household, and at Passover there is a ritual of putting a cup of wine out for Elijah. In this piece, the characters are creating their own moral universe, and the creation of their own rituals and ceremonies lies at the heart of the actions of these young people. When Elijah disappears, all the characters create their own myth about him. (It is possible that ritual might be a starting point for creating a theatrical language for the staging.)

Does Dr Pepper really fizz when you add sugar?!

Ryan had a mentor who would put sugar into his Diet Coke because he 'liked the way it fizzes' – and that little touch came into the development of Elijah's character.

Why is Kara the narrator?

Deciding the answer to this question is crucially important, and will provide a framework for the piece. It is often hard to make direct address active and therefore crucial to find a relationship between the person and the audience, or whoever they are talking to. Why are they talking? Who are the audience? Where is Kara speaking from? The audience may never know this, but it will add a necessary specificity to the delivery. Perhaps you can try different types of relationships for the Kara character – get her to try some alternatives and see what happens to her speech. Whatever decision is made about this relates to the choice about what happens at the end of the play. Kara is narrating in the past tense.

What happens at the end of the play?

Is it suicide? Did Elijah purposely ask for the match? Was he afraid of the pain? Did he know? What happens to Elijah after the bang? The workshop discussed how the stakes were higher if Elijah dies, in terms of responsibility. Is the explosion itself a 'meta-version' of the Dr Pepper and sugar idea? Ryan refused to give an answer as to what he thought or planned to happen here, as it would limit the decision-making processes of the companies.

Do you think Grace has an exit strategy?

She is living moment to moment. Ryan liked the analogy of a train gaining momentum. She is the protagonist and responds to opportunities.

Why doesn't she get out when she is given an opportunity by Elijah, in the shed?

She hasn't got what she wanted. She says they would despise him, but she is afraid they would despise her and think them both pathetic.

Did you imagine that Elijah wanted Grace to read the diary or that this is a surprise?

You could try it both ways.

Why doesn't she call Malachi?

She doesn't want to disturb him.

Did you see it on stage when you wrote it?

Normally that happens, especially when there are real-life people and real-life sets (e.g. Ryan's play *The Holy Rosenbergs* for the National Theatre). Ryan did see this on stage too, but very fluidly. Mostly Ryan lets the characters speak to him. He has an instinct but finds that if you impose a scenario upon them, you can hear it when it is read.

Are the layers in the piece intentional?

Yes, and no! Sometimes you make discoveries in the rehearsal room. Sometimes decisions are made unconsciously that you become conscious of later.

Why do the girls flush Elijah?

It is more humiliating than the boys doing it. Each character is battling with what they think being a man/being a woman is. Young people are left to decide for themselves and invent themselves in the absence of rules. This sense of foraging for a world and authority comes out in the use of phrases like 'the Feds' – which comes from TV.

Was it a conscious decision not to bring in an adult?

No, but it seems better to suggest that there are none, a little like *Lord of the Flies* – the lack of authority and adult role models influences the characters' decision making.

From a workshop led by Laurie Sansom,
with notes by Pia Furtado

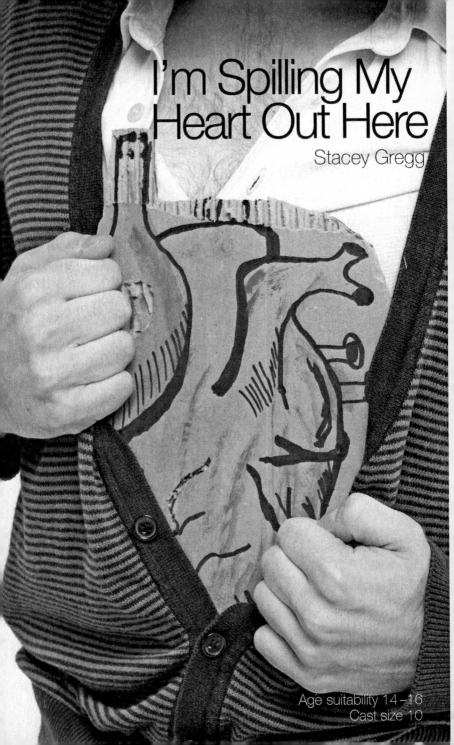

I'm Spilling My Heart Out Here

Stacey Gregg

Age suitability 14–16
Cast size 10

Stacey Gregg has been on attachment at the National Theatre Studio and was Writer-in-Residence at RADA. *Lagan* at the Oval House Theatre was Stacey's UK debut and her first play, *Perve*, opened at the Abbey Theatre, Dublin, in May 2011. She currently has commissions at Tinderbox, Watford Palace Theatre and Global Arts Corps, and has written short pieces and co-written plays for the Bush, Rough Magic, Abbey Theatre/Goethe Institut and Paines Plough. Stacey is currently developing a series with Great Meadows/BBC Northern Ireland, and has written *Spoof or Die* for Touchpaper TV/Channel 4's *Coming Up 2012*.

Characters

Karen, *fifteen*
Wilson, *fifteen*
Alexa, *fifteen*
Sean, *sixteen*
Dominic, *sixteen*
Osh, *fourteen*
Harley, *fifteen*
Sweep, *sixteen*
Ciaran, *eleven*
Jody, *fourteen*

Use of music is encouraged, the heavier and less mainstream the better. As much blood as the production allows.

Location
A small town.

Dialogue
A foward slash (/) in the text indicates overlapping dialogue, which should generally go at a quick pace.

One

A group has gathered around **Alexa**, *fizzing in anticipation. She is taking off her cardigan, back against a wall. They talk over each other, viscous, never still.*

Dom Do it.

Sweep Stand still.

Dom Now you have to breathe.

Osh In and out, in and out really –

Harley Like you're hyperventilating.

Dom Yeah, like you're about to dive.

Alexa *breathes in and out exaggeratedly.*

Harley You've got to concentrate.

Sweep You've got to breathe in and out for sixty seconds.

Dom Is it sixty seconds?

Sweep Yeah, it's sixty seconds. Who's timing?

Wilson I'm timing.

Karen Yeah, you've got a stopwatch on your phone, you do it.

Jody Omygod.

Wilson Okay, I'm timing, are you breathing?

Osh Deeper – like – (*He demonstrates.*)

Jody Yeah, that's how Kenny Gray did it.

Karen Like having a baby.

Sweep Did you see it?

Jody No, but I heard.

Harley Yeah, and I know Kenny a bit.

Jody   It's like when they do blessings at church –

Sweep   Only your freaky fundy church –

Karen   She's going a funny –

Jody   It's not fundy.

Osh   She's meant to go a funny colour.

Dom   How long's that?

Wilson   Nearly forty seconds.

Karen   Looks like she's gonna puke.

Dom   No she doesn't, right, babe?

Jody   Omygod.

Osh   Oh my God, it's mad.

Jody   This is mad.

Osh   It totally works.

Dom   It's amazing.

Osh   And after, you feel amazing.

Jody   Kenny said it was like / being stoned.

Dom   Being stoned, yeah! I heard that.

Harley   It's totally like being stoned.

Dom   How would you know, titchy-balls?

Wilson   FIFTY-THREE.

Karen   Keep breathing.

Wilson   Ready?

Dom   Someone needs to shove her in the chest.

Jody   Really hard.

Dom   Someone shove her or it won't work!

Harley   Who's doing it?

Wilson   I'm timing, it's fifty-three seconds –

Jody   You have to do it now or it won't work!

Dom   You do it.

Osh   You do it.

Harley   You do it, she's your girlfriend, Dom.

Karen   I'm not doing it.

Dom   Who's done it before?

Karen   You said you saw them do it on Kenny Gray.

Jody   Yeah, but –

Dom   You flippin' do it!

Alexa   Somebody do it!

All   Do it! Do it! Do it! Do it!

Wilson   SIXTY . . .

Jody   Do it, chicken!

WHAM. Someone pushes **Alexa** *hard in the chest and holds her against the wall.*

Alexa *drops like a stone, in a dead faint.*

A moment of silence.

Whoops, shouts, buzz. A high-five.

Two of the girls stoop to roll her over and fan her. Phones are out, taking photos and videos.

Blackout.

Two

Outside a café. **Wilson** *and* **Karen** *drinking Cokes from the glass bottle, like you get from restaurants.* **Wilson** *has got to the bottom of hers and is slurping through the straw.*

Wilson *is quietly stylish, charismatically boyish, laptop open on her knee.* **Karen** *taps her heels, impatient.* **Karen** *is most people's mate: attractive, witty, mildly alternative.*

Karen   Oh my God, what's she doing?

Wilson   She's been in there ages.

Karen   Maybe she's a hard sell.

Wilson *goes back to her laptop.*

Wilson   I'm so nearly in.

Karen   What're you doing?

Wilson   Hacking the school intranet, so –

Karen   Shut up, the staff one?

Wilson   – i.e., bitchfest.

Karen   How?

Wilson (*knowledgeable*)   Weak firewalls.

Karen *examines a split end.*

Karen   That's mad.

Kkkhh, what's taking so long?

Wilson   Maybe he's lost his mojo.

Karen   Gross.

Wilson   Never know. Diet. Depression – could be anything.

Karen   Maybe she's haggling him up.

Wilson   That never works.

Karen   Does. Sweep did it.

Wilson   Did she?

Karen   Got him up to two hundred.

Wilson   Rubbish – highest ever was Alexa and she's hot as, he would've like offered the clothes off his back for a hand job.

Karen   Maybe.

Wilson   What'd you get again?

Karen   Hundred and forty.

Wilson   Oh yeah, that's right. Reasonable. You can hold your head high at that. Fair amount of money to offer a minor for sex I'd say. Generous.

Karen   Oi.

Wilson   What?

Karen   Thought I might get one-fifty.

Wilson   Well, you don't want to look like Alexa, even if that is what they go for.

Karen   Suppose.

Wilson   And the best I got was 'are you a boy?' and a tap water. So . . .

OH – I'm in! YES. (*Typing.*) Time to troll.

Karen   What's it say? Can you access our reports?

Wilson   Depends who's askin'.

Karen   Me.

Owp – here she cooomes . . .

Jody *appears, prim, triumphant, with a fresh bottle of Coke.*

Wilson   Well?

Karen (*commiserating*)   One-ten?

Jody   Nope.

Karen   One-thirty?

Jody   Nope – hundred and thirty-fiiiive.

Karen   High-fiiiive.

Wilson   Nice one.

Karen   Wilson's got into the school intranet.

Wilson   Passwords are as alien to our teachers as personality.

Jody   What age is Creepy Martin anyway?

Karen   Don't know. Forty? Fifty?

Wilson   Thought he was in his thirties.

Karen   You got your free Coke out of him . . .

Jody   Two, baby.

Karen   Then our job here is done.

Jody   Diet. One for me, one for Alexa.

Karen   Alexa?

Wilson   Like when will he learn? No one falls for it.

Karen   I didn't know you were with Alexa.

Wilson   Wonder how many Cokes he's bought pretty girls over the years.

Jody   I wasn't. She was just there and, I don't know, crashed my party.

Wilson   Millions.

Karen   Flipping Alexa.

Wilson   Alexa gets in on everything.

Karen   Thunder stealer.

Wilson   Thunder thief.

Karen   Sounds like a superhero name. (*Hero voice.*) Thunder Thief!

Wilson   What would you be?

Karen   Average Boobs.

Super Average Boobs.

Wilson   Flippin' rubbish superhero.

Jody   Did Alexa really pass out?

Karen   What, the other day?

Jody   Yeah.

Karen   Dunno.

Jody   It was so cool she did that.

Wilson   Or did she fake it?

Jody   Dunno. She's so reckless.

Karen   Looked fake. Typical. Either way.

Wilson   Said she was out cold.

Jody   Yeah, she said her life passed before her eyes.

Wilson   Yeah, she also said she's booking a B&B for Dom's sixteenth so they can get it on, so . . .

A beat. This is juicy and disturbing.

Karen   Everyone's sayin' they've been going out for ever and she hasn't done it. Everyone's obsessed with their sex life.

Wilson   Or lack thereof. Everyone's obsessed in general – ob-sexed. I blame TV. And a lack of local amenities. Boredom leads to babies.

Jody   I believe her. She's cool. She chain-smokes.

Wilson   Pfft.

Karen   Meh.

Jody   The other day, she was like, 'Hey any of you girls want some milk? We had too much so I just brought the bottle out.' She's so cool, she didn't even care how it looked.

Karen   She was holding a bottle of milk? Like an actual pint?

Jody   Just on the street. It was mad.

Wilson   I don't care how I look . . .

Jody   Yeah, but you're . . .

*She indicates **Wilson**'s look.*

Wilson   Thanks.

Jody   Don't you want to look cute?

Wilson   I am.

Jody   I mean. Like. Sexy.

Wilson   Not if it means 'Please put your penis in me,' no.

Jody *balks.*

Wilson   That's the consensus like, definition of sexy, isn't it?

Jody   Don't you ever wear Sunday clothes even?

Wilson   Are you from the 1950s? We don't go to your church. I go to the church of Wilson.

Jody   You're so lucky you don't have to worry about looking hot. Sad you'll probs burn in hell. Want the rest of this?

Karen   Not want it?

Jody   My mum says Diet makes you more fat. It's a trick. Then I'll never get a boyfriend and die on benefits and loveless.

A beep.

All three whip out their phones as they go, fingers a frenzy of networking.

Three

Ciaran *and* **Karen** *in cycling helmets, bicycles, mooching home.*

Ciaran   Can we get chips?

Karen   No.

Ciaran   What's a BJ?

Karen *coughs.*

Karen   Uh, look, doesn't that bird look funny?

Ciaran   Yeah. But what's a BJ?

Karen *sighs.*

Karen   Why d'you ask, Ciaran?

Ciaran   Have you had one?

Karen   You shouldn't know about them. It's rude and Mum'll kill you . . . (*Styling it out.*) But yeah, probably have.

Ciaran (*thoughtful*)   Oh.

Karen   In P7 we were still making treasure maps out of pasta and stuff. Don't you do that any more?

Osh *and* **Sean** *wander across,* **Sean** *carrying a football.*

Karen *whips off her helmet, fixes her hair.*

Ciaran   I'm tellin' Mum you take off your helmet to look cool.

Karen   Shhtup – HI!

Osh   Alright?

Karen   What's up?

Osh   Sean's new. Just moved here. We're meeting up with Alexa. She's got a modelling job till five. But she said we're gonna hang out so we're meeting up with her. After. Her house is massive.

Karen   Going to youth club later?

Ciaran *mimics, flirty,* 'Going to youth club later?'

Osh   Youth club is where fun goes to die.

He notices **Sean** *and* **Karen** *checking each other out. He doesn't like it.*

Karen (*to* **Sean**)   Nice headphones.

Sean *goes to reply, but –*

Osh   They're mine. He's borrowing them cos he doesn't have any. He moved into the estate. Probably can't afford ones as nice. But I'm not prejudiced. So . . .

See ya Karen.

Sweep   Bye, Tiny.

Osh   Shuddup.

Sweep, *the scary, make-uppy girl, has joined them, munching a sausage roll.* **Sweep** *puts an arm round* **Karen**.

Sweep   No chance, bitch-features, he's so far out of your league he's in like another dimension. Are you wet for him?

Sean *is suddenly really distracted by his football. The others look grossed out.*

Karen   Sweep. My eleven-year-old brother is here.

Ciaran   Hi.

Sweep   He needs to learn.

Ciaran *nods earnestly.*

Osh (*to* **Sean**)   Are you interested in her? Cos. You're with Alexa's crowd – so what're you doing? You'll get dropped and then what? We can't hang out with her. Anyway, she's weird and hangs out with the freaky girlboy. They probably do it.

Karen   We don't, for what it's worth.

Osh (*to* **Sweep**)   Why d'you call me 'Tiny'? Is that what people think? Cos if that's what people think, you should say.

You should just let me know. Is that what people say? You should just tell me if it is. I mean, it's not like I'm insecure. I'm not insecure, do you think I'm insecure? Cos / I'm not. So . . .

Sweep   Osh, shut up, and (*to* **Karen**) you – your little heart eyes are bugging outta your head, mate.

Osh *has his phone down his pants and experimentally takes pictures from different angles.*

Karen   No rush.

Sweep (*nodding*)   Content to get yourself off for now – spoken like a true virgin. Make him jizz in the back door when you do though, 'stead of up the normal, then you won't get pregnant.

Karen   Will do.

Sweep   Has your little geek-in-my-pocket fixed my laptop yet?

Karen   Don't know.

Sweep   If I miss any coins cos of her, you'll miss your vagina once I've kicked it out your mouth into space. (*Of* **Ciaran**.) Also, tell that teenybopper to stop staring at me, wouldya?

Sweep *goes, shoving past* **Ciaran**, *whose mouth hangs open after her.*

Karen (*to* **Ciaran**)   Don't worry, she'll be dead one day. Choke to death on a bag of Hula-Hoops hopefully.

Beep.

Karen *frowns at her phone.*

Karen   Osh. Did you just Bluetooth your – ?

Osh *goes white.*

Osh   NO.

Karen   Looks like you.

Osh   NO. Shut up.

Ciaran *takes her phone and studies the image too. Then studies* **Osh**.

Osh   As if – I mean, I hardly *think* so, as if –

He squirms.

(*Shriller.*) You wouldn't even know what a – what it looks like . . .

Sean *takes a look.*

Osh (*threatening*)   If anyone tells anyone . . . (*Eventually, small.*) Does it look okay?

Karen   Yeah. (*Placating.*) It's nice.

Osh   Okay.

Ciaran (*agreeing*)   Looks like a face.

Osh   You can tell people it's nice.

Sean   It's mega.

Osh   C'mon, Sean, we're supposed to be meeting Alexa and Dom –

Karen   But Alexa was just at Creepy M's.

Osh   No she's not, she's modelling.

Karen   No she's not, I just saw her.

Osh   Whatever.

Sean *waves goodbye to* **Karen** *as they split their separate ways.*

Four

Karen *and* **Wilson** *in gym kits, accessorised as appropriate.* **Wilson** *in a fetching boy's ensemble. They peer through the gym window with toy binoculars.*

Wilson   That should be on the wildlife channel.

Karen   She needs to tame that thang.

Wilson   Think she knows you can see it peepin' out her shorts like that?

Karen   Possibly not, can't see through those jumbo eyebrows.

Wilson   Poor Sweep. PE is a cruel leveller.

They turn round and sit.

Karen   Nah, she'll find someone in her ugly band. Y'know, she didn't start wombchunks till she was fourteen? And when they did come, it was only one every four months, and with a vengeance, like she stored up four months of womb detritus and then WHOOOSH!

Wilson   That. Is. Disgusting.

Karen   True story.

Wilson *sips from a novelty coffee flask.*

Wilson   What d'y'mean, 'her ugly band'?

Karen   You know. Sweep's theory about ugly people. Everybody charts somewhere on the ugly graph, and those like, in the middle, will only ever mate with equally ug people. There's some movement downwards, but rarely up, unless you're like minted or something or –

Wilson   – the other person's blind?

Karen   Exactly. So the people at the top, the beautiful people, stick to their own and only reproduce with other beautiful people. But the ugly people will be happy too, they just need to look for someone on the same level. Not aspire too much.

That's the problem with TV and ads and stuff, everyone wants to move up the ugly spectrum, you know, by snagging someone better-looking, but it's just unnatural. Unmathematical. You know? It's like, nature. Darwin. Stuff.

Wilson   Yeah.

They refill the flask from a quarter-bottle of vodka.

Think we'll get caught again?

Karen   I've got a new excuse. Ready?

Wilson   Go.

Karen   Nosebleed.

Foolproof. Could strike anytime anywhere. They can't check.
Doesn't sound as done as period pain – anyway Miss Farnam
memorises last time you said it and keeps a diary to catch you
out instead of having a life. She's like a menstrual Rainman.
It's weird.

Wilson   Sad.

Karen   She is so so sad.

Wilson   She put you in three Friday detentions.

Karen   Adults are all the same – complete saddo sell-outs.
No sense of humour at all. All they do is talk about boring
things and pretend it's interesting when it's a complete LIE.
Makes me feel CRAZY – I mean, all growing up is, is getting
better at *lying*. 'YES I LOVE that boring thing it's SO
INTERESTING,, and suddenly you're considered 'mature' –
if you just lie. 'OH YES PLEASE let's watch a million pukey
romcoms' – relationships relationships and boringness internet
dating pathetic Bridget Jones I WANT TO KILL MYSELF,
WHO CARES ANYWAY.

A beat. **Karen** *slurps her vodka.*

Wilson   So, what's the deal with you and Seany-wauny-
woowoo?

A beat.

Karen   Nothing.

Wilson   Don't lie. You want his meat in your sandwich.

Karen   No I don't.

Wilson   How long have I known you?

Karen   For ever.

Wilson   Well, he's out of your band and he's hanging out with Alexa so he's probably douche.

Karen   Jealous?

Wilson   No way José. Just reckon if you want to lose it, don't lose it to a douche.

Karen   You know what's weird? He said 'mega'.

Wilson   People say it.

Karen   Yeah, some people say it, but not everyone, it's not common.

Wilson   And what, he said –

Karen   'Mega' –

Wilson   And you thought, 'weird'.

Karen   Yeah. Reminded me of Scott. Remember Scott?

Wilson   Oh.

Right. Yeah.

Karen   Yeah, exactly. Anyway, he seems nice.

Wilson   You talked to him?

Karen   Not really.

Wilson   You didn't talk to him.

Karen   I was looking – I saw him. I was watching him.

Wilson   You were watching / him?

Karen   I mean –

Wilson   Yeah, cos that sounds pervy.

Karen   He was in my field of vision. Is what I –

Wilson   And?

Karen   And –

I don't know.

He seems nice. Cool.

Wilson   Wow.

Karen   What?

Wilson   You like him.

Karen   No I don't.

A commotion from the gym provides a welcome distraction.

Uh oh, Sweep plus gym equipment equals GBH . . . (*Peering.*)
They've put her with the boys.

Wilson   Which boys?

Karen   (*changing the topic*)   Ahm, does Sweep know you're
using her laptop to hack the school server?

Wilson   Thinks I'm setting her up to skim credit cards.
Which I am. And she'll give me a cut. But if they ever figure
out they've been hacked, they'll trace it back to Sweep's IP.
Win win. Security in this country is a farce. International
cyber warfare will be the frontier and battlefield of our futures.
Geeks will rule / tomorrow.

Karen   Can you look up Sean on there?

Wilson *deflates.*

Wilson   Kkkhhhh, you are so underwhelming, Karen.
I bring you riches and you ask for rubbish.

Karen   Why be a notorious hacker and not use it for the
good of your fellow human?

Wilson   The hacker knows no moral code, and anyway,
we're just starved of new blood. This town's started to
intermarry. The novelty'll wear off, and he'll be just another
dick with a football. Want me to fix your binoculars?

Karen *hands* **Wilson** *her binoculars.*

Wilson *peers into the gym and sees what* **Karen** *was watching:*
Sean.

Karen   He's probs a dick, yeah. But he's okay too.

Wilson   You think he's cool.

Thought I was cool. We can't both be cool. That doesn't fit.
The world implodes, Karen.

Karen   I don't think hormones, or whatever, are aware of
the whatever social politics of our / group –

Wilson   Well, it's gonna end in tears. Don't say I didn't /
warn you.

Karen   You're getting hysterical.

Wilson   That's what I'm always telling / you –

Karen   Oh ho, the tables have turned?

Wilson   No, there's no tables. There's no tables, just –

We fundamentally can't exist together now.

Like oil and water, like cheese and pineapple.

RIP Karen and Wilson.

Karen   Getting a bit –

Wilson   So would you if –

Karen   – if what?

Wilson   Nothing.

(*Impatient.*) I'm just like questioning your moral compass, he's
everything you don't stand for. He hangs out with a gang
who call themselves the 'A-Team'. Without irony.

Karen   Why do you care?

Wilson   I don't! I don't even care. No skin off my nose. You
need to make your own mistakes. I've done all I can. Have to

let you face the real world. Good luck, child. My door will always be open.

Just thought, y'know, you and me don't run with the herd.

Karen   His hair is so *conditioned*, it floats.

Wilson (*scrutinising* **Sean** *through binoculars*)   It's okay.

Karen   Floaty. Like a baby animal.

Wilson   A rat.

Karen   Like an ad. He looked at me in the queue for mini-donuts.

Wilson   You can't ask him out. He's with Alexa's crowd. And we hate her, cos she's so goddamn-mothereffin-perfect.

Karen   I think he could be my first.

Wilson   I can't see you, let me just clean the vomit from my eyes.

Karen   Ciaran was asking sex questions. Since when did eleven-year-olds become sexually aware?

Wilson   I was.

Karen *contemplates* **Wilson**, *briefly, who looks back at her through the binoculars.*

Karen   Did you always know?

Wilson   What?

Karen   You know. (*Whispering.*) That you're a g-a-y.

Wilson   Yep.

P.S. Sean's a douche.

Karen   Do you know what a douche is?

Wilson   No.

Karen   Should Google it.

Wilson   Are you gonna ask him out?

Five

The church hall, because it's wet outside and there's nowhere else.
Jody *is mixing a bowl of gunk.* **Wilson** *and* **Karen** *are sucking the air out of big fizzy drink bottles they are just finishing, to get a headrush.*

Jody   I'm not passive-aggressive, just sometimes you guys kind of hurt my feelings –

Wilson   Push me!

Karen *obliges.*

Wilson *staggers.*

Wilson   Wooooooow, mini-headrush.

Alexa *passes with a big bag of crisps, stopping to take in* **Wilson**. *She smiles, glorious.*

Alexa (*genuine mystification*)   Why is your hair weird?

Wilson *evil-eyes* **Alexa** *as she disappears.*

Wilson   God, she is an abortion.

Karen   Yeah.

Jody   She walks like she's gliding. It's cos she's modelling and everything now. Posture. She has a walk. And your hair is weird.

Wilson   Is this avocado?

Jody   Yeah, it's always in skin creams.

Wilson   Is that egg?

Jody *mixes.*

Jody   You doubt, like Thomas the Apostle.

Karen   Noticed how much money Alexa's been throwing around?

Jody   No.

Karen   She's like buying people lunch and stuff. Dom said she actually booked that B&B for his birthday so they could do it.

Wilson   Alexa the ice queen?

Karen   Yeah.

Jody   Dom isn't gonna like it, he's OCD, bodily fluid terrifies him.

Karen   And it'll technically be rape till she's sixteen.

Wilson   You're both wrong. Heard he's gonna dump her cos he didn't wanna do it with a virgin. Too rapey.

Karen   Where's she getting the coins from?

Jody   Says her dad gives her it.

Wilson   Her dad's a massive skinflint, – remember her thirteenth? We all went to the cinema and had to buy our own popcorn, like what?!

Jody   Dom's living in a flat cos his parents hate him.

A beat.

Karen   Dom's living on his own?

A beat. Real things. Weird.

Wilson   That's scary.

Jody   It's cool, I heart him.

*She pastes green muck on **Wilson**'s face.*

Wilson   Jody, this doesn't smell –

Jody Haven't you ever used facemask?

Wilson Hello, have you met me? I spent primary school figuring out I wasn't actually a boy.

Jody Yeah. The tomboy thing is something you grow out of though, maybe.

Wilson Yeah, into a fully-grown, trouser-suit-wearing gay.

Jody *looks shy.*

Wilson You still don't believe me?

Jody No, I do. I was thinking about what you said. Did you really think you were a boy?

Wilson Wished it so much and then I just decided to ignore the fact I wasn't till I had to deal with it.

Jody Didn't you think that was weird?

Wilson No. Cos I always felt like that – so it would be weird not to. AaaaAAAHH – my face . . . my face is hot . . .

AaAAAAHHHH, *what is it?*

Karen Yo, what's wrong with her? –

Wilson *claws at her face. They watch, interested.*

Wilson Oh my God, my frigging face! Get it off! It's on fire!

Wilson *disappears, squeaking.*

Jody Wow, I've never heard her scream.

Karen Sounded like a squirrel in a blender.

Jody Think her face is melting?

Karen What if she's disfigured?

Jody She'll be our cool, gay, disfigured friend.

Karen Disfigurement is way cooler than gay.

Jody   Hey, talking of disfigurement, did you hear about Sean?

Karen   What?

Jody   That new boy you fancy. Had like a full-on heart transplant.

Karen   No way.

Jody   Yeah, and everyone's saying he's just like Scott.

Karen   Are they?

Jody   Yeah, everyone's said it.

Karen   Like when he says 'mega'?

Jody   He says 'mega'? (*Portentous.*) Did you see the hat he's wearing?

Harley *and* **Osh** *have joined them, eating sweets or carrying badminton rackets.*

Harley   Who's Scott?

Karen   Remember, Scott – that poor dude –

Jody   Oh wait, you only started youth club – He wouldn't know.

Karen   Scott was this boy who died at the funfair.

Harley   Majesto's?

Jody   That's ironic – 'Fun' fair. Not so 'fun'. Huh? 'Funfair' –

Harley   Yeah, we get it.

Karen   It was mad.

Jody   It was awful.

Osh   Sweep took pictures.

Jody   It was on the news.

Osh   I was nearly on the news, you could see the back of my head.

Jody   We all had to stay off school cos we were traumatised.

Karen   The funeral was awful.

Harley   Did you go?

Karen   No, but I saw pictures.

Osh   He was on the Fury, this ride that was advertised somewhat ominously with a Grim Reaper, and something went wrong, or he wasn't strapped in right.

Wilson *has returned, face doused and red, dabbing with paper towels.*

Jody (*calling*)   Dominic, didn't Kenny hang around with Scott That Died?

Dom, *carrying a rucksack, takes out his earphones and approaches.*

Dom   Why're you guys hangin' out at a youth club? Come to the park. For my birthday.

Jody   It's raining.

Dom   I've got fireworks and booze.

Jody   This place has radiators and snacks!

Osh   Didn't Scott go flying out of the ride and hit the like, metal, the like, frame and –

Dom   His head nearly came right off.

Harley   Dark.

Osh   That's what happened though, his head was hanging off.

Harley   God.

Dom   Like a swingball.

Jody   And that boy, Sean, is just like him.

Wilson   So?

Jody   No – Sean, the one Karen fancies, had like, a heart transplant. Don't you get it?

Harley, *intrigued by the bowl of facemask, nibbles at it.*

Osh   Haven't you guys ever heard of cellular memory?

Wilson   I've heard of it – works like homoeopathy or some wank.

Dom   It's not wank actually, my mum did a course in homoeopathy.

Jody   Ooh, at the community centre?

Sweep *has been drawn in, despite herself.*

Sweep   Can someone tell me what you lot are on about?

Dom   Can someone tell me why you're all in youth club, instead of getting wasted?

Osh   Cellular memory – this theory – when people donate organs, and the person who gets the new organ starts like acting different or remembering things they couldn't have experienced, and people believe like – some scientists and stuff think it might be cos there are cells that still have the memory of the dead person in them – and it goes with them into the new person.

Jody   That. Is. Mental.

Sweep   Still don't get it.

Dom   Need a whiteboard for the slow learner.

Sweep *jabs at* **Dom***, who dodges.* **Harley** *spits the facemix back in the bowl.*

Osh   OMYGOD, so for example, Person A is scared of water and then they die and their heart gets transplanted into Mr B, who used to be a diver and when he wakes up, he is suddenly inexplicably terrified of water.

Dom   Yeah, and it's been proven like, scientifically, there's these cells they only thought you got in your brain for making memories and things but they've discovered them in the heart I saw it on a documentary, it's true.

Jody   That is so scary.

Karen   Wait, so everyone thinks Sean is someone else?

Osh   YES.

Dom   Scott.

Karen   No way.

Jody   It is SO possible.

Wilson   No it's not.

They're gathered round now.

Jody   He was in the queue for tuckshop and he's wearing literally the most identical hat to what Scott always wore.

Osh   Scott dies horribly and has his organs donated. Sean receives a heart and it's Scott's. That's why he's so like him. Karen said the first time she met him, he said 'mega'.

Jody   I mean WHO says 'mega'?

Osh   That is incontrovertible evidence –

Wilson   – that your mum's banging the binman.

Karen   Wilson –

Wilson   What? It's full on mentalpops, complete non-science. You're all just bigging it up cos you fancy him.

Osh (*reasonable*)   Um, I don't, but some of my best friends are gayers.

Jody   It was you found his records, Wilson. You said –

Karen (*to* **Wilson**)   You're such a wang, you read his records? You hacked into them?

Wilson   You're a wang. And he's most likely a wang and Alexa's a wang and, together, they make one big superwang, so . . .

Tension. **Wilson** *looks away.*

Jody   Ask Sean if he's afraid of heights!

Karen   Why? Cos he fell off the Fury in a previous life?

Wilson   That's reincarnation, twats.

Harley   We should have a séance, contact Scott!

Jody   We can't, we're in a church.

Harley   A church hall, and it's just youth club, no one would mind.

Sean   Hi.

Alexa *and* **Sean** *have appeared on the corner of the clique.*

The group, jumpy, gawk up at him. **Sean** *is wearing the hat. He smiles at* **Karen**.

The lights flicker.

Harley   WoooooooOOO.

Jody *cuddles up to* **Osh**.

Jody   I am so freaked out right now, actually.

Dom   He is so spooky.

Alexa   What're you all talking about?

Jody   His eyes are kind of dead.

Sean *looks puzzled.* **Wilson** *shuffles guiltily.*

Wilson   Probably read it wrong. It's probably / not even–

Dom (*mock medium voice*)   Scoott, are you iiiin there? . . . Hey. Sean, show us –

Wilson   Don't –

The excitement swells.

Sweep Yeah, show us the scar.

Sean *blinks.*

Dom Yeah.

Sweep He doesn't have the heart!

A groan.

Karen That's awful.

Dom Just a flash.

Osh Don't be lobotomies, course he doesn't have a scar, right, mate? Right?

Wilson It's obviously a mistake, I think it was someone else's notes.

Osh Mate?

Sean *sighs, glances at* **Karen**.

He adjusts his top.

The scar runs down the middle of his chest.

It is very real.

A silence. A ripple of guilt.

Osh Wow.

Some moments.

Dom Respect.

Jody That is massive.

A shuffle.

Osh Does it still hurt?

Jody You'll never be able to model, does that upset you?

Sweep But it looks hot.

Jody   Scars are super hot.

Sean *fixes his clothes back, embarrassed.*

Something slips out his chest and slides on to the floor.

A gasp.

Sean's *heart. It beats. The others stare.*

Harley   Don't ya hate it when your internal organs fall out?

Sean *stoops to retrieve it.* **Osh** *nudges it with a shoe.*

Osh   Cringe.

Snickers as **Harley** *scoops it up and chucks it to* **Dom**.

Sean *snatches it back off him. Face off.*

Osh   It was just a joke Sean.

Dom   Yeah, don't take it bad.

Sweep   Aw, Sean, don't take it to heart.

Jody   Tt, so rude, Sweep –

Sweep   I didn't even mean it that time. Seriously, omygod it literally slipped out.

Jody   You did it again!

Osh   We were only messin', Sean.

Dom   Yeah, put it away.

Osh   No one made you.

Alexa   You lot are sick.

Sean *leaves them to it.*

Dom   What was that all about? Was that real?

Osh   Come on, he was playing up to it.

Alexa   Bunch of creeps.

Dom   Attention seeker or what – whose guts just fall out?

Alexa   It was his heart.

Jody   And why was he wearing that hat then?

Alexa   Tt – gonna see if he's okay.

She goes. There's a bad vibe. They wipe the blood off on clothes or each other.

Osh   Alexa gave him that hat.

Harley   Alexa gave Sean the hat?

Jody   The Scott hat?

Harley   No way, did he know Scott used to wear literally that identical hat?

Wilson   Why would she do that?

Sweep   To make drama she could be in the middle of, obvs.

Wilson   I hate Alexa.

Karen   You're just guilty, cos you humiliated him.

Wilson   I didn't know it would just fall out like that!

Jody   Cannot believe Alexa gave him that hat – she set us up.

Dom   You know she puts on a stutter so she sounds more cute?

Karen   Aren't you scared she'll hear you bad-mouthing her?

Jody   Is it cos you live on your own now?

Uncomfortable silence. **Dom** *glares daggers at* **Jody**.

Everyone looks elsewhere.

Dom   Whatever, I dumped her.

Jody   Why? Can't believe you broke up with Alexa. Omygod, if I don't get a boyfriend soon, I am literally going to die.

Dom   I'm a single man now.

Jody (*hopeful*)   You mean – ?

Dom   No.

Wilson   B&B never worked out then?

Dom   Shut up, how'd you know about the B&B?

Osh   Well, you know where she got all that money from, don't you?

Jody   What, the B&B money?

Osh   Yeah, Dom and her had this blazing row over where the funds were coming from, and she wouldn't answer. Just kept telling him these obvious like lies and he flipped out, and eventually she just started chucking things at him and said she loved him but she did it with Creepy Martin.

Jody   WHAT?

Osh   Yeah, she did it.

It hangs in the air. **Dom** *looks stony.*

Karen   What do you mean, did it?

Osh   Did it.

Dom   Jesus Osh.

They process.

Jody   But no one does it.

Karen   No one actually does it.

Sweep   Apart from me, all the time.

Dom/Wilson   You don't count.

Osh   He offered her cash and she wanted it, so she did it.

Karen   What, the whole thing?

Another beat.

Sweep   She could've just blown him.

Jody   Oh, it's horrible. Can you imagine?

Karen   Where? In the café?

Harley   Don't know. Think they went to the bogs.

Dom *gets up, restless.*

Sweep   She must've got a lot of money.

Osh   No, apparently it was only eighty quid.

Sweep   What? He never usually goes below one-ten.

Osh   Gross.

Karen   She must've done it a few times then, to get that much money . . .

Wilson   God.

Osh   Alexa is screwing Martin.

Stunned, grossed-out silence.

Jody   Is it a joke?

Karen   No.

Alexa *returns with crisps.*

Alexa   Anyone want a maize-based snack?

They stare at her.

A thump and a tinkle. A siren.

Dom *has hit the fire alarm.*

Dom   Come on bitches, to the park!

Jody   Omygoodness, he's inviting me – I am so psyched!

Six

Later. The park. Night.

Sweep *holds* **Jody** *– who has been puking – by the hair.* **Jody** *doesn't do much but hang there.* **Sweep** *occasionally swigs from a litre of cider with her free hand.*

Sweep   You're great. You get the most out of life and you don't you don't even abuse substances. Except the blood of Christ. Which as we all know is just juice.

We're not that different.

I mean I just say stuff. To speak in your language, Jodes, I bet even Jesus just said stuff. Didn't he curse that fig tree? I mean, it's not even fig season and the idiot curses it cos it doesn't have any figs – surely that's just like me? I'm always cursing things.

Believe it or not, Jodes. I've only had a semi-shag.

Don't tell anyone. Or I'll break your fucking legs. Don't know why everyone has me down as some kind of – Cos, I mean, Mum had me at seventeen, how stupid does everyone – ? I am pretty upstanding, actually. An upstanding human.

Me and Dom promised never to tell anyone. But we. Got to third base.

Then he started crying.

Just played the PS3 for a few hours.

I'm pretty conservative.

You're a good listener.

Wrote a poem last Tuesday.

Sweep *shakes* **Jody** *testily by the hair as* **Harley** *and* **Wilson** *arrive with drinks.*

Wilson   Oh good, you found Jody?

Sweep   Just getting her second wind.

Sean, *bruised and still bloodied,* **Dom** *and* **Osh** *follow, mid-debate.*

Osh   I feel sorry for her. No one actually does it with Creepy Martin, that's the like, rule.

Sweep   You lot still bitchin' about Alexa? Bored.

Osh   She is such an attention seeker. I heard she did a gang bang.

Dom   You do not 'do' a gang bang, you have one.

Osh   Like a party.

Harley   A gang-bang party. In Alexa's pants.

Osh   I gang bang, you gang bang, he/she ging bongs –

Jody *comes around momentarily to contribute.*

Jody   SHE HAS GINGBONGS AND SHE MADE SEAN WEAR THE DEAD SCOTT HAT.

A beat.

Sweep   Let's get her home.

Dom   What if her parents answer?

Sweep   They'll pray for us, it'll be heartwarming.

Osh   We can dump her in the drive.

Sweep   They have a caravan up the drive, we can put her in the caravan till she sleeps it off.

Muttering and improvising, they carry her off, as **Harley** *and* **Wilson** *appear, canoodling.* **Wilson** *looks awkward.* **Harley** *is having all his birthdays at once.*

Wilson   Kiss me.

Harley   I am.

Wilson   More. Look like you're gonna touch me up –

Harley   You're such a flippin' tease, Wilson, all this time.

Wilson   Don't talk.

Sweep *catches* **Karen**, *a word in her ear.*

Sweep   Yo – if you want a pop at gettin' with Hotty McHotHot, get in now while Alexa's not around to crush your tiny skull.

Wilson (*hissing*)   Feel me up, harder.

Harley   I can be soft, like a girl.

Wilson   Just –

*She does her best to look as though she's into **Harley**.*

Karen   Seen Sean?

Wilson *squeezes up to* **Harley***, barely acknowledging* **Karen**.
Harley *beams.*

Wilson   Nah.

*Nothing from **Karen**, who passes on. **Wilson** scowls.*

Wilson   Ow! Get off – get off –

Wilson *pushes* **Harley** *off.*

Harley   It's just raw enthusiasm, we can work on it –

Wilson   I'm done.

Harley   Seriously?

Wilson   We're over.

Harley *is devastated.*

Karen *spots* **Sean** *as the gang pass back through.*

Sweep   Think Jody's wetting herself.

Osh   Thought she didn't drink?

Dom   Well, she was lovin' them pineapple ones.

Sweep   She know they were alcoholic?

Pause.

Osh   Crap, how many'd she have?

The others drift off. **Harley** *tags on.*

Karen   Sean? Uh – ever been to Nancy's?

Sean *hangs back, shrugs, no.*

Karen   They do amazing hot chocolates.

I was gonna go. This weekend.

If you want – Just cos, they're amazing. Really, um, chocolately. And stuff.

Like crack.

But uh, friggen. Chocolatey. Not drugs.

Sean   Okay.

Karen *is elated.*

Sean *jogs off to catch up with the rest.*

Karen   Cool. See ya!

She tiny fist-pumps as she turns –

Wilson   You didn't meet me.

Karen   Oh – I forgot.

Wilson   We always meet.

Karen   I was – busy –

Wilson   Doesn't matter. Me and Harley've been hangin' out.

Karen   Okay.

Awkward.

Wilson   Hey, listen, I found stuff on the intranet. Got into notes from last year – stuff about Alexa, you know when she was off –

Karen   I'm kind of over that –

Wilson   No, it's –

Karen   What're you doing, poking around people's records?

Wilson   You asked me to.

Tension.

Karen   Do you do everything I ask?

Wilson   No. But it said Alexa was –

Karen   God, stop going on about her.

Wilson   What? I'm not –

Karen   You are. I get it, you don't like Sean. You only went on there to find crap on him – prove a point.

Wilson   No it's not – it's Alexa –

Karen   Do you fancy her or something?

Wilson (*taken aback*)   What?

Karen   Wilson, it's not fair. You're holding me back. Don't see why you hate the idea so much maybe it's just because like, because you want it too – secretly – I mean, just, be honest. You look at them and their cool clothes and their money and boyfriends and slag them but – you want to be like them and have everyone think how successful you are, even parents. The way our parents even look at – the ones who always have boyfriends and – I don't understand what's so wrong with wanting people to think I'm lucky or cool – look at *me* like that for once – why can't I have that and be friends with you too? Why do I have to flipping choose? Don't you want to be *normal*?

Wilson   You're drunk. On three blue WKDs.

Karen   Yeah, well you're a stupid lez, kissing a boy, so –

Wilson   Yeah, well you get on like you know everything but you don't know anything. You don't even know anything, even though you think you do know everything, but you don't, / know anything –

Karen   I'm SICK of your / mood.

Wilson   I'm SICK of your piny-piny-Seany face. What, you think he's the answer to your dreams? What, do you love him or something?

Karen   What would you know about love?

A beat.

Wilson   Know what – you've been a bit of a bitch lately.

Karen   I have?

Wilson   Here –

She throws something at **Karen**.

Wilson   I FIXED YOUR CUNTY BINOCULARS.

Karen *catches them, and hurls them back with force that surprises both of them.*

Wilson *shoves* **Karen**, *who grabs her by the clothes and swings her.*

And they properly fight.

A good couple of blows each.

Wilson *pulls away.* **Karen** *double takes at her.*

Wilson *looks down. Touches her chest.*

Sticky. She's bleeding. **Wilson** *scans the ground for something.*

Karen   You're bleeding.

Wilson   No I'm not.

She hides it. **Karen** *looks at her own heart. It is also bleeding.*

Karen *steps towards her, confused.*

Wilson   Just stay out of my face.

She pushes past.

Karen *picks something up.*

Karen   Wilson –

Seven

The street.

Sweep *eyeballing* **Ciaran**.

Some moments.

Sweep   Okay. Go.

She lets **Ciaran** *touch her boob, just once, one little scrunch.*

He immediately snatches back his hand as though burnt.

Ciaran (*husky*)   Thank you.

They are kind of like my mum's but smaller.

This is the best day of my life.

He sticks out a hand, earnest, and she shakes it.

Sweep   You're cute. I'm confused. Maybe I'll wait for you.

Ciaran *darts away, holding back tears.*

Sweep (*very softly*)   Put away childish things, my brave little man.

Dom   Sweep.

She turns quickly.

Seen Alexa?

Sweep   Nope.

Dom *scuffs for a second. He's troubled.*

Dom   They said she kept going back to Creepy M.

Sweep   Yeah, I heard that.

Dom *paces.*

Dom   I don't understand. Why would she do that?

Sweep   Dunno.

Dom   Everyone's blaming me. Do people know about her mum and everything now?

Sweep   Need a plaster on that.

Dom *rubs at a splodge of red seeping through his chest, and shrugs.*

Dom   Keeps leaking. 'S okay.

Police were round, askin' questions.

Sweep   I know, I was totally cooperative and then they took my shurikens, and I was like: 'That is nothing to do with you or Creepy M,' and they were like: 'Do you know what grooming is?', and I was like: 'Get out of my house, a-holes.'

Or that's what I wanted to say.

Dom   'Grooming' – shit. Is that . . . ? She hasn't answered the phone all week. Aren't shurikens those starblades Ninjas throw?

Sweep   Yeah, present from Dad.

Dom   How is he?

Sweep   He's okay . . . Asks after you. Said, when he gets out, if you ever need any more work, he can find some . . .

Dom   Cheers. Tryin' to keep straight. Might wipe my record. Then they might treat me like a human.

Sweep   Thanks for not – telling anyone. I didn't want to do the, you know? (*Mimes sex.*) With you. And I. (*Mimes crying.*)

Dom   Y'know I didn't say those things to Alexa . . . Wanted her to, you know, take her time. But she's – she's so hard to read.

Sweep *puts an arm round* **Dom.**

Sweep   You were good with Alexa. But – like, is she having a breakdown? Like her mum?

Heard about the bleeding?

Dom   Bleeding?

Sweep   Alexa. Bleeding everywhere.

Harley, **Osh** *and* **Jody** *arrive, dishevelled.* **Jody** *is crying.*

Harley   I've just been bawled out by the police and then teachers and then my parents again.

Osh   She is such a fantasist.

Jody   You can't trust her – I woke up in my CARAVAN.

Osh   She rides anything that moves.

Harley   Yeah, she's probably riding your granddad right now.

Osh   After she's done your mother.

Jody   I stayed over at her house once and she sleeps without jammybottoms. No jammybottoms at all.

Sweep   Breezy.

Jody   The police were talking to Creepy Martin, my parents freaked – I had to lie and say he just gave us the Cokes.

Sweep   No more free drinks.

Osh   Poor Creepy Martin. Alexa needs a slap, you should actually slap her –

Alexa *appears. She is bleeding from the heart.*

Silence.

She approaches, and sits among them.

No one looks directly at her.

Dom *stands, wanders away.*

Jody (*scared*)   Would you ever wash your hair?!

Harley   Why's she staring? Bet she's bleeding on purpose.

Alexa   I'm not –

Dom (*hurt*)   No one made you do it.

Alexa   I didn't – didn't mean –

Osh *has pulled something out of a plastic bag. He eggs her.*

The others are surprised, but not shocked. They fan out around her.

Osh   That's for squealing on us.

She goes to speak. But blood comes out her mouth.

Leave us alone.

Jody   Why's she doing that? I don't understand. Mum says I'm not to hang out around with you any more. You should stop it, Alexa, you're so scary, just stop it, stop it – GO AWAY.

Alexa   I can't.

Sweep   Back off, Jodes –

Harley   Throw another egg – *do it*.

Osh *pelts another egg.* **Wilson** *is suddenly there.*

Wilson   Oi – who threw it?

Osh *pulls out another egg.*

Wilson   Stop it – *Osh!*

Osh   For being a slapper.

Alexa   Dominic? Dominic –

She tries to approach **Dom***, but* **Osh** *pelts her. They erupt. Oi oi oi!*

Jody   JEZEBEL. WHORE. SLUT.

Wilson   STOP! Stop it – can't you see she's – upset.

She stays in front of **Alexa***, shielding.*

Sweep *snatches an egg out of* **Osh***'s hand and smashes it on him.*

Jody *cries.*

Harley *goes at* **Sweep***, pulling her hair.*

They brawl.

Dom *has put his headphones on and wandered off.*

Wilson (*roaring*)   STOP IT STOP IT STOP IT STOP IT!

Eight

Outside. **Sean** *and* **Karen**, *hoods up, cold. A misery date. A phone between them plays music, perhaps carried over from the previous scene, now some schmaltzy ballad. The result is thin, tinny, and adds to the general crapness.*

Karen   This is lovely.

Lovely view. Lovely pylons.

(*Quieter.*) Not awkward at all.

Nice of Sweep to break in here for us.

They kiss. It is unsuccessful. Bumpy.

Karen *pulls back, disappointed, and sighs.*

Sean *shakes his head.*

Sean   So rude.

Karen   It speaks.

Sean   Like you'd notice.

Karen   Did I miss something?

Sean   Just. You're not that great.

Karen   Ahm – you're the one who hangs around the A-team, trying to be something you're not.

Sean   Ow, I'm crying. You pretend to like me – you did nothing when they were being crappy at youth club.

Karen   Yeah, well, why'd you pretend to be a dead boy?

Sean *shakes his head.*

Sean   Don't know, I didn't – just didn't say I wasn't. Wanted everyone to think it was funny, just. You're the one using me – sucking my face.

Karen   Yeah, that's tough.

She kisses him.

Sean   You did it again!

Karen   You kissed back!

Sean   Didn't want to be rude!

Karen   Hanging round Alexa, even though she's a richbitch and you're from crapsville–

Sean   Don't talk about people you don't know, okay?

Karen   You're sticking up for Slutbags?

He slaps her arm.

Sean   Told you not to slag her – all this crap about a hat – it was a COINCIDENCE, I LIKE HATS.

She pulls away.

Karen   Wilson totally had your number. Said you were a dick the moment she saw you.

Sean   Nice. Welcoming. To your stupid town.

Karen   You don't get to say what's nice, you lied about some dead boy you never knew. You probably never even . . .

She has stopped herself.

Sean   What? Probably never what?

Karen *looks away.*

Sean *unbuttons his shirt, angry.*

He takes **Karen***'s hand, pushes it inside his chest.*

It beats. Bleeds. Some moments.

Karen   It's beating.

She allows it, respectful.

Sean   On the waiting list for months. Intensive care. Anti-rejection drugs the rest of my life, probably.

Might come as a surprise, but I don't really like to talk about it. (*Of his heart.*) They bruised it . . .

You just want to be part of Alexa and Dom and all, too.

At my old school – was off sick all the time. People don't know how to be around someone really ill. Who might die.

Just wanted to be in the whatever. Group.

Karen   Sorry.

She withdraws her hand.

He covers himself.

I mean, generally. I've been a bit of a . . .

Sean   It's okay.

Karen   Stuff just comes out my mouth.

Sean   Did you know Scott?

Karen   Not really. Nobody did.

Sean   Just seems no one's bothered to know Alexa.

Sometimes I just want to sleep through till I'm eighteen.

Karen *reaches into a bloodstained pocket.*

Pulls out another heart.

Sean   Collecting them?

Karen   Wilson's.

They consider it.

Dropped it.

Sean   You should go and see her.

Karen   Pfft . . .

Sean   What?

Karen   She's with Harley.

Sean   Yeah, right, she is. Go and fix it, doughnut-brain.

She looks at him, raising her eyebrows at 'doughnut-brain'.

She kisses him on the head.

They pull each other up, stamping heat back into their bodies, and go, arms around each other.

Nine

The church hall. **Karen** *finds* **Wilson** *screwing Pritt Sticks until the gluey bit drops out.*

They both have stains around their hearts, and are wounded and bruised.

Wilson *offers* **Karen** *a stick.*

Karen *gratefully accepts, and eases down next to her.*

They twist their gluesticks thoughtfully.

Karen   Maybe it's just a girl crush –

Wilson   I know.

In the movie of your life, you're the girl who gets the guy.

Sometimes, I am too. Dream of this blokey bloke with a sensible windbreaker, and we have a collie–spaniel cross, and everything is so easy.

And I wake up and remember – oh, I don't fancy boys.

So . . .

Karen   Not you, me. My crush. On you.

Wilson *frowns.*

Wilson   Well. Even if it is just – I don't mind –

Karen   Don't. Hate it when straight girls mess with gay ones 'just to see'.

Wilson   Well, let me know when you find the answers.

Karen   . . . Suppose I'll have to buy boy shirts. Follow Clare Balding on social media. I will always hate really gay-looking shoes though, so –

Wilson *kisses her.*

It is short, but certain.

Karen *smiles. Gives her back the heart.*

Wilson *studies it, their bloodstains.*

Karen   Is this supposed to happen?

Wilson *shrugs.*

Wilson   It's unnerving. Was killing me earlier but not as bad now.

Karen   Is it real?

She receives a text alert.

Kkkkhh, if this is Osh's knob again –

She checks her updates.

Oh. Alexa.

Wilson   She's sent out loads in the last few days.

Karen   Anyone replied?

Wilson   Don't think so.

Karen   This one's different . . .

Wilson   Think it's real?

Karen   Don't think it's a joke.

Wilson   Did you know her mum killed herself?

Karen   No.

Wilson   Read it by accident. Never managed to hack, just copied the password off Farnam's desk. Remember Alexa was off school – she wasn't in Antigua. She was in hospital.

No one knows what to do. Everyone feels bad. Everyone's angry.

Karen   Where's your phone?

Wilson *holds it up.*

Wilson   Dead. Death by egg.

Karen   She's saying she's at your house.

Wilson   What?

Ten

Alexa, *battered and unkempt, drops like a stone.*

Something slithers across the floor.

It is her heart. And maybe her stomach. It glistens.

Some moments.

Alone. Aloneness.

Alexa (*to us*)   Weird – I – Wilson left, I –

In the bathroom, trying to clean it off, egg – go to my phone to call someone – realise –

No one to call, really.

Just. Go a bit blank. Heavy.
Send a message, to everyone.
Just says, 'Help.'

Next thing, heart's just slithered out of my chest – like flipping lying – on the floor – next to me. Can't move.
Maybe I don't want to. Move.
Like, relief.

Bunch of my memories lying there.
Could end up in someone else.

She smiles at the thought.

Make better use of it.

Jody said – if I slept with Creepy M, he'd give me money, and
Dom'd love me proper. Jody stood outside, while I . . .

Don't feel much. Since Mum.

Keep doing things – tryin' to feel something. Feelin' everythin' –
nothing – it's – and I'm like this scream in my head but only
I hear it – can't seem to be scared or anything.

Till, well, now.

Her eyes close.

Wilson *and* **Karen** *burst in.*

Wilson   She putting it on?

Karen*'s down at* **Alexa***'s body, rolling her over.*

Wilson   How can you tell?

Karen   Might have to make her sick – she'll be okay. Dad
used to do this, I know what to do.

Wilson *looks at* **Karen***, surprised.* **Karen** *sits* **Alexa** *up.*

Wilson   God. Here . . .

She gingerly scoops up the organ, passes it to **Karen***, who pushes it
back in.*

Wilson   Alexa? Hey, Alexa, it's us – Wilson. And Karen.

Alexa *is shaking.*

Wilson   Want us to call your dad? We'll tell him we're just
watching TV, eating ice cream.

Alexa   I didn't uh, know where to go. Your mum let me . . .

She is wobbly, feeling her insides back in place, self-conscious.

Wilson (*joking*)   Oi, you've messed up my floor.

Karen   I'll get water.

Alexa   Salt. Salt'll get it out.

Karen *goes.*

Alexa, *recovering, examines the mess, tries to clean up. It's like a war zone. She still can't really move.*

Alexa   Thanks. For – earlier. The egg – stuff.

I was in the bathroom, trying to – went to call someone – then . . . (*Registering.*) You guys came.

Wilson   Look, I know about – your mum and all. Sorry. How'd she do it?

Alexa *looks at her.*

Alexa   Pills.

Found her in the morning.
Wanted Dom . . . when I went to, uh, the restaurant. To him.
I didn't mean . . . I wanted Dominic really.

Wilson   He's outside . . . He won't come in. Sweep brought him. Says he's sorry. I mean, everyone'll calm down. And. It'll be okay, Alexa. I didn't mean it the first time I did it either.

Alexa   It's like – a thing – a thing you carry round with you. But doesn't feel like it belongs to you. Even – like when I was talking to – him – and then it was happening . . . kept thinking, it's not real.
None of it's real.
I'm outside it.
But then, suddenly, it is.

She takes in **Wilson***.*

Wilson   What?

Alexa   Just. You seem so sorted.

Wilson   It's a front. Just decided it was funnier to find myself funny than, you know, upsetting.

Alexa   I never find myself funny.

Wilson   You aren't.

She wipes away blood from **Alexa**. **Alexa** *peers up at* **Wilson**.

Alexa   Do we have to talk to each other in school now? If we see each other in the corridor and stuff?

Wilson   Too much of a good thing . . .

Alexa   Can kill it. Good. I agree.

Wilson   We'll probably be allowed to talk to each other in our twenties.

A beat.

Alexa (*small*)   He made me feel pretty.

Wilson *offers* **Alexa** *her phone.*

Wilson   Want to text your dad?

Alexa *nods. Takes the phone.*

Karen *returns with water. She and* **Wilson** *clean the gore and pop the rest of the heart in a jiffy bag.*

Karen   Ew, slippery.

She hands **Alexa** *the jiffy.*

Karen   Think that's all of it.

Karen *and* **Wilson** *awkwardly help lift* **Alexa** *to the couch, where they sink down, exhausted.* **Karen** *perches on the arm rest. They are utterly wrecked and battle-spattered.*

Karen   Can we just watch TV till Alexa's dad comes?

Wilson *puts on TV. Something soothing, like* Friends *or* Frozen Planet.

Dom *appears, sheepish.*

Dom   Brought some. Um. Ice cream. Gone a bit melty.

He joins them, sitting carefully next to **Alexa**, *making her comfortable.*

A knock from upstairs. **Wilson** *gets up and shouts.*

Wilson   YEAH?

(*Listens.*)NO, JUST ME AND KAREN. AND ALEXA.
(*Weird.*) AND DOM.

All   HI, MRS WILSOOOONNNN / HELLOOO!

Wilson   Mum says, 'Crisps or juice?'

All   NO THANKS! / I'M OKAY, THANKS MRS
WILSON. / YES PLEEEASE.

Wilson *plops back down, going for the ice cream. They dab blood off*
each other.

Karen   Seen this one?

Alexa   Yeah, this one's good.

Dom   Yeah, it's hilarious.

Karen*'s phone rings, incongruously upbeat.*

Karen   Mum? . . . Hi . . .
Can you pick me up?
No, nothing really – just ate ice cream, watched TV.
Yeah.
Okay, see you soon, lotsa love.

They watch TV and eat ice cream . . . they look pretty happy.

I'm Spilling My Heart Out Here

BY STACEY GREGG

*Notes on rehearsal and staging, drawn from workshops
with the writer held at the National Theatre, November 2012*

How the writer came to write the play

Drawing from her own life experience, Stacey Gregg wanted
to render a truthful portrayal of adolescence – to dramatise the
trauma of daily life with its emotional turbulence and physical
change, while also expressing the trust and compassion that
exists between friends. The play seeks to capture that moment
in time when people still considered as children are navigating
very adult situations and feelings alongside intense friendships
that will not survive into adulthood.

Thinking back to her own teenage years, Stacey remembered
enjoying John Hughes's films – for example *The Breakfast Club*,
Some Kind of Wonderful and *Pretty in Pink* – and wanted to create
something that had that same bittersweet quality.

Approaching the play

I'm Spilling My Heart Out Here presents a range of exciting and
specific challenges in production. Particular areas to focus on
in preparation for rehearsal and during the process might be:

- The demands for physical proximity.
- The rhythm of the language.
- The relationship between individual characterisation and
  group identity.
- The shifting dynamics through the scenes.
- The challenge of transitioning from scene to scene.
- The practical challenge of expressing 'emotional leakage'.

Physical proximity

The play contains a number of key moments of physical proximity including kisses, fights, breast-touching. Helping the actors move into one another's personal space will be a key part of the rehearsal process for this play. From day one it may be useful to start creating an environment where contact is normalised. Warm-up exercises that help with this might be:

MAGNETIC BODY PARTS

Split the group into pairs. Assign one as leader, one as follower. Ask the actors to imagine one of their hands is magnetic and is attracting the hand of the follower. Instruct them to lead their partner around the room as if pulling the other by magnetic force, always keeping a distance of approximately ten centimetres between their hands. Remind them to be as inventive as possible about their journeys, making changes in speed, direction and height. As they gain in confidence, ask them to swap who is leader, who follower, and suggest new body parts to 'magnetise' – for example, the leader's foot leading the follower's nose, the leader's elbow pulling the follower's knee, the leader's bottom attracting the follower's bottom. Over time, bolder combinations can be tried, working up to nose-to-nose, lips-to-lips etc. Suggest they gradually reduce the gap between the body parts so there is a matter of just a few centimetres between them. This game can be played as a quick warm-up for each rehearsal, and eventually can then be used as the basis for the kissing rehearsals etc.

PUSHING WITH INTENTION

Ask two actors to face one another in the centre of a room and instruct both to push the other to the opposite side of the room while repeating a line from the play. Remind them to support their voices from their diaphragms, to connect the act of pushing to the text they are speaking, and to have concern for the safety of their partner (ensuring that the room is clear of clutter). This exercise is terrific for spring-boarding actors into imaginative, passionate contact. As the actors try to achieve their goal, encourage them to be inventive in how they push, and remind them that there are different body parts to push with. In the process of the exercise it is often the case that an interesting physical dynamic emerges that can be lifted directly from the exercise for use in a fight scene.

Pace and rhythm

Stacey Gregg's writing has remarkable energy and pace. There are few pauses in the play, and the group scenes in particular contain many competing voices, cutting in and topping one another as they vie for attention and status. This style of writing can be hard to rehearse. Observing the punctuation in the text is key. For example:

Gregg uses a dash (–) to indicate an interruption, where the next character cuts in and breaks the previous person off. The first actor speaking must make a decision about what the rest of the sentence would be in order to inflect the line correctly. The actor who interrupts will probably need to take the word before the final word as their cue in order to cut in on time.

A slash (/) indicates an overlap where the next character starts talking on top of the previous person, and the first speaker continues until their thought is complete.

The challenge for the actors is to observe the punctuation and the pace it dictates while staying in control of their performances. A problem that may arise is that, in an effort to get in on cue, the actors start speeding up everything they say, which has a snowballing, adrenalising effect on their fellow actors. The opposite problem is that actors may find it hard to come in on the cut-ins and overlaps and the rhythm of the scene settles into uniformity. Early memorisation of text (particularly the more complex group scenes) and concentrated time spent drilling the text specifically for rhythm is advisable.

The last few scenes in the play have more moments of space and air in them than the early scenes, when the characters tentatively begin to consider their own and one another's emotional lives afresh. To earn these more delicate thoughtful moments, it is important that the pace and energy of the adolescent roller-coaster is achieved beforehand.

A rehearsal warm-up exercise to help get everyone's mouths and brains working quickly while creating a sense of collective responsibility for rhythm/control might be:

MULTI-BALL

Have all ten company members throw a single ball around the circle, saying their character name when they catch the ball. They must only catch the ball once and remember the route the ball travels. Repeat the exact route of the ball with the sequence of names a few times until memorised.

Put that ball aside and introduce another ball (it must be a different size or colour from the first). This time throw the ball in a new route, saying a different sequence of words (it doesn't matter what the words are – but it may be helpful to connect them to the language world of the play, for example have everyone name a female body part; or a swear word). Again each person only catches the ball once and the route must be repeated until memorised.

Then, reintroduce the original ball and route so now two balls are running at the same time. Once this has been established, take both balls away and introduce a third (again it must look different to the other two). This time ask them to choose a new category and learn the new route. Once this new route is well established, reintroduce the previous two balls so they have all three routes running simultaneously. Encourage precision, rhythm, eye-contact and flow.

You can carry on increasing the number of balls until there are as many balls as there are people (for example ten balls, ten participants). This is an exciting game to play and watch, and the feeling of mastery the company get when they have all the balls in the air is what to aim for when playing the fast-paced opening scene of the play and others like it.

Characterisation

The relationship between individual and group identity is at the centre of this play, and there is great scope for creating detailed, nuanced characterisation, within the shifting dynamics of group cohesion/division.

There is a danger, in a group scene with characters of similar ages, for a generic 'sameness' to creep in. Giving time in rehearsals to explore the characters, their back-stories and physical identity will be valuable, helping to encourage a lively picture of difference and individuality on stage. Gregg offers this additional information about each character:

KAREN is everyone's friend. She is solid and responsible and from a stable home.

WILSON is strong, witty and independent. She proves herself to be fiercely loyal and compassionate. She is gay and boyish in appearance.

SEAN is the new boy. He is attractive and perhaps slightly older than the others. He is grounded, thoughtful and more of a listener.

DOMINIC is the best endowed of the gang and highest in the pecking order. He lives alone and has a maturity that comes from his complicated family life. He has obsessive-compulsive tendencies, as shown through his anxieties around bodily fluids. He needs to be in control.

SWEEP is full of bravado. Her bark is much worse than her bite. She is aggressive but has a vulnerable streak. She has a friendship and affinity with Dominic relating to their difficult childhoods.

ALEXA is attractive, moneyed and popular. Known as an Ice Queen, everyone has opinions about her but not many people get close to her.

OSH is a younger member of the group and looks up to Dom. He goes along with the pack and wants to be included.

HARLEY is desperate for a girlfriend and is Dom's sidekick.

CIARAN is the younger brother of Karen, which gives him access to the older kids. He is innocent but curious about sex.

JODY is naive and repressed. She wants to be a good girl and struggles to reconcile her religious beliefs with her sexual desires.

CREEPY M is an important offstage character. He is either a waiter or bartender in the café/restaurant where the girls go. He represents a dangerous adult world but until now has been treated by the girls as a dare and a joke.

Please note the writer feels that the parts should not be merged or cross-cast, since each character's gender identity is linked to the play's meaning. However, the social class of the characters is not fixed in the writer's mind in the same way and is open to interpretation.

Below are some exercises that might help your company to create their individual characters:

CREATING A BODY-MIND MAP

Take a large roll of paper and place ten human-being-sized sheets on the floor. Ask each member of the company to draw around another member's body. Label the body outlines with the characters' names. Then go through the following steps:

1 Ask the actors to find three words that capture the essence of their character. Look for the contradictions. For example, the actor playing Osh might decide Osh is blunt, insecure and popular. Next ask the actor to write each word in a different place on the body – somewhere they feel that characteristic 'lives' in his body. In the NT workshop on the play it was suggested that the word 'blunt' be written on Osh's mouth, 'popular' on his feet (perhaps he has expensive trainers and his popularity derives from that), and insecure on his genitalia. There is no right or wrong in this exercise, it is up to the actor to make choices that interest him/her and spark off thought in his/her mind.

268   Stacey Gregg

2 Ask the actor playing the character to make up a shameful,
   humiliating event in their character's past – an event that
   is defining for the character as a traumatic, low point in
   their life. Once decided, the actor can again choose a
   place on the body where this memory belongs. For
   example, one workshop participant suggested Osh has a
   traumatic memory of taking a shower after gym class and
   then reading graffiti on the toilet door saying he had a
   small penis.

3 Ask the actor to identify the one thing they fear might be
   true about themselves. For example, one workshop
   participant suggested Osh's deepest fear about himself
   might be 'I fear I am an outsider.' Other examples might
   be 'I fear I am ugly,' 'I fear I am stupid,' 'I fear I am
   unlovable.' This also should be written on the body map
   in a chosen place.

4 Ask the actor to identify what the character most wants in
   life. Where does that desire live? Perhaps one character is
   driven by the urge to belong and so writes 'I want to
   belong' on the body map in the place of his heart.

At the end of this exercise, the actor has a visual map of his
character's inner life. This should help him/her launch into
the world of this play where the body is so present.

FINDING A PHYSICALITY

Ask your actors to walk around the room as themselves,
noticing their own rhythm, breath, movements. Then ask
them to adjust their walk, allowing their character's shameful
event to inform their movement, and gradually add in their
character's wants, fears and traits, thinking about the body-
mind map they have made. Suggest they think about which
body parts lead their movement, and which they might be
trying to conceal. As they walk ask them to imagine their
character in different situations. For example, how does your
character sit, smile, run, cry? What do they do when nervous?
How might they flirt? Etc.

Scene dynamics

Each scene in the play offers an interesting set of dynamics to explore, particularly with regard to the shifting statuses of the characters. The bigger group scenes (for example Scenes Five and Six) may be hardest to shape because of their length and number of characters. For the director, it may help to break down the scenes into sections/units of action and give each a mini-title. This can help you get a grip on the dramatic development of the scene, and how it progresses. As part of this process it may also be useful to try to identify who is the leading voice in each section – which character is driving the action, and when that changes.

Below are some exercises that could be useful to make sure the scenes have dynamic development moment to moment.

INTRODUCING STATUS

To introduce the concept of status, offer the actors a collection of fruit and vegetables of different sizes, textures, colours – some small, some dull and run of the mill, some exuberant and exotic. Ask the actors to choose which fruit or vegetable is most like each character in the play. Use the 'casting' process to discuss the status of the characters – which is the biggest, most dominant in the group, which the smallest, which most beautiful/which least. For example, Karen may be an apple – familiar, unthreatening, Wilson a passion fruit – plain on the outside, and full of unseen beauty and passion within. Having assembled the 'company' you could look at a few scenes and explore how best to group the fruit/vegetable characters in a way that illuminates their status. Who is at the centre of the group, who is on the periphery, etc.? How does the group tend to shape itself around the central, highest-status character?

STATUS LADDER

Having introduced the concept of status, this exercise can be used to explore the shifting status of the characters in a scene.

Give each character a series of ten numbered pieces of paper on the floor, in a row from one to ten. This is their status ladder. Have the actor choose a place on the scale, from one to ten, which they think indicates their status at the outset of the scene. Ask them to stand beside that number. Do the same for each actor. Then play the scene, asking them to change position on the ladder each time they think their status has changed. They can move when they speak and also when others speak. There should be movement most of the time as they chart out their changing status. If not, prompt the actors to think about what they are saying, hearing and feeling, bringing attention to the detail and hidden barbs in the writing.

POINT-SCORING

Gregg talks about her play as an emotional battleground. In every scene the characters are fighting for approval, status, attention. This exercise is helpful in bringing out the sense of battle, highlighting both the pleasure of verbal victory but also the pain that comes with losing and being exposed.

Give each actor in the scene a piece of paper taped to their chest, and arm them each with a red felt-tip. Play the scene (they will need to have learned their lines), asking them to put a red mark on their opponent's papers each time they feel they have scored a verbal point against them. Explain that the object of the exercise is to score the maximum points and that they should look for every opportunity to score a point against the other characters. At the end you can count up each character's scores and discuss the emotional implications of this for their journey in the play.

FOCUS

In larger group scenes it is important to look for ways to keep the stage picture alive, varied and active. One way to achieve this is to explore the different focus points available to the actors during a scene. A useful exercise might be to replay a scene a number of times, each time asking the whole company to concentrate on one particular aspect of the scenario. For example, the opening scene could be played with everyone's attention on the stopwatch; and then played again with focus on the place on the stage where a teacher might appear; and then played again with focus on the weather (perhaps it is cold or raining); and again with focus on which other character in the scene your character finds attractive. Each time, the actors should reflect afterwards whether that particular point of focus brought the scene alive for their character. In the end each actor should choose a different main point of focus for the scene, giving the scene complexity and variety.

Design and transitions

I'm Spilling My Heart Out Here offers an unusual challenge in terms of design. Many scenes take place in unremarkable, dull environments, the predictability of the characters' external world contrasting with the vivid turmoil of their inner lives. The specifics of location are less important than the characters who operate in it, and the play has a fluid rhythm that the writer feels should not be interrupted by cumbersome scenic changes. With this in mind, it might be a useful exercise to imagine the play staged with extreme limitations; for example, consider how you would do the play if the only tools you had to tell the story of place/time were:

- Lighting (including practical lights) – perhaps the whole play can be done with one lighting object on stage per scene (with support from stage lights). For example, many mobile phones for opening scene; a café neon light for Scene Two; strip-lights for the church hall; a floor lamp for the final scene, etc.

Do the same if the following were the only tools you had:

- Written word.
- Sound/spoken word.
- Colour.
- Food/drink/fluids.
- One object per scene.

Places to sit

In small towns, teenagers often find themselves in parks or external spaces with nowhere to sit, or in youth clubs with not enough furniture, resulting in that awkward 'hanging around' feeling. Is there a way to stage the play with this idea in mind?

Additional issues to consider may be:

How the transitions from scene to scene will work. In the text, Stacey Gregg suggests blackouts, but is encouraging of other possibilities. Note that some transitions are tricky, as the same characters appear in consecutive scenes in similar spaces, making it hard to register the change in time/place. Consider the possibility of using crowds sweeping by to change some of these trickier scenes (for example, the end of the gym-watching scene could be marked by a crowd of gymkit-wearing youngsters rushing past as if the class has ended).

The borders/boundaries of the space. A number of the scenes have characters making repeated journeys across the space to and from other locations (for example, Alexa's journeys in the church hall scene). Be mindful of how to tell the story of where characters are travelling from and to.

Emotional spillage

The play exists in a world of naturalistic relationships. The dialogue is true-to-life and there is a psychological realism to the characters. Yet as the bodies and minds of the characters begin to come undone, the play enters a more surreal space. Gregg's vision is that the surreal moments of emotional spillage (heart/blood moments) happen in a seamless fashion, surprising the audience but staying rooted in the emotional reality of the characters' experience.

The practical challenges presented by these moments should not be underestimated. Realistic scheduling will be key (especially on days where there is a dress run and performance).

Creatively, the important things to decide are:

- Whether to aim for a realistic heart/blood-seeping image or an abstract one.
- How the individual heart-themed moments differ and progress.

Advice from the NT Props team includes:

Be inventive about what objects to use for the heart. What properties are important for you? Colour, shape, weight, texture, movement? Consider real meat wrapped in a condom; or look at what you have to hand and follow the tips below.

FOR THE HEARTS   Try coiled rope (like a curtain swag) or a piece of finger-bandage stuffed with cotton wool, and moulded into a heart shape. Smother with Copydex to set into place. Mix Copydex with a little paint and add another coat so it is a pink/red colour (dipping your brush in a little washing-up liquid beforehand will make it easy to wash the glue out of brushes). Perhaps fill the bandage with sand or rice so that it has a convincing weight to it. Cover with KY jelly to give it a lifelike sheen, or pour stage blood on to it.

FOR THE BLOOD SEEPAGE   Experiment with making small blood bags by folding a piece of cling film into a square of about ten centimetres, then bunch the edges up so there is a little well in the centre, put stage blood in the well, twist the top so it is a small blood sac and conceal within clothes. Do this as close to the moment it will be used as possible rather than at the start of the show. Blood capsules are also discreet and effective.

LAUNDRY   Add a little bit of washing-up liquid to the blood mixture from the start. This will help make it easier to wash out of the costumes. Alternatively, if the run is short, budget for multiple very low-cost costumes to reduce laundry pressure.

SYMBOLIC/ABSTRACT POSSIBILITIES   A piece of red velvet has a fantastic weight and texture. Can fabric be used instead of fake blood? Or ribbon drawn from the body or mouth?

Finally, do consider the following:

How slippery will your stage become after blood spillage?
Take note of when the fight scenes take place and what state
the floor will be in.

References and notes

YOUTUBE
Clips of hearts and open-heart surgery.

Clips of breath-holding and fainting.

FILMS
The Breakfast Club (dir: John Hughes).

Some Kind of Wonderful (dir: John Hughes).

Pretty in Pink (dir: John Hughes).

> *From a workshop led by Facilitating Director Sacha Wares,*
> *with notes by Kate Hewitt*

Tomorrow
I'll Be
Happy

Jonathan Harvey

Age suitability 15–19
Cast size 9

Jonathan Harvey is an award-winning playwright whose plays include: *The Cherry Blossom Tree* (Liverpool Playhouse Studio); *Wildfire* (Royal Court); *Beautiful Thing* (Bush Theatre, London and Donmar Warehouse/Duke of York's), John Whiting Award; *Babies* (National Theatre Studio/Royal Court), George Devine Award and *Evening Standard*'s Most Promising Playwright Award; *Boom Bang-A-Bang* (Bush Theatre); *Hushabye Mountain* (ETT/Hampstead); *Out in the Open* (Hampstead/Birmingham Rep); *Canary* (ETT/Hampstead) and *Corrie!* (National Tour). Television and film work includes: *Beautiful Thing* (Film Four); *Gimme Gimme Gimme* (BBC); *Coronation Street* (ITV); *Britannia High* (ITV); *Beautiful People* series 1 and 2 (BBC); *Rev* (Big Talk/BBC) and *Shameless* (Channel 4). Jonathan's first novel *All She Wants* has just been published by Pan Macmillan.

Characters

Darren, *a young gay lad. Sixteen at the beginning of the story, he has recently left his estate to go and work as a kitchen porter at a nearby holiday camp. Idealistic and full of hope.*

Marcus, *a singer at the holiday camp. Year or two older than Darren.*

Dior, *seventeen. Pragmatic. Beautiful but doesn't know it. Seems to carry a pain with her. Currently working at a local supermarket.*

Scott, *Dior's boyfriend and friend of Darren. Nice-looking. All the girls fancy him.*

Troy, *Scott's fourteen-year-old brother.*

Siddie, *used to be Scott's best mate. Has a reputation for being the local nutter and thug.*

Joanne, *Dior's friend, in love with Siddie. Finds herself fascinating.*

Cyprus, *Joanne's friend. Not much to say for herself and is often put down by the others. Always looking after her baby brother.*

Jadenne, *a girl of eighteen whom Joanne meets in prison.*

Setting

The play is set in a coastal town in the UK, present day. At the beginning of the story, the majority of the characters have not long left school.

Graveyard

An ominous rumble of thunder, which dies away. Then it's raining. Some wreaths lie on the ground, indicating a grave. **Marcus** *and* **Dior** *enter with umbrellas up.* **Marcus** *is carrying a modest bunch of flowers.* **Dior** *is heavily pregnant. They stop and look at the grave.* **Marcus** *then looks out to the audience.*

Marcus   This is such an amazing place. Clinging on to the edge of the land. Like it's going to fall in the sea. It's like you live at the end of the world. Is that the holiday camp over there? So near and yet so far.

Dior   Where did you go?

Marcus   All over. Got a job on a cruise ship.

Dior   What is it you do?

Marcus   Sing. Not very well.

Dior   You famous?

Marcus   If I was famous, you'd've recognised me last night.

Dior   I don't think I could go on a cruise. I seen that *Titanic* and thought it was well gay.

Pause.

Sorry.

Marcus   I had this fear of water. But I see something that frightens me. And I have to confront it. Stop it being scary. So I took the job on the ship. Surrounded by it.

He kneels and places the flowers on the ground. **Dior** *looks out to the sea.*

Dior   Scared now?

He looks at her. Shakes his head.

Marcus   I learned to scuba dive. In the Caribbean. There are worse places to lose your fear.

Dior   I can't sing. In my head I can. In my head I'm Adele. But I'm shy, see.

Marcus   Oh, you've no reason to be shy.

Dior   Round here. We never get a chance to escape. Else we would. So this is me. Looking at that view. For ever.

Marcus   I looked it up online. Last night. The trial. How the judge said it wasn't a hate crime.

Dior   It wasn't.

Marcus   That's not what his family think. They think it's because . . .

Dior   What, cos he was different?

Marcus   Different gets you killed, does it?

Dior   Normal counts for a lot round here. When you've got nothing. People don't wanna think that you've got something different to them. They don't like it. Anyway it wasn't that. That's just what singled him out. It was just. Too much to drink. Too much boredom. Too much madness.

Marcus   I hope so. I really hope so. Somehow that'd make me feel a bit better.

Dior   If you were his friend. He wouldn't want you to be sad.

Marcus   But what's worse? Okay, there's no hatred for what he was. So why? Because of who he was? I liked who he was.

Dior   Sometimes. Bad things just happen.

Marcus   And it was all . . . that night . . . in his school.

Dior   They shut it down. When they realised they'd given us all a shit education. Couldn't wait to brick up the place. Looks weird now. Weeds growing through the floorboards. Trees growing out the windows.

Marcus   Why did he go there? Late at night?

Dior   We don't know. No one knows.

Marcus   I got a new mobile when I went on the ship.
Texted him the new number. I couldn't work out why he
wasn't texting me back. I thought he'd changed his number.
I thought maybe I'd done something to offend him. Or he'd
met someone. Or. I just didn't know. But something inside
me was niggling away. I knew I had to come and see him.
I just didn't expect it to be like this.

Dior   His mum took his Facebook down. There was
another page. Like a tribute to him. Only some trolls ruined
it so she took that down as well. Keyboard warriors don't let
no one rest in peace.

Marcus   His mum said he was everyone's little angel.

Dior   Everyone's an angel when something like this happens.
You never hear anyone saying: 'Oh nobody liked him. He
was really weird.' Or: 'Bit of a bitch, that one.'

Marcus   He wasn't.

Dior   No, I know. I'm just saying. Everyone's perfect in
death.

Marcus   He was my angel.

Pause.

Dior   Did you know Scott?

Marcus   Scott?

Dior   Last night. At the wedding. My husband. Have you
met him before?

Pause.

Marcus   No. No.

Dior   Only . . .

Marcus   No.

Dior   Okay.

Pause.

Dior   He's good to me. He's gonna take care of me. Us. Everyone says we're too young. It won't last. But we're in this together. It's hard. Getting by on your own. But I've got him. And it doesn't seem so bad.

Marcus   Shouldn't you be on honeymoon?

Dior   We've got a caravan for a week in the summer. I'm sorry. I didn't even ask if you wanted to be on your own.

Marcus   I'm okay.

Dior   No, you should. I'll wait by the gate.

Marcus   Thank you.

Dior   See you in a bit.

Marcus   You know.

She stops. Looks back.

If you can sing. In your head. Maybe you should try out loud. Face your fear and . . .

Dior   Who are you? Simon Cowell?

And she heads off. He watches her go. Then turns and looks at the grave. He kneels.

Marcus   I got you roses. You like roses. And that white stuff you said looked like dandruff.

He starts to cry.

Oh Darren. Oh Darren. What did they do to you? You must've been so scared. You should have come with me. Why didn't you come with me?

And he kneels there crying as the lights fade.

Pub

The night before.

Music thumping out from inside. **Dior** *comes out in her wedding dress and veil and stands there, gasping for air.* **Cyprus** *comes out with a sleeping toddler in a pushchair. She has covered him with jackets.*

Cyprus   MC Alibi wants my number.

Dior   Result.

Cyprus   I told him I caught the thing.

Dior   Don't scare him off.

Cyprus   I don't think he knew what I was talking about. Are you having another thingy?

Dior   No.

Cyprus   Like, a panic on.

Dior   I just need some fresh air.

Cyprus   Dior, what's the matter?

Dior   Nothing. Nothing. Cyprus, I'm fine.

Cyprus   You ain't gonna be sick?

Dior   No.

Cyprus   You can tell me anything, you know? I don't shock. We're good mates now. We are, aren't we? We're good mates now.

Dior   Sometimes I feel like I'm drowning.

Cyprus   That's well gay.

Dior   I have to fight for my breath.

Cyprus   Well, you know why that is?

Dior   Will you just leave me alone? You never say anything. Anything. Worthwhile. So will you just shut up and go back inside? Please?

Cyprus (*chuckles*)   You're well funny.

Dior   Oh, shut up, Cyprus.

Cyprus   Ah, man. Why does everyone have to be on a downer all the time?

Dior   Cyprus . . .

Cyprus   It's your wedding night. You're meant to be the most happiest girl in the world, man.

Scott *enters.*

Scott   And she is. She's married to me now, in't she?

And he twirls **Dior** *round and hugs her.*

Cyprus   It's gonna be me next though. I caught the thing. I did.

Dior   She's gonna marry the DJ.

Cyprus   MC Alibi. He's well lush.

Scott   How's the baby?

He and **Cyprus** *look at the pushchair.*

Cyprus (*fondly*)   He's a fat bastard.

Scott   You wanna have a word with your mum.

Cyprus   I know. It's just she works.

Scott   Penny for the guy.

Cyprus   I hope he's still breathing.

Dior   Don't say that.

Cyprus   I was tryina hide his eyes from the lights. I didn't want him, like, dreaming he was tripping and shit.

Scott *looks at* **Dior** *fondly.*

Scott   Be us soon.

Dior   Things'll be all right, won't they? Things'll be all right.

Scott   Things are gonna be well good. I promise you.

Cyprus   I think she's having a panic on.

Scott   She has these bad dreams.

Dior   I am here, you know.

Scott   She wakes in the night and she can't breathe. Has to put the light on. Draw the curtains. Everything. Her old girl goes mental.

Dior   She don't.

Scott   I tell her. The worst's over. Everything's gonna be all right. But she don't listen.

Cyprus   Law unto herself. Never listens. Joanne always said it.

Scott   Well, she wants to start.

Troy *comes out.*

Troy   Scott? Dad wants to take a picture of us in our suits.

Scott   Don't he know I'm groping my hot bitch?

Dior   Don't call me that.

Scott   Right. See you in a bit. And believe me. It's all all right.

Dior   Will you stop going on about it?

Scott   And don't be too long, cos we gotta do some serious dancing.

Troy   All right, Cyprus?

Cyprus   All right?

And **Scott** *heads inside with* **Troy**.

Cyprus   I wouldn't mind if a bloke called me his bitch.

Dior   Shut up, Cyprus.

Cyprus   I quite fancy Scott's brother.

Dior   You don't have to fancy someone just cos he said hello to you.

Cyprus   I know. I so know that.

Dior   You fancy anything, you.

Cyprus   No I don't. That's so gay.

Dior   It's not.

Cyprus   I don't fancy my dad.

Dior   Cyprus. Will you shut up? Talk wanker. All you do is talk. And it's all wank.

Cyprus   Have you heard from Joanne?

Dior   No. Have you?

Cyprus   I thought she was my mate.

Dior   Only ever cared about herself, that one.

Cyprus   I've written loads. Nothing.

Pause.

Silent wanker.

And the two girls start to giggle. Just then **Marcus** *enters, carrying the flowers.*

Marcus   Excuse me. Sorry to bother you. Bit of a long shot. I'm looking for someone called Darren Williams. He lives on Fairview Road. Only there's no one in and I think I must have an old number for him.

Cyprus   Are you taking the piss?

Marcus   Sorry? No. I remember he used to talk about this pub. Wondered whether you might . . .

Dior   Are you a journalist?

Marcus   No. Why would I . . . ?

Dior   How comes you don't know what happened to him?

Marcus   What happened to him?

Dior   How d'you know him?

Marcus   We worked together. At . . . the holiday camp. I've been travelling for a bit. We lost touch and . . .

Dior   Darren's dead. He died. About eighteen months ago. He was killed. Knifed. Knife crime.

Cyprus   It's on the increase, innit.

Dior   It was all over the papers. I'm surprised you didn't know.

Marcus   I've been away. My God, that's terrible. Were you friends of his?

Dior   Yes.

Cyprus (*at the same time*)   No.

Dior   Sorry to be the bearer of bad news.

Marcus   Right. Sorry. Congratulations, by the way. I feel a bit . . . I need to sit down. Can I . . .

He motions to head inside to sit down.

Dior   Guest list only. Sorry. The pub's quite strict.

Cyprus   Yeah. And people wanna forget about Darren. It's like . . . really old news, and we like . . . So don't wanna go there.

Scott *comes out.*

Scott   Come on, babe. Everyone's asking where you've got to.

Dior   This is a mate of Darren's. He come looking for him.

*There is a slight tension when **Scott** sees **Marcus**. But they both cover it.*

Scott   All right?

Marcus   Hi.

Dior   I'm really sorry you didn't know.

Marcus   No. I'm sorry. To have intruded. On your big night. (*To* **Scott**.) Congratulations.

Scott   Cheers, mate. (*To* **Dior**.) Come on, babe.

Cyprus   See you.

And she heads inside. **Scott** *goes back in.*

Marcus   Don't you have to go back in?

Dior   Yeah. It looks like rain. Don't wanna get my dress wet. They say it's gonna rain tonight. Then all through tomorrow.

But she doesn't move.

Marcus   I thought you wanted to go.

She nods. But still she doesn't move.

What?

Dior   I could take you to him. D'you want me to take you to him?

Marcus *looks at her. Nods.*

Blackout.

Prison Nail Room

A few weeks earlier.

Joanne *is having her nails done by another inmate,* **Jadenne***. She sits with her hands in little bowls of water as* **Jadenne** *picks and files away.*

Jadenne   You got quite tough cuticles.

Joanne   Have I?

Jadenne   Done a lot of manual labour?

Joanne   I ain't never done a day's work in my life.

Jadenne   Proper little princess, aren't you?

Joanne   Let's get one thing straight, yeah? Read these. (*She indicates her lips.*) Don't come on to me.

Jadenne   Come on to you?

Joanne   Read these. (*Indicates lips again.*)

Jadenne   And why would I do that?

Joanne   I know what I look like. And I've heard stories about you.

Jadenne   I've heard stories about you, Briggsy.

Joanne   My name's Joanne.

Jadenne   Don't necessarily mean they're true. So. Let's get another thing straight, yeah? I ain't gonna come on to no one.

Joanne   My boyfriend Siddie hears about this, he'll do his nut.

Jadenne   I heard he'd been banged up an' all. What's he gonna do? Send me bad vibes?

Joanne   I know you've been badmouthing me.

Jadenne   So why come and get your nails done?

Joanne   Wanted to see you close up. See what you looked like. See you tremble.

Jadenne   Do I look scared?

Joanne   You're shaking. Not very impressive when you work with your hands, is it?

Jadenne   Maybe I was on the vodka last night. Maybe I was off my head. I get so bored, Briggsy. You know what it's like in here.

Pause.

What do you do when you get bored, Briggsy?

Joanne   I don't answer to that name. You want me to speak? You speak to me proper.

Jadenne   D'you go round murdering little gayboys? Is that how you get your kicks?

Joanne *pulls her hands away.*

Joanne   D'you know what?

She stands.

I think my hands are fine as they are.

Jadenne   Thought you was hard-faced, Joanne.

Joanne   Me? Soft as butter, darlin'.

Jadenne *laughs.*

Joanne   Don't laugh at me, mate. I'll cut you up.

Jadenne   You is well rinsed.

Joanne   Eh?

Jadenne   Man, you are so easy to wind up.

Joanne   I can't be doing with your head games.

Jadenne   You are hilarious. God, talk about paranoid.

Joanne   I ain't paranoid. You're paranoid. You've got fifteen personalities. You're schizophrenic.

Jadenne   And you ain't got a sense of humour.

Joanne   I have. I'm well funny.

Jadenne   Then see I was just having a laugh, and stick your hands back in the water.

Joanne   What, you was being funny?

Jadenne   I should do stand-up.

Joanne   That was your idea of a laugh?

Jadenne   Okay, so it backfired. Whatever. Look, go if you want. But I've only done one of your hands. You might look a bit weird.

Joanne *considers it. Then sits, and puts her hands back in the water.*

Joanne   I am funny. A lot of people say I'm the funniest person they ever met.

Jadenne   Yeah?

Joanne   Word.

Jadenne   Bit of hard skin there. Cut that out. No problemo.

Joanne   Are you wanting to be my mate? Is that what's happening here? Are you giving me some kind o' test? Is that it?

Jadenne *chuckles. She has pulled out some small scissors.*

Jadenne   Just keep your hand there.

Joanne   Is you tryina be my mate?

Jadenne *chuckles.*

Joanne   Did I pass?

Jadenne *makes a sudden lunge and stabs* **Joanne***'s hand with the scissors. Grabs the hand with the other one and stabs it again. Blood spurts everywhere.* **Joanne** *shrieks and jumps up.*

Jadenne   I wouldn't be your mate if you were the last person on this earth.

Joanne   What d'you do that for, you fucking bitch?

Jadenne   Cos the rumours were right. I am like him. And next time you step anywhere near me, I'll stab your fucking throat.

Joanne   You're mental.

Jadenne   And you better watch your back.

Joanne   And you . . . wanna check your facts, bitch.

Jadenne   Come back any time. For a facial. I'll make sure I get some battery acid in.

Joanne   You'll be in solitary for this.

Jadenne   I can be wherever I want. Cos at least I can sleep at night. Can you, Joanne? Can you? Eh?

Joanne *considers this. She steps closer to* **Jadenne**.

Joanne   What he did. Wasn't normal. You think I lose sleep over that? I don't lie in my cell crying, Jadenne. I sit there wetting myself. One less crawling the planet. You think you're taking over, but you're not. Cos for every one of you, there's ten of me.

Jadenne   You're the one who's not normal.

Joanne   Think people like your lot? They don't. They're acting. We're sick of you. Banging on about shit. I'm just a bit more up front about it.

She walks out. **Jadenne** *stands there seething.*

Prison

A few months earlier.

Cyprus *sits with* **Siddie**, *who is banged up.*

Siddie   We killed a batty, so what? He deserved it. He made the moves on Scott. Scott's like blood to me. You cross Scott, you cross me. But Scott's a pussy. He thinks too much. Sees the good. Gives second chances. So he needed a hand. To put the batty in his place.

Cyprus   Keep your voice down, Siddie. Don't let them hear you say nothing.

Siddie   Say what I like. Ain't no one gonna do nothing in here. No one's arsed.

Cyprus   You pleading guilty then?

Siddie   Nah man. Then they might just do me for manslaughter. Not the homophobic shit. You get more if it's the gay-killing shit. And I might get off. No witnesses.

Cyprus   No. No witnesses.

Siddie   Did you burn the pram?

Cyprus   Yeah.

He nods.

I took the baby out first.

Siddie   Joanne woulda been all right if she hadn't shown off on Facebook.

Cyprus   Silly bitch. But she loves you.

Siddie   Thinks she loves me.

Cyprus   No, she does. She really loves you. Soul mates, she reckons.

Siddie   I don't want it.

Cyprus   I don't think you got much choice. When she decides something.

Siddie   I have got choice. Life's all about choices.

Cyprus   So you chose to be here?

Siddie   One way or another.

Pause.

Cyprus   You scared me, Siddie. You all did. I didn't know that was gonna happen. I just thought you was gonna scare him.

Siddie   Is Joanne keeping her mouth shut about . . . the other one?

Cyprus   Yeah. Think so.

Siddie   I wanna protect him. I owe him.

Cyprus   D'you feel bad, Siddie?

Siddie   I feel jealous.

Cyprus   Jealous?

Siddie   Darren's where I wanna be.

Pause.

Cyprus   Then maybe you shoulda just killed yourself.

Siddie   When we went for the hearing. All Joanne done was cry.

Cyprus   I know. She's real good at it. Says she should be in *EastEnders*.

Siddie   I don't cry. I've never cried. When I was a kid I used to tear open my skin. Blood came easier than tears. I don't cry for me. Cos me don't deserve it. Whatever shit people have done to me. Me deserved it.

Cyprus   I don't like it when you talk like this.

Siddie   I don't care what you like or don't like.

Cyprus   Have you told them?

Siddie (*nods*)   That's why I might get off. But that night, Cyprus. That night. I dream about it. I think about it. That night, I felt . . . I dunno. Alive. So many times. So many times I'm floating. Above me. Watching.

Cyprus   That's all the bloody spliff you smoke. The weed and the pills.

Siddie   Apart from me. But that night. I was myself.

Cyprus   It's not good for your head. Not good for anyone's head.

Pause.

Have you told them about your mum?

Siddie   What about her?

Cyprus   How she kept killing herself so you'd go into care.

Siddie   I laid it on with a spade that big. I'm gonna be fine, Cyprus. Sweet as. Only thing I feel bad about. Is opening the family secrets. To get myself off. Everyone loves a sob story. But what can I do?

Cyprus   It's like the *X Factor*.

Siddie   Don't feel sorry for Darren, Cyprus.

Cyprus   I don't. What he done to Scott was disgusting. It was sick. It weren't normal.

Siddie   He humiliated him. And I know a thing or two about that. That's my trigger. My turning point.

Cyprus   Did you come up with that?

Siddie   Social worker. Good innit?

Cyprus *nods.*

Siddie   I've been vulnerable. I decided never to be vulnerable again.

Cyprus   Have you got your own telly?

Siddie   What happened to me when I was a kid. Was like a trauma. Lying inside me. Lying in my cells. Waiting to explode. They say it was only a matter of time.

Cyprus   Joanne's had her nails done. And her hair. She looks amazing. I don't think she's ever been happier.

Siddie   Life o' Riley, innit?

Cyprus   But you can't be happy, Siddie.

Siddie   Says who?

Cyprus   It'd do my nut in if I was here.

Siddie   Here makes sense. Here I belong. Here I know what I gotta do. I like it here. It's like . . . three rooms away from death.

The alarm goes for the end of visiting time.

Dior's Back Garden

A year earlier.

A washing line across the stage. **Dior** *comes on with a laundry basket of clothes and starts pegging them out. She is nervous, agitated, and the task unsettles her. She stops, takes a deep breath, then carries on hanging the clothes out. Most notable on the line is a blue tracksuit top and jeans. Just then,* **Scott** *comes out in boxers and a tee shirt.*

Scott   Dior, come to bed.

Dior   You expect me to sleep?

Scott   Please.

Dior   You expect me to sleep, Scott? After what happened tonight?

Scott   You don't have to do that.

Dior   Are you stupid? I do have to do this.

Scott   It's gonna look suspicious.

Dior   More suspicious if I'd left it. Now keep your voice down. You'll wake my mum.

Scott   Dior, please.

He looks about.

There's something burning. On the wasteland. Stinks.

He looks back to her.

Dior, talk to me. I'm scared.

Dior   We've been to a party. Spilt a drink. Smelt of smoke. So soon as I got back, I wanted the clothes washed. Simples.

Scott   People will see. It's half one in the morning. It is not normal to be putting stuff on the line at half one in the morning.

Dior   Normal. You think I know what normal is any more, Scott?

Scott Come to bed.

Dior You go to bed, you're obsessed.

Scott *looks around, seeing if anyone can see them.*

Scott No lights on.

Dior Spilt a drink. Smelt of smoke. Had to get them washed.

Scott Think we're all right.

Dior Didn't want to leave it till morning. Couldn't leave it till morning. I'm like that.

Scott I think we're gonna be all right.

Dior Three steps from the top. Creaks. Loud. Don't tread on it.

Scott Don't be long.

Dior Scott. What was he doing in the school?

Scott What you asking me for?

Dior But why did he go there?

Scott I don't know.

Dior Promise?

Scott Promise.

Dior Three steps from the top. Be careful.

He nods and heads inside. She finishes hanging the washing up. Then sinks to her knees and clutches the laundry basket, gasping for air. Just then, **Cyprus** *runs on.*

Cyprus You didn't see nothing.

Dior Fuck off, Cyprus.

Cyprus You didn't see nothing. Joanne told me to tell you. Open your mouth and she'll cut you up.

Dior *stands. She runs over and slaps* **Cyprus** *round the face.* **Cyprus** *gasps. Rubs her face.*

Dior   Get out of my face.

Cyprus   You didn't see nothing!

Dior *picks up the basket and heads inside.* **Cyprus** *runs off.*

The Old School

Earlier that night.

Darren *walks on, slightly lost, unsure where he is.*

Darren   Scott? It's me, Darren. Scott I got your text. Scott?

A torch goes on and **Scott** *is waiting for him. He is wearing the tracksuit top and jeans that were hanging on the line in the previous scene.*

Scott   All right?

Darren   Jeez, you scared the life out of me then.

Scott   Who d'you think it'd be? *(Gently.)* Knobhead.

Darren   Wasn't sure if it was a wind-up. It's a funny place to ask me to come.

Scott   Didn't want Dior knowing innit.

Darren   Is she still at the party?

Scott   Yeah.

Darren   You should be there. It's your party.

Scott   Something came up.

Darren   I told you you'd change your mind. I mean I didn't think it'd be this quick, but. *(Quickly.)* I'm not complaining.

He looks around.

This is our old geography room. Mr Evans stood here. Shouting at us to shut up. You trying to leave early. But I'd tied the straps of your rucksack to the chair.

Scott   Proper little joker, in't you?

Darren   I . . . I can't believe this is happening.

He jumps.

Scott   What's up?

Darren   Nothing. Thought I heard something.

Scott   Don't be daft. No one's gonna find us here.

Darren   No, I definitely heard something. Maybe this wasn't a good idea.

Scott   No, don't go.

Off, we hear **Dior** *calling out.*

Dior (*off*)   Scott?

Scott *panics.*

Darren   That's Dior.

Scott   I know my own girlfriend's voice.

Darren   We better get back. Sorry. I can't do this.

Scott   She ain't gonna come in the school, is she?

Darren   I thought I could but . . . Come on, let's go back to the party.

Siddie   I don't think that's such a good idea.

Darren *turns.* **Siddie**, **Joanne** *and* **Cyprus** *have come in.* **Cyprus** *has a big, blue, old-fashioned pram with her.*

Darren   Eh?

Siddie   What you two doing here then?

Darren   Oh we were just. Mucking about. Then got lost.

Joanne   You're not lost. This is our old school. You know your way round here like the back of your hand.

Darren   Not in the dark.

Joanne   Read these. (*Indicates lips.*) You are not lost.

Darren   Well, we're not now. Joanne, no, cos you can show us the way back.

Siddie   Yeah, but what were you doing here in the first place?

Darren   Nothing. Were we, Scott?

Joanne   Don't ask him.

Siddie   No, don't ask him.

Darren   I don't . . .

Siddie   Is your name Darren Williams cos you're into willy?

Darren   Piss off, I don't even know you.

Joanne   Yes, you do.

Darren   Yeah, I've seen him but I don't know him.

Siddie   Bit lippy, the battio, eh?

Darren   I ain't no battio.

Siddie   Phone.

Cyrus *gets a phone out of the pram.*

Joanne   Battio looks scared.

Darren   I ain't scared.

Siddie *shows* **Darren** *the phone.*

Siddie   These not your pictures?

Darren   They are my pictures, yes. But I still ain't no battio. Cos I don't like the word battio.

Siddie   Dress it up how you like. How d'you think it made him feel?

Darren   I dunno.

Siddie   Think.

Darren   Turned on?

Siddie *hits him round the face with the phone, knocking* **Darren** *to the ground.*

Siddie   Battio thinks he's funny. Battio not funny.

Darren   Stop calling me that. You ain't even black.

Siddie   I know I'm not fucking black. What, you think I'm blind? You think I'm incapable of looking in a mirror?

Darren   No.

Siddie   We thought we'd got rid of you.

Joanne   Thought we'd got rid of the faggot.

Siddie   But you had to come back.

Darren   Cos Scott come out of prison. I just . . .

And again, **Dior** *calls, off.*

Dior   Scott? Scott? Can you hear me?

Darren   I can hear you, Dior! Dior, help me! I'm in here!

He makes to get up, but **Siddie** *kicks him back down.*

Siddie   You keep your fucking voice down, you get me? Battios wanna be seen and not heard.

Darren   Dior!!

Dior *(off)*   Darren?! Where are you?!

Joanne   Kick the faggot in the head. Shut him up good and proper.

Darren *(to* **Scott***)*   Aren't you gonna help me?

Siddie   No one's gonna help you, mate.

Darren   Mate? I'm not your mate. You're all sick.

Siddie *pulls a knife from the pram.* **Cyprus** *had no idea it was there.*

Darren   What d'you think you're doing? You don't know me.

Siddie   You go round bumming lads. Little bumder. And you say I'm sick?

Darren   Not just you.

He stands.

Scott   What you doing, Siddie?

Joanne   Cut him, Siddie. Cut the battio.

Darren   I'm not scared of you.

Siddie   Oh, but you should be, Darren. You should be.

Darren *makes a dash for the door.* **Joanne** *trips him.* **Siddie** *plunges the knife into* **Darren***'s back.* **Darren** *screams.*

Siddie   You stupid queer faggot. Don't you ever call me sick again.

Joanne   Look at his eyes. Look at his fucking gay eyes.

She kicks **Darren** *in the head.* **Siddie** *stands back to admire his handiwork.*

Darren   What did I ever do to . . . ? I don't know . . .

Joanne   Oh, fucking shut up.

And she kicks him again. His voice is small now.

Darren   Tomorrow.

Joanne   Oh, shut up, fag twat.

Darren *is dying now.*

Darren   Tomorrow . . .

Siddie *plunges the knife in again.*

Siddie   Bit lippy, the battio.

Darren *struggles for breath and then his struggle ceases. Silence.*

Scott   What the fuck have you done, Siddie?

Siddie   Defended you, my friend. Defended you from the dark arts. Delivered you from evil.

Joanne   Battio's quiet.

Dior (*off, getting nearer*)   Scott?!

Cyprus   We should go.

Siddie *rolls* **Darren** *over so he is lying on his back. It is quite clear he is dead now.*

Siddie   Fucking leg it.

As **Siddie**, **Joanne** *and* **Cyprus** *run (***Cyprus** *taking the pram),* **Scott** *kneels and takes* **Darren** *in his arms.* **Dior** *comes in.*

Dior   Scott? What's going on? Scott?

Scott *kisses* **Darren** *on the forehead.*

Scott   Darren.

Dior   Scott, who done this?

Scott   Daz.

Dior   Scott, come on. We need to get out of here.

Scott   I didn't do anything.

Dior   You've just come out of prison, Scott. Come on.

She holds out her hand.

Scott   I messed him up. I said I would.

Dior   Come on, Scott.

Scott   I'm sorry, Daz.

He rests **Darren** *down. He stands. He takes* **Dior***'s hand and they run.*

Outside Scott's House

Earlier that evening.

A party is going on inside. Music blaring out. **Dior** *enters with*
Joanne *and* **Cyprus**, *walking down the street, heading to the party.*
Cyprus *is pushing the blue pram.*

Joanne   I hate your new pram. It's so gay.

Cyprus   It really hurts my arms.

Joanne   It's like a tank. What soldiers go in when they're
shooting and shit.

Cyprus   I know, it's a right show-up, man.

Joanne   I'm amazed I allowed myself to walk down the
street with you.

Cyprus   You're amazing, Joanne.

Joanne   Now I am liking what his mum's done with the
house.

Cyprus   His mum's gone away.

Joanne   I am liking the look of it. It's very fashion-forward.

Cyprus (*to* **Dior**)   Have you heard the latest? She is gonna
be an interior decorator.

Joanne   Designer. And I ain't gonna be. I am.

Cyprus   No, you're not. You ain't nothing.

Joanne   Your bedroom would not be your bedroom
without me.

Cyprus   You told me to move my cabinet.

Joanne   Read these. (*Indicates lips.*) Think before you speak.

Cyprus   You all right, Dior? D'you feel bad for dumping
him?

Dior   I'm just tired.

Joanne You're always saying that. I'm fucking bored of it.
'Ooh I'm tired. Ooh I'm tired. I work all day. Been on my
feet all day. I'm fucking tired.' Read these. (*Indicates lips.*) You
ain't got a job.

Dior I have.

Joanne Do you get paid?

Dior I'm not speaking to you.

Joanne Do you get a wage packet?

Cyprus Leave her alone, Joanne.

Dior I'm not sinking to your level.

Joanne Are you still on benefits?

Dior I didn't have no choice. Anyway, there might be a job
for me at the end of it. A proper one.

Joanne It's slave labour.

Dior Don't get political, Joanne. You thought Barack
Obama was where the squaddies were housed.

Cyprus I really fancy Barack Obama.

Dior (*to* **Joanne**)   I don't suppose he's gangsta enough for
you, is he?

Joanne D'you know what, Dior? I don't actually care.
Now. How do I look?

Cyprus She's gonna pull Siddie tonight.

Joanne I'm on a promise.

Dior I know. I read it on Facebook.

Joanne No harm in looking keen.

Dior 'Which bra should I choose? Siddie?'

Joanne He chose, mate.

Cyprus   Them pictures was well nice. I wish I had your boobs.

Joanne   Siddie thinks they should be bigger. When I'm eighteen I'm gonna get 'em done. He really likes the fake look? Right. Wish me luck.

Cyprus   Are you nervous, Dior?

Dior   I'm just tired.

Scott *comes out from the house.*

Scott   Dior!

Dior   All right, Scott. Welcome home.

Cyprus   Yeah, nice one, Scott. Getting out of prison and that. It's well good.

Joanne   Scott, is Siddie here?

Scott   Kitchen.

And **Joanne** *hurries in.*

Scott   You look lovely.

Dior   Who d'you think I am?

Scott   I'm sorry.

Dior   Sending me texts like that. It's disgusting. I know you've been banged up and not getting it, but I'm not Joanne.

Scott   Joanne?

Dior   She's always sending pictures of her tits to lads. You should see her pictures on Facebook. Fanny hanging out. She's got no shame. I'm not like her.

Scott   I know.

Scott *looks to* **Cyprus**, *who has got a bag of crisps out of the pram and has started to eat them.*

Scott   Cyprus, can we . . . have a minute?

Cyprus   Can't leave the baby.

Scott   Well, take him inside.

Cyprus   Pram won't fit through the door.

Scott   Fuck's sake, we'll keep an eye on him. Get inside.

Cyprus   All right.

She goes into the house. **Scott** *looks to* **Dior**.

Dior   I seen your text coming through. Stacking shelves.
I thought, 'Oh it's gonna be romantic.' But oh no.

Scott   What can I say?

Dior   'Show me what I've been missing. Send pics.' If that's
the sort of girlfriend you want, Scott, then I'm glad I ended it.
I got pride.

Scott   It was a mistake. I knew it was a mistake minute I
sent it. I was like, 'Oh no. What have I done?'

Dior   Pissed me off good and proper.

Scott   There's worse things I could do.

Dior   Nothing's secret any more. Screen-grabs and print
screening and . . . it all comes back to bite you on the arse.

Scott   I missed you. When I was away. Thought about you
all the time.

Dior   Shoulda kept in touch with Joanne. She'da sent you
pics as one for the bank.

Scott   I don't fancy Joanne.

Dior   She thinks you're some kind of hero.

Scott   I don't love Joanne.

Pause.

And you?

Dior   Me what?

Scott   What do you think?

Dior   You know what I think.

Scott   Some kind of knob.

Dior   No.

Scott   Ski-glove wanker.

Dior   Stop trying to make me laugh.

Scott   I know what I did was a show-up.

Dior   I know. I know. You've done your time. Careful. You'll turn into a country and western song in a minute.

Scott   I know you don't think I'm serious. Scared of commitment.

Dior   Think? Know.

Scott   But what if I said I was serious?

Dior   It's one thing saying it.

Scott   So what if I said. Marry me.

Dior   Are you taking the piss?

Scott   Do I look like I'm taking the piss?

Dior   Are you drunk?

Scott   No.

Dior   Are you mashed?

Scott   No. D'you hate yourself that much that you don't reckon I'm being genuine?

Dior   You always do it. You always mess with my head.

Scott   No rush. Think about it.

Dior   We're a bit young.

Scott   So you're considering it?

Dior   We're too young.

Scott   Consider it.

Dior   I'm gonna get a drink. Want one?

He nods. She heads inside. He stands there, looking up at the sky. Presently **Darren** *enters.*

Darren   Welcome home, Riot Boy. You get my text?

Scott   Yeah, mate.

Darren   Well, as you asked so nicely.

Scott   Bit of a close shave. Sent it Dior by mistake. She weren't happy. You're next to each other in my phone. Both begin with D.

Darren   What's going on with you two? I heard she dumped you when you were found guilty.

Scott   Think she's taking me back.

Darren   Oh, right. Brilliant.

Scott   In fact, Darren, I just proposed to her.

Darren   You what?

Scott   I asked her to marry me.

Darren   And what did she say?

Scott   She's gonna think about it.

Darren   So she didn't say no then?

Scott   I love her, Daz. You know I love her. You know it's complicated.

Darren   You're only eighteen.

Scott   So?

Darren   And you're throwing your life away? Just like that?

Scott   You've never liked Dior.

Darren   She doesn't like me. I think she knows.

Scott   That's in your head. Please, Darren. You knew this was on the cards. Can't you be happy for me?

Darren   What difference would it make if I wasn't?

Scott   Daz.

Darren   Don't call me that. Don't.

Pause.

I just wonder how long it'll take you to come to your senses. I just wonder how long it'll be before I get the text that says 'Meet me'.

Scott   You know what the score is.

Darren   That text'll come. I know it will. You don't, but I do.

Scott   I've never led you on.

Darren   Oh, really? Who was the first person you texted when you stepped outside that jail?

Pause.

I rest my case.

Scott   I just want you to be happy for me.

Darren   I bet they laughed. When your picture came up on the news. In the papers. Coming out of that shop with ski-gloves on. The ski-gloves boy. And that's how they see you. Not me.

Scott   I got caught up in the heat of the moment.

Darren   Huh, you do that a lot.

Scott   Shut up.

Darren   But one of them grassed you up. Someone in there. I never. Oh, d'you know what? I can't do this.

And he starts to walk away.

Scott   Where you going?

Darren   I took a weekend off work for this.

Scott   Stay. Have a drink. You're here now.

Darren   I'm gonna see my mum. Early night. May as well go back to the camp tomorrow. Take care of yourself, Scott. Last time I told you to do that, you didn't.

Scott   Darren.

Darren   What?

Pause.

Scott   If you ever need some ski-gloves.

Darren *smiles. Just then* **Siddie** *comes out. He watches them.*

Darren   Off your head, you.

And he walks off. **Scott** *watches him go, sadly.* **Siddie** *approaches* **Scott** *with a drink for him.*

Siddie   You and me need to talk.

Scott *takes the drink. Looks at* **Siddie**.

Scott   Why?

Siddie   We need to do something about him.

He indicates where **Darren** *exited.* **Scott** *takes a sip of his drink.*

Inside Scott's House

Earlier that day.

Troy *comes on struggling with a box of lagers.* **Siddie** *rushes to help him.*

Siddie   You shoulda said. I'da come with you.

Troy   Good workout for me, this. He's coming down the street.

Siddie   Is he?

Troy   I seen him.

Siddie   Is he wearing ski-gloves?

Troy   He's wearing skis.

Siddie   No!

Troy   Rinsed.

Siddie   Cheeky fucker. Was no one picking him up?

Troy   No one *to* pick him up.

Siddie   I'da picked him up.

Troy   What with? Your bare hands?

Siddie   Well, at least we're giving him a party.

Troy   I feel bad now. I'm his brother. I shoulda made sure he was picked up.

Just then **Scott** *comes in. He carries a sports bag over his shoulder.*

Scott   What's going on here, then?

Troy   Scottie!

Troy *runs and hugs him.* **Scott** *drops his bag.*

Troy   Missed you, mate.

Scott   It was nice getting some peace and quiet without you.

Troy   Jokes!

Scott   What you doing here, Siddie?

Siddie   Been kipping here for a bit.

Scott   What?

Troy   When Mum and Dad went away.

Siddie   It's only been a week, mate. I ain't nicked anything.

Troy   We've had a laugh.

Scott   It's not a dosshouse.

Siddie   And now you're back, I'll make myself scarce. All right? Jeez. Touchy since you went away, eh?

Troy   We're gonna have a party. Tonight. It was Siddie's idea. Welcome you home.

Scott   And what if I don't want a party? What if I don't feel like a party?

Siddie   I got supplies. Guaranteed a good time.

Scott *sighs.*

Scott   I need a shower. I stink of that place. Wanna wash it off me.

Siddie   Few hours from now, mate. You'll have forgotten all about the last few months.

Scott *heads off and upstairs, leaving his bag on the floor.*

Siddie   Cheeky bastard. I think your brother has a very short memory.

Troy   He's only just got in. Must be weird.

Siddie   People. They forget. Everything. But I suppose. Big things for me. Ain't big things for other people. Massive for me. Little for him.

Troy   What you on about now? Have you had a spliff?

Siddie   Social workers came. Mum'd tried to top herself again. Scott was round playing. One of the neighbours took him as the social took me. And he broke away and he head-butted the bird who had hold of me.

Troy   Nutter.

Siddie   For one of the few times in my life, I felt someone wanted me. No strings attached. Not cos of what they could get from me. Or make me do. But just cos they . . . thought I was all right. Knew one day I'd pay him back.

Troy   The party.

Siddie   The party.

Just then **Scott***'s phone beeps in his bag. They both look at it. It beeps again, and again.*

Siddie   Someone is mega-texting your bro. Some bitch wanting a booty call. I bet. Have a look.

Troy   I know his passcode as well.

He gets the phone out. They giggle.

Unless he's changed it.

He enters a number in the phone.

No, he hasn't.

They both peer over the phone, giggling. After a while the giggling stops. **Siddie** *looks horrified.*

Siddie   Which dirty queer bastard sent him that?

They look. The lights fade.

Hilltop

Six months earlier.

Darren *and* **Scott** *sit on a picnic blanket on a hill overlooking the sea, having a makeshift picnic.*

Darren   Don't hog the Monster Munch.

Scott   There's three bags.

Darren   Brilliant view.

Scott   Same as from the estate, only shunted a bit.

Darren   I've had such a nice time.

Scott   Don't be soft.

Darren   I'm just so glad you came.

Scott   A change is as good as a rest.

Darren   Will you come again?

Scott   I dunno. Might be a bit hard. We'll see.

Darren   D'you feel bad on Dior?

Scott   Can we talk about something else?

Darren   My shift starts in an hour. What you gonna do?

Scott   Meant to be going staying with my cousin in London. It's . . . like round Croydon way. I don't even know where that is.

Darren   You wanna be careful. Everyone's going mad.

Scott   I can look after myself.

Darren   I like it when you look after me.

Scott   Don't talk like that.

Darren   Like what?

Scott   You know like what, it's nuts.

Darren   You didn't mind me talking like it last night.

Scott   It's different in the night.

Darren   What d'you think to the camp?

Scott   It's not exactly Disneyland.

Darren *laughs.*

Darren   I like it. People who stay like it.

Scott   We used to come as kids.

Darren   I know.

Scott   Nick a car. Drive down. Bunk in when the bloke weren't looking.

Darren   I know.

Scott   Hour before closing. Have a go on all the rides for free.

Darren   It's different now, though.

Scott   Yeah, well. We all grow up.

Darren   You look so sad. Is that cos you've got to leave me? Cos I've got to do my shift? Cos you've got to go to London?

Scott   It's just my face, innit.

Darren   And what a face.

Scott   Darren.

Darren   If you wanna know the truth, the place is falling apart. My manager says she don't think the place'll be open next year. No one's got no money to go on holiday any more. And everyone's so fed up with having no money that when they get a couple of hundred quid together, they wanna go somewhere hot. Not here. So each weekend just the sight of sad slappers in L-plates and veils getting off their faces and pissing in the bushes. Blokes on the rampage in fancy dress. Could be any town in the country but they pay forty quid a night for the privilege. I know everyone thinks I'm the lucky one. Got off my arse and went half-hour down the road and found a job. But a year from now I could be back home and twiddling my thumbs.

Marcus *enters. He watches them for a while.*

Marcus   Darren.

Darren *looks over.*

Darren   All right?

Marcus   Been looking all over for you. Texted.

Darren   Phone's on silent.

Marcus   I wanted to say goodbye.

Darren   Oh, right.

Marcus   Who's this?

Darren   This is Scott.

Scott   All right?

Marcus   Hi.

Darren   Marcus.

Marcus   I looked for you last night but . . .

Darren   We went out. I know Scott from home. From school.

Marcus   Anyone would think you were avoiding me.

Darren   No. So you go today?

Marcus   Train's in an hour.

Darren   I don't want to make you late.

Marcus   And I can't make you change your mind?

Darren   No. You know that'd be wrong.

Marcus   You'll keep in touch?

Darren   Course. You take care of yourself now, yeah?

Marcus   I'll write. Tell you all about the fabulous time I'm having. Take care of yourself, Darren.

Darren   And you.

Marcus   Take care.

Darren *nods.* **Marcus** *leaves sadly.* **Darren** *sits, thoughtful.*

Scott   Heartbreaker.

Darren   He's going away on the cruise ships. Said he could get me a job on them too.

Scott   Why didn't you? What's keeping you here?

Darren   Do you really have to ask?

Scott   You don't like him?

Darren   No, he's all right.

Scott   Bit of a briefcase-wanker?

Darren　He's not you.

Scott　This. This is the stuff kids do. This is messing about.

Darren　I'm seventeen.

Scott　I come out here and see you and it's not real. Back there is.

Darren　This is real. It's just you're too scared to accept it.

Scott　I can't make you happy, Darren.

Darren　But don't you see? You do.

Scott　I mess you up.

Darren　You don't have to.

Scott　I always will. I send you a text, then delete it. I get in your bed, then blank you in the street. It's not good for me and it's not good for you.

Darren　Then tell her.

Scott　I can't. Can't even tell myself. It's all right for you, but I don't wanna be different. I can't be like that. I wanna be like everyone else. You don't. And being different. It gets me. Scares me. It fits you, though.

Darren　We're not different.

Scott *looks away.*

Darren　Anyway, who cares about different? Or normal. Why can't we just be, I dunno, happy?

Scott　You shoulda gone with him.

Darren　How you getting to London?

Scott　Croydon. Coach.

Darren　You wanna be careful.

Scott　Will you stop saying that?

Darren   I know what your cousin's like. And it's all kicking off up there.

Scott   It'll be a laugh.

Darren   I wish I was getting on a coach with you. Going somewhere. Anywhere.

Scott   Don't.

Darren   Let's do it. Let's run away. I'm serious. You and me.

Scott   Where?

Darren   Somewhere we can lose ourselves. I've saved a grand and a half. I'll take care of you. We'll be all right.

Scott   We can't.

Darren   Get on a coach. See where it takes us. Find a little flat.

Scott   What, you and me?

Darren   Find some work.

Scott (*chuckles*)   Now I know you really are taking the piss.

Darren   I'm serious.

Scott   And I'm a coward.

Darren *settles down again.*

Darren   I want it to be night again. You don't care then. I can say whatever I like then, and you agree. Or laugh.

Scott   That's the beer, innit.

They sit in silence for a while, eating. Drinking.

D'you hate me?

Darren   Yesterday the dishwashers packed in. All at the same time. Major drama. But instead of chucking money at it and getting 'em fixed, they're making us wash everything by hand. The new routine. Have to go out and collect the dirty plates. Take them back to our station. Then wait our turn to use the platewash. It's this old thing with brushes sticking out the water. You rub the plate on it and – Well, it ain't much fun for me. Cos I'm third station from the platewash. So by the time I get there the water's filthy. My manager, she goes: 'Don't worry Darren. This time next year, you could be first station from the platewash.' But I just know. That isn't going to happen.

Scott   I'll always mess you up.

Darren   You don't know what's around the corner.

Scott   I will.

Darren   You can be feeling lousy. Shit. But the next day everything's all right.

Scott   Darren.

Darren   So anytime I feel crap, I just tell myself.

Scott   I'll always mess you up.

Darren   Tomorrow. Tomorrow I'll be happy.

Pause.

Don't hog the Monster Munch.

Scott *offers him the bag. They eat in silence as the lights fade.*

Tomorrow I'll Be Happy

BY JONATHAN HARVEY

*Notes on rehearsal and staging, drawn from a workshop
with the writer held at the National Theatre, November 2012*

How the writer came to write the play

Jonathan Harvey: 'I wanted to write a play for young people
that spoke to them about their lives now. On top of that I was
interested in why homophobic hate crimes happen, why
people are so scared of things that are 'different' from them.
I was particularly interested in how a hateful crime such as
this might affect a group of friends. Especially if they were
somehow involved.'

Approaching the play

Jonathan said the play is about difference and the bravery
and fear associated with being different.

Structure

The timeline is significant: the play happens in reverse order.
It was suggested by the director Hettie McDonald that the
play would benefit immensely from being rehearsed in the
correct chronological order before being put back into the
way it is written. This will help make the logic of the play
crystal clear to the company.

Production

The workshop explored the key challenges that the play poses
to a director. A number of exercises were undertaken to
address the challenges which felt most significant in this piece.

Key events

In the play there are scenes we see and scenes we don't see.
In groups the workshop participants made lists of possible
events key to the plot that happen in between the written
scenes. Here is what was generated. We began by putting the
scenes in chronological order.

1. HILLTOP

- Scott gets caught up in the riots and goes to jail.
- Dior dumps Scott.
- Siddie moves into Scott's house.
- Scott accidentally sends text to Dior.
- Dior receives the text.
- Scott has been on the TV news a lot.

2. INTERIOR. SCOTT'S HOUSE – 3:15 P.M.

- Joanne puts photos of her bra on Facebook.
- Conversation between Troy and Siddie about the photos
  on the phone.
- Scott sees pictures.

3. SCOTT PROPOSES TO DIOR – 8:12 P.M.
- Siddie takes the phone.
- Siddie and Scott agree a plan.
- Siddie recruits Joanne and Cyprus.
- Siddie plants the knife.
- Scott texts Darren about school.
- Dior can't find Scott.

4. SCHOOL – MIDNIGHT
- Dior gets Scott home.
- Siddie tells Cyprus to burn the pram.

- Cyprus burns the pram.
- Joanne tells Cyprus to silence Dior.
- Dior washes the clothes.

5. EXTERIOR. DIOR'S HOUSE
- Body found.
- All either arrested or questioned.
- Joanne brags on Facebook.
- Dior accepts proposal.
- Cyprus writes to Joanne.
- Joanne and Siddie on remand.
- Marcus tries to get in touch with Darren.
- Cyprus visits Joanne.
- Funeral.
- Dior gets pregnant.
- Lots of press coverage.
- Dior maybe phones police to tell them Darren is dead.

6. PRISON
- Trial happens – convictions. (What are they convicted of?)
- Cyprus and Joanne lose touch.
- Cyprus and Dior's relationship develops.
- Wedding plans are made.
- Darren's Facebook page trolled and taken down.

7. PRISON
- Scott goes to Darren's house.
- Cyprus and Dior become friends.
- Joanne and Cyprus stand off.
- Joanne has a makeover.
- Caravan booked for honeymoon.
- New-found closeness between Scott's family.

8. PUB WEDDING

- Marcus goes wherever it is he's staying.
- Marcus and Dior plan how and where to meet the following day.
- Wedding night.
- Dior asks Scott about Marcus.
- Cyprus and MC Alibi get together.
- Marcus looks up murder on the internet.

9. GRAVEYARD

Characters

The workshop participants asked Jonathan a number of questions about characters in the play:

How do you see the characters?

I see Darren as a dreamer; Marcus as a bit posher and older (someone with a different way of life to the world of the rest of the characters); Dior as a beacon of sanity though she is not without conflicts; and Scott as being scared of being different and doing anything to fit in. Troy is a nice little brother; Siddie could be played as a monster but it's probably more interesting to go against this; Joanne would do anything for her man; and Cyprus is a sweet little thing, very susceptible to peer pressure because she is a people-pleaser.

Who is the central protagonist?

I used to think it was Darren but now I think the most interesting journey is Scott's. (Hettie MacDonald suggested that all the characters are important but identifying your protagonist is very important in terms of orientating your story.)

Is Scott gay?

Probably, but he hasn't worked it out. He would have great difficulty articulating that himself. Part of the sadness of the play is that Darren might have helped him work it out.

Does Scott use Dior as a cover for his feelings towards men?

It is not as simple as that.

Dior is the calm one but she has panic attacks – how does that fit together?

She has a lot of pressure on her – she knows what happened and colluded with Scott. I think of her as like a swan – gliding along but kicking like crazy underneath the surface.

What is Siddie's back-story?

He has definitely been abandoned by his mother and so has difficulty forming attachments. He has also been abused. When I was researching I read a lot about neglect and the impact this has. However, though this is part of his character it should not be as simple as 'he abuses therefore he becomes the abuser'. All the characters make decisions – they are not fated to end up a particular way.

Does Siddie know about Scott and Darren?

No, he doesn't. He would kill him if he did. He thinks Darren is stalking Scott. Dior knows something but is conflicted.

Does Scott collude in the attack on Darren?

Yes, though he definitely doesn't think it is going to go as far as it does.

Does Siddie know he is going to kill Darren when he comes on in the school scene?

I don't know. It is something for you to find out.

What are your thoughts on the relationship between Siddie and Joanne?

It is probably a relationship of convenience. Neither of them is very well adjusted, so it is probably not great.

Why are the parents away when Scott returns from prison?

They don't care about their children. These kids have no role models. It felt right therefore to leave them out of the play.

What has gone on between Marcus and Darren?

It was probably just a fling on the holiday camp that meant more to Marcus than to Darren.

Exercises for use in rehearsals

None of the characters in the play is a stereotype. In order to help your acting companies get to grips with this, here are a few exercises:

UNPICKING THE TEXT

Focus on one character. Write on to a large piece of paper divided into four sections:

1. Facts about you as a person (character description doesn't count).
2. Things you say about yourself.
3. Things other people say about you.
4. Things you say about other people.

Be exact about quotations used and specific about any facts. Don't worry if there are repetitions as these in themselves can be very revealing.

It is interesting to see if your characters' view of themselves matches with what others say. Do they clash? Are there patterns? Do people talk about the character a lot? Not a lot? Do we know a lot of facts about you?

BACK-STORY

Get your actors to write a character back-story from the information they already have in the play. Encourage them to go into as much detail as possible. It can be written, recorded, videoed – whatever works best for you.

HOT SEATING

Hot seating is a very useful way to develop characters. The participant must answer questions (which shouldn't be leading) in character. You can also double up characters and the questioner can choose whether to ask private or public questions. This is particularly useful in a play like this where there is a complex web of relationships to understand. As the director, try and keep the questioning in a useful area and moderate any leading questions.

Useful areas of questioning include: feelings about others (both private and public); hopes, dreams and ambitions; opinions, biographical detail; relationship histories; specific memories of another person.

STRUCTURED IMPROVISATION

Structured improvisation around the script can be very useful creating performances which are alive, nuanced and truthful.

We began by walking through the scene in the school – essentially reading through while on their feet, with script in hand. An exercise was then undertaken.

PREVIOUS CIRCUMSTANCE

In our earlier work we had identified that a scene must have taken place between Siddie and Scott which we don't see, before the scene in the school. Some basic parameters were given to define what Siddie had to achieve – to get Scott to agree to bring Darren to the school. We tried an improvisation which, on this occasion, was a little generalised. Using input from the writer and with the group observing, the logic of the situation was then tightened up – Scott would put up more obstacles, Siddie has more respect for Scott. The scene was improvised again. Midway through, the action was paused and an additional piece of plot was added which enhanced the improvisation. This exercise had endless development possibility, but if you have limited time maybe decide on what *you* think are the key events we don't see – and just do them.

Following this exercise we returned to the scene in the school. An outsider was asked to watch Scott's journey carefully during this walk-through. The improvisation had made it clear that Scott is playing a difficult game here – wanting to keep Darren there and desperate not to give away his relationship with him because the others are watching.

We then undertook another exercise. The outsider who had watched the run-through replaced the actor playing Scott. The actor playing Scott now had to be in the scene but give a constant, stream-of-consciousness interior monologue about his thoughts and feelings. This was particularly useful for Scott because after the beginning he doesn't say a lot. Going through character thoughts made him discover more about the high emotional conflict he is experiencing throughout the scene and think about how he would express it.

The way the characters speak tells you something about them. Siddie and Joanne speak in short sentences. The writer is very keen that punctuation in dialogue is observed as it is the only direct way he has of communicating with the actor. You may not understand why it is punctuated in a specific way, but if you try it you might find out.

Casting thoughts

SCOTT and SIDDIE are very important characters to cast. Think about casting company leaders in these roles, who will help lead the show and the rest of the cast by example.

DIOR is also a big challenge as she is led by her heart but is highly intelligent.

MARCUS also needs some thought because he has to open the play at a very high emotional temperature and this requires some maturity and ability. He also needs not to be a 'camp' caricature.

Other production questions

The workshop participants asked the writer and facilitating director a number of questions about the play, its plot and how to produce it.

The first scene of the play is the next day? Is that important?

Yes – very. That is where the convention of the backwards time scheme is set up. Clarity is vital.

The school in the play is left to crumble. Is it already abandoned when the play happens?

Yes. The school has closed down before the play happens.

Who is the 'other one' mentioned in the prison scene?

That is Scott.

Why is Siddie inside?

Because Joanne bragged on Facebook.

Is the baby present in the attack scene?

Yes, but you do not need to give it too much thought in production.

Why are the riots in the play?

The riots were going on about the time I was writing. They seemed to fit in with the chaotic lives the characters in the play have. Also, the story of someone getting caught stealing ski gloves, when he will probably never go skiing, tickled me.

What rights of interpretation do I have?

HETTIE: The writer is very specific about time scheme and the logic of the story. There are many production choices open to you but the play is a blueprint; if you muck about with it, it may unravel.

Can accents be changed? What about words like 'battio', which aren't familiar in some parts of the country?

HETTIE: Jonathan would like to keep 'battio' in the play because it is such a strong and vile word. There is something hideous about the fact that the character has learnt it. Also, it should be possible to perform the play in any accent.

Did the writer have a style in mind?

HETTIE: Jonathan did not have a particular style in mind. He just wanted it to be fabulous. He feels that you should aim for truthful and real performances. It doesn't feel like an abstract approach would work well. The writing is heightened, but will be best when played for absolute truth.

Do you have thoughts about the transitions?

JONATHAN: No. If I'd had a particular thought I would have written it.

HETTIE: As a director I think one of the biggest challenges of this play is finding a way to make these different locations work.

How important are the stage directions?

JONATHAN: They are very important clues which are as important to the play's meaning as the lines. Investigate what they mean. For example, in the school scene, ignoring the stage direction about Dior 'holding out her hand' would change the reading of the scene. Using this stage direction, and realising it meant she was standing at a distance, will suddenly create a more powerful tableau than when she was right beside Scott. Stage directions are story beats and should be interrogated in as much detail as dialogue.

Are you averse to changing the swearing?

HETTIE: Jonathan would be happy to have a discussion about it and enquiries should be directed to his agent.

Should the violence be realistic or could it be stylised?

JONATHAN: I think it should be real but that is probably a directorial decision.

HETTIE: The audience need to be shocked by the violence. There are different ways of achieving this. If you have an instinct that a non-realistic solution would be best, go for it.

Does the play have a religious point of view?

No.

Research

BOOK
Shattered Lives by Camila Batmanghelidjh is about children growing up in environments like those in the play.

Two gay hate-crimes were part of the writer's initial work on the play. They were: the Michael Causer killing in Liverpool, where he was beaten to death with a hardback book; and the killing of Ian Baynham in Trafalgar Square by Ruby Thomas.

From a workshop led by Hettie MacDonald,
with notes by Jonathan Humphreys

Soundclash

Lenny Henry

Beats and raps conceived by
L. H. and Akaala

Chord beds by
Benedict Westernra

Age suitability 13–19
Cast size 8
Plus 2 ensembles

Lenny Henry's work in theatre includes *The Comedy of Errors* at the National Theatre and the title role in *Othello* for Northern Broadsides for which he won the Outstanding Newcomer at the *Evening Standard* Theatre Awards. He has toured worldwide with his comedy shows *Cradle to Rave, Where You From?, So Much Things to Say, Have You Seen This Man?, Larger Than Life* and *Loud!* He was the first British comic to make a live stand-up comedy film: *Lenny Henry Live and Unleashed* was filmed before a live audience at the Hackney Empire. TV includes *The Magicians, Harry and Paul, First Love, Happy Birthday OU, Big and Small, Lenny's Britain, Lenny's Perfect Night In, The Lenny Henry Show, Little Robots, Lenny Henry in Pieces, Goodbye Mr Steadman, Hope and Glory, The Man, Lenny Goes to Town, Lenny's Big Amazon Adventure, Lenny Henry Gets Wild, White Goods, Chef, South Bank Show, Alice and Kicking, Bernard and the Genie, Lenny Go Home, The Comic Strip Presents, The Delbert Wilkins Show, Three of a Kind, Tiswas* and *New Faces*. He also voices the lead characters in *Big and Small*. He won the Lifetime Achievement Award at the British Comedy Awards and at the Black Entertainment Comedy Awards in 2003, the BMF Inspiration Award, Golden Rose of Montreux, BBC British Personality of the Year and the Golden Nymph Award at the Monte Carlo Television Festival. He is co-founder of Comic Relief.

The Set

Simple: a projection screen at the rear centre stage. Images are shown to aid transitions and support onstage action.

Black blocks could be brought on and off by cast members and assembled into tables, desks, chairs, sofas, trash cans – and eventually the sound systems themselves.

A DJ/sound operator could be in vision at all times (like the orchestra in some musical productions), flying in all tunes, jingles and sound effects.

It is possible, of course, to do the show without a projection screen. I leave it to your ingenuity to figure out scene changes, atmosphere suggestions etc. (involve the art department, I say).

Once again, back is the incredible, rhyme animal
                    Public Enemy, 'Bring the Noise'

I'm a rude boi I ain't gotta relax
I got this game in my head like dax
              Dizzee Rascal, 'Jus' a Rascal'

I came to save these new generations of babies
From parents who failed to raise em cause they're lazy!
                    Eminem, 'Fight Music'

I used to knock pounds off
It ain't nothing for me to knock nouns off
But these haters MCs are prayin for my downfall
They just, haters
                         Jay-Z, 'Hate'

Fifty K for a verse, no album out,
Yeah, my money's so tall that my Barbiez got to climb it
Hotter than a Middle Eastern climate, find it,
Tony Matterhorn, Dutty wine it, wine it . . .
                    Nicky Minaj, 'Monster'

You never thought that hip hop would take it this far
Now I'm in the limelight cause I rhyme tight
Time to get paid, blow up like the world trade . . .
                    Biggie Smalls, 'Juicy'

To all DJs, MCs, turntablists, lockers, poppers,
Hip hoppers, in life, or dreams:
LEARN THE WORDS, YOU MIGHT SING THIS . . .
              Public Enemy, 'Don't Believe the Hype'

Yeah, learn the words . . . Work on them in teams or with
friends or parents or (ulp) your teachers. If you're rhyming
to a beat, practise like crazy and remember to breathe –
          apparently it's all about FLOW . . .

                         Peace.
                         LGH, 2012

Characters

Deej (*pronounced like Fiji but without the 'i' at the end*) *is a DJ – lives for and loves music. Deej is all iPod, headphones, street dancing and spitting rhymes. He can also cut the records from side to side – scratch and rhyme.*

Sings *is a sing-jay (like Mr Vegas or Buju Banton), and can sing anything. He is obsessed with members of the opposite sex. A lot.*

Vox *loves wordplay, microphones, beatboxing, tongue twisters, flow and diction – also crazy ass dancer.*

Lox *is Vox's best mate, an expert at locking, popping, electro hip hopping and throwing out rhymes.*

Lil Kid *is a first-year, dad was a DJ and MC – and in his will gifted a legacy of records, turntables, microphone and speakers to his Lil Kid, who grieves and attempts to make sense of it all. Lil Kid hates knives and never wants to be in a gang. EVER!*

Teacher *is a deadpan, who wants not only to entertain the kids, but amuse them and get them involved with the community.*

DJ Emperor/Empress (*if it's a girl*) *is a turntablist, selector and also a rapper. Fierce, purveyor of off-the-hook rhymes and a brutal dancer – a force to be reckoned with. Wields a razor-sharp blade.* (*Rewrite any male-centric rhymes if played by a girl.*)

Others

DJ Empress's/Emperor's posse of dancers, rappers, krumpers, and hangers-on. Claughton (pronounced 'Clawton') School pupils and other classmates.

The characters can be played by anyone: male/female/black/white/Asian/able-bodied or otherwise. The only concession gender wise is that the show needs a **Big Sis** (a challenge would be to rewrite for an all-girl performance . . . good luck).

The names are iconic – which is why the characters can be interpreted however you wish.

Scene One

Against black.

SFX: a mighty lion roars three times!

Projection screen reveals street scene – a mini roadside shrine. There are flowers attached to the railings.

A **Lil Kid** *carrying plastic bags enters and observes the tableau.*

Projection screen shows the victim's school picture attached to the flowers. Candles flicker; condolence cards are tied to the railing; a hand-drawn sign says 'Stop knife crime now!'

Unseen voices sing 'Flowers on the Railing' (music by Benedict Westernra.)

Entire Cast
> Flowers on a railing
> Tied up by the road
> Candles on the kerbside
> Someone's tears have flowed
>
> And it's not for the first time
> And it will not be the last
> Said it's not for the first
> Can't we put this in the past?

Grams: a beat drops.

As **Lil Kid** *rhymes, the cast portray some of the events described in the background.*

Lil Kid
> Walkin' to school from home in the morning
> My endz so real I can never be yawning
> Gotta stay sharp, round here's not boring
> You might get blazed your mom left in mourning
> Torn and forlorn wish you'd never been born
> Council estates not nice green lawns
> Guns and a knife are just part of life
> So please don't tell me to look on the bright side

I just can't see one living round here
Just tryin' not to get tump down here
Ain't no coward just bein' realistic,
I ain't tryin' to end up as a statistic

Statistic: sutten you don't ever wanna be
Mom's raised you alone and your dad's not free
Statistic: when you've dropped out of school
Try act hard but feel like a fool
Truth be told – we ain't really that bad
Take a proper look around – it's really quite sad
We all act hard and then become scarred
Left lyin' in a coffin or locked behind bars.

Scene Two

As the song ends, **Lil Kid** *suddenly bumps into big kids – all wearing smart blazers, they are from Claughton School (male and female) and led by the fierce, Nike-sporting* **DJ Emperor**, *who blocks* **Lil Kid***'s way.*

A deliberate dance as **Emperor** *won't let* **Lil Kid** *pass.*

Claughton Crew laugh. **Emperor** *pushes* **Lil Kid**.

Other kids arrive (male and female) in Newtown School uniform (not as posh) and challenge **DJ Emperor**.

Deej (*sneering*)   I smell St Claughton school – what you lot doin' round Newtown? We ain't got no *bistros* round here.

DJ Emperor   Teachin' this first-year some manners.

Deej   That kid's wiv us.

DJ Emperor (*on guard*)   Wiv you?

Lil Kid   I'm not wiv anyone. I'm on my own.

Panicked, **Lil Kid** *bundles past* **Emperor** *and accidentally steps on his new trainers.*

DJ Emperor   Tell me you didn't.

Lil Kid (*pathetically*)   I didn't?

DJ Emperor   These was fresh out the box. Brand new. Like baby labrador puppies. (*Fury.*) I'm gonna –

He reveals a knife – and raps aggressively . . .

DJ Emperor
  Whose shoes are you steppin' on?
  Gonna need a teflon-
  Vest to protect ya neck
  From our weapons son
  Fools never learn
  I burn scalps like a perm
  My trainers cost more than a year
  Of what your family earn
  I cut you so wide, they'll need a rope
  To stitch you closed
  This is my hood here
  And everybody knows
  Makin' foes with me?
  Prepare a date for your funeral
  Shank ya man every other day
  That's my usual pastime
  Was a warrior in my past life
  Far's right now I got no cares regards life
  So you better hope you got a crew to defend you
  Cos if not, then right now, I'm gonna end you.

Emperor *throws fierce shapes throughout with his blade.*

In response the cast slow their movements right down, almost in a Matrix-*style bullet time effect – i.e.,* **Deej** *bends backwards,* **Vox** *spins away,* **Lox** *stops dead,* **Sings** *gets hold of* **Lil Kid***, who struggles momentarily and then allows himself to be protected.*

When the rhyming's done, **DJ Emperor** *sheathes the weapon.*

Everyone expresses massive relief in their own way – NO ONE likes knives.

342   Lenny Henry

DJ Emperor (*cocky*)   Yeah thought so . . . Lil Kid? (*Gestures to shoe. To* **Lil Kid**.) This stain on my new shoes don't come out, *you're* gonna be a stain . . . on the concrete.

Offstage sound of police sirens.

Emperor *leaves, his crew slipstreaming.*

Massive expression of relief from everyone once **Emperor***'s posse have gone.*

Deej   That was intense.

Vox   I wanna go to the toilet.

Lox   I just did.

Sings   See them girls? *Crisp*, you get me?

Deej/Lox/Vox   This is not the time, Sings!

Lil Kid *is creeping away,* **Deej** *blocks him.*

Deej   Where you goin', Lil Kid? We just rescued your bony arse then.

Vox   Yeah – not even a 'Thank you, Deej'?

Lox   That's correct, man – not even a (*Exaggerates.*) 'I love you guys, and I'm for ever in your debt. Here – take these socks . . . They're all I've got and they stink like Gorgonzola, but they're yours.'

The rest laugh. **Lil Kid***'s frozen.*

Sings   You should thank us – DJ Emperor was gonna slice and dice you like Ainsley on crack. We should link up.

Lil Kid *flinches – wants to go.*

Lil Kid   'Link up'? Look – I don't want to be in your gang. I just –

Deej   Ahhh man – we ain't a gang.

Lox   We don't roll like that.

Vox   We just kotch – y'knowmean? Hang? Chill? No drama . . .

Sings   We don't do violence – I'm allergic. I break out in cuts and bruises.

They laugh and boo the old joke . . . but **Lil Kid**'*s resolved..*

Lil Kid   Yeah, well. (*Makes sign.*) 'Whatever' – the whole gang thing's just not me, okay? I gotta –

But before **Lil Kid** *can vanish,* **Deej** *grabs a plastic bag, and reveals record boxes and other treasure.*

Deej   But whoa! Check out the tunes –

He opens the box and throws seven-inch singles over his shoulder as he speaks.

Deej   Never heard of it, never heard of it. 'Long Shot Kick de Bucket'? '54–46 was My Number'? 'Suzanne Beware of the Devil'? Rubbish.

He throws the tunes away. **Lil Kid** *is upset.*

Lil Kid   They're my dad's!

Deej   They're rubbish – if I didn't have sensitive skin, I'd wipe my batty with them.

Lil Kid *snatches the box back.*

Deej/Vox/Lox/Sings   OOOOHHHHH.

Lil Kid (*desperate*)   Look – I said 'thank you' for defendin' me. But I *don't* wanna be in a . . . Gangs are *trouble*. I'm going home.

He leaves. They wait a while and then follow in the same direction, like a Madness video.

Blackout.

Scene Three

Projection screen (or at least a sense of 'round the way' activity). We see an urban estate – kids skateboarding, running, playing, all within yelling distance of their houses.

Lil Kid *speed-walks, but* **Deej**, **Vox**, **Lox** *and* **Sings** *bring up the rear, relentlessly in step with him.* **Lil Kid** *stops and turns.*

Lil Kid   Will you lot just – just . . . piss off?

Deej   That's rude, man. Here's us guardin' you all the way to your yard.

Lox   Shame. No etiquette man.

Vox   He's had a etiquetectomy.

Sings   My Aunt Clarice had one of them – had to wear a corset to hold it all in afterwards . . . harsh.

They all look at **Lil Kid**. *He laughs.*

Lil Kid   I never asked you to guard me all the way to my yard. Why don't you guard yourself back to your yards, wherever your own yards are? Leave my yard alone.

Vox   He's sayin' 'yard' a lot.

Lox .   Must be a yardie.

Sings   Heh heh . . . 'Yardie', you lot should be on 'Britain's Got NO Talent'.

Lil Kid *reaches his gate, but* **Deej** *stops him with an outstretched hand.* **Lil Kid** *pushes back.* **Deej** *loses his temper.*

Deej   Enough! *This* is what happens when someone *ain't* got your back!

Deej *grabs* **Lil Kid**'s *plastic bags and upends everything on to the floor. Records fall out – as does a turntable and stylus.*

Deej, **Vox**, **Lox** *and* **Sings** *pick at everything.* **Deej** *holds up a turntable.*

Deej   You don't need this – just plug a iPod into some speakers and BOOM!

The others nod in agreement.

Lil Kid   Wouldn't sound big and fat like my dad's sound system – there's something magic about vinyl /

Sings (*interrupting*)   It's the twenty-second century, kid.

Lox   Twenty-first, you chief.

Vox *laughs.*

Lil Kid   Leave my dad's stuff alone!

Deej   Cheeky lickle . . .

Everyone grabs **Lil Kid***. They administer a wedgie, pull his shoes off and throw them into the wings. Finally* **Deej** *grabs* **Lil Kid** *on the ground, straddles his shoulders.*

Deej   You don't wanna hang with us?

He bends over, face close to **Lil Kid***'s, hawks loudly but . . . just before the gob –*

Blackout.

Scene Four

Projection screen, or just a bunch of things with sheets hung over 'em. A cellar with piled-up boxes, old records and indistinct shapes.

Lil Kid *sits, going through a box of records. Feeling 'post wedgie', he sniffles a bit.*

Lil Kid   Dad told me to take care of this stuff. I wasn't gonna let them scratch or break them. But I'm only little – what am I s'posed to do?

He takes a record from the sleeve, wipes it with a cloth and then stares at the label.

Lil Kid   Toots and the Maytals.

He turns to himself.

'Toots' – what kinda name's that? His dad musta named him after a trumpet or somethin' – or maybe he ate a lot of beans – Toooot!

Makes himself laugh.

Turns back to himself.

Shut up and play the tune!

Puts it on the turntable, presses play.

We hear 'Funky Kingston'.

He looks at the record label.

Oooh, this is *nice* . . .

He presses a button on a jingle machine – a lion roars.

Grams: 'Roar!'

Presses it again: 'Roar!'

Lil Kid   Dad had the best job in the world man.

Big Sis *is now at the door, drumming her fingers.*

Big Sis   It's time for dinner. (*Suspicious.*) Who you talkin' to?

Lil Kid   No one.

Big Sis   Was it a lickle fairy?

Lil Kid   Knock, knock.

Big Sis   Who's there?

Lil Kid   Nunya.

Big Sis (*knows the answer*)   Nunya who?

Lil Kid   Nunya bloody business.

She grins ruefully.

Beat.

Big Sis   Talkin' to yourself. (*Sucks teeth.*) They lock up people for less you know?

Lil Kid   Leave me alone?

Big Sis   You'll get a nice jacket that does up the back.

Lil Kid (*to a moron*)   I'm puttin' Dad's stuff in order. I don't want no dinner – and that's final!

Big Sis   It's Nando's.

Beat.

Lil Kid   I *said*, I'll be up in a minute!

Big Sis *laughs.*

Big Sis   Hurry up then, or it's in the bin. And – (*She softens.*) You need to get some real friends, 'stead a bein' stuck down here on your own all the time.

She goes. **Lil Kid** *talks to himself a bit more.*

Lil Kid   My dad was the best friend I ever had.

He turns to himself.

Yeah – but he's dead? He's never comin' back.

He faces out towards us.

A beat.

I really, really, really, really, really miss my dad, you know?

He begins to chant and others join him: **Deej**, **Lox**, **Vox** *and* **Sings**, **Emperor**'s *crew too.*

Projection screen: a slide show of multi-ethnic dads . . . black, white, Asian, Eastern European.

Deej
   My dad was a chief and a thief – no good

Lil Kid
My dad was a carpenter he worked with wood

Vox
My dad would come home and take a belt off the wall

Sings
My dad's in jail – I never knew him at all

Deej
My dad gave me bitch licks, didn't care what he did

Lil Kid
Dad was my friend; told me I was a special kid

Sings
I never met my dad

Lox
I never met my dad

Deej
My dad's long gone and good riddance, in the wind, he never ever

Vox
Bloody creep

Deej
He used to hit my mum

Lil Kid
He used to kiss my mum

Sings
He walked out on my mum

Deej
He'd never talk to my mum

All
My dad!

Deej
    Really, really, really, really messed me up

Vox
    My dad!

Lox
    Only ever showed up when he was bruk

All
    My dad!

Deej
    Dads of the world – what are you doin'?
    I really ain't got a clue what it is that you're pursuin'
    You wanna make babies – then leave us alone
    Even when you're in the home, always busy on the phone
    We need your guidance – but you won't supply
    Too busy with your woman on the side lookin' fly
    So you fly the nest and leave us in limbo
    You're not the real thing – you're just a symbol
    Now your kid's moving vicious
    Since you broke up with your missus
    Feelin' empty – and we needin' somethin' to fulfil us
    And we're angry, self-harm or act like thugs
    But Dad? All we needed was your love.

Slow fade out on everyone except for **Lil Kid**.

Lil Kid   My dad died.

He walks up to an indistinct shape covered in a dust sheet, reveals the front of some decks – a lion's head design.

And all he left me was these records and tapes. Said I'd figure
it out when I was older. (*Feels lion shape.*) He made all this
himself. But I don't know what to do with it . . .

He looks confused.

Lil Kid   You *do* know there's a chicken dinner upstairs with
your name on it?

He turns to himself.

Do I look stupid to you?

He turns back.

You *do* look a bit stupid, yeah.

He turns on himself.

Wanna fight, cheese breath?

Back on himself.

Wanna pick your teeth up with a broken arm?

Turns back.

What did you say?

Once more he turns to himself.

You're so ugly the only way they could get a puppy to play with you is to hang pork chops off your ears.

He grabs himself by the throat – falls to the ground – rolls to the left once, then to the right. He's enjoying this 'fight amongst himself' immensely.

Give in now.

Rolls over laughing.

No – *you* give in.

Big Sis *enters.*

Big Sis   If you don't come upstairs in five minutes – (*Sees* **Lil Kid**'s *self-strangling.*) Oh for *God's sake*!

Blackout.

Scene Five

Projection screen or any signification that we're at Newtown School.

Lights up.

A chaotic schoolroom.

Deej, **Sings**, **Vox** and **Lox** and other kids playing cards, having an impromptu street dance contest, etc. A boombox plays (this should be fun and can take as long as we like − dance-offs etc.).

Some kids wear headphones, one kid wears just pants, one dances on a desk, another strobes (hip hop shaking), a couple snog, someone yells into a phone, one genius pokes his finger into his laughing mate's forehead repeatedly. One kid naps under a desk.

Teacher *enters − ready to inspire, but then spies chaos, and so attempts to restore order.*

Heads to the front of the class − points at various offenders, and barks monosyllabic instructions.

Teacher   Sit. Stop. Off. Up. Here. Calm. Down. Quiet.

One kid does sit-ups in his jockey shorts. Girls watch.

Trousers. (*To observers.*) Disperse!

Beat.

Okay, good. Now, *quickly* so I can actually *teach* you something this afternoon. The mayor's exhibition −

He clicks a remote. A slide − 'Caribbean Culture in Our Community − What's the Caribbean Ever Done for Us?' − appears on screen.

− is soon, very soon, and Newtown School have been asked to present a 'Caribbean-style entertainment'. I believe another school have assembled a Jamaican sound system.

Deej   What?

Teacher   Yes, a sound system, who'd have thought it? Well *they* did obviously, because they've been rehearsing. And − Joy of Joys! Guess what? they require a *challenger* − for what they used to call − a sound clash.

He presses the remote and reveals a picture of two sound systems facing each other.

No point having a 'sound clash' alone, is there? Why d'you think that is? (*Waits for an answer.*) *There'd be no clash!* Would there? So – I thought you lot might like to do that. (*To* **Deej**.) You're a DJ, aren't you?

Deej *jumps up.*

Deej   What? Is the Prime Minister posh? Does a bear poop in the woods? Is Greece broke? Does Michelle have bigger biceps than Barack? Am *I* a DJ? Listen – Lox? Do it.

Lox *pushes play on the boombox. A heavy beat drops.* (*This is a bragging-style rap –* **Deej** *and co. are generally sweet – they act tough . . . but it's generally acting.*)

Deej
    We come in the door makin' our own law
    All you hear is:

All
    Please don't hit me no more

Deej
    We come in the door makin' our own law
    All you hear is:

All
    Please don't hit me no more

Deej
    Cos this goes out for those that choose to use
    Disre-spectful views – I'm the king a' this school
    We're so real DJs and MCs
    We're straight Gs
    Step up with your bait crew
    We're like –

All
    PLEASE!

Deej
    You can't cut, can't rap, can't mix
    I plug in my *iPod*, you're like ah sh –

Write it down cos town for town
Round for round, pound for pound
You know – we run this town
Sittin' down cos pound for pound
You know we run this town

All
Please don't hit me no more

Deej
We come in the door makin' our own law
All you hear is:

All
Please don't hit me no more.

Ends.

Teacher   I *thought* you'd like that. If only you were this enthusiastic about geography. It'll be up to you to supply your own turntables, records etc . . . No iPods allowed for this.

Deej*'s face falls . . .*

He clicks on remote and we see detail of the sound system. Two dreads man the controls.

Teacher   Sound systems traditionally were known for their insistence on the most up- to-date music, wardrobe-sized speakers etc. Prehistoric technology of course but effective – blummen loud too . . .

He snorts a laugh, but no one's listening to him. They're all focused on **Deej** *as he paces the floor.*

Deej (*thinking aloud*)   They're gonna have MCs and singers, and dancers – we gotta come correct, we gotta be sick.

Teacher   Yes – well . . . you'd better get cracking. You *can* locate the appropriate equipment, can't you?

Deej   Yeah – I know just where to go an' all . . . I think.

Deej, **Vox**, **Lox** *and* **Sings** *all stand . . .*

All   We was born to do this, man!

Blackout.

Scene Six

Projection screen: we're back in the cellar.

Lil Kid *performs a ritual with his dad's records.*

He takes great care to wipe the vinyl, then places it on the turntable. Does the same with another one.

The following is almost meditation/spoken word – not a rap as there's no beats . . .

Lil Kid
Dad said: 'Careful kid, else the dust will bust the needle.
Relax, an' breathe, bob and weave, soon you'll soar jus'
   like a eagle.'
He said: 'All tunes must sound pristine and clean;
Explosive like home-made nitroglycerine;
Ferocious like a hung-over Wolverine . . .
Make you crazy bounce like you're on two-leg trampoline,
Drop a beat and blast you to smithereens.'

He plays a tune – puts headphones on and then, with increasing confidence, mixes back and forth between this tune and the next. Like Grandmaster Flash giving a demonstration . . .

He gets all excited – the beat is fast. He raps:

Lil Kid
So strong when I mix like a Jet Lee kung-fu kick
Little boys don't want this –
See I'm proud when it's loud and the music blares
And the whole crowd stares and it ain't really fair
Cos I show dem – my bars are golden
I'm old school like Saxon, Trojan

Grew up with the sound systems and the toasters
My dad showed me that this is my culture
This is the root of so much that you do
Gotta give credit where it is due
Gotta give credit where it is due
Respect this!

Deej, **Vox**, **Lox** *and* **Sings** *appear – they're looking through a convenient window into the cellar.*

Deej/Vox/Lox/Sings   Oooooooooooh!

Lil Kid *whips round but they've disappeared and then:*

Sound of door buzzer.

Big Sis (*offstage*)   Door! Mates of yours from school!

Lil Kid   Mates from school? I haven't got any –

Deej, **Lox**, **Vox**, *and* **Sings** *troop into his domain.*

Lil Kid *is terrified.*

Lox *checks everything.*

Lox   This is dank, man.

Sings   A *proper*, old school, and serious sound system. (*Dons headphones and poses.*) 'Dread at the controls!'

Sings *starts singing and sorting a pile of records simultaneously.*

Lil Kid *stands in front of his dad's stuff – a knight defending the castle.*

Lil Kid   Don't any of you touch my dad's things.

Deej (*gestures at everything*)   We need to borrow *alla* this.

Lox   For this show we gotta do.

Lil Kid   No.

Deej   No?

Lil Kid   No!

Vox   No?

Lil Kid   Yeah – no!

Lox   Yeah?

Lil Kid   No!!

Deej/Lox/Vox/Sings   Why?

Lil Kid   Cos he *gobbed* on me!

A beat drops and he raps.

> I'm a first-year and I've had my worst year
> Wanna settle down and just do my work yeah?
> Without your depressin' pressin' me to be
> I'm not your possession – I'm steppin' solely
> I don't wanna join with none a' your gang
> I've seen how that story ends and it's sad
> With my name on a railin' with flowers and my name
> My own mother wailin' and steamin' in wild pain
> That's not me, it might be you –
> Please keep that for you and your crew
> You spat in my face, now this sudden change of view?
> But I refuse to be used – so please just move.

Deej *and the others listen and react throughout.*

Deej   Sweet.

Lox   You got lyrics.

Sings   Like Doctor Seuss but, a short-arse.

Vox   You gots to link up wiv us.

Lil Kid   I don't wanna be in no gang! Jeezum pease – how many times?

Lox/Sings/Lox   Jeezum pease?

Deej (*patient*)   We ain't a *gang* – we're like spars, mates, compadres – we got each other's back – tha's all.

Lil Kid   Yeah, right – turn my back and you jook me in it?
I'm staying solo, the answer's no – so forget it, you arseholes.

They all bristle at this cheek, then:

Big Sis *enters.* **Sings** *reacts – a back flip, spinning on his head, an arooga sound? He fancies her.*

Big Sis   Nice language – I'm never letting you watch
CBeebies ever again.

Sings *flirts with* **Big Sis***: takes off his cap, puts it back on, smiles . . .*

The others recognise the symptoms.

Sings (*smitten*)   We was just asking if we could borrow this
equipment. We've got this sound clash competition thing?
And we reckon with this sound system? We could win . . . By
the way, you are the most righteously crisp girl I've ever seen.
You're cris' like smoky bacon, man.

Grams: a semi-dance hall beat kicks in.

The guys bounce in time:

Deej/Lox/Vox
  Oh no no – it's – happening again.
  Oh no no – it's – happening again.

Sings
  You walked in the place and I can't think straight
  I'm gettin' so hot that I just might faint
  The shape of your waist and your neat pretty face
  Enough to make a bad words cuss by a saint
  Gyal you look good I don't mean disrespect
  I just want to make you sweat.

Deej/Lox/Vox
  Oh, no no, it's happenin' again.
  Oh, no no, it's happenin' again.

Sings
  Where you get that body cos you body it's so – good
  The prettiest young gyal I ever saw in this – hood

Your Cola bottle shape all around the place
Bruk out, bruk out gyal – you have the shape –

He reaches out to touch **Big Sis**'s *shoulder.*

Grams: kung-fu fight music.

Big Sis *flips him over on his back,* Zhang Ziyi-*style.*

Grams: a mighty beat drops.

Big Sis (*with skip load of attitude*)
The name's Big Sis
Aka out of your reach
You wanna like me? That's sweet
But please don't touch what you can't afford
I'm bored, I've heard this – all before
But what I can tell you, you wanna borrow them decks
You better take my little brother with you, that's respect
Cos he knows the A sides, B sides, mixing and scratching
Puttin' in work while you're relaxin'
He's mastered the craft perfected his art
When it comes to flows, you know he stands apart
So it's real simple, you want the equipment
Then my little brother comes with it –
It's just business . . .

Everyone stares in wonder.

Lox   Fierce.

Vox   Mighty.

Deej   Gorgeous.

Sings   Ugggnnnh . . .

Big Sis   Listen you lot, since he died, all my brother's got is
Dad's sound system. It's more than just two turntables and a
microphone . . . it's family.

Deej   Didn't know your dad was gone – sorry.

This is a huge admission of guilt.

Vox   Sorry, man.

Lox   Yeah. That's shit, man. Total darkness.

Lil Kid *looks down at his feet – still scared, but now* **Big Sis** *is here he's gathering some courage.*

Lil Kid   I don't want you guys anywhere near my dad's stuff.

Deej   Hey, know what? Teacher said learn about Caribbean history. This stuff here's like a museum – but people can't hear or see what your dad built, cos it's stuck down here gatherin' dust – just trust us, yeah?

Big Sis *is moved. She takes* **Lil Kid**'s *hand.*

Big Sis   Look – he's right, his stuff's been down here since Reeboks was popular . . . You should let 'em use it, set it up and let it roar. Dad'd love that – if he was here he'd say 'Yes'.

Lil Kid   What?!

Big Sis   It's true – he never got the chance to really hear what this stuff can do. They only did a couple of gigs before he died.

Lil Kid   But . . . these boys –

Big Sis   They look all right to me.

The boys assume a pose – most squeaky-clean boy band on earth.

Lil Kid's *thrown.*

Lil Kid   Well they look like that *now*, but that one over there (**Deej**) *gobbed* on me.

Deej *withers under* **Big Sis**'s *gaze.*

Big Sis   That's disgusting. Is that true?

Deej *shrugs.*

Big Sis   Are you mentally ill?

Deej   I probably am as it goes, yeah.

Big Sis   Well – that's all right then. He wasn't in his right mind so – probably didn't mean it.

Lil Kid   What?!

Big Sis   Look – these guys might just help you get out the house. You're always down here with these old records and your imaginary friend – it's weird.

Lil Kid   No, I'm not, that's not true.

Turns to himself.

(*Quietly.*) Will you shut up and let her talk?

He turns back to himself.

Everyone's a bit weirded out by this.

But Dad wanted me to look after his stuff.

Big Sis   Yeah, I know – he told you to 'take care' – he didn't say 'get stuck', though, did he? Stuck down here with all this old stuff. (*Beat.*) What's best for you is to get this stuff out the house and *do* something with it.

Sings   And we have to take little Frodo too, yeah?

The guys go into a huddle and have a mimed conversation – lots of arm waving and pointing at **Lil Kid***.*

At one point it all stops as they turn and stare at him for a while – then whip back to the huddle.

Then they turn and look at **Big Sis***, who waits, tapping her foot patiently.*

A decision is made. **Deej** *turns to* **Lil Kid***. He's very earnest.*

Deej   Alright – after a heated debate, we're all agreed. I'm sorry for pickin' on you. I dunno why. It's just a 'growin' up round here' thing, I guess. (*An idea.*) Know what? I'm gonna let you – hit me – right now, yeah? *Hard* – in the *face.* Yeah – let's count it down: 5–4–3–2 –

Everyone waits expectantly.

Lil Kid *explodes.*

Lil Kid   Do I look like a complete chief? I'm not gonna punch you in the face. That's the stupidest idea I've ever heard. I keep tellin' you – I'm not into violence.

Deej   Good job cos I woulda box every last one a your teet down your throat.

The others nod.

Lox/Vox/Sings   Yeah, he woulda / No mistake / Teet woulda bin snackin' on undercrackers for real.

Deej (*to* **Big Sis**)   No offence – So look, we'll call you 'Kid Selector', yeah? (*Points to the rest of them.*) He's Sings, cos he sings, that's Lox cos he can lock and pop, he's Vox cos he's got a distinctive set a' pipes and I'm Deej cos I'm a DJ and MC . . .

Lil Kid   'Kid Selector'?

Deej   Yeah, cos in a sound system crew the selector's the one who chooses all the records.

Lil Kid (*very excited*)   'Kid Selector'?

Vox   Yeah, man, don't go all postal – do you want to do it or not?

Sings (*cajoling*)   We'll take you for a meal at – (*Sings last vowel like Jesse J.*) Nandoooooooooooooooooooooo's.

Beat.

Lil Kid *looks up at the screen: a thought balloon appears featuring a Nando's chicken dinner (make a thought balloon with a gorgeous chicken dinner at its centre). It disappears.*

Lil Kid (*a beat, then a huge smile*)   Whatever you guys did, the Nando's feast sealed the deal . . . The Kid Selector is totally in!

He presses the jingle machine. A lion roars!

Beat.

He smiles, presses it again.

A lion roars again.

They stare at him.

Beat.

One thing though? You guys have to promise – keep me away from that DJ Emperor fruitcake. I don't wanna end up stabbed up like that kid last week. Or the one the week before that.

Deej   We don't business with them anyway. We don't want nothin' to do with knives. Get me?

Lil Kid *nods.*

Beat.

Lil Kid   Wanna hear some records?

Time passing sequence.

Projection screen: record boxes being opened.

Deej, **Lox**, **Vox** and **Sings** *reacting like they've discovered the holy grail.* **Lil Kid** *watches proudly.*

A dance sequence as they pass records and venerate each one.

Everybody's skankin' to the tunes – and then **Lox** *stops dead . . .*

Lox   What we gonna call ourselves?

Lil Kid *walks over to a covered box, removes the dust sheet. A lion head is revealed.*

Lil Kid   That Claughton knobhead's called DJ Emperor – We should be kings – 'Lion Sound Crew'.

Deej/Vox/Sings   Oooohhhhh!

Lox   I dunno – I ain't feelin' lions, you know?

Vox   You *like* lions!

Lox   I don't wanna *be* one though, get me? Anyways right, the lionesses do *all* the work. Them guys just sit around all day combin' out their Afros.

Deej   Lions ain't got no Afros – and they can't use a comb cos they ain't got no thumbs – you chief! (*Attenborough commentary.*) 'The pride approaches . . . We know the males by their Afros as they bob over the horizon – there's the Jamaican lion, of course, as we can see by the customary dreadlocks and woolly hat.'

They all laugh – except for **Lox**, *who's still thinking.*

Lox   Peacocks are cooler than lions, tortoises and hares – they're blatant, flamboyant – all them colours flyin' out their bumhole.

Vox   I am not bein' in no crew that's got pee and cock in its title, get me?

They laugh.

Lil Kid   'Lion Sound' was the name of my dad's system. If you really want me in? We're gonna be called 'Lion Sound'. For my dad.

The others look at each other – a silent agreement – then extend hands into a team gesture, one hand on top of another.

Deej   On three, yeah? 'Lion Sound' – one, two, three . . .

All   LION SOUND!

Scene Seven

Projection screen:

CARIBBEAN CULTURE IN OUR SOCIETY
WHAT'S THE CARIBBEAN EVER DONE FOR US?

Come and enjoy all things Caribbean including jerk chicken and a reggae sound clash! Newtown vs. St Claughton's.

Then: a slide show of pictures that kids have painted featuring all things Caribbean: flags, islands, Bob Marley, carnival, bananas, cricketers, sugar cane, etc.

A tiny carnival procession passes through. A couple of little kids are dressed in bizarre carnival costumes. Soca music plays . . .

Applause.

Deej, **Sings**, **Lox**, **Vox** *and* **Lil Kid** *enter, start setting up.*

DJ Emperor *and the Claughton crew enter and start setting up their equipment on the opposite side of the stage.*

Deej   Check out the competition.

DJ Emperor *looks across and leers . . . then sees* **Lil Kid** *and holds up his muddied trainer – still dirty.*

Beat.

Lil Kid *panics.*

Lil Kid   That's it. *I am toast! Oh God!* I'm toast with no butter or jam or Marmite – not even a scrape of Utterly Butterly – just the dry toast – DJ Emperor's gonna cut me into triangles!

Deej   Relax, man.

Lil Kid: Relax? DJ Emperor wants to jab holes in me like a Tesco's microwave dinner. *Relax?* I'm going home. Before I get jooked. See ya!

Vox *grabs* **Lil Kid**'s *collar.*

Vox   Chill, munchkin. No one's jookin' no one in here.

Lox   With all these big people round?

Sings   He'd have to be as nutty as squirrel doo-doo.

Deej   That's well nutty.

Sings   So refrigerate – and let's get it together.

Lil Kid   I'm going to the toilet.

He slips off, but on his way, bumps into **DJ Emperor**, *stepping on his other superwhite trainer.* **Emperor** *goes Defcon One, but a minion pulls him away.*

Claughton Kid   Leave it – he ain't worth it. (*Beat.*) My Liege.

Emperor *walks off haughtily – but* **Lil Kid** *is now very frightened indeed, and runs away.*

Music underscores the exhibition continuing. **Big Sis** *enters and* **Sings** *jogs up to her and chats excitedly . . . The others react.*

Meanwhile, elsewhere.

Spotlight on **Lil Kid** *as he enters dragging a big container along.*

The lid is raised and reveals a sign that says 'Skool kraft baskit – keep out!'

Lil Kid *rummages around. There's the sound of clattering metal on metal. The lid goes down and* **Lil Kid** *stands up, stuffing shiny sharp scissors into his waistband. He looks at us, scared but determined.*

He pushes the basket off.

Blackout and lights up on another part of the stage.

Scene Eight

An explosion of soca music.

Teacher *takes centre stage and taps the microphone to make sure it's on.*

Lox   Go on, sir – spit some lyrics!

Vox   Go on, sir – dance-hall style!

Teacher *momentarily does the 'running man' dance.*

Everyone roars their appreciation – it's so incongruous it's funny.

Teacher   That's enough of that.

Lox   That was so sick it needed hosp-ita-li-sation!

More laughter.

Teacher (*mimicking*) I'll be seeing you later on in after-school det-ten-shun.

Boos and jeers – no one likes detention.

Teacher Thanks to everyone who's taken part today – especially St Claughton School and – (*Looks at pad.*) DJ Emperor – also our lot from Newtown School – (*Cheers and boos.*) who are called – (*Looks at pad.*) Lion Sound!

Lox Still not feelin' that name, you know.

Deej, **Sings** *and* **Vox** (*in unison*) Shut up, man!

Teacher Okay . . . Let's just 'chillax', let's just refrigerate for a moment. (*Laughter.*) I want to read something to you – that an anonymous Newtown pupil wrote – here it is: (*Reads*) 'I've really enjoyed working on this exhibition. It just proves we can all unite and create something positive – we're not just gang members or teefs. We're creative too.' (*Folds paper.*) Thanks to Shaniqua Shepherd for – (*Realises.*) Oh, you . . . wanted to . . . remain anonymous.

Ah. Shit. Sorry, Shaniqua. Right – well, onward. Ahhh . . . Big clap, come on!

Applause.

Big Sis Yes! Hallelujah! Whoo! Genius!

Teacher *does running man dance again.*

Laughter.

Teacher Stop – *Hammertime*! (*Laughs.*) Okay, here we go – the moment you've been waiting for, sound clash part one: here's St Claughton and DJ Emperor's crew!

Big cheers and some boos from the crowd.

Claughton dancers ready themselves on the floor.

Emperor *is behind the decks.*

He drops a beat and suddenly – the dancers move, military style with utter precision; heads snap to the right and left in unison. This is no drill.

Emperor's *on the mic. He spits rhymes with his usual ferocity.*

DJ Emperor

Claughton, it's the crew most important
Move like soldiers the wars that we fought in
Exploding rage, we step to the stage
The beats and the rhymes that'll leave you in the shade
When we bus a move – there's only a few who
Could do what we do – I thought that you knew

That the sound system, the sound system
The sound system, the best sound system

Big bass lines – that's what we're about
Speakers as tall as – Peter Crouch
Dance floor bubblin' bass is thumpin'
It's like a big fight everybody wanna jump in
I'll tell you somethin' there's only one king
Forget your man girl, you gotta dump him
And jump in with a real G from Claughton
It's my sound system, we're most important

The sound system, the sound system
The sound system, the best sound system

Yeah, you wanna know exactly who we're better than?
Biggie, Jigga and Nas and Eminem
And we dance better than alla the Jacksons
And like Guy Ritchie we're bringin' the action
So stop, flee, leave, please
How many more young mothers must grieve
For their fake sons who can't MC?
And they try and they try but it never will be

Cos the
The sound system, the sound system
The sound system, the best sound system.

All danced out, the Claughton crew stare arrogantly at us, then turn to **Deej**'s *crew with utter contempt.*

Teacher *takes to the stage.*

Teacher   Well that was very . . . organised. Okay, so, there'll be a break while we all have a lie down . . . and then we'll have Newtown's very own Lion Sound crew!!

Big Sis *whoops, cheers and claps – the audience join in.*

Lil Kid *is totally embarrassed.*

Meanwhile, the Lion decks have been set up – they look impressive.

Blackout and then:

Loud UK hip hop plays . . . underscoring:

Projection screen: more slide show. A collage featuring Bob Marley, palm trees, and Pele, Nelson Mandela, Darth Vader, Ainsley Harriott, pictures of Caribbean islands – girls in bikinis, dreadlocks playing drums, slavery images, Jimmy Cliff's 'Harder They Come' poster, and Levi Root's Reggae Reggae Sauce. It's impressive, colourful work.

Meanwhile, the Lion Sound crew – **Deej**, **Lil Kid**, **Lox**, **Vox** *and* **Sings** *wait.*

Teacher *re-enters and stands centre stage, a spotlight hits him, and he taps the mic.*

Teacher   I don't know why I keep doing that – I know it's on. Well, the question on everyone's lips is, can Newtown School compare to St Claughton School's mighty Emperor Sound? Well this *is* a sound clash. We have a *challenger.* (*Whoops.*) I present – Newtown School's very own – Lion Sound system.

As he reaches the word 'sound':

Grams: the loudest lion's roar we've ever heard – ever.

Vox   LION SOUND IN THE PLACE!

Grams: a wicked grime / reggae combo-style beat . . .

Projection screen: shows almost subliminal flashes of each character/
subject in the rap. Newtown School dancers, including **Vox**, **Lox**,
Sings, **Lil Kid** *and* **Deej** *take turns to dance throughout.*

Deej
 What has Caribbean culture – ever done for me?
 It's influenced everything we do – quite massively
 Cos reggae music's at the root of everything that's
  popular
 Today it influences the way we think, the way that we
  behave

Vox
 See the core of the music, heart of a rebel
 Slave maroons, when the Jacobins, the Africans were
  took away
 Ska, if it's punk, if it's drum'n'bass or dubstep
 Caribbean culture's at the root of the success
 Even if it's hip hop, please – let us not forget
 Kool here, he came from where? Yeah, that's correct
 It's so vital, Toots and the Maytals –
 How many tunes spiralled from them livin' so ital

Lox
 Prince Buster was popular, long before Sean Paul
 When Aswad made Warrior Charge they come to school
 The carnival at Notting Hill, people movin' how they feel
 Changed this whole country for ever, we're just bein' real
 Not just music, it's food, it's a way of talkin'
 A way of thinkin' you've got to live it and walk it

Sings
 Cos everything we're comin' with the people wanna
  follow it
 And by the time they catch up with us, you know we're
  done with it
 We come with it, they covered it, everybody is lovin' it
 All the styles you're seein' it, you know we mothered it

Lil Kid
What do they call me now? Kid Selector!
Sit you'self down come an see the lecture
My dad passing on to me, now I'm passin' it on to you
What is the source of the things you see?
Every sound that you hear, it's true
And when a sound clash some get mash
Run up you mouth get more than a scratch
Caribbean culture's at the root
And that's a natural fact!

Newtown crew link arms – yell:

All   LION SOUND SYSTEM!

Lil Kid *presses a button on the jingle machine – we hear:*

Grams: 'We run tings, tings don't run we?'

ROAR!

Huge cheers. **Teacher** *re-enters the stage. Despite the mic he has to yell to make himself heard over the cheering.*

Teacher   Well, thank you very much, Lion Sound crew – very educational. Alright then – here's the big moment: by cheering, who was the best? Was it DJ Emperor?

Crowd cheer, especially Claughton posse.

Teacher   Okay – very loud indeed. But we're not done yet . . . was it the Lion Sound crew?

And he's drowned out by an almost unanimous yell of approval from the crowd, who are shouting out 'More' and 'Rewind' and 'Yeah'.

Big Sis   Whooooo! Whooooooooo!! Ha hahahaha! I think I've jus' wet myself but *I don't care! Woooooo!*

Lil Kid *almost dies with embarrassment, but is hugged out of it by his posse. At last he's happy.*

Teacher   That's it then, it's unanimous – Lion crew are the winners. Well done, Newtown School – it was all my idea, of course . . .

More cheers, jubilation as Lion crew high-five each other, then turn to face **DJ Emperor**'s *mob.*

The next bit happens in oil – not slo-mo but not overly rushed: it's a dance.

Lil Kid *gives a mock bow.* **Deej**, **Sings**, **Vox** *and* **Lox** *laugh.*

Emperor's *furious – runs over to start some shit.*

Lil Kid *sees* **Emperor** *coming, panics, then reaches behind to his waistband.*

As **Emperor** *reaches* **Lil Kid** *and bumps him hard . . . Pauses, then steps back, facing upstage.* **Lil Kid**'s *looking at the audience.*

DJ Emperor (*loud*)   I'm gonna teach you some respect – I'm –

But everyone's looking at his stomach.

DJ Emperor   What?

He looks down, turns round to face us. He has a pair of scissors sticking out of his stomach. There's blood.

Emperor *drops to his knees, tries to stop the blood.*

DJ Emperor   What? I don't –

He looks at **Lil Kid**, *who is fascinated by his right hand, which is covered in blood.*

Big Sis *screams.*

Emperor *collapses.*

Music underscores – dream-like and strange.

Lights fade. Silhouettes run in slo-mo, people on phones, there is chatter, but all we hear is the word 'ambulance'. It's over now . . .

Blackout.

Against black:

A cell door slams, echoes into the distance.

*A stern **Judge**'s voice, all business and matter-of-fact, seeps in and out.*

Judge   . . . boy died because of *you* . . . Make an example . . .
Custodial sentence . . . Regret your actions . . . rest of your
life . . .

*Fade up, and we see a spotlit **Lil Kid** wearing remand clothes, staring
at us – shocked and isolated.*

Fade out and then up again . . .

*Projection screen: bunches of flowers on railings – from afar at first –
with cards of condolence, headphones tied there too.*

*The victim's photograph – it's **DJ Emperor** – a normal kid . . .
smiling, in smart blazer . . .*

*Simultaneously, the cast have taken their places on stage, all with lit
candles. **Deej**, **Lox**, **Vox**, **Lil Kid**, **Big Sis** and the rest face us.*

Deej
>Every single day – mad potential is wasted
>That's the way it is, when you're livin' in this matrix
>Another brother gone, another mother's lost
>Another son has left us – now what a cost?

Vox
>From the anger that we're livin' in
>The pain and the strain
>What I really wanna know is
>Now – can it change?
>Only if we turn around this sick mentality
>Only then can we begin to affect our reality

Lox
>Reverse all the tragedy; it will be gradually
>Not be willing to fight each other so casually
>Fill our kids with happiness
>Let them sing a different song
>The world's way bigger than the estate that you are
>   livin' on

Sings

    Light a candle for the flowers on the railing
    But let's focus our mind on how to change it
    Light a candle for the flowers on the railing
    But let's all focus our mind on how to change it.

And the rest of the cast (with lit candles) add their voices to his, singing:

    Flowers on a railing
    Tied up by the road
    Candles on the kerbside
    Someone's tears have flowed

    And it's not for the first time
    And it will not be the last
    No it's not for the first time
    Can't we put this in the past?

The lyrics fade.

And we –

Fade to black.

Soundclash

BY LENNY HENRY

*Notes on rehearsal and staging, drawn from a workshop
with the writer held at the National Theatre, November 2012*

How the writer came to write the play

Lenny Henry writes:

When I was writing this play, I thought at first that I was
gonna write about a Soundclash between rival school sound
systems.

All very exciting.

But as the story poured out of me, first of all I realised that
not only was there going to be a magic realist element to it,
but also there was going to be a big hip-hop thread running
through the whole piece. Lastly – the way it turned out– it
became about knife crime.

I can't imagine being fourteen now, living in a city where
young people fighting a turf war over a postal code is a
common occurrence.

I want this play to be funny, funky, fresh, hip hop and
incredibly moving. It's about a scared but talented kid who
ends up throwing everything away because of his fear of
being bullied.

I wonder if we can't do something about this?

Background to the play

Paulette Randall, the director, began the workshop by
speaking about personal memories that reminded her of the
play. She recalled that, when she was younger, at weekends
the furniture in her family home would be moved upstairs,
the carpet would be rolled back and speakers and decks
brought into the house. The light bulbs would be changed to

red and blue, and the party would last all day and night. Lenny Henry said that in Jamaican culture these are called rent parties. This was their introduction to hip hop. Officially, hip hop began in the sixties.

Paulette also spoke about a sound system in Jamaica where part-way through the music someone tells a story. It is an oral tradition in Jamaica. Lenny explained that hip hop is essentially a form of storytelling: hip-hop artists dramatise stories through their lyrics, and exaggerate situations.

Approaching the play

Movement director Simeon Qsyea described how hip hop has evolved. It started in America, so when it came to this country UK rappers and MCs would speak with an American accent. Eventually they began to use their own voices and different regional accents and dialects. Therefore, wherever your play is set, encourage your performers to use their own voices and delivery style.

Simeon also asked 'What does it mean to be hip hop?' and 'How can you embody hip hop?' Traditionally, the early hip-hop artists' movement originated from mimicking gangsters and pimps in America, walking low in order to hide from the police. However hip-hop artists from the west coast of the States have a more flashy physicality, walking high and proud, even using canes.

Simeon suggested directors and actors look at how people walk around in their own area and then create their own hip-hop movement, one that is true to the group and to the environment. Minimal movement, even a style of walking, can create a hip-hop feel.

Research the history of hip hop, and about hip hop today. Lenny encourages companies to research hip-hop culture as part of the rehearsal process. Set it as a research project for the group to present.

Themes

Lenny spoke about what he thinks are the themes within the play, and what inspired him to write it. He says the themes are:

- What has Caribbean culture done for us?
- Photos of the dead, and flowers on the railings.
- I don't wanna die.
- Following your own path.

Language

Anthony Anaxagorou, spoken-word artist and poet, came to speak to the group about what he does, and to offer an alternative style of delivery for the rapping within the play. He said Bill Hicks regards his performance as poetry; and poetry, like rapping, is all about storytelling. He spoke about the difference between rhythm and rhyme: often the poetry he performs doesn't rhyme, but it has a clear rhythm, much like the speech within the play. Anthony encouraged companies to think about how to bring a story to life with only voice and words. He suggested letting the words breathe, and not concentrating on when to take a breath.

Here are a few words that appear in the script, and their definitions:

TOASTER: the person who raps over the tracks.

SELECTOR: the person who selects the tracks.

SHANK: knife.

CLAAT: cloth.

KOTCH: stay.

Characters and characterisation

Get the actors up on their feet as early as possible to allow the script to get into their muscle memory. This will help them to learn lines.

ANOTHER KID is Lil Kid's imaginary friend. He is someone for Lil Kid to talk to. Maybe s/he can look similar to Lil Kid – they may be dressed in a similar way or share the same movement. This will show the audience that s/he is Lil Kid's imaginary friend and part of his brain.

Lenny described LIL KID as lonely like an open wound. He is scared he's going to get targeted because he isn't in a gang. He keeps himself to himself to avoid this, but consequently ends up doing the thing he feared the most.

EMPEROR and his gang should be slick, soldier-like, militarised, regimented and choreographed. Emperor has to be different to the Newtown kids.

There should be something visually different between the two schools and their pupils. Lenny says Claughton is definitely the posher school. This should be apparent in the way they dress. That difference may invade their bodies as well. Let it get into the characters' physicality, how they walk and move together.

Production, staging and design

Hip hop is about making something from nothing.

Simeon suggests putting a group of actors together and giving them simple movements to do at the same time: this shows unity and is an easy way to create a gang. 'Locking and popping' is incredibly popular in hip-hop culture and Simeon demonstrated how that particular style of movement lends itself to this storytelling.

Movement can tell stories. Think of it as a way to create images and shapes rather than as dance or choreography. These are simply other tools for telling the story.

Lenny says feel free to change the melody for the raps or compose them with different instruments if that suits your group. You could even get performers to create sound effects.

Keep the staging simple. If you can make your own set, sound and lights – do so!

In the stage directions Lenny uses projections to show the locations of the scenes. Lenny uses projections a lot in his own work, so audiences can see what he is talking about as he speaks: he says it, they see it. But you don't need to do that. You can create your piece any way you want to. This attitude is very strongly rooted in the history of hip hop. You make use of what you have. The simplicity of hip hop is represented in this play.

Simeon showed the group a video of his dance company BirdGang creating human turntables. If you don't have decks to hand, this may be an alternative option. He also suggested using lighting to divide up the stage. This would work particularly well at the end when locations change in quick succession. Think about how to create scene settings with bodies rather than set and, when introducing movement to a company, don't scare them with words like choreography or routines.

Style and technique

Lenny urges companies to find the comedy within the play. The gangs can work as a unit and the comedy may come out of their movement together. Paulette says the language in the script is heightened, so allow the movement also to be bigger than in real life.

Lenny suggests that sometimes the comedy comes from the reaction rather than the joke or the person delivering the line. He says most importantly it's all about telling the story – through music, movement, rhythm and rhyme.

Exercises for use in rehearsals

Stand in a circle. You will need a few beanbags. Make eye-
contact with someone in the circle, say their name and then
throw them a beanbag. Repeat. As the beanbag is being
passed around the circle, introduce another beanbag. You
may have three or four beanbags being passed around the
circle at the same time. This game is helpful to learn names
and create focus within a group.

Place two chairs facing each other. Person A sits in one chair
and makes movements while Person B sits in the other chair
and mirrors A. At the same time B answers simple maths
questions from C, standing to their left-hand side, and
personal questions from D, standing to their right-hand side.
Keep the questions simple.

In pairs, stand at opposite sides of the room. A is accusing B
of stealing their phone. A and B can only communicate using
gobbledegook language. A realises they were wrong and B
tries to get A to apologise, again only communicating through
gobbledegook.

In pairs, tell each other a story. Think about surroundings
and mental state. Shake your head while reading. See if this
projects dissatisfaction in the voice. Make your intention
physical, or show attitude/emotion while speaking.
Physicalising the emotion while speaking the line can inject
the tone and intention into the dialogue.

Lenny suggests actors learn raps using pictures for lyrics, like
a picture dictionary. Draw a picture beside the lyrics, as a
visual way to learn.

Introduce the language into your vocal warm-ups. Replace
tongue-twisters with lyrics from Eminem or Jay Z songs.
The language is difficult to deliver, almost Shakespearean, so
introduce breathing exercises early in rehearsals.

One person tells a monologue to the rest of the group. If the
audience don't believe the storyteller, they must turn their
backs and walk away. The storyteller has to fight harder to

get the group to face them, using only their voice and the words they have been given.

Get a pack of cards. Ace is highest and two is lowest. Everyone in the group chooses a card but cannot look at it and must place the card on their forehead. The group walk around the room and greet each other. They should each try to work out from the others' responses what their status is. Ask the group to line up in order of status. Then ask the group to think about status within the play. Think about who is high and who is low status. How do characters view themselves and how do others view them?

Walk around the space. When speaking, stop, stand still and deliver lines while the rest of the group continue to walk around the space. Maybe add a rhythm to the exercise. The stillness of the person speaking draws the audience's focus to them. If the rest of the group walk in time to a beat they become one.

You can create gangs by 'flocking': one person is the leader, and everyone else flocks. The leader can change as the flock changes direction. Whoever is front of the pack leads.

There was a lot of discussion about Shakespeare in this workshop. Exercises used to unlock Shakespearean text may also apply to *Soundclash*.

Suggested references

Research knife-crime statistics, including looking at www.parliament.uk

The Dozens http://en.wikipedia.org/wiki/The_Dozens

Hip Hop: Beyond Beats and Rhymes (a 2006 documentary film).

Black Consciousness Movement.

RAPPERS
Professor Green.

Eminem.

Grandmaster Flash.

John Cooper Clarke.

Rude Kids: 'Cotton Buds'.

Dot Rotten.

ON YOUTUBE
Kool DJ Herc: 'Merry-Go-Round'
http://youtu.be/Hw4H2FZjfpo

Lady Leshurr
http://youtu.be/u18VL5iwAxs

Freestyling Rap Rhyme Words
how to create freestyle rap lyrics naturally, by Mike Min
http://youtu.be/KqNzXX7uC0I

Shane Koyczan: 'The Crickets Have Arthritis',
Words Aloud 2007, Canada
http://youtu.be/6VrZE8MCnIA

BirdGang : 'Human Turntables'
http://youtu.be/uNv8WXkSav4

ARTist, created by Mukhtar O.S. Mukhtar
http://youtu.be/QT6HWJGeO0w

From a workshop led by Paulette Randall,
with Movement Director Simeon Qsyea, with notes by Laura Keefe

Don't Feed the Animals

Jemma Kennedy

Age suitability 13–19
Cast size 16
Plus ensemble

You get from the clowns just what you bring to them . . .
they bring a great baggage of old mockeries and deflations
that are as old as our conceits and self-delusions.

Ernest Hemingway

Jemma Kennedy was Pearson Playwright at the National Theatre Studio in 2010 and part of the inaugural Soho 6 writing scheme with the Soho Theatre Company in 2011. Her plays include *The Seagull* (adaptation, Tabard Theatre), *How to Remember the Dead* (Radio 4 Afternoon Play), *The Prince and the Pauper* (Unicorn Theatre) and *The Grand Irrationality* (Lost Theatre Studio, Los Angeles). Her novel *Skywalking* was published by Viking Penguin in 2003 and she has three films in development with Objective Productions and Focus Features. Jemma is also a writing tutor and a mentor for the Koestler Foundation. She recently wrote the National Theatre's 'New Views' online playwriting course for young writers.

Author's Notes

The Circus Show at the end (Act Three) should be about ten minutes long. It's the climax of the play, and should provide a spectacular finish, hopefully confounding the audience's lack of expectation about the gang's ability to pull it together and deliver something amazing. Think about subverting the audience's expectations, as well as the traditional notion of what a circus is. The dramatic role of the show is to demonstrate that the gang has learned co-ordination, discipline and form – all the things they lacked at the beginning of the play – and how they use this in the show to create meaning for themselves.

The show should above all be entertaining. It should hopefully include movement, colour, music and humour. I've included basic action for each section, but you can improvise around this, add, embellish and develop. Be as daring and ambitious as you like. If there are dancers, acrobats or jugglers in your company, use them!

Having said that, it's important to stress that 'real' or professional circus skills aren't necessary to make the show work. It's about harnessing the natural characteristics and qualities of the gang members (and actors), and turning them into a performance, where everyone pulls together. Think about the idea of showing *organised chaos*. As long as you look like you know what you're doing in the show, and more importantly, that you're enjoying it, then anything goes!

Props
Can be anything and everything. They could include standard gym props, e.g., benches, crash mats, a trampette or mini-trampoline; bales of hay, ladders, ropes, juggling balls, batons, hula hoops, as well as the individual gang members' personal items, e.g., the skateboard, the iPod, Raj's box of chicken, a bicycle, etc. You can be as imaginative or as utilitarian as you like.

Music

Music is integral to the show. A different track can be used for each routine, or a single piece of music might accompany the whole thing up until the animals' prison dance. My suggestion for this final part of the show is for something that's definitely *not* in the circus tradition, but contemporary and urban, which reflects the taste of the gang. (Suggestions are 'Pon de Floor' by Major Lazer and 'Boyz' or 'Paper Planes' by M.I.A.) But you can choose music that suits you and provide context. It might be rock'n'roll, jazz, drum and bass – whatever you think works with the tone of the show. If you have a live band in your school or group, you might want to get them involved in providing the show soundtrack.

The Ring

Can be imagined or literal – i.e. formed with props, materials or people. Be imaginative. What does the circle represent to you metaphorically? What does it represent to the gang and the performers? How can you show that physically on stage?

Sound Effects

Aside from specific musical tracks that might accompany the show, sound can be used to help create meaning throughout, e.g.

- A live drummer or band might be brought onstage to create cues or backing tracks for the various routines.

- Specific sound effects to indicate the voices of the judge or policemen might include drum rolls, buzzers, swanee whistle or kazoo. (See the opening of Charlie Chaplin's film *City Lights* for ideas.)

- You might also want to use audio tracks to create animal noises, audience applause, police sirens, etc.

Characters

Zack
Missy
Pozzo
Pedro
Pip
Tinkerbelle
Spike
Chloe
Raj
Diz
Billy
Alex
Midge
Lulu
Charlie
Boy

Most parts could be either gender.

Setting
A circus big top, interior and exterior.

One

A blast of circus music as lights go up. We're on an airfield, somewhere in England, outside the artistes' entrance to a big-top circus tent. Red velvet curtains conceal the interior. A fence prevents visitors coming in to the artistes' enclosure . . . or performers from getting out. A gaily painted circus sign reads: SPARKES CIRCUS: THE FUNNIEST SHOW IN ENGLAND.

A clown, **Pozzo***, lurches through the curtains. He's a traditional, white-face clown, with a red nose, red eyes and red wig, dressed in a striped harlequin outfit. From inside the tent, the sound of booing drowns out the tinny music.*

The clown makes a rude gesture towards the big top, pulls a hip flask from his costume and drains it. He staggers towards the fence and stops beneath the circus sign. As the music reaches its grand finale, he clutches his heart and falls down dead.

Zack *runs out of the tent through the curtains: a boy of fifteen, small and wiry, dressed in a Robin Hood costume. He kneels, checks the clown's pulse. He bows his head, then takes his hat off and solemnly places it over the dead man's face.*

Another clown, **Pedro***, runs out through the curtains. He is an Auguste clown with a pink face, white eyes and mouth, red comedy nose and enormous clown shoes. He stops dead. He crosses himself.*

Zack   You'd better get Pappy.

Pedro *takes off his hat, shakes his head, makes a cut-throat gesture.*

Zack   Please, Pedro. We've got to get him out of here before anyone sees him.

Pedro *sinks to his knees, begins to cry silently. A third clown,* **Pip***, runs out of the big top. He's a Hobo clown: bowler hat, baggy trousers and a cane.*

Zack   He's gone, Pip.

Pip *picks up* **Pozzo**'*s flask, examines it, and throws it down in frustration.*

Zack   He's been hitting it hard since Tiny got sold. You should have tried to stop him.

Pip *shrugs and mimes – what could he do?*

Zack   You can't *both* refuse to talk!

Both clowns nod their heads – yes they can.

How long does the mourning period last?

Pedro *holds up an index finger.*

Zack   A day?

Pedro *shakes his head.* **Pip** *holds up seven fingers.*

Zack   A week?

Pedro *nods. He mimes digging a grave.*

Zack   Until the funeral? But tomorrow's the biggest show of the year. We need you.

Pip *shrugs, then presses his hands to his heart. He kneels at* **Pedro***'s side, and mourns over* **Pozzo***'s body.*

Missy *runs out through the curtains. She's a year older than* **Zack***, dressed in a Maid Marian costume.*

Missy   What the hell's going on? The crowd are going mad in there. Pozzo, stop fooling around and get back in the ring.

Zack   He can't hear you, Missy. Pozzo's done his final turn.

Missy   What happened?

Zack   He got tired of being funny.

Missy   It's his job to be funny!

Zack   Not any more. I think he was missing Tiny.

Missy   We're all missing Tiny. That doesn't stop us going out every day and putting on a show.

Zack   Where's Pappy?

Missy   Trying to calm down the audience. They all want their money back.

Zack   It's over, isn't it? We're finished.

Missy   Don't say that.

Zack   It's the truth. Our main attraction's been sold, half our acts have gone over to Cox's, and now our best clown's carked it.

Pip *and* **Pedro** *pick up* **Pozzo***'s body.*

Missy   Where are you going?

Pip *points beyond the circus tent.*

Zack   They won't talk, not until he's buried. It's clown tradition.

Missy   What about circus tradition? (*To the clowns.*) The one that pays your sodding wages!

The clowns ignore this and carry **Pozzo** *away.*

Tinkerbelle *comes out through the curtains. A tiny, Eastern European woman dressed as a fairy. A child's body. A voice woven from Benson & Hedges and cherry brandy.*

Tinkerbelle   What in name of holy fug happened out there?

Zack   Pozzo's had a heart attack. He's dead.

Tinkerbelle   Fugging typical.

Missy   Is that all you can say?

Tinkerbelle   What else to say? The crowd goes bananas. Somebody throws toffee apple, it hits me in fugging tits.

Missy   Keep your hair on, Tinkerbelle –

Tinkerbelle   Why should I? Thanks to Pozzo, this circus is laughing stock.

Missy   Don't exaggerate.

Tinkerbelle   You saw! He puke all over ringside seats, then he piss himself. Who wants to pay good money for that? People get same for free on High Street every Saturday night.

Zack   He missed Tiny. She held everything together. She was bigger than all of us.

Tinkerbelle   Of course she was! She was fugging elephant!

From inside the tent, another wave of boos and hissing from the crowd.

Tinkerbelle . Hear that?

Missy   Pappy will talk them round.

Tinkerbelle   Like hell he will. I not put up with this shit no more. I going.

Zack   Going where?

Tinkerbelle   Cox's Circus. They offer double salary and my own trailer. No more share with Princess Zuzu and her fugging python.

Missy   Please, Tink –

Tinkerbelle   Sorry, kids. Tell your grandfather he owes me week's pay. Fugging tightwad.

She exits. **Zack** *and* **Missy** *look at each other.*

Zack   What did I tell you? Finished.

Missy   Get a grip, Zack. We'll keep going somehow.

Zack   What's the point? Audiences don't care about us any more. They want what Cox's are offering.

Missy   Extortionate ticket prices and sugarfree candyfloss?

Zack   Projections. Lasers. 3D.

Missy   We're sixth-generation circus folk. Don't our traditions mean anything to you?

Zack   It's the twenty-first century. We should have modernised. Moved on.

Missy   You mean given up.

A pause. They stare at each other.

Zack   It's the busiest night of the year tomorrow, Missy.
And now we're three clowns down and our fairy's flown the
coop.

Missy   Pappy will sort it out.

Zack   No he won't. He'll do what he always does when
there's a crisis. Lock himself in his trailer with a bottle of rum
and play horrible old show tunes.

Missy   Then we'll have to take charge ourselves.

Zack   And do what?

Missy   Find someone to replace the clowns and Tinkerbelle.

Zack   Where?

Missy   I don't know . . . from the circuit.

Zack   Why does everything have to be so hard? (*Beat.*)
Don't you ever just want a normal life?

Missy   I'd rather die.

*A record starts up somewhere beyond the big top: 'Congratulations'
by Cliff Richard.*

Zack   Pappy's off.

Missy   Come on.

They exit through the curtains.

*A gang of local kids appears around the side of the big top. Their
entrance should have the same energy as a crowd of circus tumblers, but
totally unco-ordinated. They jostle and push each other, generally get in
each other's way. They wear school uniforms hidden under hooded tops
and disguised with accessories.*

Spike *takes the lead, with a lopsided swagger.* **Chloe** *is never far
from his side.* **Raj** *has a box of take-out chicken.* **Diz** *swigs from a
can of lager.* **Alex** *does tricks on his skateboard.* **Billy** *clowns around*

for the benefit of **Midge** *and* **Lulu**, *who share headphones on an iPod and sing tunelessly to whatever song they're playing.* **Charlie** *is in a world of his own, always on the periphery, usually ignored.*

As they walk, they talk incessantly – curses and insults fly around like stones. Individual lines can be assigned to characters as necessary.

Gang　That was shit.

That was wack.

That was dry.

You're dry.

Dry up.

Watch this.

What now?

Oy, you lot.

'S wrong with you?

Nothing.

Get off.

Oy, you lot. Watch this! You lot!

Alex's *skateboard trick goes wrong. He lands on his back. The* **Gang** *howls with laughter. They gather in front of the fence.*

Diz　What do we do now?

Billy　Throw some shit at the animals?

Spike　They ain't got any left.

Diz　Not a proper circus without animals.

Raj　You're an animal.

Diz　You're an animal. Eat so much chicken, you should be clucking.

Midge　Chloe's clucking.

Lulu   She wants to lay an egg with Spike.

Chloe   Shut up!

Alex   I'm a cheetah.

Billy   I'm a goat.

Midge   I'm a peacock.

Lulu   I'm a bunny rabbit.

Gang   Aaah!

Chloe   I'm a cougar!

Gang   Grrrr!

Diz   I'm an Indian tiger.

Raj   That's racist.

Spike   And I'm king of the jungle!

Gang   Oooh!

Pause.

Diz   So what do we do now?

Chloe   Yeah, this is boring.

Raj   You're boring.

Billy   Boring I'm snoring.

Alex   Let's go down the park. I can't work on this grass.

Spike   Park's got CCTV now.

Diz   What about the youth centre?

Raj   Closed down, innit.

Midge   Let's go *somewhere*.

Lulu   I want to see the rest of the show.

Spike   They closed the show, you mushroom.

Billy   What for?

Raj   Clown went mental, innit.

Diz   Clown gave me the finger.

Alex   Clown was off his tits.

Chloe   This circus is shit.

Spike   All circuses are shit.

Raj   Why, what we still doing here, then?

A pause. Nobody knows.

Zack *enters and hangs a sign on the fence:* 'CLOSED UNTIL
FURTHER NOTICE'.

Spike   Oy. Robin Hood. We want our money back.

Raj   You think you been robbing the rich, boy, you wrong.

Diz   You deaf?

Alex   You a mong?

Billy   Speaka da English?

Zack   Go away.

Gang   Oooh!

Spike   Hear what we said, boy? Cough up.

Zack   I don't hold the dinari.

Diz   Di-whatty?

Zack   Ask at the box office.

Spike   You're in the show, ain't you?

Raj   Or your mum dress you like that?

Zack   My mum's dead.

Alex   Poor little circus boy.

Zack   Shut up.

Gang   Oooh!

Spike *steps forward.*

Spike   I ain't taking orders from someone in tights.

*He vaults over the fence. The **Gang** cheers.*

Zack   You can't come in here, it's artistes only.

Spike   You mean piss artistes. That clown of yours was lashed.

Zack   I'll get Pappy.

*The **Gang** howls. One by one they scramble over the fence to join* **Spike**.

Gang   Pappy, he said Pappy.

Sappy Pappy.

Pappy wear a nappy.

Pappy not happy.

*As **Billy** lands, he falls over. When he stands up, his trousers, which are normally hanging halfway off his arse, fall down completely. The* **Gang** *howls with laughter.*

Diz   We got a volunteer for you, circus boy.

Spike   Billy the Kid, our resident jester. You should give him a job.

Billy   What about Midge and Lulu? (*Pointing.*) The skeleton twins.

Raj   Dyslexic anorexic. Put 'em in your sideshow.

Midge   Raj the fat man.

Diz   Like a corn-fed turkey.

Spike   Diz boy, ugly as sin, the human gargoyle.

Diz   What about you, man? Spike's got a tiny head.

Lulu/Midge   Pinhead!

Chloe   Shut up!

Alex   And Chloe's a tattooed lady, innit Chlo?

Chloe   Piss off, Alex. Scab-kneed rubberman freak.

Gang   Oooh!

Charlie *steps forward as though anticipating his turn to be insulted, but everyone ignores him.*

Zack   Go home, can't you. The show's over.

Spike   Cos your clown in trouble?

Zack   The clown's dead.

Billy   Dead?

Diz   He laugh himself to death?

Raj   I weren't laughing.

Zack   If you didn't like it, why did you come?

Spike *approaches, threatening.*

Spike   We came *here* to collect our dough. You gonna pay up, or am I gonna have to Robin Hood you?

*He grabs **Zack** by the scruff of the neck.* **Missy** *comes out through the curtains.*

Missy   Pappy's taken Pozzo to the – What's going on?

Spike *lets go.*

Zack   Nanti. (*Nothing.*)

Diz   Nanti, he said nanti!

Billy   Nanti, nanti, stick it up your panty!

Missy   Need a hand?

Zack   No.

Missy   Then what are these chavvies (*kids*) doing backstage?

Spike   Chavvies? Is that gyppo?

Zack   We're not gyppos.

Spike   So why she talking pikey?

Raj   Yeah, she chattin' three kinda shit, bwoy.

Spike   Who is she?

Zack   My sister.

Spike   She's fit.

Gang   Oooh!

Diz   Spike gonna have a big fat gypsy wedding!

Chloe   Shut up!

Zack   They want a refund.

Raj   Yeah, cos your show was wack.

Diz   Cos your circus is wack.

Chloe   Cos all circuses are wack.

Missy   If you want a refund, go to box office. This is private property.

Spike   Not any more.

Missy   Who the hell do you think you are?

Spike   I'm Spike. This is my gang.

Missy *laughs.*

Missy   Gang? (*To* **Zack**.) Put a call out on the Tannoy. There's a kindergarten class who've lost their teacher.

The **Gang** *bristles.*

Chloe   Shut up!

Diz   We don't go to school.

Billy   We left school.

Raj   We *over* school, man.

Spike   We're anarchists!

Gang Yeah!

Pause.

Diz What's it mean again?

Charlie *taps something into his phone, shows his phone to* **Midge** *and* **Lulu**.

Midge 'Anarchy: non-recognition of authority'.

Lulu 'A state of disorder'.

Midge 'The absolute freedom of the individual'.

Gang Oh.

Diz Yeah, we rebels.

Alex We soldiers.

Billy We rioters.

Chloe We outlaws.

Lulu We make trouble.

Midge On the double.

Missy Is that right?

She whips **Billy**'s *tie out from under his jacket.*

Missy St Matthew's. Thought so. Schoolkids on the bunk.

The **Gang** *shuffles, embarrassed.*

Spike So? We're still anarchists.

Zack How?

Lulu/Midge We on strike.

Missy Why?

Raj Protest at school, innit.

Missy Over what?

Billy Stuff.

Missy   What stuff?

Alex   Cuts and that.

Missy   What cuts?

Chloe   Cuts. Stuff. Funding shit. Who cares?

Missy (*to* **Zack**)   Poor little things. They're rebels without a cause.

Spike   Piss off. We know our rights.

Gang   The right to be bored.

The right to bunk off.

The right to fool around.

The right to do nothing without people breathing down our necks.

Missy   And you call that a protest?

Spike   What's it to you, bitch!

Gang   Oooh!

Missy   More than it is to you.

Spike   You don't even know us.

Missy   I've met you before.

Raj   No you ain't.

Missy   Yes I have. Every town, every county, wherever we pitch up. 'Look, gyppos. They don't wash. Don't go to school. Different. Weird.'

Spike   Well, aren't you?

Missy   We're circus folk. We know more about anarchy than you ever will. Right, Zack?

Zack (*unsure*)   Right.

Spike   You? Anarchists don't dress up like nonces.

Missy   No? What about Dionysus?

Diz   Who?

Missy   Bottom?

Diz   Bottom, she said Bottom!

Missy   Punch? Yorick? Pantaloon?

Alex   What?

Missy   Charlie Chaplin and Buster Keaton? Homer Simpson and Peter Pan?

Zack   Missy!

Missy   I'm giving the kids a lesson. (*To the* **Gang**.) Our people have defied authority since time began. In royal courts and village squares. At carnival and midsummer fair. We fly through the air, we dance on ropes, we unmask power and pull down its pants. See, people think they're laughing at us, but all the time the joke's on you. And you lot? You're just a bunch of sheep pretending to be wolves. (*To* **Zack**.) I'm going to get Pedro. (*To the* **Gang**.) If you're not gone by the time I get back, you'll see how angry a real clown looks beneath his make-up.

She stalks off. Silence.

Raj   She on the rag?

Chloe   Shut up!

Lulu   She going to grass us up for bunking off? I'll lose my pocket money if my mum finds out.

Alex   I'll be grounded.

Billy   I'll be suspended.

Spike   I'll be expelled.

Raj   Three strikes and you're out!

Chloe   Don't tell no one you saw us, okay?

Zack   Who am I going to tell? By tomorrow we might be closed.

Alex   How come?

Zack   We've already lost half our acts to Cox's. If we can't do the show, we'll go under.

Billy   Cox's is cool! They got a laser show.

Zack   I know. (*Close to tears.*) And now Tiny's gone and Pozzo's dead. Nobody wants what we've got any more.

The **Gang** *shuffles, uncomfortable.*

A young boy struts on with a tape measure. He measures the fence, writes in a notebook.

Boy (*officious*)   Afternoon.

Zack (*drying his eyes*)   Who the hell are you?

Boy   Health and Safety.

Zack   What?

Boy   My dad works for the council. We're going to shut you down.

Zack   WHAT?

Boy   Your circus draws a rough crowd, he says. Performers don't have visas, he says.

Zack   But –

Boy   Circus is anti-social, he says. When he's mayor, he says –

Midge   Wait, is your dad Mr Grey?

Boy   Councillor Grey. He's going to clean this town up and bring back some order, he says.

Midge   Grey's the one who shut down the playground where my brother goes.

Diz   And the library.

Alex   And the skate park.

Chloe   And the youth centre.

Boy   Dad says they're unnecessary. Unsanitary. A waste of public resources, he says.

Spike   Well, we say he's wrong.

Boy (*peering at* **Spike**'s *uniform*)   St Matthew's? You're on walk-out. Just because Dad shut down the drama club.

Billy   Why'd he do that?

Boy   Sacrifices must be made, he said. Dad's on the board of governors. He'll have you kicked out. (*He brandishes his notebook.*) Name?

The **Gang** *look at each other, panicked.*

Spike   He can't do that! And we don't care about the drama club!

Boy   Yes, he can. Rebel forces have got to be controlled, he says. Name?

Zack   Wait. They're not part of the walk-out. They're working for me.

Gang   Wha –

Zack *silences them with a look.*

Boy   For you? Doing what?

Zack   They're part of my show.

Boy   But they're hooligans.

Zack   No. They're acrobats. Jugglers. Clowns.

Boy   I don't believe you.

Spike *steps forward.*

Spike   You calling him a liar?

Boy (*shrinking back*)   No . . .

Spike   Good. You heard what the gaffer said. Now get off our land.

Boy   I'll be back for the show tomorrow. We'll see who's lying then.

Spike   You do that, and bring your dad. We're gonna give you a show all right.

He turns to **Zack**.

Spike   Right?

Zack   Right.

He turns to the **Gang**.

Zack   Right?

Gang (*astonished*)   Right.

Blackout. Music: 'Oh What a Circus', by David Essex.

Two

A makeshift circus ring has been fashioned out of props / bags / coats, etc. In the middle, **Diz** *stands on a step-ladder or scaffold, poised to jump off. The* **Gang** *stand below, forming a human safety net. Everyone has changed into practice clothes. A clothes rail is nearby, covered with a sheet.*

Diz (*quaking*)   I can't!

Zack   You can.

Diz   I'm scared of heights!

Zack   Then jump down, like I showed you. First, say, LISTO! That tells the catcher you're ready.

Diz   But I ain't!

Zack (*to the* **Gang**)   Then we say READY so he knows we are.

Gang   Then what?

Zack   Then, HEP! He jumps. And we catch him.

Diz   What if they drop me?

Zack   You won't drop him, will you?

Raj   Depends.

Zack   On what?

Raj   On whether or not we feel like a laugh.

The **Gang** *laughs.*

Diz   See?

Zack   If you want to be in the show, you have to learn trust.

Spike   I don't trust no one, man. What's the point?

Zack   You can't go it alone. Circus is about teamwork. Faith. Focus and calm.

Diz *spots something offstage and points.*

Diz   Oi, Zack! Your sister's coming.

Everyone panics.

Zack   Come down, then, quick.

Diz   Aaagh! Listo!

Gang   Ready!

Diz   HEP!

He jumps off the ladder and is caught safely by the **Gang***.*

Diz *(euphoric)*   That was sick! Can I do it again?

Zack   Later. Remember, if she asks, you're just helping out backstage.

The **Gang** *start working: sweeping up, polishing the fence, etc.*

Missy *enters. She looks suspiciously at the* **Gang***, who try to act inconspicuous. They are terrible actors.*

Missy   Isn't it past their bedtime?

Zack   They're giving me a hand.

Missy   With what?

Zack   Maintenance.

Missy   And what's this? (*The practice ring.*)

Zack   I was practising. How's Pappy?

Missy   Worse.

Zack   Oh?

Missy   Listen.

In the distance a blast of The Brotherhood of Man singing 'Tie a Yellow Ribbon Round the Old Oak Tree'.

Zack   Shit.

Missy   That's not all. We've lost the rest of the company.

Zack   What?

Missy   I've just spent two hours trying to talk them round. But they've gone.

Zack   Where?

Missy   Boris and Doris have defected to Cox's, Carmen and Juan have left for Spain and Zuzu's gone to Butlin's.

Zack   So that leaves –

The **Gang** *leans in eagerly.*

Missy   Us. You and me.

The **Gang** *withdraws, disappointed.*

Zack   You're saying we need a whole new company?

Missy   No, I'm saying we need a miracle.

Zack   I've got an idea . . .

The **Gang** *lean in again.* **Missy** *takes out an address book.*

Missy   And I've got Pappy's address book. I'm going to call everyone we've ever worked with.

Zack   It's midsummer weekend. They'll all be in shows of their own.

Missy   We're circus folk, remember? We stick together. And tell your friends to go home. We don't train animals here any more.

She exits.

Diz   When you gonna tell her you've found a new team?

Raj   Yeah, stop being a pussy.

Zack   I need to talk her round slowly.

Billy   You said we ain't got time to go slowly.

Lulu   You said you could show us some skills.

Zack   It's not just your lack of skills that's the problem. You're flatties.

Spike   What?

Zack   You're not circus folk. You heard her. She thinks we should keep it in the family.

Spike   Now wait a minute. First of all, I got skills. Chloe knows!

Chloe (*pleased*)   Shut up!

Spike   And second of all, I ain't a flattie. I got height. And depth. And volume.

Gang   Yeah!

Zack   Don't blame Missy. It's hard growing up in the circus. You learn not to trust outsiders.

Diz   I just trusted you!

Zack   I know. But audiences have changed. They get bored. And when they get bored, they get mean.

Midge/Lulu   Mean? What d'you mean, mean?

Zack   It was different when we were kids. When you looked out of the ring what you saw was a circle of awe. Lips parted so wide you could toss in a coin and make them swallow gold. Faces all flushed, heads thrown back as you tread the air, and the sound they make – AH! – like they're watching fireworks, only *you're* the whoosh, the fizz, the spray of stars . . .

Billy   And now?

Zack   Heads down. Checking BlackBerrys. Phones. And the O's now yawns, not gasps, 'cause they've seen it all before on a screen at home.

Spike   They won't be doing that when we come into the ring.

Zack   Show me then. What did you say? Height. Depth. Volume.

Spike   That's right.

Zack   Then catch!

Zack *tosses a juggling baton or ball up in the air for* **Spike** *to catch.* **Spike** *drops it. He tosses it to* **Raj**, *who does the same. The baton gets fumbled around the group as* **Zack** *continues trying to improvise a routine.* **Charlie** *tries to join in, but inevitably gets left out of everything.*

Zack   Now, jump!

He effortlessly leapfrogs over a member of the **Gang**. **Spike** *attempts to do the same, but falls over. The rest of the* **Gang** *follow suit, knocking each other down.*

Zack   Now, balance!

He steps on to the linked hands of two **Gang** *members, who lift him up into the air. He strikes a graceful pose, then jumps down.* **Spike** *attempts the same thing . . . and tumbles, flattening the others.*

The **Gang** *by now are a giant sprawling, moaning mess. They lie on their backs like upturned beetles, elbowing each other, cursing.* **Zack** *stands and regards them.*

Zack   You've definitely got volume.

They pick themselves up.

Spike   You're cheating, man. You been doing this for years.

Zack   I never said it was easy.

Raj   What else we gonna do? I ain't no acrobat.

Zack   What else *can* you do?

Spike *pulls the covering off the clothes rail. It's hung with clown costumes.*

Spike   We can clown about!

The **Gang** *clusters round the rail.* **Charlie** *is elbowed out of the way.* **Spike** *takes down a costume.*

Spike   Who's this?

Zack   That was Pozzo's. The white-face clown.

Raj   White-face? That's racist.

Spike   I remember. White face, red nose and wig.

Billy   Like Ronald McDonald?

Zack   No. White-face is a tyrant.

Spike   Yeah?

Zack   His wits are sharpest. His costume's the best. His aim with the pie –

Spike   Deadly?

Zack   Perfect.

Spike *starts putting on the costume.* **Raj** *takes* **Pedro**'s *costume off the rail.*

Zack   Auguste clown.

Raj   You what?

Zack   The fool.

The **Gang** *turns as one and points at* **Billy**.

Gang   Billy the Kid!

Billy   I ain't playing a fool.

Zack   He's no fool. He's the master of slapstick.

Billy   Master?

Zack   He's the butt of all jokes. Takes the pie in the face. The slap and the stick. But he still keeps going.

Midge/Lulu   Auguste's got guts.

Alex   Auguste's got nerve.

Diz   Auguste won't be beaten, boy!

Billy   I'll do it!

Billy *grabs the costume from* **Raj**. **Zack** *takes down* **Pip**'s *costume*.

Zack   Last, the Hobo.

Raj   Don't tell me. Another Caucasian.

Zack   No, this one's a dark-face.

Raj   Dark-face? That's racist!

Zack   He's a tramp.

Diz   Like Chloe.

Chloe   Shut up!

Zack   A traveller. Simple. Lives by his wits.

Midge   Wait, why these clowns all *boys*?

Zack   You can change the rules. That's what circus is all about.

Midge *steps forward and takes the costume.*

Lulu Midge!

Midge Hobo don't give a shit about what people think!

Billy Hobo don't need nothing.

Alex Hobo Zen, man!

Zack Black paint on face, white around eyes and mouth, bowler hat.

Spike, **Billy** and **Midge** *go behind the rail to finish putting on their costumes.*

Raj What about us?

Zack I don't know. What else you got?

Charlie *puts his hand up, but nobody notices.*

Diz I can text with my tongue.

Alex I can skate like a pro.

Chloe I can do my eyes like Marilyn Monroe.

Lulu I can't do nothing without Midge.

Gang Aah!

Zack But can you pull together? Focus? Take direction?

Gang Yeah.

Raj Except from your sister. Stuck-up bitch.

Missy *comes back in. The* **Gang** *jump to pretending to work again.*

Zack Well?

Missy Nobody's free. You were right. We're finished.

Zack Don't say that.

Missy It's the truth. We'll have to pack up. Three hundred years of Sparke's snuffed out in one day.

The **Gang** *moves in closer.*

Zack Missy, listen.

Missy   What?

Zack   The gang wants to help.

Missy   Good.

Gang   Yeah?

Missy   They can clean out the toilets. Pappy disagreed with the rum.

Gang   Ergh!

Raj   Now wait a minute! I ain't no cleaner! I'm a circus artiste.

Diz   And me.

Alex   And me.

Billy   And me.

Chloe   And me.

Lulu   And me.

Charlie *steps forward but is ignored.*

Missy   You what?

Zack   Why can't they be in the show?

Missy   Have you lost your mind? They're flatties.

Raj   Chloe ain't a flattie.

Chloe   Shut up!

Missy   Number one. They're kids. Number two. They're morons.

Zack   Number three, we've got twenty-four hours to devise a new show.

Missy   They wouldn't last an hour.

Spike   Says who?

He steps out from behind the clothes rail in his clown regalia, followed by **Billy** *and* **Midge**. *The* **Gang** *howls.*

Raj   It *is* Ronald McDonald. And his two McNuggets!

Gang   You look dumb.

You look wack.

You look gay.

You look . . . different.

The laughter falls away. Pause.

Spike   What's the matter?

Chloe   You're not Spike no more.

Zack   He's not supposed to be. He's playing a part.

Alex   But they could be anyone –

Lulu   We could be anywhere –

Diz   Any old clowns from any old town –

Billy   We're not us.

Spike *takes off his hat and wig.*

Spike   I wanna do something else.

Missy   Go on then. There's the ring. Step inside and show me what you got.

Spike   All right, I will!

Spike *steps into the ring. The* **Gang** *cheers.*

Missy   Well?

Spike   Well what?

Missy   What are you waiting for? Entertain us.

Spike *pulls up his hood. He spits. He shadow boxes.*

Gang   Go on, Spike.

Show dem, Spike.

Do your thing.

Make it happen.

Spike *keeps limbering up, stalling for time. The* **Gang** *get restless.* **Missy** *starts a slow clap. The* **Gang** *join in. The clap gets faster and faster.* **Spike** *gets more and more stressed out.*

Chloe *stands up.*

Chloe   Think you're better than us, do you?

Missy   Er, yes.

Zack   No, we don't.

Missy   Whose side are you on?

Zack   It's not about sides. It's about the show.

Missy (*to* **Chloe**)   So? What can you do? A backflip?

Chloe   Shut up!

Missy   An Arab Spring?

Chloe   Get lost.

Missy   The splits? A headstand? A cartwheel?

Chloe   I can do a cartwheel, bitch.

The **Gang** *cheers her on.*

Gang   Go, Chlo!

Do it, girl!

Show us your knickers!

Chloe   All right, I will!

Chloe *enters the circle and does a very bad cartwheel. The* **Gang** *cracks up.*

Raj   She not the tattooed lady, she the *bearded* lady!

Chloe   Shut up!

Missy (*to* **Zack**)   Looks like it wasn't such a good idea after all. Anyone else want a go?

Charlie *puts his hand up again.*

Missy   Who is that kid?

Diz   That's Charlie.

Raj   He don't talk.

Zack   Why not?

Gang   He's weird.

He's a loner.

A loser.

Anti-social.

ADHD.

Alex   We let him hang around cos he's got the best phone.

Missy   And that's the best you can all offer? You can't act. Can't do tricks. You've got nothing.

Gang (*defeated*)   Oh.

Zack   Forget tricks. (*To the* **Gang**.) Everybody's got something to put in the ring.

Lulu   Like what?

Zack   You tell me. What do you feel? What you do want to say?

Raj   Feel? We don't feel. That's gay.

Missy (*to* **Zack**)   You're wasting your time. We earned our place here. What have they ever had to fight for?

Lulu   Everything!

Gang   Yeah!

Midge   They want to fill you with crap. Make you fat, so you're hemmed in, pinned down, can't run.

Lulu   You got to stay light as air. Live on smoke and foam. Slip through cracks, out of their grasp, over their heads.

Diz   They want to break you. So you got to stand your ground.

Raj   Don't budge. Stay strong. Muscle and fat. So they can't see inside.

Alex   They want you to lock your wheels.

Chloe   Hobble you. No make-up, boyfriends, heels, just rules.

Missy   Who's they?

Lulu   Everyone.

Gang   We hang in the street and they make us go home.

We plug in our Pods and they say that we're were thick.

We pull up our hoods and they label us thugs.

So we roam and skate and push and shove.

We talk in code so they can't listen in.

They think we're animals but they don't know nothing.

Zack (*to* **Missy**)   See? They've got plenty to say. We just need to figure out how.

Missy   Why should we? They don't care about our circus . . . or that a piece of England's dying right before their eyes.

Raj   Your circus ain't English. That fairy girl was a Ruskie!

Missy   Ukrainian. And she's not a girl, she's forty-five.

Spike   Who cares if England's dying, anyway? England's shit.

Missy   So why don't you do something to make it better, instead of just taking the piss?

Raj   Cos we're good at it, that's why.

Gang   Yeah!

Too right!

It's a free county, innit?

Missy   Freedom's wasted on you. You've got no discipline. No imagination. No focus.

Gang   Pikey!

Bitch!

Nazi!

Spike *tears down the Sparke's Circus sign.*

Spike   We offered to help you! You deserve to go under.

Alex   You're as bad as Mr Grey.

Missy   Who the hell's he?

Alex   The councillor.

Diz   The controller.

Billy   The shut-downer.

Spike   And I say we're staging a walk-out!

Gang   What?

Spike   A strike.

Missy   You can't go on strike, you're not employed.

Spike   Don't matter. We know our rights.

Gang   The right to not be bored.

The right to let off steam.

The right to experiment without people breathing down our necks.

Diz   We want to do something.

Midge   Be someone.

Alex   And you won't let us!

Spike   So as of now, we're on protest. Zack? You with us?

Missy   Well, Zack. Are you a circus boy? Or a flattie?

Zack   I – I –

Gang   Come on, Zack!

Come cotch with us.

Choose us, not her.

Zack   I – I –

Missy   Six generations, Zack. Family tradition. Us and them.

The catcalls between **Missy** *and the* **Gang** *get louder and louder . . . until* **Zack** *loses it.*

Zack   I'm sick of this! I'm sick of fighting, and I'm sick of apologising for who I am, and I'm *sick* of wearing tights!

Everyone looks at him.

Sorry. (*To* **Missy**.) Not everything old should be saved. Empty seats in the big top? Clowns too angry to be funny and a ringmaster too drunk to crack his whip? Pappy's old, Missy. We're not.

He hesitates, then walks towards the **Gang**, *who draw him in, patting him on the back, ruffling his hair.*

Gang   Go, Zack!

Nice one!

Our mascot!

Good man!

Pause.

Diz   So what do we do now?

Spike   We walk out. And show her we mean business.
Come on.

He leads the **Gang** *and* **Zack** *off.*

Charlie *lingers, unnoticed by* **Missy**, *who sits down and buries her
face in her hands.* **Charlie** *approaches. He taps her on the shoulder.*

Missy   Piss off, why don't you, and join your friends.

Charlie *shakes his head. He whispers in her ear.*

Missy   Congratulations? For what?

Charlie *whispers in her ear again.*

Missy   Turning them into true anarchists? How?

Charlie *taps something into his phone, shows it to* **Missy**.

Missy   'Totalitarianism. Authority. Oppressive control.'
Oh.

Charlie *nods.*

Missy   What was I supposed to do? They're a bunch of
animals.

Charlie *shakes his head and whispers again.*

Missy   Put them in the ring?

Solidarity?

Community?

Conscience?

Who wants to see a show about that?

Charlie *points at himself.*

Missy   Really?

But they're on strike.

Charlie *gestures: give him a minute. He steps into the ring. He opens his mouth – and ROARS – a proper MGM lion's roar that makes the big top shake.*

Missy   How the hell d'you do that?

Charlie *whispers in her ear.*

Missy   Practice?

Charlie *nods and smiles.*

The **Gang** *and* **Zack** *enter.*

Gang   What was that?

That was wild.

That was sick.

Who got eaten?

Missy *faces the* **Gang**.

Missy   Listen. Look. Maybe I was wrong.

Spike   Go on.

Missy   You have got something. It's untapped. It's unfocused. But it's strong.

Diz   Is it in Raj's bottom?

Raj   Get lost!

Missy   It's in all of you. But you have to tame yourselves. You can't fight people with chaos. Only with form.

Zack   A new form? Not animals doing tricks, or clowns doing tired routines? A show that means something?

Missy   That's right.

Diz   So how do we do it?

Missy   Be yourselves. People are the new animals. Just ask Charlie.

Everyone looks at **Charlie**. *He nods.*

Gang   *People* are the new animals?

People are the new *animals*?

People are the new animals!

They start to caper around excitedly.

We're wild.

And angry.

But we ain't dumb.

We got form.

Full of surprises.

Know our enemies.

Defy authority.

We tame ourselves, boy.

Charlie *takes a whip out of his pocket and gives it to* **Missy**. *She cracks it. The* **Gang** *stops.* **Missy** *grins.*

Missy   Well? Are you ready to work or not?

Gang   Yeah!

Missy   Then gather round, beasts. I think I've got an idea!

The group huddles together around **Missy** *as the lights cut to blackout.*

Music: 'Copacabana' by Danny La Rue.

Three

The music carries over. Lights up on the ring. We're now inside the circus big top. A new sign has been made: THE PEOPLE'S CIRCUS.

The music cuts abruptly as if the record has been ripped off the turntable. The ringmaster enters with a flourish – it's **Missy**, *wearing a top hat.*

Missy   Ladies and gentlemen, boys and girls, welcome to the greatest show on earth – the circus. A place of thrills and danger, euphoria and hilarity, and family fun.

Crowd applause.

Look around you at the happy faces in the audience. See the bright eyes of the children, their parents, and grandparents. So contented, so peaceful, so –

A missile flies on stage and hits **Missy** *in the face (it could be a vegetable, a shoe, anything . . .)*

Missy   You'll pay for that, you little beasts! (*To the audience.*) Sorry, ladies and gents. Now, sit tight, hold on to your hats, and remember, whatever you do, don't . . . feed . . . the animals!

She runs off. The clowns' intro music strikes up, and the three clowns run on: **Spike**, **Billy** *and* **Midge**.

CLOWN ROUTINE

Spike *now wears a grey suit jacket, grey tie and grey trilby hat, with grey face paint (a parody of Mr Grey).* **Billy** *the* **Kid** *is a clown 'youth' (an exaggerated version of himself) in baggy pants halfway down his arse, massive over-sized trainers, iPod and baseball cap.* **Midge** *as the* **Hobo** *is a homeless person in a dress made of cardboard, a bottle of booze and a begging bowl.*

The basic action of their routine is outlined below, but the company can improvise and embellish as necessary.

Greyface *discovers* **Hobo** *begging, demonstrates his contempt for her, and shows his own authority.* **Greyface** *attempts to move* **Hobo** *along. The* **Kid** *comes along, tries to intervene and prevent* **Greyface** *from hauling* **Hobo** *off to be punished.* **Hobo** *and the* **Kid** *form an alliance in order to challenge* **Greyface**'s *authority. They bamboozle, outwit and finally depose him. The skit climaxes with* **Greyface**'s *public humiliation.*

*The emphasis should be on physical speed, slapstick and farce –
movements are exaggerated and could incorporate tumbles, somersaults
and pratfalls. The* **Kid** *and* **Hobo** *might jump on* **Greyface***'s
back, steal his hat and toss it between them, terrorise him with the
music on the iPod, strip him of his outfit, etc. They might eventually
carry him off, or leave him wearing the* **Hobo***'s outfit and arrest him.*

*Props can be used as necessary. Each clown might also have a single
line of dialogue that they can repeat as often as necessary, or
communicate with a particular sound. I suggest:* **Greyface***, 'It's a
disgrace!' The* **Kid***, 'Believe!'* **Hobo***, 'Spare any change.' But these
can be changed or omitted as desired.*

The clowns leave the stage to applause. **Missy** *comes back on.*

Missy   And now, ladies and gentlemen, for the most daring
part of the show. I introduce you to – the animals!

Diz, **Raj**, **Lulu**, **Chloe** *and* **Alex** *enter at her flourish. They
wear animal masks (chimp, dog, tiger, camel, etc.) and prowl, snarl,
scratch, fight among themselves. They might perform some chaotic
animal acrobatics.*

Missy   Such wildness. Such depravity. Such insolence!
We must tame them into docile subordinates! Or chaos . . .
will . . . reign!

Zack *runs on – the animal trainer. He cracks a whip. The animals
cower, terrified.*

ANIMAL-TAMING ROUTINE

New music starts up for this routine. **Zack** *begins to marshal the
animals through a series of movements. They jump through hoops,
balance on bins or chairs, perform choreographed movements. Each time
an animal completes a trick,* **Zack** *gives them a reward – money
(a coin or note), a can of beer, a cigarette, a mobile phone, etc. The
animals grab at them excitedly, sniff them, pocket them.*

The clowns reappear. They start to interfere with **Zack***'s routine,
teasing the animals, provoking them.* **Greyface** *steals the whip and*

tries to discipline them. The **Kid** *gets in the way.* **Hobo** *steals the animals' food.*

Zack *tries to rally round but the manic energy of the clowns is too much for him. The show has by now descended into chaos, with the animals getting wilder and wilder as their 'treats' are confiscated and stolen.*

A police siren sounds in the background. **Missy** *runs on, carrying a flashing blue light. (She might be accompanied by other policemen played by* **Pozzo**, **Pedro** *and* **Pip**.*) She manages to chivvy the animals into a circle, and lassoes them with a rope. She leads them around in a circle, and takes them into a prison. (The prison can be created with lighting, props or actors.) The circus music ends with a flourish as the animals' imprisonment begins.*

The animals stand in their cell, dejected, while a sentry keeps watch outside (a policeman or a clown, perhaps **Greyface**). **Missy** *appears, wearing the robes of a judge, and passes sentence on them, again without using words.*

ANIMAL DANCE ROUTINE

The animals prowl the cage. They begin to fight among themselves, scratching, snarling, biting. Then, from the animals' midst, **Charlie** *appears. He wears a hoodie, pulled up to obscure his face – another prisoner. He takes out an iPod and presses play. A new musical track starts up. This one is very different in tone from the previous ones. It's rhythmic, spare and urban (see notes at end for suggestions).*

Charlie *begins to move to the music – he is graceful, elegant and very controlled.*

The animals stop fighting each other to watch. Eventually, they begin to copy **Charlie**'s *movements. At first they're clumsy, but they soon get the hang of it. They become a group, not just a gang; they are synchronised, focused, fluid.*

Outside, the guard covers his ears. He summons the judge and the other policemen. They attempt to constrain the group inside the prison walls, but the group eventually outmanoeuvre their oppressor and break through the walls of the prison. (This should be done without violence, but keeping to the discipline of the dance routine.)

The prison vanishes. **Missy**, **Zack** *and the authority figures exit. The animals remove their animal masks and continue with their routine, which grows in scope and confidence. This is* **Charlie**'s *big moment to perform as the leader of the gang and the star of the show. His turn might include acrobatics, juggling, breakdancing, skateboarding – whatever the actor's talents are. Whatever they are, the act should be surprising and spectacular. Or surprising and hilarious!*

At the climax of the animals' act, the clowns run back on . . . They may have all swapped clothes now, or **Greyface** *might be chasing* **Kid** *and* **Hobo** *in a reversal of their earlier routine. They carry a box or bundle. They put it down.* **Tinkerbelle** *bursts out and cartwheels across the stage – the grand finale.*

Zack *and* **Missy** *run on, astonished.*

Zack   You're back!

Tinkerbelle   Fugging right. Cox's sucked.

She curtseys. The whole company bow to rapturous applause from the audience.

Four

Backstage. The **Gang**, *minus* **Missy** *and* **Zack**, *explode through the big top curtains. They shake hands, hug, kiss, dance. They are jubilant. They are artistes!*

The **Boy** *enters, and stands outside the fence, watching.*

Spike   Well? What's your dad got to say to that?

Boy   Dad's gone home. He's a laughing stock, he said. He won't run for mayor now, he said.

The **Gang** *high-five each other.* **Zack** *and* **Missy** *enter.*

Zack   We've broken our record at the box office!

Missy   There's an agent in the audience, he wants the show for a UK tour!

The **Gang** *whoops.*

Boy   Can I join your circus? Please?

Pause.

Spike   What can you do?

Boy (*dejected*)   Nothing.

Spike *smiles.*

Spike   That's what we said. (*He goes to the fence and lifts the* **Boy** *up on to it.*) Say listo.

Boy   Listo.

Spike (*to the* **Gang**)   Ready?

Gang   Ready.

All   Hep!

Lights cut to black before the boy jumps.

Don't Feed the Animals

BY JEMMA KENNEDY

*Notes on rehearsal and staging, drawn from a workshop
with the writer held at the National Theatre, November 2012*

Why the writer came to write the play

Teamwork   One of the reasons Jemma Kennedy wrote the
play was to investigate hierarchy and status. In the course of
the story these considerations have to be put aside, the gang
has to work together and form new collaborative relationships.

'People are the new animals'   Jemma spoke about this central
metaphor of the play: the way young people are controlled
and contained. Creativity is about instinct, not academia.

This play is about letting the cast discover their creative
instincts but then giving them the structure, self-discipline and
focus to transform these instincts into a great production.

Location/language/local issues

This play is not location-specific. Jemma is happy for you to
adapt the play and the language to suit your local idioms.
The key is to use your groups and see what they bring to it.
The rule of thumb from facilitating director Angus Jackson
was: if you are going to substitute words, make sure that the
flow/rhythm of the line isn't disrupted. Any substitute words
should therefore be of similar length. The key for Jemma is to
keep the meaning.

If locations are mentioned, you can feel free to change them.
If there is a local issue connected with government cuts and
closure of a local community centre, for example, then by all
means insert it when the gang talk of how there is nothing for
them to do and nowhere for them to go. The kids walk out
from school because the Drama Club has been closed down.

Any local issue you think will connect with your actors and the audience can be substituted for this.

Approaching the play

In the workshop we read through the play and talked through the facts. What do we know? What has just happened? What can we infer about the kids and their lives?

These interesting facts and questions came out of the read-through and accompanying discussions:

- Tiny the elephant has just been sold. When?

- Elephants cost between £12,500 and £65,000, depending on size, age, experience. They cost around £300 per week to keep.

- How long has Pozzo been drinking? Has he rapidly sunk into fatal alcoholism or has it been a slow decline? What has he just done in the ring to make the crowd boo him off? Angus suggested that the more recent this descent into alcoholism, the less time Zack and Missy have had to deal with it and come up with a solution. This makes the stakes much higher and their problem more immediate. The higher the stakes the more dramatic the situation. The stakes are the fuel for the action, they motivate each character.

- Research the different types of clown: the White-Face, the Auguste, the Hobo.

- Google 'circus lingo'. Here's one link: http://filmwaterfor elephants.wordpress.com/bigtop/circus-lingo/

- Zack and Missy don't have to be brother and sister, but they should be family – cousins perhaps.

- The biggest show of the year is the next day. Decide which bank holiday it is, and establish the timeline.

- Jemma did not mind if the 'show tunes' were changed.

- What act are Missy and Zack performing? It can be changed but must be something that is traditional and recognisable. Cal McCrystal, clowning director, suggested a crossbow routine.

- The gang's lines need to be generally heard in the scenes when they are spoken by individual characters, but when spoken by the gang as a group they can overlap. These lines can be shared by an ensemble of actors.

- Can Raj be played by a middle-class white kid? Yes, a white Raj could be playing the part of a 'street' Asian kid, like Etonians speaking with South London accents. He could be trying to be cool. This is just an example of a character choice; it is up to the actor and director to decide.

- Don't be tempted to change the lines for the characters of the gang. If they don't seem to suit the actor, examine what the line tells you about the character, how that might be a character trait and how it might inform the choices of the actor playing them. However, sometime kids say stuff just to entertain each other and the lines are not there to give us some huge character insight.

- The gang wants a refund. Did they pay to get into the circus? Probably not.

- *The Boy.* Who is he? How old is he? Why is he not at school? These are questions that you will have to find the answer to yourselves. He can be a she. However, this character needs to be a genuine threat to the gang, someone they cannot touch. For Cal the casting of this part is crucial: it needs to be someone with presence and charisma, someone who can stand up to the gang.

- Why does Zack not tell Missy about signing up the gang to help out? Why did he sign them up in the first place?

- *The Flop.* Clowns go into the ring to be funny. If they do something that doesn't get a laugh and then acknowledge the failure, you may get a laugh out of that.

- *The Insisting Gag.* Clowns must always enter with a sense of optimism. If the gag fails, it is this optimism that makes them try again. As the gag is repeated, it can sometimes get funnier even though the audience know what it is.

- *Chorus work.* The gang are a unit but that doesn't mean they are not individuals. Take time to find out who they are, make their characters unique and don't let them just pick up on each other's rhythms and pace.

- Should the initial entrance of the gang be choreographed? It was felt that it should not be highly choreographed so that it formed a greater contrast with the circus show at the end.

- If you have some circus skills then teach them to the cast. You don't need to teach them pratfalls or traditional clown gags. They have to find their own clown, starting with their own physicality.

Cal McCrystal on approaches to physical comedy

There's no getting away from it, the last section of the play needs to be funny. For this to work, the actors need to create their roles and the routines. The director of the piece will need to create a safe place for this to happen.

Start with a question for your performers:

> Steven Spielberg meets you in the street and wants to cast you in his next movie. He asks you what your dream role is. What do you say? What sort of character do you want to play and what is it about that character that makes you want to play it?

You want your actors to be playing their dream role now, in this play. It also helps them to articulate why they want to perform. Look into your actors' personalities; find the characters in the actors and not the script.

Games are a safe way to get actors to perform, taking the pressure off them to create.

Use the following exercises to unlock the final scene.

Exercises for use in rehearsals

THE FASHION SHOW

- The group sits at one end of the room. Place two upturned tables to form an entrance at the other end of the room.

- One at a time, walk down the room as if you are on a catwalk. Once you reach the audience, walk from one side of the room to the other. On the way out, just as you are about to leave you must 'bust a move'.

- There should be fun, pumping music but not anything too cool as that will make them pose. Naff pop music is best.

- Look for the pleasure in doing it. The clown never wants to leave the stage.

- If you have a part of your body that you normally feel uncomfortable with, exaggerate it. This now becomes your sexiest body part: flaunt it.

- Don't be afraid to go for it. You cannot be over the top. That is what we enjoy.

- Everyone has to do it.

- We want the audience to laugh *at* you, not with you.

- We want the audience to feel superior to the clowns. We love them because they are not afraid to make fools of themselves, they are open and vulnerable.

STATUS — THE EUROVISION SONG CONTEST

Four friends decide to enter the Eurovision Song Contest. They are selected to perform and go to the finals. They are very excited and can't wait. They take the stage to perform – and only at that moment realise that they haven't chosen a song to sing. Each expects one of the others will come up with something; only problem is that they all think that they are the lowest-status person in the group.

- Don't act, let it come, a song will appear.

- Choose the friends. Send them out and play some introduction music.
- Announce the group and get the audience to cheer wildly.
- Get the group to enter, stand in a row facing the audience.
- See what happens.
- Make sure that no one leads or consciously starts the song.

Ask the audience, who is the most intelligent? Who is the most stupid? Who has status?

THE SHAKESPEARE SPEECH

- Choose an actor who knows a speech from Shakespeare. They are the lead. They must deliver this speech with as much seriousness as possible to the audience.
- Meanwhile another actor is sitting on the stage waiting for their time to enter the scene. This performance is in the Brechtian style so the actors are on stage the whole time.
- The other actor must make sure that the audience is concentrating on the speech. If they feel that they are being watched by the audience they must make sure that the audience knows that they should be watching the other actor. They must do this while trying to stay ready and in character and without disturbing the other actor.
- Clowns are funnier when they are trying to help and not trying to mess things up.

In this game the major and minor roles are reversed. The minor character is the lead in this instance, because our attention is completely on the actor waiting to go on.

THE TORTURE

This is the iconic clowning exercise. If you attempt it, make sure that all the group are supportive and in a safe place.

- One at a time enter the room and be funny in front of the rest of the group.

- If you flop, which you will, take it. You might get a laugh. You can't be clown or comedian unless you have flopped.
- The clown is the most vulnerable part of who you are and the most elusive to find. Every clown finds it a real pleasure to perform; they don't want to be anywhere else.

PLEASURE

- Choose an actor to walk into the room and see how long they can sustain real pleasure in being in front of the audience. Ask the audience to say how long it lasted.
- Repeat the exercise but tell the actor to imagine that it is their birthday and all the audience have arrived just to see them. How is it different? It's hard to act pleasure, it needs to come from the inside.

GRANDMOTHER'S FOOTSTEPS

We know the rules. This is a great game to play as everyone who plays is in a constant state of readiness and pleasure to be there. That is the state they need to be on stage with.

ROMEO AND JULIET

- Choose someone who knows the words to a silly song. They need to know enough of the words that they can perform them as a speech.
- This actor will now play Romeo.
- Choose an actor to play Juliet. Juliet will lie next to Romeo as if she is dead.
- Romeo is to find her dead body and, with as much reality as possible, he is to recite the words of his silly song as if they are the lines written for him. He is to take the poison and die.
- Perform it as seriously as possible. The more seriously you play it, the funnier it will be. Seeing a clown trying to be a good actor is funny.

WHO KILLED KING JOHN?

This should come under the heading of 'games to make you look stupid'. It's a great icebreaker between teachers and pupils.

- Stand in a circle. Number round in a circle from King Cal (for instance) through Number One, Number Two, etc., to the last person in the circle.

- The game goes like this

    King Cal asks Number One: 'Who killed King John?'

    Number One: 'Not I.'

    King Cal: 'Then who killed King John?'

    Number One: 'Number Three killed King John.'

    Number Three: 'Not I.'

    Number One: 'Then who killed King John?'

    Number Three: 'Number Five killed King John.'

    Number Five: 'Not I.' *Etc.*

- When someone gets it wrong, they move to the bottom of the group and everyone moves up a place.

- It should be speedy, which means there will be more mistakes.

ARE YOU SENSITIVE?

Get three people to walk into the room and stand in front of the audience. Ask the audience many and various questions about the performers.

- What type of car are they?
- What animal are they?
- Who looks the most stupid?
- What piece of furniture are they? Etc.

One-third of who we are is what we think of ourselves. Two-thirds is what other people think of us. For the clown it is best to know what people think of you and how they perceive you.

Ask the performers what is it about them that their friends laugh about behind their backs? To know your weaknesses is essential for the clown.

HOT SEATING

It's great to get the actors to talk about their characters before they have had a chance to think too much. They may discard some of what they say when hot seated but most of it will stick.

THE LYING GAME

Choose four people.

- Ask them to think about some unusual skill they have or some amazing experience.
- Ask them to leave the room and tell each other their secrets.
- They have to decide on one of the secret skills/experiences. Don't discuss the details of the skill or experience. Choose the one that is the most extreme.
- Ask them to come back into the room.
- The four people now have to convince the audience that they are the one who has the skill or had the experience.
- We now ask them questions. Our task is to find out who is lying and who is telling the truth.
- When answering the questions, try not to block. It is easy to say 'No'. The danger is in saying 'Yes'; we then have the pleasure of seeing you try to be inventive.

DANCING

Get your actors to dance. It's fun to see people enjoying their own stupidity. Get them to dance as if they fancy someone on the other side of the room.

IMPERSONATION

Get the actors to speak their lines impersonating the worst actor they know. How does this liberate their performance? It may free them up.

THE CLOWNING SCENE

Ways of starting:

- Choose five performers.
- Go behind the screen and then enter.
- Your aim is to come in and perform a clowning scene.
- They only have one chair as the set.
- All the clowns have to be optimistic.
- Don't play clowns, play yourselves.
- Try and work together.

Just try stuff out, be aware of what the audience react to and try it again. See what happens.

Once you have tried this, you can then structure it, cast the characters. In our session, for instance, we chose two brothers, and two parents with a young daughter who fancied the younger brother; the older brother fancied the young girl but she didn't like him. The parents didn't want her near the boys. Play it again and see what happens.

This is a great way to start. Send groups away to devise routines and see what they come up with. Then you can work from that.

Questions for Jemma, Cal and Angus

How much physical contact can there be?

Cal suggests that there should be as much as possible. Practise stage fighting, slaps, kicks up the bum, hair grabs, etc. Violence should not be gendered. Make sure you approach stage combat and violence with appropriate expertise and take health and safety very seriously. Try searching online for local fight directors.

Can you teach timing?

'Timing' is knowing when the audience want you to do that funny thing, deciding whether you want to give it to them, and if so when.

Does the relationship have to be between Spike and Chloe?

No, but we need that dynamic in the group so move it to another pair of characters if necessary.

Final words

Have fun with the play. It is about letting the performers show off their skills. The final act is about them throwing themselves into it and seeing what happens. The aim is for them to feel free and uninhibited.

From a workshop led by Angus Jackson
with Physical Comedy Director Cal McCrystal,
with notes by Drew Mulligan

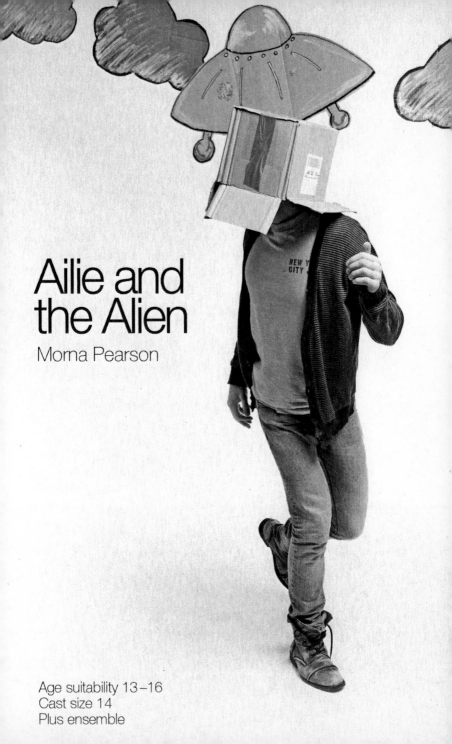

Ailie and
the Alien

Morna Pearson

Age suitability 13–16
Cast size 14
Plus ensemble

Morna Pearson is from Elgin and currently lives in Edinburgh. Her first full professional production was *Distracted* at the Traverse Theatre in 2006, which won the Meyer-Whitworth Award 2007 and was nominated for a CATS Award. Morna was given the inaugural Rod Hall Memorial Award in 2006. Her other plays include: *Elf Analysis* (Òran Mór), *McBeth's McPets* (BBC Radio Scotland), *Side Effects* (BBC Radio 3/Bona Broadcasting), *The Company Will Overlook a Moment of Madness* (adaptation, NTS/Òran Mór), *Skin; or How to Disappear* (short, Agent 160), *The Artist Man and the Mother Woman* (Traverse Theatre).

Characters

Ailie, *female, sixteen*
Beth, *female, sixteen, Ailie's best friend*
Claire, *female, sixteen*
Darren, *male, twenty, Beth's boyfriend*
Ericson, *PE teacher (written as male but can be adapted to female)*
Finn, *alien male, sixteen/seventeen, clumsy, not used to his human body*
Grant, *male, seventeen, kept back a year*
Harrison, *Geography teacher, male or female*
Igor, *male, fifteen, advanced a year*

Other school pupils include **Pupil One**, **Pupil Two**
Alien *family,* **Mum**, **Dad** *and little* **Sister**

Some characters only have a couple of lines so can be doubled if need be.

One

ON THE COUNTRY BUS

A school bell rings; it's the end of the day. The sound of pupils spilling out of the building. **Ailie** *is first on the bus,* **Claire** *close behind her.*

Claire   Oh my God, I thought the day was never going to end.

Ailie   Tell me about it.

Claire   Eh, was I speaking to you?

Ailie (*looking around her, there's no one else there*)   Yes?

The bus starts filling up fast. **Ailie** *is trying to save the seat next to her for* **Beth**. *Several* **Pupils** *try to sit on it.*

Ailie   No, saving it . . . Saving it . . . Beth's seat . . . It's taken . . .

Eventually, the only other seat left is next to **Claire**, *who is on the seats adjacent to* **Ailie**. **Beth** *finally gets on the bus.*

Ailie (*enthusiastically waving and shouting*)   Beth! Saved you a seat. Beth!

Claire (*coolly*)   Sit next to me, Beth.

Beth *sits next to* **Claire**.

Beth (*to* **Ailie**, *awkwardly*)   Sorry.

Claire   So, like, tell me all about Darren. Is he rich? Does he play football? Does he have a hairy chest? He totally does, doesn't he?

Beth   Ehm . . .

Claire   How old is he?

Beth   Twenty.

Claire   Wow, that's so mature.

Beth   Hm . . . yeah . . . suppose he is.

Claire   So . . . what else is he like?

Beth   He's really spontaneous. Like, we can just be sitting around on a boring Sunday and he'll suddenly be all, 'Let's drive to the beach,' 'Let's drive to the mountains,' 'Let's drive by pigeons and throw bricks at them.'

Claire   So he's got a car? That's totally cool.

Beth   Yeah. He is cool.

Beat.

Here, I've got a photo.

Beth *shows* **Claire** *a photo on her phone, and they engage in gossip.* **Igor** *is the last to get on the bus. He makes a beeline for* **Ailie**.

Ailie   Oh great.

Igor   Ah, *ma cherie*, we meet again. I just did a mean experiment in the Chemistry lab.

Ailie   Really?

Igor   I detect a lack of inquisitiveness in your tone, however I shall carry on regardless. Mr Hans had clearly had a liquid lunch, he didn't know what he was doing. At one point, he just stared at his reflection in the departmental television and cried. So I took it upon myself to lock him in the cupboard with his bottle of scotch, and take charge of the class myself. I thought I'd get them excited about science again and show them how to make fire without a match or lighter. Potassium permanganate and glycerine, and a drop of water to accelerate the reaction. There were singed eyebrows all round. Well, not mine, as I was the only one wearing goggles. It was absolutely mint, though.

Ailie   Mint?

Igor   Or whatever slang word for exceptional the kids are using these days. So, I've been thinking –

Ailie   Oh no –

Igor   I think you and I should go to the cinema. We'll have to go out of town of course, unless you want to see some god-awful-piece-of-fluff Vince Vaughan vehicle. (*Snorts.*) My mum can drive us. And she'll want to escort me anyway. She won't let me on dates alone because she's scared I'll lose my innocence before I'm sixteen.

Ailie   I think you're safe there.

Beth *interrupts* **Igor** *and* **Ailie**.

Beth   Hey, Ailie, have you done tomorrow's Geography homework?

Ailie   Yeah.

Beth   Can I copy it?

Ailie   Ehm . . . I don't have it on me.

Beth   Hey, why don't you bring it round tonight? Yeah, do that. See you at six.

She starts talking to **Claire** *again, not giving* **Ailie** *a chance to answer.*

Ailie   But I don't know if my dad can –

She tuts, then exhales loudly.

Igor   She's not listening. Welcome to my world. Nobody listens, nobody cares, nobody understands what it's like to be a genius stuck inside the body of a fiercely underdeveloped fifteen-year-old boy, forced to rot his brains at a frighteningly low-achieving school.

Ailie   Shut it, Igor.

Igor   I shall rise above the name-calling. The irony is that Grant, the joker who named me Igor, and his friends are too ignorant to know that in reality I would've been Dr Frankenstein and someone like Grant would be my hunch-backed dumbo assistant. (*Snorts.*) But I expect more from you, Ailie. I'm disappointed.

Ailie   Sorry.

Igor   So, are we going to the cinema or what?

Ailie   Oh look, it's my stop.

Two

AILIE'S HOUSE

Ailie *has arrived back to a quiet house. Lights are on, the feeling that someone should be here, or has just left. An empty glass sits on the kitchen counter.* **Ailie** *lifts it and smells it.*

Ailie   Dad?

A lonely silence. She puts the TV on and channel-flicks, eventually turns it off.

Dad?

Pauses for a reply or some sign of life. There isn't one. She picks up her Geography homework book, puts it into her school bag, puts the bag on her back.

Three

CYCLING TO BETH'S

Ailie *gets on her fairly rubbish bicycle. She starts the journey to* **Beth***'s farmhouse, three miles away. The road is narrow, rarely straight, and undulating.*

Four

BETH'S BEDROOM

Ailie *arrives, windswept, sweaty and out of breath.* **Beth** *and* **Darren** *are lying on the bed.*

Ailie   Hi Beth –

Darren   Hi babe.

Ailie (*surprised when she notices* **Darren**)   Oh!

Beth   Ailie!

Ailie   What's he doing here?

Beth   I forgot . . . Did we say six?

Ailie   Yeah, but I'm early.

Glances at **Darren**.

Ailie   It's not usually a problem.

Beth   My mum and dad went out, so Darren came round.

Darren   Don't worry, there's room here for one more.

He pats the bed and winks. **Beth** *gives him a death-stare and* **Ailie** *is visibly creeped out.*

Ailie (*to* **Beth**)   Is Darren leaving soon?

Beth   No, probably not.

Ailie   You could've told me. I've just cycled all the way for nothing.

Beth   Did you bring your homework book?

Ailie   Yeah.

Beth   Well, it's not for nothing then.

Darren   What's this all about? Homework? I never did any homework and I'm okay.

Ailie   That's debatable.

Darren   I've never been out of work.

Beth   But you work for your dad.

Darren   And . . . ?

Beth   Nothing.

Ailie (*taking homework book out of bag*)   Here, just take it.

She throws the book on to the bed. **Darren** *reaches for it and starts looking through it.*

Beth   Thanks. I'll give it back first thing tomorrow.

Ailie   You better.

Beth   I will.

Ailie   At least get a thesaurus and change a few words. See you tomorrow, Beth.

Beth   Cool.

Darren   Bye, Ailie.

As **Ailie** *leaves the house, she hears them laughing. She suddenly feels a bit paranoid.*

Five

CYCLING HOME

Ailie *notices it's getting dark. She goes to switch on her bicycle lights, only to find they don't work. Suddenly, the sky starts to rumble.* **Ailie** *jumps on her bike to try and beat the rain. Moments later, the rain begins to pour down.* **Ailie** *is soaked, exhausted and cold, still pedalling away as the thunder turns to lightning. Then, a rumble – a different sound from the thunder – begins, gradually getting louder. Bright lights seem to be approaching from above.* **Ailie**, *still cycling away, looks up just as a spaceship flies low over her head. The force and the shock knock her off her bike. The spaceship crash-lands in the next field.* **Ailie** *remains unconscious on the road. Four little green* **Aliens** *cautiously toddle towards* **Ailie**, *nattering away in a squeaky alien language. Three of them come to a halt a little distance away, while one carries on moving closer to her and touches her head.*

Six

NEXT DAY AT SCHOOL

*At break. There's the usual amount of noise and chatter going on. New boy **Finn** sits alone in the corner. **Beth** speaks to **Claire**.*

Beth   So I heard Darren speaking to someone on his phone last night – saying something about Amsterdam and wanting to keep it a secret from me . . .

Claire   Oh my God!

Beth   I know! I think he's going to surprise me on my birthday.

Claire   Wow. Does he have any mates that I might like? Y'know, but totally much better-looking?

*Igor approaches **Finn**.*

Igor   Greetings new boy. Bijeghbe chugh vaj biHegh!

Pronounciation: bee-JEGH-bey-choogh-vaj-b-KHEGH; translation: 'Surrender or die!'

Finn   Pardon?

Igor   Ah, you don't speak Klingon. You have failed my friendship test. That said, beggars can't be choosers. Come on, I'll show you round.

Finn   Great. (*Stands up, a bit wobbly.*) I'm a bit wobbly on these legs.

Igor   What's the matter? Have you had an operation?

Finn   Yes . . . well . . . sort of.

He smiles.

Ailie *enters, she has a large plaster on her forehead, perhaps a bandage on her arm. She approaches **Beth** and **Claire**.*

Ailie   Hi. What have I missed?

Claire   Certainly not the branches on the ugly tree you fell out of.

Ailie   Funny.

Beth   What's happened to you?

Ailie   I think I must've fallen off my bike. I remember leaving yours last night, and it started to rain and then I woke up in bed at half nine this morning. I don't know, I must've blacked out but somehow got home.

Beth   Jeez, do you think it was a hit-and-run?

Ailie   Suppose it could've been.

Beth   Is your head okay?

Ailie   Yeah, I think so. Dad thinks I might need stitches though –

Claire   Ugh, I'm bored. It's always about you.

She walks away.

Ailie   Oh well. Did you have fun last night?

Beth   Yeah, Darren's taking me to Amsterdam.

Ailie   Oh wow. When?

Beth   For my birthday. I mean, I think. It's not definite.

Ailie   I thought we were going to Fat Willy's Fancy Dress Roller Disco for your birthday?

Beth   But I can't really say no to a holiday. He would've put a deposit down and everything.

Ailie   But I've put a deposit down for our costumes . . .

Beth   Sorry.

The bell rings.

Seven

GEOGRAPHY

Igor *and* **Finn** *are sitting next to each other as other pupils continue to enter the classroom.* **Grant** *enters and sits behind* **Igor**.

Igor   So, where are you from, Finn?

Finn   Kind of all over.

Igor   I see.

Finn   I probably won't be here for long. It's kind of an unscheduled stop. But my parents are keen that I don't miss out on my education, and they want me to experience all sorts of cultures before the war to end planet Earth and all humankind begins.

Igor   Ha ha. Good one. Well, I'm not sure your parents have made the right choice. There are too many dunces in this school, they hold us over-achievers back. For instance –

Turns round to **Grant** *who is drawing graffiti on the table.*

Igor   Grant. What nationality is Stephen Hawking?

Grant   Who's Stephen Hawking? Your boyfriend?

Igor *turns back to* **Finn**.

Igor   And I thought he was going to say American. My expectations of him could not get any lower.

Grant   Igor, if you were on *Mastermind*, would your specialist subject be wedgies or crying like a girl?

Ailie *and* **Beth** *enter.* **Ailie** *sits next to* **Finn**. *They have an instant attraction to each other.*

Igor   Ah, Finn. Meet my girlfriend, Ailie –

Ailie   Not your girlfriend.

Igor   Not yet. Ailie, meet Finn. He's a bohemian gentleman of the travelling community, and he doesn't speak Klingon.

Ailie   Like any normal person.

Igor   That's harsh. Perhaps fair. Anyway, how's your knowledge on glacial features, Finn?

Ailie   Oh yeah – (*Turns to* **Beth**.) Beth, can I have my homework back?

Beth   Oh shit.

Ailie   No, you're joking.

Beth   I forgot it.

Ailie   Oh my God, we're so in the shit.

Beth   Well, I'm not. I just forgot yours.

Ailie   What?!

Teacher **Harrison** *enters the room, clearly in a bad mood.* **Ailie** *stands, desperately wanting to escape the room.*

Harrison   Oi, you. Sit down.

Ailie   Sorry. I was just –

Harrison   Sit. (*To* **Finn**.) You're a new one.

Finn   Yes.

Harrison   Oh well. Homework to the front. Now.

Everyone passes their homework jotters to the front of the class, except **Ailie**, *who looks uncomfortable.*

Harrison   Where's yours?

Ailie   I think I . . . left it at home.

Harrison   Detention.

Ailie   I've done it, but it's just . . . not here.

Harrison   Two days' detention.

Ailie   But I can't, I'll miss the bus and my dad can't pick me up –

Harrison   A week's detention.

Finn *has ducked down as if to pick something off the floor. He has magically produced* **Ailie***'s homework book.*

Finn   Excuse me. Is this it?

Ailie   How did it – ?

Finn   You must've dropped it on the floor.

Ailie   Oh . . . right . . .

Beth   That's really weird because I left it at –

Ailie (*elbows* **Beth**)   Yes, it's weird . . . because . . . I never . . . drop . . . things.

Harrison   Okay. Give it. The whole class gets extra homework to make up for the time Ailie has wasted.

Everyone groans, apart from **Igor***.*

Igor   Yes!

Ailie *stares in disbelief at* **Beth***.*

Eight

ON THE BUS

Finn *sits next to* **Ailie***.* **Igor** *is disappointed when he sees* **Finn** *has taken that seat, but he takes the adjacent seat.*

Ailie   Hi, Finn.

Finn   Hi.

Ailie   So, how did you do that trick?

Finn   What trick?

Ailie   Where my homework jotter magically appeared from nowhere.

Finn   I don't know what you're talking about. I just found it on the floor.

Ailie   Really? That's your story and you're sticking to it.

Finn   Got you out of trouble though, didn't it?

He smiles.

Ailie   Hey, Igor, want to go to Fat Willy's Fancy Dress Roller Disco with me next weekend?

Igor   Well. Look how the tables have turned –

Ailie   It's not a date. I'm only asking you cos I don't know anyone else that would be seen dead wearing a Star Wars costume on a Saturday night. And I don't want to lose my deposit.

Igor   Oh, how I'd love to spend a romantic evening with you, Ailie, however, despite my many talents, the ability to roller skate eludes me. I wouldn't want to scrape my knees.

Ailie   But that's okay, cos you'll be wearing an inflatable Jabba the Hutt costume.

Igor   Oh, okay then. That'll please Mother – I'll literally be wrapped up in cotton wool.

Ailie   Great.

Igor   And will you be dressed up as . . . oh lord, I'm getting tingly just thinking about . . . Princess Leia?

Ailie   No. Chewbacca.

Igor   Damnit. That's only half my fantasy realised then.

Some time passes on the bus. Things are thrown, pupils standing up, swapping seats, being pushed, laughing, shouting, gossiping, someone opens a packet of sweets and offers one to the person next to them. That person takes one from the packet and passes the packet on to someone else, and so forth, until the packet has travelled round the whole bus and gets back to the original person, but it is empty – no sweets left for them.

Ailie   Excuse me, Finn. This is my stop.

Finn   Yeah, it's my stop too.

Ailie   Is it?

Finn   Yes.

Ailie   Is it?

Finn   Yes.

They both get up to get off the bus.

Ailie   Are you following me?

Finn   Looks like you're following me.

They exit the bus. The bus drives away, leaving them alone at the side of the road.

Finn   Why didn't you ask me to go to Fancy Willy's Dressy Disco?

Ailie   Fat Willy's Fancy Dress Roller Disco?

Finn   Yeah, that thing.

Ailie   I don't know you. That's why.

Finn   So, you don't ask people to go places unless you know them?

Ailie   Yes.

Finn   Can we get to know each other then?

Ailie   See you, Finn.

Ailie *walks towards her home.*

Finn   See you tomorrow?

Ailie   No doubt.

Finn *watches her go, then heads home himself.*

Nine

ALIENS

Mum   How was school, dear?

They laugh.

Sister   You look stupid.

Finn   It's really strange, but –

Dad   I imagine it is.

Finn   But it's really fascinating. The humans are so . . .

Sister   Fat?

Mum *and* **Dad** *laugh.*

Sister   I think their eyeballs will taste like chicken.

Finn   Hey, d'you know they cook chickens before they eat them?

Mum   No way.

Dad   That's crazy.

Finn   I know.

Sister   But then the feathers would be all crunchy.

Finn   They don't eat the feathers, they pull them out first. And they don't even eat the giblets.

Dad   But that's the best part.

Mum   What a waste. They have no taste.

Ten

PSE CLASS

Ericson, *PE teacher, is also one of the school's Personal and Social Education teachers.*

Ericson   Okay. Pipe down. Pipe down. I have just been informed that these PSE classes are actually for teaching Personal and Social Education, and not for running a fantasy football league. So, scorecards away everybody, I'm going to teach you the facts of life in about . . . (*Looks at watch.*) twenty seconds.

Everyone groans / mumbles.

Okay, boys, fingers in your ears.

The boys put their fingers in their ears.

Girls. The male of the species will do anything, will say anything, will wear anything, will buy anything, will lie about anything in order to get access to your private areas. You have been warned. Now cover your ears.

The girls put their fingers in their ears, the boys uncover their ears.

Boys. The female of the species will do anything, will say anything, will wear anything, will buy anything, will lie about anything in order to get access to your private bank account. You have been warned.

The boys and girls eye each other suspiciously.

Now, I've given you some straight advice, cos that's the kind of straight guy I am. I suggest any . . . non-straight advice . . . for instance, about musicals and such . . . should be directed towards Mr Faraday in the Maths Department.

The pupils gasp, whisper.

Oh, is that not common knowledge? Oops.

Igor *puts hand up to speak.*

Igor   I believe Mrs Green's PSE class got some careers advice.

Ericson   You want careers advice?

A few nod.

Igor   Oh no, I don't need advice, but perhaps my peers do.

Ericson   So you've got your career worked out, have you?

Igor   Indeed I have. I'm going to study Chemistry with Nanotechnology, then do a PhD research programme, then a NASA postdoctoral fellowship, then a –

Ericson (*snores*)   Bored. And you? What do you want to be?

Grant   Formula One racing driver.

Ericson   No chance. Try washing cars. You?

Pupil One   A top chef.

Ericson   Ha. Try washing dishes. You?

Pupil Two   An architect?

Ericson   No way. Forget it. You?

Claire   I want to be a celebrity and sing and dance and present TV shows and –

Ericson   Ha ha ha. You?

Ailie   Probably a nurse or something.

Ericson   Thank God, that's more like it. You?

Finn   Not sure, I haven't really thought about it.

Ericson   Good man. Thinking is dangerous. You?

Beth   I want to run my own hair, nail, beauty and well-being salon for dogs.

Ericson   Lord help us all. So to sum up, my careers advice, in short, is aim lower. In fact, that's my advice for life. Aim low.

Eleven

IN THE HALLWAY

Finn *and* **Ailie** *are in the hall.* **Ailie** *is wearing a bright, patterned jumper.*

Finn   Hello, Ailie.

Ailie   Hi.

Finn   Can I talk to you?

Ailie   Of course. What about?

Finn   I don't know. What do people usually talk about?

Ailie   What about . . . why are you everywhere I go?

Finn   What do you mean?

Ailie   You're everywhere. You're in all my classes. You're on the bus. You follow me in the corridors. You're even in the changing rooms, pretending you didn't know it was females only. Why are you everywhere?

Finn   If you like someone, you stand beside them, don't you? At least, that's what we do where I come from.

Ailie   Where do you come from?

Finn   It's a long story, for another time. I want to stand beside you. Always.

Ailie   What does that mean?

Finn   I should get the blessing of your father, yes?

Ailie   Very funny.

Finn   Was it?

Ailie   No.

Finn   I'm confused.

Ailie   Good, cos so am I.

Finn   I like you Ailie. That's all I wanted to say.

About to walk away.

Ailie   Well . . . do you want to go to the cinema this weekend or what? I mean, I'm not bothered if you don't –

Finn   The cinema. That's where people sit in lines in the dark and stare at a moving picture, yes?

Ailie   That's right . . .

Claire *swans past with a group of other pupils.*

Claire   You know, Finn, we were just saying that if you grew your hair a bit longer, you'd look even more fit.

Pupil One   Like that's possible.

Pupil Two   We think you'd look like Bieber.

Finn   What's Bieber?

Claire *laughs really loudly. She touches his arm.*

Claire   You're so funny!

Ailie   He's not that funny.

Claire   Oh my God. Check out Ailie's jumper. My granddad's got the same one.

Her group of friends laugh. **Finn** *looks at* **Ailie***, sees she is embarrassed.* **Everyone** *in the hall freezes, except* **Finn***.*

Finn (*stares into the eyes of* **Claire***'s friends*)   There's nothing wrong with Ailie's jumper. I really like it. In fact, it's the best jumper I've ever seen.

Everyone *unfreezes.*

Pupil One   I really like your jumper Ailie.

Claire   What?

Pupil Two   The pattern is really funky.

Ailie   Oh, thanks.

Claire   They're joking, Ailie. Your jumper is rank.

Pupil One   I really like it.

Pupil Two   Yeah. It's the best jumper I've ever seen.

Claire *drags her friends away.*

Ailie   Wow. That was really weird.

Finn   Was it?

Ailie   Nobody disagrees with Claire. Nobody.

Finn   Well, now they do.

Twelve

BETH'S BEDROOM

Darren *lounges on* **Beth***'s bed, as usual.*

Beth   So . . . should I be keeping next weekend free?

Darren   Don't know. Should you?

Beth   You know fine.

Darren   How should I know fine?

Beth   Ha ha. Very funny.

Darren   What?

Beth   Shut up. You know fine, it's my birthday.

Darren   Is it?

Beth   Have you got a surprise for me?

Darren   Oh shit. Next weekend? I'm going to Amsterdam next weekend.

Beth   Are you now? And who might you be taking with you . . . ?

Darren   Bazza, Ronnie, Mark, Beany and Steve.

Beth   What? Seriously?

Darren   Yeah.

Beth   What for?

Darren   What d'you mean?

Beth   Why are you going?

Darren   It's a holiday, isn't it?

Beth   Don't you want to go with me?

Darren   I'll take you somewhere nice in the summer. Like Belgium or Stonehenge or something.

Beth   Do you have to go? I don't trust them.

Darren   Who? The Danish? No, I don't trust them either, babe.

Beth   You mean the Dutch.

Darren   They're all the same.

Beth   I meant your friends. I don't trust your friends. After all the stories you've told me –

Darren   But you trust me babe, don't you?

Thirteen

AILIE'S BEDROOM

Ailie *is in bed, sleeping.* **Finn** *sits beside her bed and watches.* **Ailie** *stirs.*

Finn   There's a reason you all look different. It's beautiful. It must make life more interesting. You're beautiful. Not like us. We're functional. For a greater purpose, we're told.

Pause.

It's fascinating.

Ailie (*slowly wakes*)   What?

Finn   You have so many mirrors.

Ailie (*still not quite aware of who is talking/where she is*)   What?

Finn   Not just you. I mean everyone. All humans. Mirrors. Everywhere.

Ailie (*becoming more conscious*)   Finn . . .

Finn   Always looking. At yourself. At other people.

Ailie   Finn?!

Finn   Hi.

Ailie   What are you doing here?

Finn   Don't panic.

Ailie   Jesus Christ –

Finn   Shh. You'll wake your dad. He's resting.

Ailie   What d'you mean, resting?

Finn   He's fine.

Ailie   What's happened?

Finn   He's okay now.

Ailie (*calls out*)   Dad?

Finn   Shh. Just leave him to rest.

Ailie   Has something happened?

Finn   He collapsed.

Ailie   Oh my God.

Finn   Don't worry, he's fine.

Ailie   Heart attack?

Finn   He's fine. I fixed him.

Ailie   Fixed him?

Finn   He was broken. Now he's fixed. He's resting in bed.

Ailie   He needs a doctor.

Finn   No. A doctor won't find anything wrong. I fixed his body.

Ailie   Like – how? You just fixed him, like that?

Finn   No, not that easy. It took a lot of my power to do so. I'm too weak to go home right now.

Ailie   Sometimes you almost appear to be normal, but then I realise . . . you're not normal at all.

Finn *pulls* **Ailie** *close and hugs her.*

Finn   Trust me, Ailie.

Ailie   Looks like I'm going to have to.

Pause, she gets up and puts the light on.

Do you want a cup of tea? Or juice?

Finn   No.

Ailie   Thank you.

Finn   What?

Ailie   'No, thank you.' You never say thank you.

Finn   Okay.

He picks up a large jar.

What's this?

Ailie   Ugh, stick insects. They're a nightmare. You can have some, if you like. They keep multiplying like . . . well, stick insects. In fact, you can have them all if you want. I'm over them.

Finn   Okay.

Pause.

Thank you.

Ailie   I'm just going to check on Dad.

She exits.

Finn   Okay.

He looks at the jar, at the stick insects crawling around. He takes the lid off to have a closer look. He puts his hand in to touch one. He

*pauses for a moment, then grabs a handful of the insects and shoves
them into his mouth and chews them. He likes them. He eats another
handful. And another. He looks into the jar and sees that there are
none left. He puts the lid back on and puts the jar down.* **Ailie** *enters
the room.*

Ailie   He's sleeping so quietly. Not a sound. Like he's really
at peace, for once.

Finn   Good.

Ailie   What's your family like?

Finn   Hm. They're a strange bunch.

Ailie   Aren't they all, though?

Finn   Mine especially.

Ailie   Who do you live with?

Finn   Mum, Dad and sister.

Ailie   Is your sister at our school?

Finn   Our school.

Ailie   What?

Finn   Just sounds nice.

Ailie   Okay.

Finn   No. She decided to be home-schooled.

Ailie   Oh, right. Still. Must be nice to have people at home.
My dad is . . . he's hardly ever at home. But when he is . . .
he's not really here, you know? He's on another planet. You
know?

Finn (*nods*)   Yeah.

Ailie   Hey, you've got something in your teeth.

Finn   Oh right. (*He picks a tooth.*) Is that it?

Ailie   No, the one to the left.

Finn (*picks at another tooth*) Is that it?

Ailie   No. I'll try and . . .

She tries to pick the thing out of his tooth.

Got it. Ugh, it's like a . . . leg . . . or something – Oh my God –

She rushes to lift up the stick-insect jar.

Oh my God, Finn! What have you done?

Finn *looks sheepish.*

Fourteen

SCHOOL HALLWAY

Ailie *and* **Finn** *stand in the corridor holding hands.* **Igor** *spies them and makes a beeline towards them.*

Igor   Morning, Ailie.

Ailie   Hi.

Igor (*makes evil eyes as he looks at* **Finn**)   Finn. Or should I say . . . frenemy.

Finn   Ah, that's sweet.

Ailie *shakes her head to indicate that it's not sweet.*

Finn   Oh.

Claire *approaches the group.*

Claire   FYI Ailie, Beth isn't coming to school today. Her and Darren had, like, a totally huge fight last night cos apparently he's totally going on holiday to Amsterdam with his mates and not her. Beth thought he was planning a birthday surprise for her. But he, like, totally isn't.

Ailie   How do you know all this?

Claire   Cos she, like, totally phoned my phone last night. Cos I'm her friend. And I, like, totally listen to other people's problems and shit.

Igor   I hope not literally.

Claire   What you saying, Igor?

Igor   Nothing.

Finn   What's Amsterdam?

Igor   It's a place where groups of alpha males go and morally dubious if not downright illegal acts occur. It's unsavoury at best.

Claire   You're unsavoury, Igor.

Igor   Thanks. You really dug deep for that insult.

Ailie   Hey Finn, you're going to miss your library induction.

Claire   Who needs books when you look this pretty –

She runs her hand over **Finn***'s bicep.*

Claire   Right, Finn?

Finn (*looks alarmed, as does* **Ailie**)   Think I better get to the library.

Finn *leaves.* **Ailie** *is about to follow him when* **Igor** *pulls on* **Ailie***'s arm.*

Igor   Ailie. Come walk with me for a minute.

Ailie   Okay . . . What is it?

Igor   We need to talk.

Ailie   Do we?

Igor   Look, my love. This isn't working out.

Ailie   What's 'this'?

Igor   And I'm prepared to stand aside if you can honestly say, hand on heart, from the bottom of your soul, that Finn is the better man.

Ailie   Okay. That's very kind of you.

Igor   I don't want to stand in the way of true love. I'm not prepared to be Lady Diana to your Charles and Camilla.

Ailie   Okay, that's great. Thanks.

Igor   What's great?

Ailie   That you're . . . standing aside.

Igor   Oh.

Ailie   What?

Igor   That was quite quick. Don't you need time to think?

Ailie   No.

Igor (*looks upset*)   Very well. Well. He's going to break your heart, Ailie.

Ailie   Sorry –

Igor   That's all I've got to say.

Fifteen

ALIEN FAMILY

Dad   Son. You're getting awfully comfortable in your human body, aren't you?

Finn   No, it's just a hassle to keep changing back, that's all. I don't want to waste energy.

Dad   But you are surely using a lot of your power to maintain it, no? I'm worried about you, Finn.

Finn   Why?

Dad   When I was your age, I was hell bent on the destruction of the human race. But you're so mild-mannered. I'd even go so far as to say you are being extremely pleasant.

Sister   Ooya, burn.

Finn   Sorry, Dad. I've been a bit out of sorts since we got here. Maybe it's the air, or something in the water, or those yummy little biscuits with the jammy middle.

Sister   Humans smell funny.

Finn   They smell like rose petals and strawberry ice cream.

Sister   They smell like the gaseous cloud formation just outside Uranus.

Mum   Well, anyway, the ship is nearly fixed so we can leave Earth soon. We've been given a new assignment. Far away from here, thank goodness. I don't think I could stomach another chicken.

Sister   I want to try them stick insects Finn was telling us about.

Dad   Hush up. Finn, we basically need to move on soon, as the invisibility shield is coming to the end of its life. If you give me a hand in the control room, I think we could leave sometime in the next few days. Perhaps as soon as tomorrow.

Finn   Tomorrow?

Dad   If you help me.

Mum   Is that a problem, dear?

Finn   No.

Beat.

No.

Sixteen

BETH'S BEDROOM

Beth *and* **Darren** *are lying on the bed.*

Beth   And will you call me?

Darren   When?

Beth   When you're in Amsterdam.

Darren   Dunno. There's like a time difference and everything.

Beth   Yeah, only an hour difference.

Darren   Just shut up about it. You're doing my head in.

Beth   Sorry.

Darren   If I feel like phoning you, I will.

Beth   So, what will you be doing the whole time? Drinking?

Darren   A lot of that, yes. Also, y'know, cultural wanderings and that. Y'know, Anne Frank's gardens for a start.

Beth   What about girls?

Darren   Well, you know the boys. They're all single and ugly as sin so they'll be taking what they can get.

Beth   What will you do when they're . . . doing stuff?

Darren   Thinking of you, my little Pooky.

Beth   Ah, that's nice.

Darren   Can't say I won't be tempted though.

Beth   What?

Darren   I mean, when you're offered sex on a plate, it's hard not to lick it clean.

Beth   What are you saying?

Darren   I'm saying, it'll take all my willpower, but I can't make any promises –

Beth   Please, Darren –

Darren   Unless . . .

Beth   What? Anything. What is it?

Darren   If I had a photo of you, y'know, to stave off any moments of weakness.

Beth   I've got a spare passport photo you could keep in your wallet.

Darren   Not that kind of photo.

Beth   What kind?

Darren   The kind of photo that says you love me. You do love me, don't you?

Beth   Yes.

Darren   And I love you.

Beth   I know, but –

Darren   But what? What's the problem, babe?

His voice is gentle, but there's something sinister in his tone.

Beth   Nothing.

Darren   That's right. There's no problem.

*He strokes **Beth**'s hair. His hand comes to rest around her neck.*

Seventeen

SCHOOL

There seems to be a lot of excitement, pupils crowding around phones. **Ailie** *walks in with* **Finn***.*

Finn   Ailie, I need to talk to you about something –

Ailie (*noticing the noise and excitement*)   Wow, what do you think's going on?

Finn   I don't know. Can we go somewhere quiet to speak?

Grant *rushes up to them.*

Grant   Here, dudes, have you seen Beth this morning?

Ailie   No, why?

Grant *holds his phone screen towards their faces.*

Grant   Now you have.

He laughs.

Ailie *is shocked at what she sees. She grabs his phone, drops it and stamps on it.*

Grant   What did you do that for? You mad bitch.

He pushes **Ailie***, but as he bends down to pick up the pieces of his phone she pushes him back and he falls to the ground.* **Finn** *puts his arms around* **Ailie***, to protect her but also to hold her back. Suddenly, everyone's attention has turned to them.*

Ailie   How did you get that, you pervert?

Grant   Oh, I'm a pervert, am I? Well, so is everyone in the whole school then. Everyone's seen the photos. They're on the internet, if you want a look.

Ailie   Take them off then.

Grant   It wasn't me. And anyway, they've probably been copied a million times already.

Ailie   Darren?

Grant   Bingo.

He walks away and the crowd disperses.

Ailie   I've got to go to Beth's. I've got to phone her.

She speed-dials.

Come on . . . come on . . . answerphone.

Finn   Wait a minute, what's happened?

Ailie   Are you dumb? Darren's put naked photos of her on the internet.

Finn   You're upset.

Ailie   Of course I am.

Finn   Because she's your friend.

Ailie   Finn, you're not helping. I feel sick. I need to see if she's okay. Let's get a taxi.

Finn   Wait – can I borrow your computer?

Ailie   What for?

Finn   I think I can help.

Ailie   (*taking her laptop out of her bag*)   I didn't know you were a computing genius.

Finn   Well, I'm not. Yet.

Everyone, including **Ailie**, *freezes.* **Finn** *uses his power to erase the photos having been uploaded and people's memories of it being done. A moment later, everyone unfreezes.*

Finn   Ailie, I need to talk to you about something –

Ailie   Okay.

Finn   Can we go somewhere quiet to speak?

Grant   Here, dudes, have you seen Beth this morning?

Ailie   No, why?

Grant   Her better half was going to lend me *Happy Hardcore Ibiza Megamix 5* on vinyl. See, I'm a DJ now.

Ailie   Wow . . .

Beth *enters, happy as usual.* **Finn** *is pale and exhausted.*

Ailie   There she goes.

Grant *rushes up to* **Beth**. *She gives him a record.*

Ailie (*to* **Finn**)   Are you okay? You look really –

Beth   Hi. I slept in and totally missed the bus. A bit weird, that's never happened before.

Ailie   I've been meaning to ask, do you want to do something for your birthday now that you're not going to Amst –

Beth   No. I think I'll just stay in.

Ailie   What? And wait by the phone?

Beth   No, I just don't feel like doing anything.

Ailie   Great. So I've still got a date with Igor then.

Beth   It'd be a shame to let him down . . .

Eighteen

AILIE'S KITCHEN

Ailie *arrives home. In the kitchen, there is an empty glass and an empty vodka bottle.*

Ailie   Dad?

Pause.

What's the point?

She puts the bottle in the bin and the glass in the sink. She opens up her laptop, switches it on. She starts typing . . .

Nineteen

ALIEN FAMILY

*Meanwhile, over at **Finn**'s spaceship . . .*

Dad   Where have you been? I was hoping you'd help me fix the ship.

Finn   I had to help a friend.

Mum   You don't look well. Let me get you a few pigeons. I've just broken their necks, they're still warm.

Finn   No, I'm fine.

Dad   'Fine', are you? That's what the humans say, isn't it? Hm. Finn, why don't you start up the ship? Not from the control deck. From here, using your powers.

Finn   I can't.

Dad   You can't, or won't?

Finn   I can't. I'm too weak right now.

Mum   Why's that, dear?

Finn   I've been helping a friend. She really needed my help.

Dad   You've been abusing your power?

Finn   If that's what you call it, then yes.

Mum   Whatever you've done, you do know it can't stay that way for ever? Once your power has gone, everything will unravel.

Finn   I know. That's why I need a bit more time. I need to let her know.

Dad   You can go, but quickly. And without your power. Until we leave this planet, you cannot be trusted with it.

Finn   Please let me keep my human body, until I come back.

Mum   Very well. But you must come back and you'll be confined to the ship until we leave. Else you know what happens to deserters. They will find you.

Sister   Ha ha.

She blows a raspberry.

Finn *starts running towards* **Ailie**'s *home.*

Twenty

AILIE'S KITCHEN

Meanwhile, **Ailie** *is still on her computer in the kitchen . . .*

Ailie (*typing*)   Wait a minute . . . (*Shocked.*) What . . . the . . .

Finn *runs in, he's out of breath.*

Ailie   Finn! Have you seen this? 'Ailie's Fugly Jumper Hate Page'. Four hundred and nineteen 'likes'. How long has this been here? I'm going to kill her.

Finn   I'm sorry, Ailie, I thought I'd have more time.

Sound effect of a low heart monitor beep begins, gradually getting louder until end of scene.

Ailie   You're sorry? It's not your fault Claire's such a tool.

Finn   I have to go now. I'm leaving.

Ailie   What?

Finn   For ever. I'm leaving for ever. And I have to tell you fast because this body I'm in isn't going to last much longer, and I have so much to tell you, and I know it's going to be hard to listen to. But your dad is very ill, he's in the hospital and he's been there for a while now.

Ailie   No he's not. He's home. He was just in here before I got back. Because I put his glass in the sink –

She looks in the sink, there is no glass.

Oh. Well, I definitely put the bottle in the bin –

She looks in the bin, there is no bottle.

Where did it go?

Finn   That's just it, everything I've done to help you is coming undone. I was trying to make it better for you. I was trying to make you smile more.

Ailie   What? . . . So my dad is . . . Oh God! His heart? What's happened?

Finn   He's going to be fine though.

Ailie   How do you know?

Finn   Well, I don't, but he's in the hospital and there's someone else who really needs your help right now.

Ailie   My help?

Finn   Beth is in trouble. Go to Beth's now. Call an ambulance and go to her.

Ailie   (*she rummages in her school bag for her phone*)   And you?

Finn   I have to go.

Ailie   (*upset*)   I can't do this.

Finn   You can. You're stronger than you think you are. Trust me. I didn't realise it at first, but you're much stronger than I thought you were.

Noise or music drowns out any voices. **Ailie** *dials 999 and speaks to an operator. As she does so* **Finn** *hugs her.*

Twenty-One

BETH'S BEDROOM

Meanwhile, over at **Beth**'s *farmhouse . . .*

In her darkened room, **Beth** *is lying on her bed. She is unconscious. Her laptop is open, a soft blue screen light illuminates her face. An empty bottle of pills lies not far from one of her lifeless palms. A blue flashing light of an approaching ambulance streams through her window.* **Ailie** *runs in, distraught. She tries to lift her up. She can't take her weight, but she keeps trying and trying.*

Twenty-Two

HOSPITAL

Saturday evening, a few days later. **Beth** *is lying in a hospital bed.*
Ailie *enters, holding a cupcake with one unlit candle in it.*

Ailie   Happy birthday.

Beth   Thanks.

Ailie   Some birthday.

Beth   It's not my best.

Ailie   How are you feeling today?

Beth   Fine. Managed to eat breakfast.

Ailie   Good. And how are you feeling about . . . everything?

Beth   Fine.

Ailie   Yeah?

Beth (*nods, becomes upset*)   I thought he loved me –

Ailie (*hugs her*)   I know.

Beth   I can't ever go back to school.

Ailie   Yes, you can.

Beth   You know the dicks that won't ever stop, they won't
let it go. It's just a laugh to them. How can I go back to that?

Ailie   You can go back cos I'll be with you. Every single
moment of every single day.

Beth   My parents . . . they think it was an accident.

Ailie   Okay . . .

Beth   I said I had toothache and couldn't remember how
many I'd taken.

Ailie   Toothache?

Beth   I'll tell them eventually. Just not now. How's your dad?

Ailie   He's doing well. I've just been to see him, think he'll
be getting out tomorrow.

Beth   Great.

Ailie   Yeah. He's actually better than I think I've ever seen
him before. Sounds bad but, I think he really needed this
shock. Without it, nothing would've changed. Says the first
thing he's going to do when he gets home is throw out all his
drink. And he's going to teach me to play golf. I've no idea
why, but I'm not going to complain.

Beth   And how's you and Finn getting on?

Ailie   He's gone.

Beth   Oh.

Ailie   Yup. Life goes on though.

Beth   It does.

Ailie   Anyway, it's about time you made a wish.

She lights the candle on the cupcake.

Music fades in.

Ailie *holds* **Beth***'s hand as she closes her eyes, about to blow out the
candle.*

Elsewhere, a spaceship ascends into the night sky.

And, somewhere in town, **Igor** *is waiting patiently in his Jabba the
Hutt costume, looking at his watch every now and again.*

Ailie and the Alien

BY MORNA PEARSON

*Notes on rehearsal and staging, drawn from a workshop
with the writer held at the National Theatre, November 2012*

Approaching the play

This play presents a chance to be really theatrical with little
or no budget. It is not naturalistic and there are opportunities
for humour, innovation and ensemble work. There are also
serious themes of family and romantic relationships appropriate
for Citizenship and PSHE classes.

The starting point for writing the play was an attempt to
grasp the intensity of being at school, where experiences seem
to be magnified. In the classroom, in school corridors or on
the school bus, you can feel trapped with people you don't
like and who don't seem to like you. Morna Pearson mentions
her experience of teachers who seemed to hate children and
should not have been teaching.

Casting

Ideally, the cast will be interested in exploring their characters
fully and have time to understand the whole play. Particularly
in this play, supporting and non-speaking roles are important
for telling the story, creating its world, and depicting the
different settings.

Youth theatre performers will often be of a similar age, which
can make casting characters of different ages seem tricky.
It can be helpful to think about the qualities (good and bad)
that each character represents and how performers might
deal with them. Vocal qualities and body language are also
worth considering, especially when casting adult characters.

It is worth bearing in mind that audiences will go along with
the world that is presented on stage and use their imaginations

to help it make sense. For instance, adults don't have to be
tall, Finn doesn't have to be handsome. Morna is open to the
idea of cross-casting (girls playing boys and vice versa).

Casting Darren might be problematic because of his treatment
of Beth and their subtle differences in age. The performer
should be someone who can access the darker side of the
character, but also be friends with the performer playing
Beth. Both performers should be able to talk through the
ideas and problems involved in their characters' relationship.

Characters and characterisation

The script offers clues even about characters with very few
lines. There's room for imaginative interpretation rooted in
the text. A useful exercise to start developing characterisation
is to list a) what the character says about him/herself; b) what
others say about the character; c) what the character says
about others.

Working on characters' back-stories also helps build up the
present life of the play. Simple question-and-answer sessions
can generate material for back-stories. Other exercises
include improvising past events in characters' biographies,
hot seating, and naming a single event for each year of their
lives ('When I was one I . . . ', 'When I was two I . . . ', etc.).
While back-stories undoubtedly lead to new discoveries about
the setting, the characters themselves and their relationships,
it is still important to remember that this is supporting work
and it's crucial for any production to focus on the present
action of the story.

There is a sense that all the characters are aliens in their own
way. Morna describes how the aliens crash-land on Earth by
mistake and are on an undisclosed sinister mission, perhaps to
another planet. There's room for manoeuvre in depicting the
alliances – it is more important to set up and follow through
the aliens' characters and narrative than making sure they are
'little green aliens' as written. Likewise, it is possible to

present the whole alien family in human bodies as long as it's clear for the audience that they are different to the human characters.

The difference between human and alien characters can stretch further than costume design – they might be different in movement, behaviour, body language, voice, make-up etc. These are also aspects that might help show how Finn keeps a family resemblance to the other aliens and does not always have full control of his human body. One possible approach is for Finn's alien body to reveal itself gradually throughout the play, lending the character a clear visual narrative.

In the workshop, participants listed words and qualities of behaviour we might associate with each character:

AILIE   Open-minded, sarcastic, humorous, vulnerable, wanting to connect, social status.

BETH   Weak, selfish, desperate to be cool, social status, naive, trusting, vulnerable, contradictory.

CLAIRE   Divisive, manipulative, needing power, insecure, attention-seeking.

DARREN   Controlling, insecure, sexualised, laddish, transparent, manipulative, immature, stupid, buffoon, bravado.

ERICSON   Bitter, nostalgic, light relief, lazy teacher, bad role model, nervous, cool, risqué, like Miss Trunchbull from *Matilda*.

FINN   Naive, innocent, idealistic, caring, outsider, black sheep of family, humane, curious.

GRANT   Intimidating, joker, threatening, inadequate, knowledgeable, loner, plonker.

HARRISON   Moody, abrupt, impolite, disrespectful, power-hungry, tired.

IGOR   Intelligent, geeky, self-aware, sad, endearing, kind.

ALIEN FAMILY   Familiar family unit, familiar gender roles, supportive, protective, quirky.

NB: The text is not explicit about why Ailie's mother is not present and Morna is happy for that to be decided in the making of each production.

Structure

A clear sense of how the play is structured will help guide both the company and the audience through the story. For instance, there's a repeated sequence of morning, afternoon and evening scenes as the story progresses through Ailie's daily routine over a week. This can impact on aspects as diverse as lighting and character tempo.

Writing up a map of the play is a handy guide – a simple list or table of each scene, with a title assigned by the director or whole company, detailing the time of day, what happens, the characters onstage. With these basic facts at your fingertips, you can make each scene your own and fit it to your production's interpretation.

Exercises for use in rehearsals

Moving as a group is helpful for building an ensemble. Simple exercises like walking around the rehearsal room or filling the performance space can be enhanced by direct movement (walking in straight lines, turning at sharp angles) and/or indirect movement (walking and turning in curves). One of the challenges of creating lifelike group scenes is preventing uniform movement, so giving different instructions to smaller groups can help stimulate different rhythms.

Acting is taking action – doing one thing to achieve another. It is important for performers to have clear tasks: e.g. focusing on a light/heavy, direct/indirect quality of movement. Company members can begin to create a character from these specific physical tasks, which can then be built on to refine and detail.

A physical warm-up or game can really help bind a group before working as a chorus. Other exercises that support this work include shoaling and counting one to ten as a group.

Staging

There's no need to be literal in the settings of this play – the options for staging are left open by the text. Audiences can understand a lot about where a scene is set from a few small imaginative prompts. The playful tone of the play encourages a playful approach to staging.

It's worth thinking carefully about the order in which you work on scenes. It's tempting to start at the beginning and work chronologically through the text, but it's sometimes helpful to tackle the trickier scenes first (e.g. the spaceship crash-landing) to work out a visual vocabulary for the production. It is also useful to have pictures on the rehearsal room wall as visual inspirations for creating the world of the play.

There are lots of locations and many quick scenes, offering the chance to switch locations in imaginative ways. Blackouts are nearly always not the answer. An audience's experience is interrupted by blackouts while the storytelling stops. Other solutions include using a split stage, interpolated transitions or movement sequences, use of sound or live music. Finding a stage language or style the company feels comfortable with is important and this can be explored by trying out different approaches to the same scene– for instance, using as few objects as possible, perhaps just chairs or boxes.

Think laterally to achieve lighting effects on a small budget – e.g. mobile phones or torches. Likewise, foley techniques are useful for sound effects – e.g. dried peas in a sieve for rain.

Performers also often have other skills such as playing musical instruments or imitating sounds. This can also serve a purpose by giving a large company more engagement with the show and can save tech time, which is particularly useful when transferring to a new venue with time of the essence.

Freeze-frame tableaux offer a way of building up the visual language of a production. These can be directed or devised by performers. In the workshop, participants created scenic images using only chairs and handheld objects in the room. A tableau of the school bus used different levels, vocal sound effects and added movement to create a sense of the bus journey.

Other devised sequences included the spaceship crash-landing (an extra-terrestrial atmosphere can be supported by lighting and sound effects) and Ailie cycling down the road (her forward motion might be suggested by other people or objects travelling backwards across the stage). Thinking about the perspective through which the audience experiences the scene is important – e.g. heightening Ailie's breath as she's cycling helps an audience focus on her subjectivity and draws us closer to the character.

In the workshop, participants explored ways of staging scenes using paper as a primary design tool. Seaside-style cut-outs offered ways for one performer to play more than one role in a scene; Ailie's bicycle and the storm clouds can be made of paper, while tapping another sheet creates the sound of rain. Reusing props and set pieces in different parts of the show can help save money and is also satisfying for the audience, as they use their imaginations to join in creating the world of the play.

Sample scene: Scene Sixteen

In the workshop participants staged Scene Sixteen, to address the concerns of several directors. The relationship between Darren and Beth might be challenging to stage for companies of any age because of the characters' attitudes.

The structure of the scene and how it is played can have a major impact on its interpretation. For instance, if Darren's intention (or 'objective') throughout the scene is *to take a photo of Beth* and his action is to seduce her, he will seem manipulative and predatory. This changes if the scene is structured with a turning point on Darren's line 'Unless . . .' If his intention beforehand is *to stay inside and get warm* or *to watch television* and the idea of taking a photo first occurs to Darren only at this point, he immediately seems less threatening.

Similarly, Beth's intentions can be gauged to emphasise the sense that she's being exploited or to give her more influence in the relationship – e.g. Beth's intention could be *to seduce Darren*. Other intentions could be *to humour* or *to tease*.

Where the scene is set is also up for discussion and will affect its meaning. The couple might be 'lying on the bed' as written or they might be sitting on the bed or at a table. Where the characters are will change what is at stake for them both. How the scene is staged will also impact on how an audience reads the situation.

Finally, a sense of danger is necessary for the scene and the story as a whole. But how dangerous it becomes is a choice for each production. The final stage direction – '*His hand comes to rest around her neck*' – does not insist on violence, but gives an indication of where and how far the relationship might develop.

Suggested references

My Parents Are Aliens
'The Bash Street Kids'
Twilight
Mork and Mindy
Grange Hill

The Wizard of Oz

The Big Bang Theory

Bad Education

The Inbetweeners

Our Day Out

Waterloo Road

The Ketchup Effect

Gregory's Girl

Skins

Matilda

These can be useful ways for performers to relate to the characters and their situation. YouTube, TV and films are helpful and accessible research tools. Young people can also find reference points in real life, for instance, at their own schools. 'Who are the characters' equivalents in real life?' 'Who would be in the ideal fantasy cast?'

From a workshop led by Jemime Levick,
with notes by Matthew Evans

Forty-Five Minutes

Anya Reiss

Age suitability 15–19
Cast size 8

Education, education, education.
Tony Blair

Anya Reiss was born and brought up in London, and wrote her first play when she was fourteen, having become a member of the Royal Court Theatre's Young Writers' Programme. Her debut play, *Spur of the Moment* (written when she was seventeen), opened at the Royal Court Theatre in July 2010, winning the Best New Play at the 2010 TMA Awards and Anya the Most Promising Playwright Award at both the 2010 *Evening Standard* Awards and Critics' Circle Awards. Her second play, *The Acid Test*, also debuted at the Royal Court in May 2011. Most recently her adaptation of Anton Chekhov's *The Seagull* opened at the Southwark Playhouse in 2012. She also contributed to the Bush Theatre's Sixty-Six Books in 2011 and the Old Vic's Children's Monologues in 2010.

Characters

Nathan, *sixth form*
Darrel, *sixth form*
Alex, *sixth form*
Georgie, *sixth form*
Trent, *sixth form*
Lara, *sixth form*
Louise, *year ten*
Michael, *year ten*

Setting
The school's computer room

Nathan *and* **Darrel** *are sitting together at two computers,* **Alex** *separately on another.*

Nathan   Read it out then.

Darrel   All of it?

Nathan   No the key points bit

Alex   Can you please shut up?

Nathan   It'll help you too

Alex   I know what it says

Darrel   Why can't you just read it to yourself?

Nathan   Read it out loud

Alex   Don't Darrel

Nathan   Ignore her

Alex   Oh fuck you

Nathan   Read it out Darrel

Darrel   'Explain why you want to study the course you are applying for. If you mention your personal interests and hobbies, try to link them to the skills and experience required for the course.'

Alex   Oh 'cause you didn't know that?

Nathan   Shut up. Go on

Darrel   'The personal statement could be used as the basis for an interview, so be prepared to answer questions on it. This may be your only written work that the course tutor sees before making a decision . . . '

Nathan   Fuck

Darrel   'Make sure it is organised and literate.'

Alex   Oh what a surprise

Nathan   What is the matter with you?

Alex   You're talking

Nathan   About the form, we're talking about the form

Darrel   'Get the grammar, spelling and punctuation right.'

Alex   Oh my God

Darrel   That *is* a stupid thing to put up there

Nathan   What?

Darrel   That is a stupid thing to put up there, you're not going to try and get it wrong are you?

Nathan   You got to do it on a computer anyway Darrel

Darrel   So?

Nathan   So obviously you're gonna get spelling and everything right

Darrel   Not all words are on a computer

Nathan   Yeah well not like swearing and names and stuff

Darrel   They have swearing

Nathan   No they don't

Darrel   Yeah they do

Nathan   No they don't, the red line comes up

Darrel   No, they have it in the dictionary, they just don't offer it to you on spell-check suggestions

Nathan   No they don't

Darrel   Look, I'll show you

Alex   We have forty-five minutes and you are doing that?

Nathan   Why do you care? Just do your UCAS

Alex   I'm doing my UCAS

Darrel (*about the computer*)   Look, well they don't have 'shite' but they have everything else, see?

Nathan   Someone must have added them

Darrel   No. Look, just look at 'cint', it don't suggest 'cunt' as a correction but it knows that cunt's a word

Alex   Can you shut up!

Nathan   Go to the library if we're annoying you

Alex   It'll be full by now

Nathan   You're Sixth Form

Alex   They don't listen, the new kids

Nathan   Course they will

Darrel   Nah it's true Nath' this lot just don't give a fuck

Nathan   Get Miss Barrett to chuck them off then

Alex   I don't have time to go to the library, we've got forty-five minutes!

Darrel   I swear it was next week

Nathan   Darrel, if you say it again, if you say that again . .

Darrel   I told you, I'm sorry. I thought it was next week, I thought it was midnight next week!

Alex   Oh my God please just be quiet

Nathan   Go to the library!

Alex   It's too loud in the library

Darrel   What?

Alex   Miss Barrett's always shouting at everyone to shut up, she's more annoying than you

Nathan   If you care so much, why did you leave it till now?

Alex   Because I've been off sick!

Nathan   So?

Alex   I thought it was next week too

Nathan   I don't understand why *you* wouldn't have done this weeks ago

Alex   I've been off sick you know that

Darrel   How sick?

Nathan   You going to give it to us?

Darrel   I can't get sick, I'm going away at the weekend

Alex   You're not going to get sick

Darrel   What did you have?

Alex   Nothing

Nathan   Why can't we catch it?

Alex   'Cause you can't

Nathan   What is it like cancer?

Alex *ignores this.*

Nathan   Jesus Alex sorry it isn't, is it? Jesus . . .

Alex   Of course it's not fucking cancer Nathan

Georgie, **Lara** *and* **Trent** *come in.* **Lara**'s *in tears,* **Georgie** *slams down at a computer and turns it on.*

Trent   See Lara they're here as well

Georgie   Just oh my fucking, fucking God, that fucking bitch, she's . . .

Trent   Don't break the thing

Georgie   Why aren't you angry?

Trent   Course I'm angry but we've got forty-five minutes don't break a computer

Georgie   Hope she dies in hell the stupid fucking . . .

Alex   Whatever's the matter Georgie can you shut up, I have forty-five minutes to finish . . .

Georgie   So have I Alex! So have I!

Alex   Well you should have done it before

Georgie   I thought the deadline was next week, she said she said didn't she, Lara?

Lara   She said

Darrel   I knew it! I told you it wasn't my fault

Nathan   What? He did say the deadline was next week then?

Georgie   They all said it was for next week, all of them, they said we should give it in at the end of this week and school would check them first then it was deadline next week

Darrel   She told me I got it wrong and screamed at me for telling Nathan the wrong thing

Nathan   And screamed at me for not checking

Darrel   The bitch

Georgie   I know she is such a bitch

Trent   Yeah alright guys, alright but we still got forty-five minutes whoever's fault it is, we've all got to do it

Nathan   I thought you guys weren't in today

Trent   We were late for class, she said she'd let you lot off to do it too

Darrel   Lara sit down and do the thing don't just stand there crying

Lara   There's no point

Alex   You can't miss the deadline Lara

Nathan   It's the school's fault. Lara your dad can sue them

Lara   He's not that kind of lawyer

Nathan   What kind is there that can't sue?

Lara   He just works there

Trent (*turning on a computer*)   Lara sit down!

Nathan   They will get sacked for this

Darrel   They don't sack anyone at this stupid school

Alex   They sacked Mr Dallaway

Nathan   Because he tried to kiss that girl in Year Eleven not because he was stupid

Georgie   Which girl?

Nathan   Some Year Eleven girl, I dunno

Darrel   Maria Santez

Georgie   Her? She's disgusting

Lara   They didn't even sack Mrs Wells who told everyone that they were going to go to be crucified in Hell

Trent   Yeah, and everyone in my class failed French last year because Mr Gords taught the wrong book, he's still here

Georgie   You were in the bottom group Trent that's why you failed

Trent   No he taught the wrong book

Georgie   It's French Trent how different can the book be?

Darrel   Lara fucking open your UCAS

Lara   There's no point! They read my statement said it was terrible, said I did it all wrong and Miss Hall would do it with me next week!

Alex   You haven't finished your statement!

Nathan   Yeah nor have me or Darrel

Trent   Mine's still fucked up

Alex   How can you not have done them!

Nathan   I got some bullet points

Alex   Oh my God

Nathan   If you've done it, why are you here?

Alex   To finish the form I hadn't put my results in and stuff. I'd done my statement!

Nathan   They don't care really about statements, they know the teachers have done them

Lara   They haven't done mine!

Georgie   In Cambridge they throw them in the bin

Alex   Yeah well lucky I'm not trying for Cambridge then isn't it?

Darrel   Why didn't you fill in your results and stuff before, that's the easy bit

Alex   Don't have internet at home

Nathan   What?

Darrel   What?

Trent   You don't have internet at home!?

Georgie   What the hell Alex? How do you do your homework?

Alex   Er I dunno like every person before the millennium

Trent (*seeing she still hasn't started*)   Lara!

Georgie   Why did they tell us the wrong fucking deadline?

Alex   Georgie forget about that for now

Georgie   You didn't see her just then, you didn't see Miss Leal we came in, me and Trent and Lara, we came in and she was like, 'Oh bet everyone feels relieved now the forms are sent off,' got no shame

Trent   Yeah she went so red

Georgie   So fucking red because I was like 'Er what the fuck that's next week,' and she was like 'No, that's what Darrel and poor Nathan thought too.'

Nathan   'Poor Nathan'

Georgie   Yeah and she was like 'Oh, well you better go and polish them off then, you've only got forty-five minutes till the deadline.'

Trent   No fucking shame

Georgie   No fucking shame and we wasted like a year looking for Miss Hall for Lara

Darrel   Why do you need Miss Hall? She's almost as dumb as Miss Leal

Georgie   No one's as dumb as Miss Leal

Lara   She promised to help me with my statement but she wouldn't even come because she's got the Year Sevens' parents' evening in a bit

Darrel   Fuck the Year Sevens man, this is your future

Georgie   I know that's what I said

Alex   What fuck the Year Sevens?

Georgie   No but they don't teach you anything you need to know till like Year Nine

Nathan   Exactly! That's why it's all so screwed up. They don't teach you anything and they don't give a shit until like Year Nine. Then Year Nine you have to choose your GCSEs, then take them, then your AS, then A-levels and you have to do your UCAS at the same fucking time

Darrel   And none of them matter except your UCAS

Nathan   Exactly

Alex   Er and your A-levels and GCSEs

Trent   No they don't, that's what they always say

Georgie   Yeah it's all like 'Fail your GCSEs and you'll never get a job, oh wait they don't matter it's your AS-levels, no wait forget them it's A-levels, oh no no, no one cares as long as you get into a good uni'

Lara   And get a good degree

Georgie   Exactly

Louise *and* **Michael** *come in.*

Georgie   No sorry fuck off we're on these

Michael   Those are free

Nathan   Fuck off we're doing UCAS

Louise   Those were meant to be done ages ago

Nathan   Thank you for that

Louise   My sister sent hers off last month

Nathan   Who's your sister?

Lara   She's Beth's sister

Trent, Darrel *and* **Nathan** *start laughing.*

Georgie   Shut up

Louise   What?

Nathan   Darrel you know Beth

Darrel   Shut up man

Nathan   You know Beth hey he knows your sister

Louise   Yeah and I know him, you're Darrel

Nathan   Oh yeah how do you know him?

Louise   He fucked my sister

They laugh.

Michael   We won't distract you

Alex   Sorry guys but seriously we need to do this

Louise   We won't talk

Michael   You can't stop us

Georgie   Jesus Christ this is our whole future, can you like have a little respect?

Michael   You left it till now

Darrel   Can everyone stop fucking saying that?

Georgie   We got like ten minutes to do this okay

Lara   What!

Georgie   Practically

Trent   Can you log in for God's sake Lara, I got to do my own shit here

Michael   Why do you have 'like ten minutes' to do it?

Alex   Because we just found out the deadline's at five

Louise   Shit

Georgie   You know the drama teacher Miss Leal, she just told us, just told us to go and do it now while we've got the chance, they all got it wrong

Louise   Really?

Lara   And the school was meant to read our statements before you send it but they can't now

Louise   What are you going to do if you miss the deadline?

Lara *looks for a second, seems distressed.*

Trent   Shut up kid why don't you just run off okay? We got to do this

Louise   You're talking to me all about Darrel and my sister

Louise *and* **Michael** *have flounced down on to a seat.*

Georgie   Nah nah nah sorry no

Alex   Yeah guys go away

Michael   We've only got till five to do this stuff. We have to help at the parents' evening

Darrel   You're not allowed in here after school

Michael   Yeah but we have to do this

Darrel   But you can't come in the computer room after hours until Sixth Form

Michael   They sent us to do this okay?

Darrel   But you're not allowed in . . .

Michael   We have permission

Darrel   But it's the rules you're not allowed . . .

Nathan   Shut up man shut up okay shut up

Darrel   Alright mate chill

Nathan   Stop saying they're not allowed in here. I got to do this?

Georgie   We've all got to do it Nathan

Nathan   I got to do my personal statement okay, okay? So shut up

Darrel   So have I mate calm down

Nathan   No you've nearly done yours look, look yours is nearly done

Darrel   I dunno how to finish it

Nathan   Just shut up you all sitting there going 'Oh my god please go away in case you distract us kids.' You lot are fucking chatting anyway

Alex   Exactly

Nathan   Oh fuck off Alex

Alex   Sent

Nathan   What?

Trent   For real?

Alex   Yeah I'm done so 'bye guys

Georgie   You're done?

Alex   Yup like have fun and everything

Lara   Oh my God no this is going to happen, everyone is just going to send theirs

Alex   I think that's the idea

Lara   No and it's gonna stress me more

Alex   Why? Just do it

Lara   No oh my God no, I'm just gonna sit here and everyone will finish and leave me here and I'll miss the deadline

Alex   We only have forty-five minutes

Darrel   She's got a point

Nathan   Like thirty minutes now

Lara   Oh my God

Alex   Okay guys have fun

Nathan   No Alex wait

Alex   What?

Nathan   Alex

Alex   What?

Nathan   Help

Darrel *laughs.*

Nathan   Shut up, help me

Alex   Oh yeah because you were so quiet and helpful when I wanted you to be

Georgie   Trent when did we do our GCSEs?

Trent   Hm?

Nathan   Shut up guys, Alex please

Georgie   Oi don't tell me to shut up

Nathan   Georgie fuck's sake please shut up for a minute, Alex?

Georgie   Why you telling me to shut up man I want to know when we did our –

Nathan   Shut up

Georgie   No why you telling me to shut up, you can't tell –

Trent   2011

Nathan   Because I'm trying to talk to Alex okay

Georgie   You can talk to her and I can ask Trent when we did our GCSEs at the same time

Nathan   No you're talking over me

Georgie   We ain't talking to the same people

Nathan   Why can't you shut up for a minute?

Trent   2011

Georgie   Why you being so fucking rude?

Nathan   I'm talking to Alex / and you're just interrupting me talking balls about your GCSEs like work it out yourself okay I just need a minute of silence just to ask Alex to give me a hand okay and you're fucking around shouting out like a stupid little –

Georgie   / Yeah I know you're talking to Alex okay you can talk to her as I ask Trent a fucking question about what year we did our GCSEs in okay because I'm not dumb I didn't leave my statement till now I'm just doing the form.

Nathan (*completing his sentence*)   – bitch.

Georgie   Oh you call me a bitch now?

Trent   2011!

Nathan   I'm saying you're acting like a bitch

Georgie   Do you know how offensive that is?

Trent   2011 Georgie!

Nathan   Oh I don't give a shit okay? This is my future and you're chatting away . . .

Georgie   Oh you know what fuck you Nathan

Darrel   Please guys shut up

Nathan   I don't want to have a fight with you . . .

Georgie   Oh you don't want to have a fight with me but you call me a bitch? You call me a bitch?

Nathan   Because I'm trying to talk to Alex okay and you're shouting stuff out

Darrel   Guys shut the hell up

Trent   2011 Georgie

Lara   2011

Georgie   I was asking a question okay? I'm allowed to ask a fucking question when I want okay, this isn't *your* computer room

Nathan   Why you making a big drama okay I just want you to shut up

Georgie   You know what Nathan you're going nowhere mate you're going nowhere

Nathan   I'm going nowhere?

Trent   Okay guys, stop now 2011 Georgie

Georgie   Yeah you're going nowhere because you're dumb Nathan. You should have done your statement weeks ago

Nathan   That's why I'm asking for her help and you start shrieking about . . .

Georgie   I was just asking when we did our GCSEs!

Darrel (*slamming his hand down on her keyboard repeatedly*)   2011!
2011! 2011!

A pause. They all look at him. **Georgie** *is outraged.*

Darrel (*back to his computer*)   Jesus Christ

Trent (*to* **Georgie**, *who is puffing up in anger*)   Don't, just
don't

Louise   I thought you guys had like ten minutes

Lara *bursts into tears again.*

Trent   You shut up and do your little project

Nathan   Alex

Alex   Oh remembered me?

Nathan   Please

Alex   Why should I?

Nathan   Please genuinely okay I got what? Like half an
hour? I got a paragraph okay, please you're good at this kind
of stuff

Alex   So?

Nathan   Come on don't be like that, this is like whether
I get in or not okay? I gotta get in 'kay? I got to

Alex   What are you applying for?

Nathan   Community Studies

Alex *and, over in the corner,* **Michael** *and* **Louise** *snort.*

Nathan   Oh you fuck-off little idiots you wait till you're
here, you still think GCSEs are scary, no one gives a shit
about them

Michael   Er yeah they do

Nathan   No they don't

Michael   Yeah they do, unis look and employers

Alex   No one cares about your GCSEs they're a waste of time everyone knows it

Nathan   Alex help me

Alex   What you even going to say for Community Studies?

Nathan   I dunno just please okay

Trent   Otherwise you're just going to go back to class Alex

Nathan   Yeah back to Miss Leal

Alex (*sighs*)   Fine.

Alex *comes to look at* **Nathan***'s computer.* **Darrel** *is very aware that* **Georgie** *has been staring at him since the keyboard bashing.*

Darrel   Stop looking at me okay

Georgie   You just broke my computer

Darrel   No I didn't

Georgie   What if you had?

Darrel   But I didn't

Georgie   What if I had lost everything?

Trent   It's fine Georgie just get on with it

Georgie   This is stupid those kids are right they can't just tell us we have forty-five minutes I mean for fuck's sake what if we hadn't gone to drama! I don't usually go to drama. What if we hadn't gone to drama and Miss Leal hadn't told us?

Trent   Not being harsh Lara but your crying is really distracting me

Lara   It's no good

Trent   Be fine just stop crying and do it

Lara   I can't do it

Georgie   Alex why don't you help Lara?

Nathan   She's helping me!

Trent   Yeah but she's crying man

Nathan   You want me to cry? I'll fucking cry if you want me to mate at least she's done hers, she's got words on a screen

Lara   But it's all wrong she said it was all wrong

Alex   I bet it's not

Lara   No it's all wrong I didn't even get the pack I only just borrowed Beth's now

Georgie   Her 'pack'?

Lara   All the stuff with what you're not allowed to say, Miss Hall said I'd done everything you weren't supposed to

Darrel   Then shut up and change it

Lara   I can't! I don't know any words

Darrel   Well I haven't done mine either

Lara   Georgie?

Georgie   I can't help you babe I'm shit with words as well

Lara *looks to* **Trent**.

Trent   No I'm doing my statement too

Lara   Please

Trent   I'm applying for Sports Science I can't help you

Darrel   Fuck off you are

Trent   Yeah

Darrel   Why you doing that?

Trent   Because I want to be a Scientist of Sport

Darrel   What?

Trent   I want to be a sports teacher

Darrel   Why?

Trent   What are *you* doing?

Darrel   Management and Leisure . . . what? What?

Trent   Nothing man. You knock yourself out folding bed sheets

Darrel   It's not like that

Lara   Alex please

Nathan   She's helping me!

Lara   But she's the only one any good at English

Nathan   She is helping me for fuck's sake. She is helping me!

Lara   But like okay Alex, just tell me another word for 'and' okay?

Alex   What?

Nathan   She is helping me! I got like eighty words okay?

Lara   Another word for 'and'?

Alex   'Also'

Lara   I've used that

Alex   'In addition to'

Lara   I used that like fifty times

Alex   Oh um . . .

Louise   'Furthermore'

Lara   What?

Louise   'Furthermore'

Georgie   I thought you weren't going to speak

Michael   She's trying to help

Georgie   I thought you weren't going to speak either

Louise   Fine okay I won't help

Lara   No please how do I say 'I've always had a passion for France and the language has always fascinated me'?

Georgie   Why you talking about France?

Lara   For background interest stuff

Louise   What's wrong with that?

Lara   Wrong with what?

Louise   What you just said

Lara   I'm not allowed to use the word 'passion' or 'fascinate'

Trent   Or 'always'

Lara   What!

Trent   You're not allowed to say 'always' look at the list

Lara   What! What why can't I say 'always'? What the hell, why can't I say 'always'?

Darrel   Can you shut up Lara! Use the thesaurus on the computer

Lara   But why can't I say it?

Darrel   Just look it up man

Alex *is typing for* **Nathan** *by now and they have swapped seats.*

Nathan   That's really good

Lara   See Alex why won't you help me!

Nathan   Lara look it up on the computer

Lara   But I don't see why I can't say 'always'. What's wrong with 'always'?

Nathan *comes over to her computer and leans over using it.* **Lara** *is looking at the list.*

Lara   And 'mistake'! I'm not allowed to say 'mistake' or 'hate' or 'nothing'! What the hell! What the hell! Why can't I say the word 'nothing'? What is wrong with the word 'nothing'?

She puts her head on her desk.

Nathan (*reading from the computer*)   'For ever, for all time, for eternity, for the end of time' . . .

Trent   What you saying?

Nathan   Other words for 'always'. Lara. Lara

Lara   What?

Nathan   Here are other words for always: 'for ever, for all time, for eternity, for the end of time' . .

Lara   I can't use them

Nathan   Why not?

Lara   'I've for eternity had a passion for France and the language has for the end of time fascinated me'

Nathan   Alright fine but I'm saying there's a thesaurus on the computer so stop trying to steal Alex

Lara   I'm not trying to steal her! I just need some help okay, she's writing yours for you! She's not allowed to do that

Alex   I'm not writing it for him

Nathan   What are you doing then?

Alex   I'm writing some bits you got to put it together yourself

Nathan   Alex I don't have time for this, okay? You can't play jigsaw with it and test me

Alex   Yeah but I don't know everything about you. I can't put all the personal stuff in

Nathan   Like what?

Alex   Like your GCSE grades

Nathan   I can't put them down

Alex   You had to in the form

Nathan   Yeah but I'm not going to draw attention to them am I? They were all like Cs and Ds

Trent   Where you applying man?

Darrel *laughs.*

Nathan   [*Choose a university.*]

Georgie   [—]?

Nathan   Yeah, so?

Georgie   I didn't even know they had a university

Alex   Well like what's your extracurricular stuff?

Lara   You, girl? Beth's sister

Louise   Louise

Alex   Nathan?

Lara   Come help me please

Nathan   Haven't done any

Alex   Well what am I meant to put down?

Nathan *shrugs.*

Louise   I have to do this

Lara   Please?

Louise   Like if we haven't got this done they'll be really mad

Lara   This is my UCAS!

Louise   I'm not going to be any good at it

Michael   Louise!

Louise   Yeah and I got to do this

Lara   Please like my whole life depends on this

Michael   Then you shouldn't have left it till now

Nathan   If I hear one more person say that okay? One more person! What's your name?

Michael   What?

Nathan   What's your name?

Michael   Michael

Nathan   Okay Michael, if I hear one more person called Michael saying that, I'm going to put their face through a computer okay?

Alex   Shut up Nathan if you're going to start bullying the Year Nines I'm not helping you

Michael   Year Ten

Alex   Oh Nathan go over and smack him cheeky little bastard

Darrel   I said didn't I, they have no respect these new ones

Lara   Louise?

Darrel   And you stop begging a kid to come over and help you with your uni application, a thirteen-year-old shouldn't be better than you

Michael   Fourteen

Alex   *I'm* going to come over there and put your face through a computer if you don't shut up

Nathan *laughs appreciatively.*

Georgie   Wait wait what the fuck? Trent what's the reference bit? Trent? Trent?

Trent   What?

Georgie   What is the reference bit?

Alex   You don't need that.

Georgie   You sure?

Alex   Yeah.

Georgie   Then why's it there?

Alex   For independent people, it's fine ours is our school.

Darrel   'Kay that's gotta do

Nathan   What!

Darrel   Fuck it I'm sending that

Nathan   You finished it?

Darrel   Kind of, we got what like twenty minutes forget it

Alex   Use your time

Darrel   No I can't make it any fucking better than it is now

Nathan   What the hell man?

Darrel   What? Sorry!

Nathan   You've finished it?

Trent   I'd read it through first mate

Darrel   No I've had enough of this shit I'm sending it

Lara   No no I said this would happen

Darrel   What?

Lara   Everyone's just gonna finish and leave us to it till it's just me and I'll never get it done

Darrel   Don't be stupid

Lara   No none of you will help me

Trent   None of us can help you

Lara   No. Can everyone stop sending them off okay?

Trent   Only Alex has

Lara   No! No more, no one else okay

Georgie   We got like . . .

Lara   I know okay I know but please can we just all wait

Georgie   Why?

Lara   Can we just all fucking wait and then when the bell goes we send them together okay?

Trent   Why?

Georgie   Okay fine.

Trent   Why?

Lara   Please

Trent   Why!

Lara   'Cause else you all sit there and are finished

Trent   Whenever we send them we'll still be done when we're done

Georgie   Just say yes Trent

Trent   But why, it's dumb

Darrel   Yeah why wait? I just want it gone

Lara   No Darrel don't you dare

Darrel   What's the problem?

Georgie   Just leave it Darrel who cares? Just say yes to her okay, it doesn't matter

Lara   Otherwise everyone will be –

Georgie   Just say yes to her for God's sake

Lara   I don't want to be . . .

Georgie   Trent

Trent   Okay yes okay whatever

Lara   You'll wait?

Trent   Yeah okay

Lara   You promise?

Trent   Yeah fine whatever

Lara   And you guys too? Nathan? Nathan?

Nathan   What?

Georgie   Just say you'll wait to send your form and we'll send them all off together okay?

Nathan   What? What?

Georgie   Just promise her

Nathan   Okay fine whatever

Lara   Darrel?

Darrel   I don't see why

Georgie   Just fucking promise her okay! What difference does it make? You're only going to go back to class if you're done so just say yes

Darrel   But . . .

Georgie   You've not filled out your employment anyway

Darrel   What?

Georgie   On the form, you can't even send that

Darrel   Why do I have to put that down? Why do they care where I've worked? I'm going to study, not work there

Alex *laughs, the others ignore.*

Trent   It's so they can see what kind of person you are

Darrel   What?

Trent   Like hard working, 'done work experience' that kind of thing

Darrel   It's none of their business!

Georgie   Get over it Darrel

Darrel   Nah 'cause I'm a kid okay and they're already judging me on everything I've done. What they're not going to take me because I haven't worked at Pizza Hut or something?

Georgie   It's not like that

Lara   I've never worked at Pizza Hut

Alex   Oh God's sake shut up Lara and do your statement

Lara   I never worked anywhere except at my mum's salon

Darrel   Yeah well exactly

Lara   And she didn't pay me so that doesn't count

Nathan   You've worked Darrel

Darrel   No. I'm not filling that bit out

Trent   Don't be stupid man

Darrel   No. I hate this shit it's none of their business where I've worked or if I have or haven't, makes no difference to whether I can do my course

Trent   Well if you'd worked in a hotel or something –

Darrel   Is that another crack about my course?

Trent   No but I mean shows you want to do it, you know what I mean

Darrel   No this is fucked! This is just like when you're little and the teachers make you draw pictures of your family and describe your bedroom and shit, they're just nosy

Alex   Darrel I don't think they read the UCAS like it's *Heat* magazine

Georgie   I told you they throw them in the bin

Darrel   No. I'm not filling it out, I'm sending it

Trent   That's such a bad idea

Lara   Darrel!

Darrel   Ah what the hell?

Georgie   It won't send unless you check the box to show that you have finished it

Darrel   But then it looks like I've never done any work

Georgie   Yeah if you won't fill it out, it will look like that

Darrel   This is such bullshit

Michael   Okay guys, guys, not being funny or anything but what we're actually doing is important too and all you lot are just talking and arguing and stuff and it is really distracting so can you keep it to like a whisper at least if you have to talk?

Pause. They all look at him.

Louise (*hitting him*)   Fuck's sake. (*To the rest*) Sorry sorry. He's really sorry

They're all still looking at him.

Michael   It's true you know. You're all making this big fuss about it, why don't you just all shut up and get on with it?

Louise   Michael!

Michael   Like you're having a go at us for distracting you but you're all doing it yourselves., it's really kind of childish

Louise   Michael shut up!

Michael   I don't see why they should get whatever they want just because they're older and say it's important, when we're going to get in loads of trouble if we don't finish this

Louise   Don't hit him, he bruises really easily

Michael   But . . .

Louise *puts her hand over* **Michael***'s mouth.*

Louise   He won't talk any more I promise

Michael *tries to protest but she just grips his face more.*

Louise   Promise

Trent   Okay okay

Darrel   What?

Trent   Okay fine whatever

Nathan   Alex please why have you stopped?

Georgie   Trent it's so not okay

Trent   Okay fine you sort it out. I'm going to try and get into university okay?

Lara   Oh my god just what's the point?

Georgie   Don't start

Darrel   Lara just stop moaning, let me see what you've done

He goes over to her computer.

Lara   Like nothing. I changed that one sentence but I just don't know how to make it good

Darrel *(about a big folder on the desk)*   What's in here?

Lara   All the notes she gave me –

Darrel *picks it up.*

Lara   – to make it better, but I can't even read her writing properly so it's pointless

Darrel *walks up behind* **Michael** *with the folder. He smashes* **Michael** *round the head with it. Some pages come out.*

Darrel   Fuck you

Nathan *notices but is too stressed to laugh.* **Trent** *and the girls laugh,* **Louise** *does too, a bit.*

Michael   That really fucking hurt

Lara   You haven't broke my folder have you?

Darrel   You won't need it in like half an hour

Lara   Bring it back

Michael   That really hurt

Trent   Shut up mate

Lara   Bring it back Darrel!

Louise   You okay?

Michael   Don't alright

Darrel   Even Louise is laughing

Lara   Give it back

Darrel (*giving the folder back*)   Here. Alright, here

Lara   What's the point? I don't even want to go

Alex   Obviously none of us want to go

Trent   What? I want to go

Georgie   Yeah same, what you talking about Alex?

Alex   What? Like obviously you want to get in, but none of us want to *go*, right?

Georgie   No I want to go

Alex   What? What do all of you want to go?

Trent   Yeah

Darrel   Yeah

Alex   Why?

Pause.

Darrel   'Cause like . . . (*Looks to* **Trent**.)

Trent   Like to study and meet people and stuff

Darrel   Like girls and stuff

Trent   Get a good job

Alex   Lara you don't want to go?

Lara   Well like, I don't want to do this but yeah I want to go

Georgie   If you want to be anybody you have to go

Alex   No you don't. Loads of people don't go

Georgie   Yeah like plumbers and stuff

Nathan   You're the only one who will get in for sure

Georgie   And Trent

Darrel   He's doing 'science'

Nathan   Yeah but you know what I mean, she's gonna like get into somewhere really good

Georgie   So will Trent

Trent   Shut up Georgie

Nathan   What do you mean you don't want to go? You're just trying be different

Alex   Well do you want to go?

Nathan   Yeah that's why I'm doing this

Alex   If you so wanted to go why did you leave it till now? Why did all of us leave it till now?

Georgie   Because she told us the wrong date

Alex   Why didn't you send it weeks ago like Beth, like everyone else?

Lara   Because it's hard

Alex   I don't believe any of you want to

Nathan   Course we do, why don't you?

Alex   Because it's going to be . . . it's just so boring!

Lara   No you don't even have to go to the lectures or anything

Georgie   Yeah you like just have to do a few essays

Lara   And the first year doesn't even count

Georgie   Yeah my sister says the first year doesn't even count

Alex   Why you going?

Georgie   Oh come on Alex. What do you want to do? You want to go out and get a job and shit now? Why?

Alex   Why do you wanna go?

Georgie   Like they say the job and the parties and stuff

Alex   'Eighty per cent of employers would take someone with work experience over a graduate.'

Darrel   Where you get that from?

Georgie   Work experience as what?

Alex   As whatever you want to be

Georgie   I'm doing sociology what work experience is there for that?

Alex   Well what do you want to be?

Georgie   Sandra said my job options are counsellor, housing manager, teacher, further education lecturer . . .

Lara   Did you get Sandra? I got this guy called Ted

Trent   Yeah I got him, said he could tell I'd be a really good sports teacher

Georgie   Yeah Sandra was really good

Alex   So what you want to be?

Georgie   She said counsellor, housing manager, teacher . . .

Alex   Yeah but what do you want to be?

Georgie   I dunno. I got three years before that

Alex   But do you want to do any of those jobs?

Darrel   Imagine Georgie as a teacher

Georgie   I wouldn't be a teacher

Alex   What housing manger?

Georgie   What's wrong with that?

Alex   There's nothing wrong with that if that's what you want to do

Georgie   She said loads of stuff. I've got it written down

Lara   What do you want to be?

Alex   Journalist

Nathan   Yeah so you got to get your English degree, please stop screwing around and help me

Alex   No, but I don't *need* a degree

Nathan   Then why did you apply?

Alex   Because my parents made me

Darrel   Aw your parents made you

Trent   Alex shut up

Alex   Fine, okay do your work

Trent   No I mean shut up about 'your parents made you and you don't want to go, you obviously do

Georgie   Human resources officer, charity fundraiser, youth worker

Alex   I don't

Georgie   Probation officer

Alex   But you know you want to be a sports coach?

Trent   Yeah

Alex   Exactly and you have to go to uni, you're fine it makes sense for you

Georgie   Like loads of options

Alex   Like Trent you're fine

Lara   I don't know what I want to be

Alex   That's probably why your personal statement is bad

Georgie   What! Of course you know what you want to be

Lara   No

Georgie   Then why the hell are you applying for accountancy if you don't want to be an accountant?

Darrel   You're applying for accountancy!

Lara   Because I told Ted I want to make a lot of money and he said 'cause I got an A for maths I could take it for A-level and then when I saw him again he said universities have really good employment graduate history for accountancy

Alex   And that's why you picked it!

Lara   Yeah

Alex   But you don't want to be an accountant?

Lara   I dunno, maybe

Louise   And you are writing about France in your statement?

Nathan   I know what I want to do Alex, does that mean you'll write my fucking statement please?

Alex   What do you want to do?

Nathan   Get into uni!

Alex   Oh my God

Nathan *pushes her out of the way and starts on the computer himself.*

Alex   Why did you apply?

Lara   I dunno, everyone else was

Trent   Right, done

Georgie   Really?

Trent   Whatever. Can't concentrate with all this, I'm going to send it

Lara   No!

Trent   Alright alright.

Georgie   You're done?

Trent   How much you done?

Georgie   Like nothing, will you help me?

Trent   Yeah okay

Lara (*to* **Darrel**)   Why you just sitting there?

Darrel   I've done mine

Georgie   What? When?

Darrel   I'm finished

Lara   But . . .

Darrel   No Lara I ain't sent it. But it's done okay?

Lara   No employment?

Darrel   Yeah

Georgie   Oh Darrel

Lara   So what everyone's done theirs?

Georgie   I haven't

Lara   Yeah but yours is just the form, what am I going to do?

Alex   Give up

Lara   No I can't

Trent   Don't tell her to give up

Alex   She obviously doesn't want to go

Georgie   No you don't want to go

Trent   She says

Alex   I don't, I hope I don't get in

Darrel   Then why did you send it?

Alex   Because my parents made me, everyone in my family went to university I had to apply, they'd think I was stupid or something if I didn't, I tried not to! I been off sick thought I might miss the deadline

Georgie   They'll think you're even stupider if you don't get in

Alex   I don't really care any more

Trent   Then why did you send it?

Alex   I dunno I shouldn't have. It was just, like, expected.

Lara   I know practically our whole year, even my parents expected me to and they didn't go

Georgie   Nor did mine

Alex   But makes no difference it's so stupid

Nathan   Can you shut the hell up Alex!

Alex   You were the one saying the system's screwed up

Nathan   I don't care alright? Maybe your whole family is like fucking Cambridge graduates or something but I've got to get in okay? I dunno why I was screwing around before. I've got to, so can you either help me or fuck off?

Alex   Why you so desperate to go?

Nathan   My family wants me to

Alex   See? Same as me

Nathan   No 'cause no one in my family's been to uni. That's why they want me to

Alex   So?

Nathan   What do you mean so?

Alex   Oh sorry is it worse because no one's ever been in your family and they all have in mine? It's the same thing

Nathan   No it's not

Alex   Yeah it is. I know what you're trying to say. I know exactly how you're trying to make it out Nathan but you're not Ryan fucking Atwood, you know it's exactly the same

Nathan   I don't know what you're chatting about

Alex   Oh yeah?

Nathan   I don't watch *The O.C*

Alex   Then how do you know Ryan Atwood is in *The O.C.*?

Nathan   My sister

Alex   Oh yeah?

Nathan   My sister watches it

Alex   But you still know what I mean

Nathan   No I don't

Trent   Who is Ryan Atwood?

Georgie   She means like Will Smith in *The Fresh Prince of Bel Air*

Nathan   I'm not being like that

Alex   Well if you so wanted to go you would have done it before, all of them did their personal statements

Nathan   Darrel didn't

Alex   He's done it now

Nathan   And I'm trying to do mine, you're meant to be helping me

Alex   Yeah and I will, but don't act like it's so important for you when your family's made you just the same as me

Nathan   My mum wanted me to

Alex   Yeah so does mine

Darrel   (*or whoever is closest of the Sixth Formers*) *kicks her.*

Alex   What? She does

Georgie (*indicating* **Nathan**)   Alex

Alex   Wha . . . Oh shit, sorry, sorry Nathan I forgot. Wasn't thinking, sorry

Nathan   It's fine.

Alex   Sorry, sorry

Nathan   It's fine.

Alex   Do you want me to help again?

Nathan   No it's fine, whatever.

Darrel   Don't be stupid man let her.

Distracted again, **Louise** *and* **Michael** *have been watching. They whisper.*

Nathan   Okay fine

Michael (*audibly*)   Oh

They look over.

Louise   Sorry. Beth told me

Michael   Yeah sorry for your loss

Nathan   Fuck off

Michael   Just like, yeah, sorry

They turn back to their computers.

Alex   Are you sure you haven't got any extracurricular I can put in?

Nathan   No

Alex   You work at the shop at the weekend yeah?

Nathan   Yeah

Alex   How long?

Nathan   Like since last September

Alex   Okay I'll put that in

Darrel   No don't put his fucking job in

Alex   But he's got nothing else

Darrel   So? It's none of their business

Trent   Nothing in the personal statement is their business

Darrel   Exactly.

Georgie   Trent can you help me?

Trent   It's easy

Lara   Will someone please help me!

Trent   I'm shit at English

Darrel   Same

Lara   Louise please

Louise   What?

Michael   No we've just been through this

Lara   Please, please, I'll do anything. I'll buy you cigarettes or like alcohol or whatever

Michael   She has an older sister for that

Lara   Please!

Michael   This is important too

Darrel   What the hell are you guys even doing that you keep saying is *so* important?

Michael   Just work, but it doesn't mean . . .

Darrel *has come over.* **Michael** *tries to cover the screen.*

Trent   That a teacher let you come in here for?

Darrel   Oh fuck off

Michael   No get off

Darrel *and* **Michael** *struggle*

Darrel   Trent come here

Trent *comes over, they hold* **Michael** *to the swivel chair and push him over to the other side of the room. They're enjoying themselves,* **Michael** *is not.*

Trent   Fucking hell

Darrel   Lara Lara come here hold him, shit hold him. Lara!

Michael *comes off the seat.* **Trent** *and* **Darrel** *sit on him.*

Trent   Lara

Lara (*screaming*)   I'm doing my personal statement!

Georgie   It's alright

Darrel   Jesus

Trent   Sorry Lara

Michael *tries to get back to the computer, the boys stop him.*

Darrel   We just want to see what you're doing

Trent   Stop making a big deal out of it all, okay?

Darrel   You've already upset our friend causing all this trouble and making noise. (*Off the computer.*) 'The Buddha's birth, enlightenment and death'

Trent   RS! You two are stressing over RS?

Louise   Darrel please get off him

Darrel   No one bothers with RS mate it's a joke

Louise   No it's not

Trent   It's like General Studies or something

Georgie   I like RS

Darrel   Okay fine whatever but Mr Gorge is a pussy, you don't have to stress

Louise   Okay fine. Will you let him up?

Michael   It's not for Mr Gorge

Darrel   Miss Hall is an even bigger pussy she'd just cry if you don't give it in or something

Lara   Don't even talk about Miss Hall to me!

Michael   It's for Mr Patts

Trent   What?

Darrel   Why?

Georgie   Why is it for Mr Patts?

Trent   You do your form.

Georgie *sighs, turns back.*

Trent   Yeah but why the fuck is it for Mr Patts Martin?

Louise   Michael

Trent   Michael why the fuck is it for Mr Patts? He doesn't take classes

Darrel   Unless you're on probation, you on probation?

Michael   No

Trent   Then why's it for Mr Patts? She can't be on probation

Louise   We're not on probation, just let him up

Michael   Assembly

Darrel *and* **Trent** *are delighted. They lean down to talk to him underneath them.*

Darrel   Assembly?!

Trent   Fuck off you're doing assembly

Darrel   You little pussy man. You both doing it?

Michael   Yes

Darrel (*to* **Louise**)   And I thought you were okay, I thought you were normal

Louise   We got asked

Nathan   Guys keep it down

Trent   You little neeks

Darrel   Even Alex never done an assembly

Trent   It's like you want to get beat up

Darrel   Did you choose that as a subject too?

Trent   Oh my God did you choose Buddha?

Darrel   Oh my God did you?

Trent   You chose Buddha?

Michael   Mr Patts is doing all the world religious festivals, he asked me and Louise to do Buddhism

Darrel   Jesus Christ man you're such a loser

Trent   Such a waste man

Darrel   Going 'Oh this is so important'

Trent   'This is important too'

Darrel   We're doing our fucking UCAS there, that's our future

Michael   It's for the headmaster. It is important

Louise   Oh shut up Michael

Darrel   See even Louise telling you to shut up

Michael   Get off me

Trent   You're right you know they got no respect these Year Nines

Michael   Tens!

Darrel   Yeah shut up Michael unless you want to go back to learning about Buddha

Michael   Get the fuck off me

Trent   Georgie stop watching we've done ours.

Georgie   Eurgh

Georgie *turns back again.*

Alex   I can't concentrate with all this

Nathan   Alex can't concentrate

Louise   Look get off him, I'll help Lara if you get off him

Lara   Get off him Trent!

Darrel   She doesn't need some thirteen-year-old's help

Louise   Fourteen

Lara   Get off him Trent. Thank you Louise

Michael   Get the fuck off me

Louise   Shut up Michael

Nathan   Darrel shut him up Alex can't concentrate

Michael   It really hurts, get off me

Trent   You promise you'll help Lara?

Louise   Yeah

Michael   I'll tell Mr Patts

Trent   What?

Darrel   You'll what?

Nathan   Michael shut up!

Michael   I'll tell Mr Patts if you don't get the fuck off me now

Louise   They are Michael

Darrel   No we fucking aren't, not going to do what some little thirteen-year-old pussy tells us to

Michael   Fourteen! I've fucking said and said. I'm fourteen!

Nathan's *come over, leans down, hits the back of his head so* **Michael** *smacks his face on the floor.* **Darrel** *and* **Trent** *get up.*

Georgie   Nathan!

Nathan   She can't concentrate

Nathan *goes back to his seat.*

Darrel (*to* **Michael**)   Fucking little waste gash

Michael's *nose is bleeding.*

Trent (*to* **Nathan**)   Did that a bit hard

They both look a little uncomfortable but don't give in to it.

Alex   You didn't have to do that

Nathan   Pissing me off.

Michael *sits on the floor a bit stunned.*

Trent (*to* **Louise**)   'Kay go on, help her then

Louise   Fine. (*Getting up, to* **Michael**.) You okay?

Michael *doesn't answer.*

Trent   Michael?

Louise   You okay?

Darrel   Michael? Nath' you smacked his brain out

Alex   See now look what you've done?

Louise   Michael?

Nathan   You alright?

Lara *passes him a tissue.*

Michael (*to* **Nathan**)   You care just because you don't want to get into trouble

Louise   Obviously

Michael   You're meant to be doing the assembly with me

Louise   Yeah but it can wait we've done loads of it

Michael   Fine

He gets up.

Darrel   You're not going to tell Mr Patts are you?

Alex   He's not an idiot

Michael   No

Trent   Yeah you're fine mate, you just do your project thing and shut up okay?

Georgie   'Cause we're doing our UCAS here

Michael   Yeah I know. I know you're doing your stupid fucking UCAS. I don't care, you shouldn't have left it till now, I don't care what you all say none of you deserve to go, you're all idiots and shouldn't have left it till now

Georgie   Do you want another smack?

Michael   Fuck off I don't care, you all think you're cool but you're just a bunch of no-hope losers who'll never get anywhere because you think it's neeky to do an assembly for the headmaster. But I'm going to have something to write in my UCAS rather than a job in a shop or that I want to meet girls at uni

Trent   Oh fuck off man

Darrel   Fuck off

Louise   Michael please. I'll be like ten minutes okay? Let me just help her okay? Then I'll come back

Michael   We're meant to be . . .

Louise   I know, sorry

Lara   Sorry Michael

Louise Do you want another tissue?

Michael *nods.* **Lara** *passes one to* **Louise**, *who passes it to* **Michael**.

Lara Thank you Michael

Michael *sits.* **Louise** *comes over to* **Lara**.

Trent Your boyfriend's stroppy isn't he?

Louise Show me then

Lara All this bit I've highlighted I have to rephrase

Louise 'Kay

Darrel You good at English like Beth then?

Louise *shrugs.*

Lara That's why she's helping me, she's good. Aren't you? Aren't you good?

Louise I'm okay

Lara Oh

Georgie She's being modest, you are good aren't you?

Louise I dunno

Georgie What you get last year?

Louise Like ninety-something

Trent Fuck off, really?

Darrel Yeah. Beth is really clever too

Lara Okay then please will you look at this?

Louise Okay

Darrel Can't believe you're getting a thirteen-year-old to write your UCAS

Lara She's fourteen

Darrel And you're applying for maths and stuff. I don't get it, you're clever

Lara I just can't do this kind of thing

Georgie She studies loads, she's book-smart

Lara Yeah

Trent Lara you're not meant to agree with that

Lara Why not?

Trent 'Cause you don't want to be book-smart. You want to be clever

Lara What's the difference?

Darrel Love the way no one's doing their own UCAS any more

Georgie I haven't finished mine yet!

Trent Oh for fuck's sake, move then

Georgie Thank you

Darrel See?

Nathan Yeah that's really good

Alex Do you really have nothing else? Like no books or anything you've read I can put in?

Nathan No

Darrel It's Community Studies mate relax

Nathan Yeah

Darrel Like you passed an exam, that makes you more qualified than anyone else applying

Nathan Yeah that's fine

Alex Okay just tell me some hobbies then, make up some

Nathan Like what?

Alex   Anything.

Nathan   Football then

Alex   Okay

Nathan   No but I never played at school

Alex   They're not going to check it, you need something Nathan

Nathan   Okay

Darrel   I'm bored

Nathan   Well fuck off then Darrel we're all working

Lara   No we're all waiting to send them off together!

Darrel   Which is stupid

Louise   It's not that bad

Lara   What?

Louise   Your statement, it seems fine

Darrel   Course it does to you

Lara   Darrel stop it

Darrel   She's thirteen years old

Louise   I'm fucking fourteen Darrel you know that

Trent   Oooo

Darrel   Shut up Louise

Louise   Pissing me off

Darrel   Fuck off Louise

Louise   Talking about me like I'm not here and being like that to Michael

Michael   You're talking about me like I'm not here

Trent   Oooo

Lara   Stop it Trent, look he's sorry okay? Louise can you please . . . ?

Louise   Why you starting? I'm trying to defend you

Michael   No you're not

Louise   Yes I am!

Michael   You weren't before

Trent   Trouble in par –

Georgie   You're meant to be helping me Trent, leave the kids alone

Trent   It's just the form . . .

Michael   Can you stop calling us the kids?

Darrel   Oh shut up Mike you want another slap?

Georgie (*to* **Michael**)   You talking to me?

Louise   Darrel stop thinking you're the big man

Lara   Please can you just help me Louise?

Darrel   Think I'm the 'big man'?

Georgie   Oi Martin are you talking to me?

Louise   Yeah

Michael   Michael!

Darrel   Do you know how stupid you sound?

Michael   I've told you my fucking name is Michael!

Louise   I sound stupid? Is this how you are around your friends? Like all loud and shouting at me and shit

Georgie   Trent? Trent can you do something about this kid?

Darrel   Oh what are you talking about?

Lara   Darrel leave her the fuck alone!

Trent   Leave me out of it

Darrel   You only want her to help you with your UCAS

Lara   Yeah of course I do

Georgie   You're totally useless

Trent   I'm trying to help you with your form

Alex   Nathan I can't do it with this –

Nathan   Okay guys!

Darrel   You think I'm going to let some stupid little girl –

Louise   Oh yeah carry on Darrel

Darrel   Why are you talking like you know me?

Louise   I do know you Darrel

Nathan   Guys please

Georgie   Oi Michael

Trent   Why don't you leave the kid alone?

Michael   I'm not a kid!

Georgie   You let him talk to you like that?

Darrel   What? Just 'cause I been round your house you know me?

Trent   Leave it

Louise   Beth's told me all about you

Darrel   And what the hell's that meant to mean?

Georgie   You're so pathetic Trent you're just sitting there with that little . . .

Trent   I feel bad, look at his nose

Georgie   You're such a pussy

Michael   You're such a bitch

Trent *laughs.*

Georgie You . . . are you laughing? Trent are you fucking laughing at him saying that to me?

Darrel What the hell's that meant to mean?

Nathan Guys shut the fuck up! Shut up

Darrel What the hell's that meant to mean?

Nathan Darrel! Darrel man shut up, chill, chill just for a sec

Darrel But, what the hell –

Louise You don't scare me

Nathan You shut up too

Georgie You're fucking laughing at that?

Nathan Georgie! Georgie! Georgie!

Georgie Why's that funny?

Trent It's not funny

Lara Darrel sit back down

Nathan Shut up all you three shut up for a minute

Georgie You don't stand up for me he calls me a bitch and –

Trent I don't have to stand up for you you aren't my fucking girlfriend

Georgie . . . I know

Trent So stop bossing me around

Darrel So what the fuck was that meant to mean?

Nathan No shut up, guys please

Georgie I'm not bossing you around

Trent Yeah you are and whining and shit

Georgie   No I'm not

Darrel   Louise don't ignore me

Nathan   Please just send your fucking forms you're all like done aren't you?

Lara   I'm not, so Darrel stop –

Louise   It's fine Lara just send it

Darrel   You gonna talk to me then?

Louise   I am fucking talking to you

Georgie   See Trent! This is what I mean look they've got no respect these Year Tens

Michael   Respect for what?

Nathan   Now I really mean it you all shut the fuck up! We got like five fucking minutes, five fucking minutes to do this

Darrel   So what you saying?

Louise   You know what I'm saying

Lara   Darrel!

Darrel   What you saying?

Louise   That you're trying to act the big fucking man and making fun of me and Michael and my sister but you didn't even fuck her

Trent   Wow what!

Nathan   Guys please!

Georgie   Now you're talking to him

Darrel   Yes I did. What you saying?

Lara   She told me, told me you couldn't, said you were too drunk and then started crying about it 'cause you're still a virgin

Trent   Fuck off!

Darrel   What? What you chatting about?

Lara   Louise please help me

Nathan   Shut up all of you!

Louise   I've told you you're done Lara just send it

Darrel   Why you saying lies?

Trent   You never slept with Beth?

Nathan   Five minutes till our fucking future is gone and you lot give a shit about that?

Michael   They're all done. It's just you

Nathan   You kid have got some sort of death wish

Trent   Darrel you gone red as fuck man

Darrel   Why you telling fucking lies about me?

Georgie   Trent can you talk to me?

Lara   You sure it can go?

Alex   Nathan –

Nathan   Just all shut the hell up!

Georgie   Trent!

Alex   Nathan –

Nathan   I know. I'm trying to make them shut up

Darrel   I dunno why your slut of a sister said that, that next fucking pussy

Georgie   Trent!

Louise   Oh yeah yeah whatever Darrel, whatever you say

Georgie   Trent

Trent   Stop saying my name!

Alex   It's done, it's finished, you can send it

Georgie   Why you being like this?

Lara   Can I really send it?

Nathan   You done it?

Alex   Yeah

Ecstatic and in thanks, **Nathan** *kisses* **Alex***. Only* **Michael** *notices at first. He looks around to see if the others have.*

Trent   Just leave me the / hell alone

Darrel   / Lying little . . .

Lara   Louise!

Louise*, who is trying to get away from* **Darrel***, sees them coming out of the kiss. Her focus distracts* **Darrel** *and* **Lara***, who also look.*

Darrel   And what the fuck is going on here!

Nathan   Thank you!

Trent   Look I'm not saying you've done anything wrong but stop shouting at me like I'm your little bitch, okay?

Georgie   I ain't doing nothing like that

Darrel   Nathan you know her sister's been lying her fucking face off

Nathan   Man who cares?

Darrel   I'm going to talk to Beth later

Georgie   Trent I ain't doing nothing like that

Louise   Oh you're going to talk to her?

Darrel   Look you little bitch . . .

Michael   Leave her alone

Lara   Leave it Martin

Michael   Michael!

Darrel   I had enough of you two now

Trent   Fine.

Georgie   Don't just say 'fine' because . . .

Michael   Don't shout at her

Darrel   'Don't shout at her'

Lara   Darrel that's mean

Darrel   'That's mean'!

Alex   Why don't you all just send your fucking UCAS?

Michael   You're such a joke

Darrel   Oh am I little man?

Michael   You know what I should do, pull the plug on your computer

Darrel   Go ahead man it's saved

Michael   Oh yeah?

Darrel   Yeah go on but see what happens

Michael   Yeah?

Darrel   Yeah I'll do a lot more than smack your face on the floor

The bell goes, they all stop.

Alex   That's the forty-five minutes up.

Lara   Shit.

Georgie   Shit.

Trent   Actually?

Alex   Yeah you gotta all send it.

Lara   Oh my god. It's so not ready

Darrel   None of ours are really ready

Nathan   Fuck.

Georgie   If only you'd all shut up we could have done them properly

Nathan   Says you!

Trent   We better send them

Lara   But they're so bad

Alex   It's alright

Nathan   We needed longer

Louise   You can't miss the deadline. Maybe you should all just . . .

Georgie   Oh fuck I don't want to

Darrel   Right just fucking do it

He doesn't, none of them can. **Alex** *leans over* **Nathan** *and sends his.*

Nathan   Ah

Alex   'Kay come on guys

She walks down along, and sends them all for everyone.

Alex   Okay? There's nothing else you could have done, you can't miss the deadline.

Michael (*reading*)   'Please remember your application must be received by UCAS by midnight (UK time) on the 15th January. If you apply past the deadline, check with your chosen university first to see if they are still willing to consider you for your chosen course.'

Pause.

Lara   Where's that from?

Michael   Your pack.

Georgie   You're fucking joking right

Michael   'By midnight (UK time) on the 15th January –'

Lara   But it's the . . .

Darrel   I said I fucking, fucking, fucking said it was next week! I said it was next week!

Lara   Oh my God

Trent   It's next week, but we . . .

Georgie   Oh my God I'm going to kill her

Nathan   It's next week

Lara   Back! Back? How do we get it back?

Nathan   We can't get it back

Lara   But it's shit! It's all shit, the teachers haven't looked or anything. It's shit. I thought, I thought we only had –

Georgie   I'm going to kill her, I am going to get her fucking sacked! She can't do this! She can't have done this to us!

Trent   Are you sure we can't get it back?

Darrel   There must be a way to get it back

Michael   'If you want to withdraw your application, phone UCAS.'

Lara   We'll do that

Michael   'If you withdraw, you will not be able to make another application during the academic year, and you will not be eligible for the Clearing system.'

Trent   Where are you getting this shit from?

Michael   Your pack.

Darrel   How did you get that?

Michael   'Cause you hit me round the fucking head with it. Louise let's go

Darrel   You known all that time?

Michael   Known what? Louise

Louise   Did you know all that time?

Michael   What? We have to go to parents' evening

Georgie   Did you fucking know that it was next week? And you let us send that shit off and we all thought we had forty-five fucking minutes and we had a week more

Lara   And the deadline is at midnight anyway

Georgie   And school hasn't checked it or anything and you let us send it

Michael   'Cause when are deadlines at five p.m.? When is stuff ever actually strict in the real world? You're all pathetic it's not school. There are always idiots like you who miss deadlines they make allowances for that in the real world. Nothing's ever final in the real world

Nathan   You knew?

Michael   If you hit me again I'll tell Mr Patts

Nathan   You can tell fucking Buddha kid I don't give a fuck

Michael   It's right in front of you, why did none of you check? Anyone with half a fucking brain cell. Miss Leal told you the deadline was now? She's a fucking drama teacher what the fuck would she know?

Georgie   She said

Michael   You should have checked

Darrel   I'm going to kill you

Michael   Anyone would have checked

Georgie   Right!

She slams her fist down and chases **Michael***, who runs out of the room.*

Georgie   Trent!

Trent *and* **Darrel** *get up and chase after* **Michael***.* **Lara** *makes a little noise.*

Nathan   I swear if you start crying Lara

Alex   There's no point crying

There's shouting outside from the others.

Louise   They're not going to really hurt him, are they?

Nathan   Probably not, but I am

Nathan *goes to leave.*

Alex   Nathan don't. What's the point?

Nathan   Oh shut up Alex. You don't even want to go

Nathan *goes. It gets louder outside.* **Louise** *goes to save her computer but* **Lara** *jumps up and beats her to it, turns it off.*

Louise   Lara!

Lara   Fuck you and him

Louise   I didn't know, I was trying to help you!

Lara   None of these kids have got any fucking respect

She goes out.

Louise   What do we say to Mr Patts?

Alex *shrugs. There's a yell.* **Alex** *goes to open the door but* **Michael** *pushes his way in. They've taken his trousers, he slams the door after him and holds it shut.*

Michael (*yelling through the door*)   You shouldn't have all left it till now! And listened to a fucking drama teacher, should you? Louise help me!

Louise *and* **Alex** *sit back, giving up.* **Michael** *struggles to keep the door shut.*

Michael   When I do it I won't leave it so I got forty-five minutes! I. Take. Responsibility. For. My. Own. Education.

The door almost opens.

Forty-Five Minutes

BY ANYA REISS

*Notes on rehearsal and staging, drawn from a workshop
with the writer held at the National Theatre, November 2012*

How the writer came to write the play

'The play was written for the actors, with no worries about
scene changes. Keep it simple. It's about the weird
phenomenon of how people react in a pressure-cooker
situation, the pressures of time and consequence.'

Anya Reiss

The moment of completing and sending in a UCAS form is
critical in a young person's life: perhaps the first time that an
individual is asked to present himself or herself to the adult
world, and to address a system of priorities and values that
will be significantly different from those shared with their
peers. Personal information and the all-important personal
statement need to be codified and adapted to fall in with a
new adult audience. How will the UCAS form (and by
extension, you), be viewed by the outside world where the
governing prerogatives, standards and principles are different
from those of the sixth-form common room? The applications
panel of a university is unlikely to be concerned with how
many internet followers you have, how many parties you've
been to and your all-time favourite dance track. Suddenly,
in this new context, the long-cupboarded skeleton of once
being a highly decorated Girl Guide, of being the village's
most reliable paper boy or that occasional job in the corner
shop have suddenly circumstantially grown in significance
and worth.

The group, led by director Lyndsey Turner and writer Anya
Reiss, discussed the fact that the UK has a higher frequency
of exams and assessments than almost any education system
in the world. These tests are fulcrum moments socially as well

as academically in a young person's development; it is at these times that the year group is 'reshuffled' like a pack of cards. Other moments of 'social reshuffling' include moving from primary to secondary school, subject choices at GCSE, the decision as to whether to go into further education or higher education. The fallout from these choices will restructure a young person's life and begin to define them as the choices necessarily become more precisely focused.

Lyndsey Turner suggested it would be worthwhile, when investigating the characters of the play, to examine three 'selves': the TRUE SELF (the private and emotional self of the character, the person they see in the bathroom mirror every morning); the FACEBOOK SELF (the constructed, media self, a projection of how one would like to be perceived: cool, well-liked, sociable, fashionable); and the ADULT WORLD SELF (the self as evaluated by the 'grown-up world' and its perceived merit system of work ethic, reliability, maturity, intellect, utilitarianism). *Forty-Five Minutes* interrogates the interplay between these three 'selves', and dramatises a group of people at the moment when the deck of cards which has remained stable during the sixth form reshuffles once again.

Try setting up Facebook pages for the characters: decide what they would say about themselves, how they would prioritise that information and what photograph they might choose to post on the internet. How do they want to be understood or distinguished?

Approaching the play

The relatively small cast, tight structure and naturalistic real-time element of the play had attracted many of the workshop participants. It allows for a character-driven production, an opportunity to develop and investigate characters more deeply. There are no musical numbers or big images to worry about, but the text offers the opportunity to focus on the humour, timing and tonal qualities in the play, a chance to explore and discover different layers 'without having to worry about scene changes'. What Lyndsey Turner described as the 'closed-time, closed-space' format of the play means that highs and lows, peaks and troughs need to be found through the acting rather than special effects.

There was excitement about this chance for young actors to play characters close to their own age, in many cases the same age, to use familiar-sounding dialogue and contemporary styles and patterns of speech, but along with this attraction there was a concern that their cast could end up 'playing themselves'. Lyndsey Turner agreed that there is always the danger of young actors 'bringing the character to themselves' and also of painting characters with broad brush-strokes, going for the obvious and generating stereotypes, or of the actors presenting a generalised 'impression' of a character type (the bully, the swot, the cool kid, the teachers' pet). She hoped that character exercises, like those described below, could aid the specificity and particularity of individual character creation and help to avoid categorising or stock school characters. Try sporadically swapping roles around during the early stages of rehearsal, see what comes of having different actors playing very different roles, try to avoid persistent rhythms and character interpretations, play around and avoid stereotypes at all costs.

Characters and characterisation

These character descriptions have been drawn from notes by Anya Reiss, with some additional information discussed during the workshop.

NATHAN   Outside this room he is high-status, popular, alpha, someone who usually doesn't care, but in this context his power is lost and he's the underdog. He's the one whose stress is probably the most authentic; it is this that makes him vulnerable and his vulnerability makes him volatile.

Examine how Nathan may react when parents are mentioned.
He may veer away from the subject, but it doesn't negate an
'internal flinch'. Play around with the politics and protocol of
this sidestepping while silently acknowledging the loss. What
are the 'rules' and expectations of behaviour around a young
person who has recently lost a family member? How much of
a persistent spectre is it? How wary are the other characters
about using the word 'mum' in his presence?

His is the most authentic, gut-churning worry, a visceral fear.
Cast an actor who can bring some status to the part.

DARREL   The last to start and the first to give up in any
given situation. Of all of them, he is the one for whom the
situation feels the least real; he has talked and joked and
complained about UCAS so much that he finds it hard to
realise that this really is his last chance. He's probably a bit
of a stoner.

The relationship between Darrel and Nathan is an important
one, probably the longest-standing friendship in the room.
Try to cast someone with some comic flair as Darrel. Nathan
and Darrel don't need to be beautiful, but a bit of swagger
wouldn't go amiss.

ALEX   In the sixth form people find their status changes. Alex
is a recent graduate to medium-/high-status as, now the
group is older, her sarcasm and intelligence are better
appreciated. She probably comes from the 'best' background
but not by a mile; she is the one least likely to see the others
outside of school.

Anya said she was anxious about a reading of Alex limited to
marking her out solely by her social class; she shouldn't be
played as posh, as this is not a play about social stratification.
Her character evolution and costuming should be carefully
considered, as there is a potential stereotyping pitfall to be
avoided. Consider how much of an outsider she is and has
been, and how this may have changed recently as the pack-
reshuffling of the sixth form has moved her up the pecking

order. She has found a new, weird coolness and has consequently been propelled up the ladder to be the most valuable player in the room. Make sure she doesn't become an absolute angel.

GEORGIE   Her loudness and friendship with Trent have made her more of a boys' girl than a girls' girl. She isn't unkind, just self-righteous, usually at the expense of others, and uncomfortable when hers isn't the voice being listened to.

TRENT   The most contained of the group but still reasonably high-status, the kind of guy you don't really pay much attention to but would never want to interrupt. He's centred; this attracts people, but his identity is based on being well liked rather than a defining trait. He takes the path of least resistance every time.

Trent is well centred with effortless high status. He doesn't speak a great deal but this endows what he does say with conspicuous weight.

LARA   Outside the room she is a girlier version of Georgie and a bit of a force to be reckoned with, hiding behind her tastes and femininity. I imagine she is the youngest of a large family and has found that crying usually brings results.

Lara is a pairing with Georgie. She defines herself by the bands she likes and the fashions she adopts, and she uses this projected image as a shield; hers is an imposing, well-preened 'Facebook Self'.

LOUISE   Because of her older sister, she is less impressed by the sixth-formers being older, and is also forearmed with knowledge about them from her sister. Despite being confident in the room, she would normally tend to blend in within her own year, and it's because of this that she tolerates so much before she finally becomes too frustrated at Darrel and blurts his secrets out.

MICHAEL   Of everyone, Michael has the least front; he hasn't developed a character or a shield or a filter, he's just himself. A strong believer in what is right and what is fair, it is this rather than bravery that makes him so stubborn. I imagine he comes from quite a serious, hard-working family and finds the sixth-formers vaguely ridiculous.

'Take responsibility for your own education' is one of his most significant lines.

Lyndsey Turner described Michael as a David Attenborough character and the sixth-formers as a strange species that don't wholly make sense to him. He is not necessarily a brave young man, but he can stand up for himself when the need arises. His respect and reverence/fear of teachers shouldn't be ignored; he isn't up-to-date with or maybe even aware of the fashions and trends around him. Beware of playing him as simply *weird*, an obvious outsider; allow the character to evolve through what he says and does during the play and try to resist the temptation to mint a shining new oddball dynamic the moment he enters the fray but to let his otherness unfold. The director and writer both agreed that this is a difficult role to cast and that it would be wise to choose an actor who could understand the complexity of the character.

Exercises for use in rehearsal

Exercises for feeding back-stories and developing character

TOP TRUMPS

Draw up top-trump-style cards for each character and give them a rating/answer for each category; some of them won't be easy to numerically quantify so you may need to develop a scoring system. An important element in this exercise is choosing which categories to use, so discuss which could be helpful to begin the construction/creation of the characters.

During the workshop, different category suggestions were:

• Coolness calibre – actual and projected/perceived.
• Weirdness rating.

- Popularity with teachers.
- Number of people kissed.
- Number of brothers and sisters.
- Parent(s)' education: how well schooled are the characters' mums and dads? Are the characters in the play their respective family's higher-education pioneers?
- GCSE/AS exam results: how well did they do in their last academic tests?
- What are their predicted A-level grades?
- Number of suspensions.
- Extent of worry/care about exam results – actual and projected/perceived.
- Degree of pressure from family to succeed.

DIAGNOSTICS

Choose two opposite walls/points in the rehearsal space, one wall representing DEFINITELY YES 100% BRILLIANT, the opposing wall representing ABSOLUTELY NO 0% TERRIBLE. The actors should then position themselves on the imaginary linear scale running between the two poles in response to questions about their characters; avoid choosing yes/no questions but choose ones to which answers can be measured or quantified in some way. Also avoid questions that are wholly subjective, so instead of 'How good-looking are they?' use 'How good-looking do they think they are?'

Try to urge actors not to hover consistently around the middle of the scale – they must feel strongly about something. Similarly, be wary of characters who are always placing themselves at the extremes, always all-or-nothing; Lyndsey Turner suggested the frequent consequence in performance of these extremes of character is a lot of angst and shouting. Don't rush this exercise, and encourage your actors to be considered and precise. The choices are not absolute and may modulate, so try the exercise at intervals during rehearsals, perhaps leaving the deeper, more searching questions until later in the process.

Questions tried out during the workshop were:

- How healthy is your diet?
- How easy is it for you to get a good eight hours' sleep?
- How well do you sleep before an exam?
- How much do you like animals?
- How well do you get on with your parents?
- How happy/confident/terrified would you be presenting a school assembly?
- How likely are you to cry under pressure/with frustration?
- How willing would you be to watch a horror film on your own in the dark?
- How comfortable are you with the sex you are attracted to?

Try to avoid actors always doing this exercise in methodical silence. The questions may fuel thoughts and mental imagery for the actors, so ask them what they are thinking, what made them make that choice, what is it in the text (if anything) that informed that choice? You may find unexpected affinities/ bonds ('I didn't know you loved Lady Gaga, me too!') and disagreements ('I can't believe you hate Lady Gaga!') develop between characters, so consider encouraging dialogue between the characters as the actors get used to this exercise.

Exercises for playing with tone

To investigate more unconventional and unexpected ways of performing the text, the group was divided into groups of three and each group looked at the first two pages of the script. Each group was asked to present this same section of the play but in different recognisable styles, in this case familiar TV genres ('cool yoof' drama, Channel Four foreign film, classic British sitcom, kids' TV, an ITV cop drama such as *The Sweeney* and a Nordic detective drama), to see what different approaches and playing styles might unpredictably throw up for further investigation. The exercise revealed lots of potential for brief moments of surrealism, stylisation and significant rhythmic changes. Young people have a wide range of references and allusions available to them through mass communication and media, so this might be a useful and fun launch-point for rehearsals. Maybe try using a 'remote control' that can jump around different genres and styles: horror movie, Greek tragedy, music-hall, silent movie, infomercial.

STATES OF TENSION EXERCISE

The group members were taken through the stages of an imaginary morning preparing for a university interview. The exercise went through six stages of tension moving through gentle early-morning semi-consciousness, planning the day, preparing for the interview, getting behind schedule, waiting for buses, losing CVs, missing trains and ending in helpless frantic panic. Try developing progressive narrative scenarios that shift and crank up your actors' tension and anxiety; see how they respond physically as well as emotionally; see where the tensions manifest themselves in their bodies.

During the workshop, the participants then immediately went on to try and complete a UCAS form of their own while in varying states of tension. How easy is it to be distracted when you're really relaxed and which characters in the play are the most likely to be diverted from the UCAS job in hand? How easy is it to write or type and think clearly when you are in a state of high anxiety: how many mistakes are made and does the tension impede accuracy? Observe how the body unconsciously develops places of tension, look for micro-behaviour during these exercises and see if they can be used to inform the performances; small, often hidden, details such as which parts of the body are held during moments of anxiety, the characters' tension points, can add much desired detail. While completing the UCAS forms in character, consider

which parts of the form your character would complete first:
would they choose the easy sections to get them out of the
way or the more complicated sections to have more thinking
time to get them right?

POINTING

This is an exercise to highlight specific moments of the text
like the *events* mentioned below, examining how they could be
accentuated or momentarily spotlit or suspended without
interfering with the impetus of the action.

The company was divided into two groups. The first group
looked at the moment in the play when Alex announces she's
sent off her form and were asked to experiment with different
ways of focusing on this moment. First of all the group
stylised the moment, having all the actors turning to look at
Alex simultaneously following her announcement 'Sent',
crisply holding the moment and then returning to their own
tasks. The group then tried marking the moment with Alex
standing up, all eyes upon her, and almost exiting, to change
the stage picture completely. They then tried using a prop (in
this case a paper aeroplane) thrown on the word 'Sent',
suspending the activity as the characters watched the plane's
flight. It was observed that this could also have been
interpreted as resembling the sending/flight of the email.
Finally the group experimented with ways that tight
spotlighting of individual characters could be used to draw
precise and dramatic focus.

The second group looked at a moment that isn't indicated in
the text – an unwritten stage direction which everyone agreed
was important: the moment when Michael realises the
applicants have got the date wrong and they have indeed still
got another week. When might this happen and how could it
be 'pointed' for the audience. For this the group chose a
moment om page 537:

LOUISE: Do you want another tissue?

MICHAEL *nods.* LARA *passes one to* LOUISE, *who passes it to* MICHAEL.

LARA: Thank you Michael

MICHAEL *sits.* LOUISE *comes over to* LARA .

The group thought that here would be an interesting time for Michael to realise the mistake of the others. Rather than it being a genuine and immediately shared discovery after the forms have been sent, putting the discovery here would mean that Michael is 'sitting on' this significant information for ten pages of text. What might hanging on to this secret say about him? Why does he select that moment for the revelation, and why does he choose to make it at all?

The group showed this epiphany in two ways: first, a very brief stylised choral *hallelujah* to mark the realisation; and second a more naturalistic attempt to quietly bring the news to Louise's attention as she '*comes over to* LARA'. Michael failed to get Louise's attention and only the audience noticed this moment, because the characters onstage were all too busy, but the audience knew something was amiss and were in collusion but unsure precisely with what.

The directors were encouraged not to ignore the deadline-date discovery but to experiment with when and how it is made. Playing around with film genres, tempo and rhythm, trying momentarily slowing the action down and experimenting with exposing and portraying the characters' inner emotions, the character's 'True Self' at moments of significance were all suggested for investigation.

Structure

The shape of the play: topography
Forty-Five Minutes is not broken down into acts or scenes. Lyndsey Turner suggested that it may be helpful to examine the hidden internal architecture of the play by looking at the sequence of significant, pivotal *events* in the action, and the *chapters* that connect these important moments of change.

When dividing the play into manageable chapter-chunks it will help to give each chapter a title. This should help determine the focus of this passage of activity, and each significant moment should manifest a change of energy leading towards the next event. When using this technique be careful that the dynamic and drive of each chapter doesn't wane as it approaches the next event. But keep the energy up, don't let the changes of chapter become rehearsed points of rest. The decision why and where to put the events that trigger the changes of chapter could be a start for good detailed debate for the company as they start to look at the shape of the play.

Suggestions for the first six chapters and TITLES were:

- Chapter 1: NATHAN AND DARREL SETTLE IN – from opening of the play until

- Chapter 2: ARRIVAL OF GEORGIE, LARA AND TRENT – from *'Georgie, Lara and Trent come in'* until

- Chapter 3: ARRIVAL OF LOUISE AND MICHAEL – from *'Louise and Michael come in'* until

- Chapter 4: ALEX SENDS HER FORM BUT IS THEN PERSUADED TO STAY – from 'ALEX: Sent' until

- Chapter 5: THEY GET DOWN TO WORK – from *'Alex comes to look at Nathan's computer'* until

- Chapter 6: MICHAEL POKES HIS NOSE IN NUMBER ONE – from 'MICHAEL: Louise!' until 'LARA: Can we all just fucking wait . . . '

The play is full of tensions and anxieties, with each character experiencing frustration, annoyance and worry at different times, and this tension-baton needs to be passed around the characters, ideally with someone always in some form of panic/anxiety at any given moment and the other characters experiencing varying levels of tension.

To help investigate the pulse-rate of each character and the calibration of different levels of tension throughout the group, Lyndsey Turner gave each group a large piece of paper marked with three vertical columns, each column representing a 'chapter' of the play. The x-axis indicated the progression of time and the y-axis the level of distress, from calm at the base to haemorrhaging anxiety at the top. In cast-sized groups the participants each chose a character to follow through the designated three chapters and drew a line representing their character's state of tension through these chapters. Using the same sheet of paper the group marked the progression of each character with peaks denoting moments of high anxiety and troughs periods of calm, with the stipulation that at all times one character must be in the top quarter of the distress scale.

This exercise again will promote discussion and teamwork within a company, as the states of all the characters need to be considered in relation to one another to achieve calibration and distribution through the levels of tension. This will hopefully aid the investigation of the musicality and rhythm of scenes and avoid all the characters experiencing periods of calm or anxiety simultaneously Try and find the high and the low notes.

On their 'pulse line' on these scene maps, the participants also marked the moment they thought their character has the most control of the room. You could also try marking at what point the character feels least in control, dominant or effective. Lyndsey Turner encouraged directors to consider mapping the whole play in this manner, making it a document that was constantly updated and a continuing project that could become the subject of debate, discussion and negotiation for a company, so that the overall shape of everyone's collective input was being debated and tackled as a team.

The text and language

The writer accepts that some companies/audiences may have a problem with the use of swearwords in the play, but she would prefer that the offensive words were removed rather than sanitised – substituting something like 'frick' for 'fuck', for example, should be avoided. Certain sections of the play's strong language should not be altered: please avoid changes to pages 493–7, 505–6, 509–10, 514–15, 520–1, 533–7, 540–50. The word 'cunt' on page 495 could be changed to something else, but the chosen word should still be striking and not used elsewhere in the play.

The square brackets on page 513 can be filled with a place of your choice. For the purpose of regional accuracy, the titles of examinations and academic school year groups can also be changed.

The use of the slash mark (/) indicates overlapping dialogue.

Casting

Trent and Michael could both be female characters but the mode of violence used against Michael would need to be adapted and modified. In these cases the writer acknowledges the need to change the word 'he' to 'she'.

Production, staging and design

The 'closed-space, closed-time' structure is and will be a challenge for directors. Lyndsey Turner encouraged them to persevere with sifting truthful but also vibrant ways of staging the play, to be ambitious and to find the potential for physical movement in the piece: to avoid a static play of talking heads.

It was agreed that careful consideration of the different possibilities for staging should be an ongoing process throughout the initial stages of rehearsal. The directors were encouraged not to get tied down to an onstage seating plan/layout too early, but to allow the *mise en scène* to be decided through experimentation. Try putting furniture on wheels to see if the configuration could even be altered mid-performance. Do the characters all have to remain in their starting positions?

During the workshop cardboard boxes were used to represent computer monitors placed on the participant actors' knees, and chairs were moved into different configurations to investigate each shape's merits and problems. The group tried placing all the characters seated in a straight line across the stage; then in classroom up/down rows facing downstage as if to an imaginary teacher's desk; in two up/down rows stage left and right with all characters facing offstage; in a delta formation with all characters facing offstage; an arc with all characters facing downstage; in pairs dotted around the stage. Each configuration had its advantages and drawbacks, sightlines and characters being blocked being the most persistent snags.

The characters are all distracted at some point from their UCAS task, some more frequently than others, and distinct physical choices such as having to turn round or cross the stage to talk to someone could be much more interesting than the turn of a head, so careful consideration should be given to where the different characters are placed in relation to one another. What are the interesting avenues of dialogue? See what the effect might be of additional furniture, shelves, bags, desks. Where's the window? Is there a window? Experiment with having no cardboard boxes/monitors and just using keyboards, or try using frames to represent computer screens. Or do you need to represent the computers physically at all?

Sound effects

The use of sound effects is open to development and experimentation but shouldn't be intrusive. It might be interesting to experiment with what 'realistic' sounds could be used, such as the sending of an email, a computer error message and what activity there might be outside the room after the school bell goes.

From a workshop led by Lyndsey Turner,
with notes by Phil Sheppard

Participating Companies

Aberdeen Arts Centre
Act One Theatre School
Altru Youth Theatre
Aquinas Youth Theatre Company
Arnold Academy
artsdepot youth theatre
ArtsEd
Ashcroft Technology Academy
Astor College
Barbara Priestman School and
    Technology College
Bedford College
Benenden School
Berzerk Productions
Bexhill College
Birmingham Metropolitan Academy
    of Performing Arts (BMAPA)
Bishops High School
Blatchington Mill School
Bodens Youth Theatre
Brentford School for Girls
Brewery Youth Theatre
Bridgend College
Brigg Sixth Form
Cabinteely Youth Theatre
Cambridge Regional College
CASTEnsemble
Castleford Academy
Chichester Festival Theatre
Chichester High School for Girls
Chingford Foundation School
Chorlton High School
Christ's Hospital School
Cirencester College
City of London Academy –
    Southwark
Cloakroom Theatre
Cockburn School
Colbury and Ashurst Youth Theatre

Coleg Powys
Collision Youth Theatre
Coulsdon Sixth Form College
Craigholme School
Creative Industries in Salford [CRIS]
Crisscross Productions
Dame Allan's Schools Theatre
    Company
De Aston School
Deafinitely Theatre
Debden Park High School
Denbigh High School
Derby College
Dorchester Youth Theatre
Drama Lab, Jersey
Dramaplus Youth Theatre
Drummond Community High
    School
Duck Egg Theatre Company
Dukes Theatre
East Berkshire College
Eden Court Creative – Isle of Skye
    Youth Theatre
Eden Court Young Company
EF International Academy
Elizabeth Garrett Anderson School
Erith School
EXIT 25 Theatre School
Explosive Arts
Felixstowe Academy
Flying High Theatre Company
Fowey Community College
Fulham Cross Girls' School
Fusion Youth Theatre
George Green's School
Glenthorne High School
Gloucestershire College
Greenfield Community College
Gresham's School

Griese Youth Theatre
Groundlings Theatre
Halesowen College
Hampton College
Heaton Manor Theatre Project
Hertswood School
High-Jinks Creative Drama
Highly Sprung Performance Co.
Honley High School
Horsecross Arts
Hove Park School
HT Productions
ICIA, University of Bath
Ilkley Grammar School
ingenius theatre
InterACT Youth Theatre
Ipswich High School
Jigsaw Arts
John Cabot Academy
Junk Shop Theatre Company
Key Youth Theatre
Kildare Youth Theatre
King's Company
King's Lynn Academy
Kings Youth Theatre
Kingsley School
Kingussie High School
Lakeside Arts Centre
Largs Youth Theatre
Lightbulb Youth Theatre
Llanelli Youth Theatre
Lochaber Youth Theatre
LOST Youth Theatre Company
Lowton High School
Ludlow C of E School
Lyceum Youth Theatre
Lyme Youth Theatre
Lyric Young Company
M6 Theatre
Maiden Erlegh School
Marshalls Park School
Meridian School

Misbourne School
Montage Theatre Arts
MorePies Productions
Mountview Academy of Theatre
    Arts – Young People's
    Programme/Young Performers
    Company
Nescot College (Up Stage Right)
New College Nottingham
New College, Swindon
Newcastle College
Newent Community School and
    Sixth Form Centre
Nidderdale High School
North Durham Academy
North Lanarkshire Youth Theatre
One Theatre Company
Orange Tree Theatre
Ormiston Sudbury Academy
Oxford Actors Company
PACE
Parabola Arts Centre
Park High School
Peer Productions
Perfect Circle Youth Theatre
Pump House CYT
QE School & Sixth Form
Queen Elizabeth's School
Quilley School of Engineering
RBL Foundations
Redruth School
Reed's School
RFD Campus, Gloucestershire
    College
Ricards Lodge High School
Ridgewood School
Rodillian School
Rokeby School
Rotherham College of Arts and
    Technology
Royal Berkshire Academy
Royal Exchange Theatre

Rushcliffe School Arts Council
Sacred Heart High School
Sgioba Dràma Òigridh Inbhir Nis
Shenfield High School
Sheringham High School
Sirius Academy
Slow Theatre Company
Smestow School
South Wirral High School
Spotlight UK
St Brendan's Sixth Form College
St George's Academy
St George's School Ascot
St Mary's Calne
St Monica's Theatre Company
St Paul's Catholic College
Stafford Gatehouse Youth Theatre
Stage Tynemouth
Stephen Joseph Youth Theatre
Stockport School
Stoke Damerel Community College
Stopsley High School
Tanbridge House School
The Blue Coat School Oldham
The Boswells School
The Bridge Academy
The Canterbury Academy
The Crestwood School
The Customs House Youth Theatre
The Discarded Nut Theatre
    Company
The Farnley Academy
The Garage
The Langley Academy
The Lincoln Young Company
The Lowry (two companies)
The Manor Academy
The Marlowe Theatre
The Regent Theatre Academy of
    Performing Arts

The SAVVY Young Company
The Snaith School
The St Ives Youth Theatre
Theatre Akimbo
Theatre Royal, Bury St Edmunds
Theatre Royal Young Company
Thurso High School
Tower House School
Trent College
Trinity Youth Theatre Company
Tyne Valley Youth Theatre
Tytherington High School
Upstaged Theatre Company
UROCK Youth Theatre
Warwick Arts Centre Senior Youth
    Theatre
Waterhead Academy
Wellington School
West Thames College
Wester Hailes Education Centre
Westwood Girls' College
Whitmore High School
Wildern School
Winchmore School
Winstanley College
Winterhill School
Winton School
Woodbridge High School
Woolwich Polytechnic for Boys
Wootton Upper School
Worthing College
Yew Tree Youth Theatre
Young and Unique Theatre,
    Callington Community College
Young Dramatic Arts Theatre
    Company
Young Persons' Theatre Company
Ysgol Aberconwy
Ysgol Morgan Llwyd
360 Youth Theatre

Partner Theatres

artsdepot

Brewery Arts Centre, Kendal

Bristol Old Vic

Chichester Festival Theatre / The Capitol, Horsham

Eden Court

Greenwich Theatre

Lyceum, Edinburgh

Lyric, Belfast

Lyric, Hammersmith

Marlowe Theatre, Canterbury

Northern Stage, Newcastle

Norwich Garage

Norwich Playhouse

Royal & Derngate, Northampton

Sakisbury Playhouse

Sheffield Theatres

Soho Theatre

Stephen Joseph Theatre, Scarborough

The Lowry Centre, Salford

Theatre Royal Plymouth

Wales Millennium Centre, Cardiff

Warwick Arts Centre

West Yorkshire Playhouse, Leeds

Performing Rights

Applications for permission to perform etc. should be made,
before rehearsals begin, to the following representatives:

For *The Guffin*:
Casarotto Ramsay
Waverley House
7–12 Noel Street
London W1F 8GQ

For *Mobile Phone Show*:
A.J. Associates
Higher Healey House
Higherhouse Lane
White Coppice
Chorley PR6 9BT, Lancs
info.ajassociates@talktalk.net

For *What Are They Like?*:
The Agency
24 Pottery Lane
London W11 4LZ

For *Soundclash*:
PBJ Management
22 Rathbone Street
London W1T 1LA

For *We Lost Elijah*; *I'm Spilling My Heart Out Here*;
Don't Feed the Animals; *Forty-Five Minutes*:
United Agents
12–26 Lexington Street
London W1F OLE

For *Tomorrow I'll Be Happy*:
Independent Talent
Oxford House
76 Oxford Street
London W1D 1BS

For *Ailie and the Alien*:
Knight Hall Agency Ltd
Lower Ground Floor
7 Mallow Street
London EC1Y 8RQ